Story

Hier findest du lustige und spannende Texte über die *friends* in Greenwich.

Action UK!

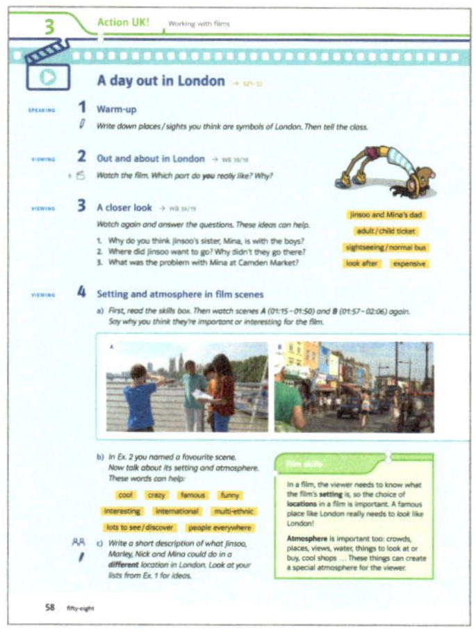

Und hier gibt es tolle Filme aus Greenwich!

Across cult

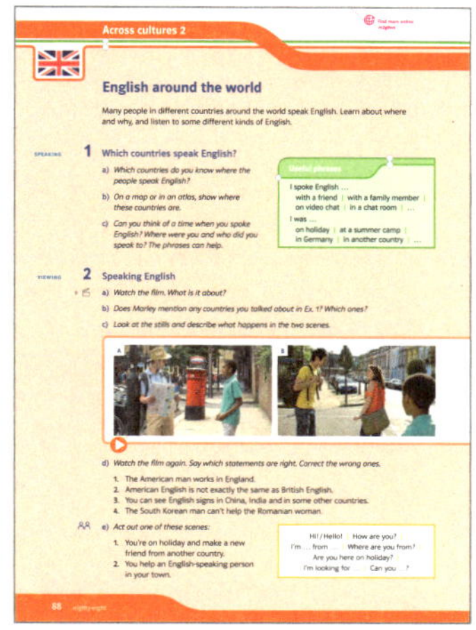

Vergleiche auf diesen Seiten deinen Alltag mit der Alltagskultur und der Geschichte Großbritanniens.

Diff pool

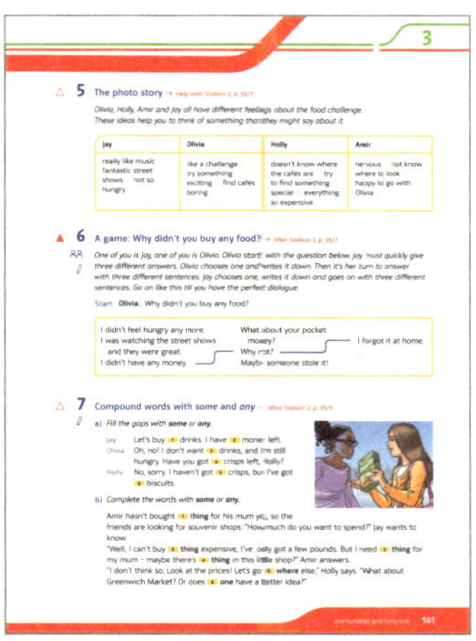

Skills

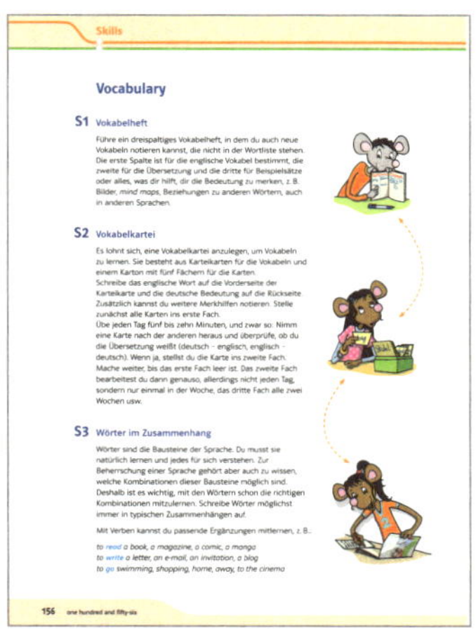

Grammar, Vocabulary

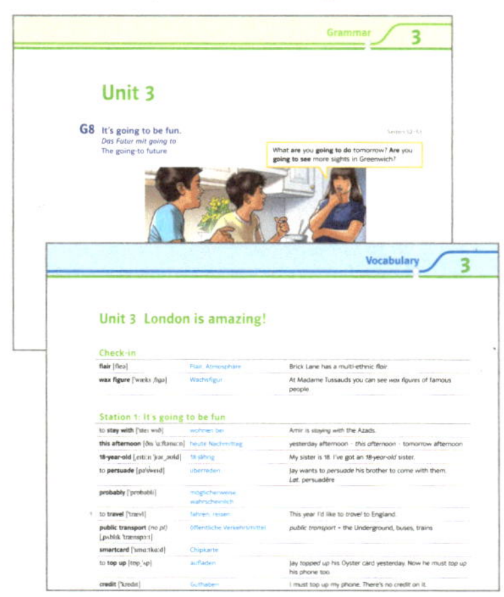

Im hinteren Buchtei stehen dir hilfreiche Anhänge zur Verfügung. *Diff pool, Grammar* und *Vocabulary* kennst du schon aus dem letzten Jahr. Neu ab Green Line 2 ist der *Skills*-Anhang. Hier findest du zu den Lernbereichen *Reading, Writing, Speaking, Listening, Viewing, Mediation* und *Vocabulary* allerlei Lernhilfen und Methodentipps. Die gelben Verweise → S17 bei den Unit-Aufgaben sagen dir, dass es sich lohnt, dort nachzuschlagen!

Symbole

→ △ 124/1	Verweis auf leichtere Aufgaben / Hilfen im Diff pool
→ ▲ 124/2	Verweis auf anspruchsvollere Aufgaben im Diff pool
→ WB 7/4	Verweis auf eine Übung im Workbook
→ G2	Verweis auf die Grammatik im Anhang
→ S2	Verweis auf die Skills im Anhang
	Partnerarbeit
	Gruppenarbeit
	Hier entsteht ein Produkt für dein Portfolio.
	Schreiben (geschlossen / einfach)
	Schreiben (offen / kreativ)
S1/14	Verweis auf die Schüler-CDs (Audio)
L1/19	Verweis auf die Lehrer-CDs (Audio)
	Verweis auf die Lehrer-DVD (Film)
	Code auf www.klett.de eingeben und Zusatzmaterial nutzen
2	Übungen, die die Unit task besonders vorbereiten
	Across cultures

Green Line 2 G9 für Klasse 6 an Gymnasien

Herausgeber: Harald Weisshaar, Bisingen

Autorinnen und Autoren: Marion Horner, Ipswich; Carolyn Jones, Beckenham; Jon Marks, Ventnor; Alison Wooder, Ventnor sowie Paul Dennis, Lahnstein; Barbara Greive, Dortmund; Cornelia Kaminski, Fulda unter Mitwirkung von Manuela Brumme, Stuttgart; Monique Kunhar, Schwaikheim

Beratung: Paul Dennis, Lahnstein; Cornelia Kaminski, Fulda; Nilgül Karabulut, Aachen; Hartmut Klose, Seevetal; Antje Körber, Merseburg; Jörg Nieswand, Berlin; Jörg Schulze, Dresden

Für besondere Unterstützung danken wir herzlich Ms Susan Bolton von der **Thomas Tallis School**, London.

Zusatzmaterial für Schülerinnen und Schüler zu diesem Band:

Workbook + Audio-CD + Übungssoftware	978-3-12-854228-7
Workbook + Audio-CD	978-3-12-854225-6
Fit für Tests und Klassenarbeiten mit Lösungsheft und Audio-CD	978-3-12-854227-0
Das Trainingsbuch mit Audio-CD	978-3-12-854302-4
Vokabellernheft	978-3-12-854282-9
Vokabeltraining aktiv	978-3-12-854332-1

sowie eine Reihe von abgestimmten *English Readers*

1. Auflage 1 5 4 3 2 1 | 2019 18 17 16 15

Alle Drucke dieser Auflage sind unverändert und können im Unterricht nebeneinander verwendet werden.
Die letzte Zahl bezeichnet das Jahr des Druckes.
Das Werk und seine Teile sind urheberrechtlich geschützt. Jede Nutzung in anderen als den gesetzlich zugelassenen Fällen bedarf der vorherigen schriftlichen Einwilligung des Verlages. Hinweis § 52 a UrhG: Weder das Werk noch seine Teile dürfen ohne eine solche Einwilligung eingescannt und in ein Netzwerk eingestellt werden. Dies gilt auch für Intranets von Schulen und sonstigen Bildungseinrichtungen. Fotomechanische oder andere Wiedergabeverfahren nur mit Genehmigung des Verlages.

© Ernst Klett Verlag GmbH, Stuttgart 2015. Alle Rechte vorbehalten. www.klett.de

Redaktion: Michael Mattison; Anette Dangelmaier; Lektorat editoria: Cornelia Schaller, Fellbach
Herstellung: Anita Bauch; Cristina Dunu

Gestaltung: Petra Michel, Essen
Umschlaggestaltung: know idea, Freiburg; Koma Amok, Stuttgart
Illustrationen: Peer Kramer, Düsseldorf; jani lunablau, Barcelona *(Maskottchen und Story)* sowie Christian Dekelver, Weinstadt *(Karten)*
Satz: Satzkiste GmbH, Stuttgart; Mediengestaltung Elke Kurz, Waiblingen
Reproduktion: Schwaben-Repro, Stuttgart
Druck: PASSAVIA Druckservice GmbH & Co. KG, Passau

Printed in Germany
ISBN 978-3-12-854220-1 (fester Einband)
ISBN 978-3-12-854221-8 (flexibler Einband)

ausgemustert

Line 2 G9

von
Marion Horner
Carolyn Jones
Jon Marks
Alison Wooder
Paul Dennis
Barbara Greive
Cornelia Kaminski

herausgegeben von
Harald Weisshaar

Ernst Klett Verlag
Stuttgart · Leipzig

Unit 1: My friends and I

Unit 2: Let's discover TTS!

‹ Story 2 ›

Across cultures 1 🇬🇧

Inhalt

Unit 3: London is amazing!

Unit 4: Sport is good for you!

Inhalt

Legende

L	Listening	W	Writing	VOC	Vocabulary	(UK flag)	Across cultures
S	Speaking	M	Mediation	SK	Skills	< >	Fakultativ
R	Reading	V	Viewing	(puzzle icon)	Kompetenzaufgabe	R	Revision

Find more online: ny827k

Unit 1

My friends and I

Your classmates – CAUGHT ON CAMERA!

Jay, don't you know that embarrassing outfits always end up in the yearbook? LOL!

Dave, Olivia and Luke after a round of boxing. Ouch, those red noses! Oh, wait – it's Red Nose Day, of course! (Nice cake, mmm…)

SPEAKING

1 Talk about the yearbook photos

What can you see? Where are the girls and boys? What do you think they're doing or saying?

LISTENING

2 Caught on camera

L 1/1

a) *Listen to the dialogues. Which photo are the characters talking about? (There is no dialogue for one of the photos.)*

→ S18–20

b) *Listen again and then answer the questions.*

1. How does Jay feel about the photo of himself and Holly? 2. Which two characters are on the yearbook team? 3. Who is doing which pages in the yearbook? 4. Why does Holly like the photo of the three boys?

In Unit 1 you learn

… how to talk about special activities in the past and how to give information about places. You learn:

- words about feelings
- the simple past
- words and phrases that describe and compare

C

The eyes say it all for lovebirds Holly and Jay. (The camera never lies!)

D

Luke, Dave and Jay are practising for the class trip. Hey guys, we know that you're funny – but now we know that you're silly too!

SPEAKING

3 Feelings → WB 2/1–2

happy | shy | excited | embarrassed | proud

a) *Take turns to act different feelings. Can the others guess your word?*

b) *Look at the photos again. Say how you think the characters feel and why.*

Example: Photo D: I think Dave feels happy because he's having fun with his friends.

→ △ 108/1

c) *Make a mind map for 'feelings'. Add new words to your personal vocabulary.*

Across cultures

Yearbooks are an American tradition, but now they are popular in British schools too. Students on a yearbook team work together to make a fun book for their class, with photos of students and reports about activities during the school year. How do you collect the highlights in the school year?

L 1/2

I love Red Nose Day

YES, IT'S RED NOSE TIME AGAIN!

RED NOSE DAY
DO SOMETHING FUNNY FOR MONEY

Here at TTS we always do our best for COMIC RELIEF. Two years ago we raised lots of money, but this year let's raise even more! Check the TTS website for more information.

COMIC RELIEF is a great charity. It helps people in need in Africa and also the UK. The comedian Lenny Henry started Comic Relief – that's how it got its name – and on the first Red Nose Day in 1988 people wore red noses, did fun activities to raise money and watched a big comedy show on TV. That was many years ago, but today we still do the same things!

I love Red Nose Day. So when I saw the poster on the school noticeboard last month I felt really excited. My friends and I had lots of crazy ideas about how to raise money. In the end we made and sold cakes with funny faces. After school we went into Greenwich and did our own comedy show in the street. Luke's dog Sherlock was a real star, and lots of people gave us money for the TTS collection. It was great fun! I can't wait till next time.

Olivia Fraser

READING

1 Charity work: Olivia and her friends

→ ▲ 108/2

Look at what Olivia writes about Red Nose Day. What things sound fun to you?

Across cultures

People in the UK often help **charities**. What charities in Germany do you know about?

LANGUAGE

2 Irregular simple past forms → WB 3/3 → G1

a) *Look again at Olivia's text and find the past forms of these verbs. Make a list.*

be ✔ do ✔ feel get give go have make see sell wear

Verb	Past form
be do feel	was / were did …

There are no rules for irregular past forms. You must learn them by heart.

→ △ 108/3

b) *Put in the correct past forms. (The list of irregular verbs on page 239 can help you.)*

Two years ago the students **1** (do) fun activities and **2** (get) money for Comic Relief. They **3** (bring) the money to school. Then the school **4** (put) all the money together and **5** (give) it to the charity. Red Nose Day **6** (be) a non-uniform day, so everyone **7** (come) to school in different clothes. But they all **8** (wear) something red. Of course they all **9** (have) red noses too. Some students **10** (take) funny photos for the school website.

GUAGE

3 Find the rule: Regular simple past forms

a) *Look at the example. Find the rule for regular past forms and write it down.*

Example: Lenny Henry **started** Comic Relief in 1988. Last time we **raised** lots of money. In the evening we **watched** the big TV show.

L1/4

b) *Be careful how you say* ***-ed****. There are three different sounds. Listen and say:*

→ 109/4
→ S14

1. [d] Two years ago we organis**ed** a great Red Nose Day. I lov**ed** it. We plann**ed** lots of activities.
2. [t] First we help**ed** to raise money. Then we watch**ed** TV. I lik**ed** Lenny Henry's jokes!
3. [ɪd] I want**ed** to look funny so I paint**ed** my face. I need**ed** a red nose too, of course.

GUAGE

4 The friends' comedy show → WB 3/4–5

Look at the picture and write 5–6 sentences about the comedy show. Choose from these verbs and use the simple past.

play | do | chase | watch | collect | dance | laugh | act

Example: The friends did the comedy show after school.

GUAGE

5 The star of the show → WB 4/6, 5/7

→ 109/5

What does Sherlock tell his dog friends the next day?
Write the text again in his words, with the verbs in the simple past.
Check if the forms are regular or irregular.

Start: I **did** lots of great tricks in the comedy show yesterday.

Sherlock *does* lots of great tricks in the comedy show. First he *jumps* over a big box. Then he *runs* around and *chases* his tail. After that he *dances* on a skateboard, and when Olivia *starts* to play the sax he also *sings*. The people *love* it. They *laugh* and *clap* and *give* lots of money for Comic Relief. Luke and his friends *try* to do their best too but everyone's eyes *are* on Sherlock. He *feels* happy and proud – he *is* the real star of the show!

Look at G1 on page 142. You must be careful with the spelling of some regular forms.

SPEAKING

6 Play a game: Something funny for money

People often pay money when you do funny or hard activities for charity. Take turns to say what you did on Red Nose Day. Roll two dice, for an activity and a comment.

Example: 2 + 5 I went everywhere in pyjamas. I enjoyed the day.

Activities	Comments
1 turn off my phone for the day	1 have lots of fun
2 go everywhere in pyjamas	2 find that hard
3 swim for 30 minutes	3 feel great
4 eat baby food	4 do my best
5 try not to laugh all day	5 enjoy the day
6 speak in a funny voice	6 raise lots of money

If you like, you can think of new ideas for activities and comments.

WRITING

7 Your turn: A report about a special activity

→ △ 109/6

Write a report about an activity that you did with your friends or family. Write 6–8 sentences.

Example: Last year my friends and I helped to tidy a park. We …

Useful phrases

When? Last week / A month ago / In July / …
Who? My friends and I / My dad / …
What? We did a project / show … | We organised a … / made … / helped …
Feelings? It was fun / I felt happy / nervous / proud / …

MEDIATION

8 A flyer in a German classroom

→ S17

Answer a British student's questions.

1. I know 'groß', so I can see this flyer is about something big. But what is it?
2. Who wants to sell cakes? And why?
3. Is the sale here in the school building?
4. 10th October – that's the date of your sale, right?
5. What's this about Africa?

Mediation skills

A **quick answer** helps to keep the conversation going.

Don't worry **if the answer isn't in the text**. Just say there's no information.

GROSSER KUCHENVERKAUF

++ Wichtige Ankündigung! ++

Wir brauchen noch Geld für unsere Klassenfahrt. Deshalb planen wir einen großen Kuchenverkauf. (Erinnert ihr euch? Letztes Jahr haben wir auf diese Weise viel Geld für eine Schule in Afrika gesammelt.) Lasst uns also bald wieder in der Küche fleißig werden und viele leckere Kuchen backen!
Um zu besprechen, wann unser Kuchenverkauf stattfindet und wer was macht, treffen wir uns am 10. Oktober in der ersten Unterrichtsstunde. Merkt euch bitte dieses Datum – und bringt viele Ideen mit!

L 1/5

How did they know?

Luke: Only ten days till our class trip! I can't wait!

Dave: Sit down and help us, Luke! It's our group's job to think of games to play on the coach.

Luke: Hey, what about puzzle stories?

Holly: I don't know that game. How do you play it?

Dave: I know it! Great idea, Luke. Someone tells a little story with missing information. Then the others ask questions to try and find the solution. Here's a puzzle story for you …

After an anonymous phone call the police went to an address to arrest a dangerous man. They didn't know what the man looked like. They only knew that his name was John and that he was at that address. When they got to the house they found four people at a table in the kitchen: a taxi driver, a mechanic, a farmer and a postman. The police didn't ask any questions and the other people didn't say anything, but right away the police arrested the postman. How did they know that they had the right person? Why were they so sure?

Luke: Did the police really arrest the right person? — Dave: Yes, they did.

Luke: Were there any photos of the man? — Dave: No, there weren't.

Holly: Did the postman try to run away? — Dave: No, he didn't.

Luke: Did the other people help the police? — Dave: No, they didn't.

Holly: Was it the man's home? — Dave: I don't know. But that isn't important.

Luke: Was the man's name a clue? — Dave: Yes, it was.

→ Solution on p. 15

AKING

9 Talk about games

Do you like guessing games? What ideas have you got for games on a coach trip?

GUAGE

10 Ask and answer questions about the puzzle story → WB 5/8 → G2–3

1. Did the phone call help the police?
2. Was the man's name Peter?
3. Did the police ask any questions?
4. Was the man dangerous?
5. Were the four people in the kitchen?
6. Were the other people postmen too?

Yes,	he it they	was. were. did.
No,		wasn't. weren't. didn't.

LANGUAGE

11 Find the rule: Differences between present and past → G2-3

*Look at the sentences in the present and the past. What are the differences for **questions** and **negative sentences**? Write down the rule.*

Simple present	Simple past
Do you like the story? What does she say? I don't know the game. He doesn't want to play.	Did you like the story? What did she say? I didn't know the game. He didn't want to play.

LANGUAGE

12 Guess what we did

→ △ 110/7
→ ▲ 110/8

Think of a fun activity that you and a friend did on a coach. (It needn't be true.) Your partner guesses what you did.

Example:
Did you tell puzzle stories? – No, we didn't.
Did you count all the red cars? – No, we didn't.
Did you send funny texts? – Yes, we did!

LANGUAGE

13 Problems on the coach → WB 5/9

*Complete the sentences. Use **didn't**.*

Example: I felt hungry but I (not have any food) → … but I didn't have any food.

1. I wasn't happy because my best friend (not sit next to me)
2. I helped a girl with her bag but she (not say thank you)
3. It was very loud on the coach so some people (not hear our puzzle stories)
4. The driver was friendly but he (not speak much English)
5. I needed the toilet but the coach (not stop)
6. The coach was slow so we (not get there till late)

LANGUAGE

14 Make fun questions and answers → WB 6/10-11 → G2

a) *Work in groups of three or four. Think of six fun questions. Start with question words and use the simple past. Write each question on a piece of paper.*

How? Why? What? Where?
Who? laugh? get? see?
be? meet? …?

Examples:
What did you find in your schoolbag?
Why were you in a tree all day?

b) *Swap questions with another group and write funny answers to their questions.*

c) *With the other group, look at all the questions and answers. Choose the three best ideas and read them to the class.*

AKING

15 Revision: Who am I? → WB 7/12

Think of a famous person. It can be a real person (e.g. singer, sports star) or a character from a film or book. Your partner must guess who you are.

Example:

Are you a real person? – No, I'm not.
Can I see you in a film? – Yes, you can.
Is the film a comedy? – No, it isn't.
Do you do dangerous things? – Yes, I do.
Does Daniel Craig act your role? – Yes, he does.
I know! You're James Bond. – Yes, that's right.

You can only ask questions with yes/no answers.
Are you ...? Have you got ...?
Do/Does ...? Is ...? ...?

ENING

16 Luke's dream

L1/6
→ S18–20

a) *Listen and find five pictures that go with Luke's dream. (One picture is wrong.) Put the five pictures in the correct order.*

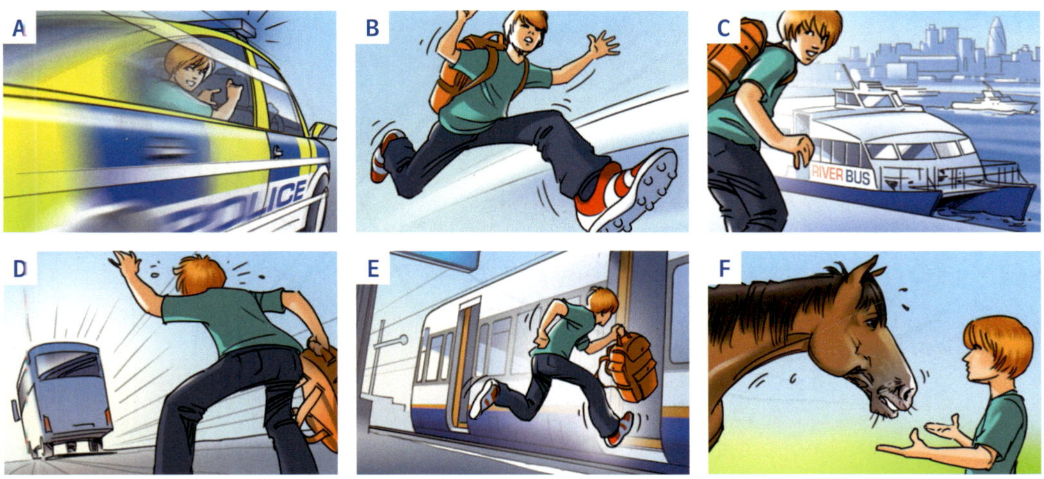

b) *Listen again and answer the questions.*

1. What was Luke's problem with Sherlock? 2. How did Luke feel when the coach went without him? 3. Who did Luke ask for help first? 4. Why were the police suddenly too busy to help Luke? 5. Why didn't Luke stay on the train? 6. What did Luke find out about the horse in the past? 7. Why didn't Luke find out the end of his dream?

RITING

17 Your turn: Your puzzle story

Write your own short puzzle story (5–6 sentences).
You can use your own idea or maybe you already know a story like this.
Can your friends guess the solution?

Solution to the puzzle story on page 13: There was only one man in the house – the postman. The other people were all women.

L 1/7

Everyone can enjoy a challenge

Home | About us | Courses | Activities | Events

Ty'n y Berth is an outdoor centre near Snowdonia National Park in Wales. With its mountains, forests and lakes, Wales is great for outdoor activities. We organise adventure courses for school groups. We believe our activities are as important as lessons in the classroom. A course at TYB is not only the most exciting project of the year for students – it also helps them to learn new skills, to work in a team and to be more confident.

Some of the most popular adventures are mountain walking, climbing and gorge scrambling. Younger students do easier routes than older students, but everyone can enjoy a challenge – the hardest challenges are often the favourite activities. There is always something exciting to do, even in the worst weather. That's why at Ty'n y Berth you can see the happiest smiles in Wales!

SPEAKING

18 Talk about the outdoor centre

a) *Close your books. Say what you remember about Wales and the outdoor centre.*

b) *Would you like to go there? What looks fun or interesting to you?*

c) *Your turn: Tell the class about a challenge that you had.*

Across cultures

Wales is an important part of the UK, but it's also a separate country with its own Celtic culture. Many people there speak two languages, English and Welsh. Ty'n y Berth is a Welsh name. You say it like this: [ti:n‿ə 'bɜ:θ]

LANGUAGE

19 Find the rule: Comparative and superlative forms → G4

a) *Copy and complete the grid. Look in the text for the missing forms.*

b) *Collect more examples from the text and add them to the grid.*

c) *Write down the rule for comparative and superlative forms of adjectives.*

adjective	comparative	superlative
hard	harder	…
big	…	biggest
easy	…	easiest
popular	more popular	…
confident	…	most confident
bad	worse	…
…	…	…

UAGE

20 Practise the new forms

→ △ 110/9

a) *Say the comparative and superlative forms of these adjectives.*

proud good interesting funny dangerous quiet brave excited

b) *What do you think about these things? Compare your ideas.*

Example: A: I think mountain walking is the **most exciting** outdoor activity.
B: Oh, I think climbing is **more exciting than** mountain walking.

exciting outdoor activity | good place for a holiday | interesting hobby | (any more ideas?)

UAGE

21 Say it in different words

→ WB 7/13, 8/14–15 → G5

→ △ 111/10

Use a different adjective and a different form.

Example: 1. Wales is **smaller than** England.

1. Wales isn't as big as England. (small)
2. The weather today isn't as good as yesterday. (bad)
3. Route A is harder than route B. (easy)
4. The courses are cheaper than most people think. (expensive)
5. I'm more confident than I was about new challenges. (nervous)

JLARY

22 Find adjectives to describe what you can see

→ WB 8/16

→ △ 111/11
→ ▲ 111/12

Take turns to describe. Use comparative or superlative forms or '(not) as … as …'

fast small low big slow tall high

S1/3–7 L1/9–13

It was amazing

This text and the exercises help with the Unit task on pages 22–23.

1 Before you read

→ S5–6, 8

Look only at the words in blue in part A of the text. What do you think the text is about? Collect ideas.

Dave Preston's report for the class yearbook:

A It was a trip to a different planet! We came from a place with busy streets and shops and lots of people, but in this new place there were only mountains and lakes and lots of sheep …

Everyone on the coach was excited when we started our class trip to the Ty'n y Berth Outdoor Centre that Saturday morning. Even our teacher Mr Swindon was excited. "Who wants to go to Wales?" he shouted. "We all do!" we shouted back.

It was a long way from Greenwich, but we played games and ate our sandwiches, and when at last we saw the big sign "Croeso i Gymru" we all clapped. Now the roads were quieter. Everything looked green and the villages and farms had strange Welsh names. Soon we were in the mountains.

B At last the coach stopped in front of an old grey building next to fields and trees. Lots of the buildings in Wales are grey.

A man with a friendly face met us at the door of the building. "Welcome to Ty'n y Berth, everyone!" he said with a smile. "I'm Will, one of the instructors at the centre. And this is your home for the next few days."

Years ago it was a village school. But now it's all different inside. The biggest room is for meals and free time activities, and most of the smaller rooms are bedrooms for people on courses at the centre.

I was in a bedroom with five other boys. Right away there was a problem because Luke and Jay wanted the same bed near the window. "Maybe you can take turns," I said. They thought that was a good solution, and Luke slept in the bed first. For all of us that night it felt a bit strange to be in a new place without our families.

C Most of the time at Ty'n y Berth we were too busy to think of home. Every morning and afternoon there were new and exciting activities to try. Then in the evening we usually played games.

Everyone loved gorge scrambling. It was funny when Olivia, Holly and I tried to help each other to get across a little river. In the end we just helped each other to fall *into* it. The water in mountain rivers is very cold!

We all found some activities harder than others. For me, climbing was the greatest challenge. But our instructor Ceri was great. She gave me lots of tips, and then I felt more confident.

Late one evening there was a surprise. Will gave everyone a torch and we went for a walk in the dark. "Don't talk, just listen," Will said. So we listened and it was amazing because it was so very quiet. In Greenwich there's always noise, even at night. Then we all turned off our torches and that was amazing too. It was much darker than in London so the stars looked much bigger and clearer.

D Too soon it was the last day, but when we went to bed Luke whispered to me, "I've got a torch so let's go for a night walk again. Just you, Jay and me." We knew it was against the rules, but we wanted one last adventure. We waited till the others were asleep. Then, as quiet as mice, we tiptoed from the bedroom.

It was very dark outside, but with Luke's torch we found our way across a field and through some trees. Then Luke turned off the torch. Well, I thought he did, and I didn't know why. "Er, Luke – it's a cloudy night so we can't look at the stars, you know. I can't even see you," Jay said. "I know," Luke's voice answered. "The torch needs a new battery."

Oh no! Now we had a problem. The night was as black as – well, as black as night. We tried to be cool but we didn't feel it. Which was the way back to the centre? We had no idea. We started to walk. We just hoped it was the right way. Then suddenly – "Hoo-hoo!" What was that? The strange noise made us nervous. "Hoo-hoo!" It was nearer now. What was it? We started to run, but in the dark it was dangerous. Jay fell over something. "Help! It's moving! It's a monster!" he shouted. We tried to run away together. Something awful hit my face and I shouted too. We were really scared. It was crazy. I don't know how we got back to the centre again. We were so happy to see that old grey building. We tiptoed to the door and – oh no, the door was locked! What now? We didn't want trouble, but we needed to get back to our beds. How did we do it? That's a secret.

E Early the next morning the coach came to take us back to Greenwich. We were sad to say goodbye to Wales, but we've all got great memories of our amazing class trip. (And now everyone knows why Luke, Jay and I were tired and slept all the way home!)

ADING

2 Questions about the text → WB 9/17–18

a) *Take turns to ask and answer questions about Dave's report.*

Example: Where did the students go for their class trip? – They went to Wales.

What …?	the students / go for their class trip	Dave / find the hardest challenge
Why …?	everyone / get to Ty'n y Berth	the stars / look so big and clear
Where …?	the girls and boys / eat their meals	the three boys / go for a night walk
How …?	Luke and Jay / want the same bed	Luke's torch / need?
When …?	the students / do on the course	(*your own idea for questions?*)

b) *Something to think about: What do you think these things were?*

1. the "hoo-hoo" noise (line 97) 2. the monster (line 102) 3. something awful (line 104)

SPEAKING

3 The secret → WB 9/19

a) *In the report Dave doesn't say how he, Luke and Jay got back to their beds. How do you think they did this? What ideas have you got?*

→ S16 → △ 111/13

b) *Role play: Work in groups. Think of an ending and write a short scene. Act your scene for the class.*

WRITING

4 How to: Plan a travel report

→ S7

a) *In one or two sentences say what each of the five parts of the report (A–E) is about.*

Start: Part A is about how the students got from Greenwich to Wales.

b) *Find two or three key phrases in each part that can make good headings for that part.*

Example: Part A: Our class trip – A long way from Greenwich – Croeso i Gymru

→ S10–13

c) *Use your ideas from a) and b) to make Dave's plan for his report. Use a grid to show the five parts and the main ideas in each part.*

Part	Main ideas
A	class trip – from Greenwich to Wales – long way
B	

Writing skills

Always **make a plan** for a text. A good plan shows how many **parts** the text has got and also the main ideas in each part.

Try to **make your text interesting** for the reader. Think of a special way to start the text. Choose good words and phrases that help the reader to see and feel what you describe.

VOCABULARY

5 How to: Make a travel report interesting

→ S13

a) *Talk about the first sentence of Dave's report. Do you think this is a good way to start a travel report? Why/why not?*

b) *A travel report needs different kinds of words and phrases. Look at the lists below and find more examples in Dave's report. (Some examples can go in more than one list.)*

1. words that explain 'when': that Saturday morning (line 9) – at last (line 22) – …
2. words that describe places: everything looked green (line 18) – busy streets (line 3) – …
3. words that show feelings: excited (line 11) – we all clapped (line 17) – …
4. words that make a text exciting: a different planet! (line 2) – Oh no! (line 91) – …

How to use a dictionary

Think! Do you really need a dictionary? What do you do first when you see a new English word? What do you do if you don't know how to translate a German word into English?

1 Talk about different kinds of dictionaries

a) *Match A–E to the right kind of dictionary. (Some sentences are correct for all three kinds.)*

Online … | In a book … | In an electronic dictionary …

A. the words are in a list in alphabetical order.
B. you write in the search box to look up a word.
C. you can see the different meanings of the word.
D. you can hear the word's pronunciation.
E. there are two parts: first words in one language and then words in the other language.

b) *What other information do the different dictionaries give?*

c) *Which kind of dictionary do* ***you*** *like to use? Explain why.*

2 Practise with the alphabet → WB 10/20–21

a) *Revision: Take turns to say the alphabet in English.*

b) *Work with the first sentence in part C of Dave's report on page 18. Put all the words in the sentence in alphabetical order. (Be careful with words that start with the same letter – look at the next letters too.) Then check with your partner. Is the order correct?*

3 Find the correct meaning → WB 10/22

a) *English → German: When you find more than one meaning for a word, choose the right meaning for the sentence. Look up the words in blue and translate them into German.*

1. Take the second street on the right. That's the right way for the station.
2. I haven't got time to sit and chat today. We can chat when I come next time.
3. This is a very small room. There's room for only one bed.

b) *German → English: Sometimes you need different English words for the same German word. Look up the German words and complete the sentences.*

1. ***tragen***: a) The students … a blue uniform.
   b) They … their books to school in a bag.
2. ***treffen***: a) I often … my friends in the park.
   b) Try to … that tree with your ball.
3. ***Karte***: a) Can you find Wales on the …?
   b) Look at the … for our special lunch.

Our travel report

For your yearbook, work in groups of four and write a short travel report about a class trip. It can be a real trip – or a fantasy trip! It needn't be as long as Dave's report on pages 18–19, but it's important to make it interesting for your readers.

Step 1

Choose an idea for your trip → WB 11/24

a) *What kind of class trip can your group write about? Do you want to use one of these photos? Or have you got your own great idea? Discuss different ideas and then choose* ***one*** *idea for your travel report.*

1

2

3

1. rafting | paddle | current | to capsize
2. science fiction | aliens | planet | spaceship
3. sightseeing | youth hostel | party | trouble

b) *Work with a placemat to collect ideas for your report. You each think about one of the four topics below. Write down ideas in your part of the placemat.*

1. The place: How did you get there?
2. The people: Who is in the report?
3. Typical activities: What did you do or see during the first part of your trip?
4. A special adventure (e.g. problem, surprise): What happened? What did you do?

c) *Choose which ideas you want to use and write them down in the middle of the placemat.*

For help with questions in the simple past, look back at **Station 2**.

For help with new words, look at the **Skills page**.

For help with placemats look at page 139 in the **Skills section**.

rafting ['rɑ:ftɪŋ] Schlauchbootfahren | **paddle** ['pædl] Paddel | **current** ['kʌrnt] Strömung | **to capsize** [kæp'saɪz] kentern | **to go sightseeing** ['saɪtˌsi:ɪŋ] eine Besichtigungstour machen | **youth hostel** ['ju:θ ˌhɒstl] Jugendherberge

Step 2

Plan your travel report → WB 11/25

For help with how to write a plan, look at the **Story** again.

a) *Your report has got four parts.*
Together, write a plan that shows the key ideas in each part.

Part 1: The beginning: Here you describe how you got to the place.
Part 2: The first day(s): Here you describe typical activities for this kind of trip.
Part 3: The special adventure: Say what happened, but don't tell the whole story. This part of the report finishes with a problem or an exciting situation.
Part 4: The ending: Explain how the adventure finished; find a good ending.

b) *Decide who writes which part of the report.*

Step 3

Write your part of the travel report

Do you remember the four kinds of words for travel reports? Look back at the **Story** exercises.

For help with the simple past, look at **Station 1** and **Station 2** again.

Station 3 helps you with adjectives.

a) *Work with the plan from Step 2 and make notes about the information in your part. Don't write sentences – just important words and phrases.*

b) *Read through your notes. Have you got interesting ideas and words?*

c) *Now write your part of the report. Don't forget to use the simple past.*

Step 4

Improve your part of the report → WB 12/26

Work with a partner from your group. Check each other's texts. Help each other to improve the texts.

Look at page 133 in the **Skills section** for tips on how to check texts.

Step 5

Finish your travel report → WB 12/27

a) *Put the four parts together and read the whole report. Are you happy with it? If not, discuss it and improve it.*

b) *Now think of the best way to present your report. Use photos or pictures too.*

The new boy → S21-22

VIEWING

1 Film scenes → WB 13/28

1 a) *Watch (00:00-03:01). Look at the headings for Scene A and B and at the phrases in the box. Match the phrases with the right scene.*

Scene A: After school **Scene B:** The new boy

sneaking around | a bad day? | friends again | why lemons? | trouble (between friends)

b) *Jinsoo and Marley want to know why Nick is buying all those things. What do **you** think Nick is up to? What happens next? Talk about your ideas and then watch the last part of the film (03:02-04:45).*

c) *Do you like the film's ending? Explain why/why not. Write two or three sentences.*

Example: I think the ending is nice / funny / surprising / boring / … because …

VIEWING

2 Film and music

a) *Before you read the box on the right, watch (01:58-04:45) again and listen to the music in the different scenes. What can you say about the music? Why do you think the filmmakers use music that way?*

b) *Now read the box. Then look at the photo. Which adjectives describe the mood and the feelings in the scene? What kind of music would **you** use for the scene?*

Film skills

Films don't work the same way as texts. A film tells a story with words – *and* with **pictures**, **sounds** and **music** too. So you have the story in a film, and you have different ways to tell that story. These are called the audio-visual effects of a film.

Examples: If you want to show that a person is sad, you can use slow and sad music. For an action scene, you can use loud and fast music.

Mood / Feelings:

excited | sad | tired | happy | angry | unfriendly | hurt | silly | …

Music:

funny | slow | loud | aggressive | sad | fast | sweet | happy | cool | scary | …

→ Solutions p. 241

Can you …

1. talk about activities that you did? — I went to … | We played / sold …
2. find out what happened? — Did you see …? | Why was he …? | How did she …?
3. say how you felt? — I was / felt embarrassed/… | It was exciting / …
4. compare things? — It's bigger than / as big as … | It's the most exciting …

UAGE

1 The yearbook team

Look at the list of jobs for the yearbook team. Write down what they did yesterday. Make sentences with the correct past forms.

Start: They talked about … They …

- talk about the 'dreams' page
- put the sports pages together
- look at Jay's ideas for the music pages
- collect ideas for the puzzles page
- take a photo of the yearbook team
- make a list of jobs for next week

UAGE

2 Put in the correct past forms

Holly: I [1] (go) swimming in the sea at Southend yesterday.
Dave: Wow! [2] (be) it your mum's idea to go to Southend?
Holly: No, it [3] (not be). Olivia's family [4] (invite) me.
Dave: Lucky you! [5] (you go) on the train?
Holly: Yes, we [6] (do).
Dave: You [7] (be) brave to go in the sea at this time of the year! [8] (be) the water cold?
Holly: Yes, it [9] (be). So we [10] (not stay) in the water for more than a few minutes.

UAGE

3 What are the questions?

Olivia calls home from Ty'n y Berth. Her dad wants to know more. What does he ask?

1. Olivia: We *got up* early this morning.
   Dad: When did you …?
2. Olivia: We *went* for a long walk.
   Dad: Where …?
3. Olivia: We *saw* lots of interesting things.
   Dad: What …?
4. Olivia: My classmates *laughed* at me.
   Dad: Why …?

UAGE

4 Comparative and superlative forms: Pet profiles for the yearbook

1. Luke's dog Sherlock is the (crazy) animal in England. There's nothing (funny) than when he chases his tail. It's always (fast) than he is!
2. The (cute) pets for Holly are her two guinea pigs. Mr Fluff likes to explore. He thinks a trip in a bag is (interesting) than a game on the floor! Honey isn't as (brave) as Mr Fluff.
3. Cats are the (popular) pets in the class. Dave's cat Sid brings presents for the family. Some presents are (good) than others. The (bad) thing for Dave is a mouse in his bed!

S 1/8–12 L 1/14–18

Middle school: How I got lost[1] in London

Rafe Khatchadorian is not very popular with his classmates, and his best friend Leo only exists in Rafe's imagination. A lot of things go wrong for Rafe, especially on a school trip to London to study Living History (when you visit special museums where they show how people lived in the past). When they go to see a famous London wax museum, he makes some silly mistakes, and his popularity score – a sign of how much the others like him – falls and falls.

The big event of the day was a tour around Madame Fifi's House of Wax. Now, of course we were excited about seeing the main attractions – Will and Kate! David Beckham! Rihanna! – but we were *really* excited about the basement[2]. Because in the basement was Madame Fifi's Temple of Terrors, where you could see beheadings[3], people on spikes and other horrible things. In other words, all the blood[4].

Yeah, yeah, we saw all the famous people. But do you *really* want to stand eye to eye with Tom Cruise? *You do?*

Not me. I wanted stuff from *my* world. So I stayed longest at Henry VIII (he had six wives[5] and beheaded two of them!), Winston Churchill (he said "We shall never surrender"[6] to Adolf Hitler!), Charles Darwin (it's thanks to him we know that we come from monkeys[7]!), Guy Fawkes (he tried to blow up[8] Parliament ... Wait: should[9] we like him or not?)

I was sad to leave the upper floors. And also ...

"Scared ...?" Leo whispered.

"No, of course I'm not scared," I said.

"Frightened?"

"Frightened is the same as scared," I told him. "And no, I'm not frightened."

But, let me tell you a secret: I *was* nervous.

"Is everyone ready?" Gordon, our tour guide, asked.

"Yeah," we all replied.

I remembered my popularity score today (-11) and decided to be brave, so my "Yeah" was the loudest. "YEAH!"

"Right, then, let's go," Gordon said. He opened the door but then stopped. "Does anybody in the group have a weak heart[10]?" he asked.

"No," we replied.

"NO!" came my voice, the loudest.

"And everyone knows about the haunting[11]?"

"YEAH!" I shouted, really enjoying myself.

Everyone looked at me – Gordon too.

"What is your name, young man?" he asked.

1 to get lost [get 'lɒst] verschwinden; verloren gehen | **2 basement** ['beɪsmənt] Keller | **3 beheading** [bɪ'hedɪŋ] Enthauptung | **4 blood** [blʌd] Blut | **5 wives** [waɪvz] Ehefrauen | **6 we shall never surrender** [wi ʃæl ˌnevə sr'endə] wir werden uns nie ergeben | **7 monkey** ['mʌŋki] Affe | **8 to blow up** [bləʊ‿'ʌp] in die Luft sprengen | **9 should** [ʃʊd] sollten | **10 weak heart** [wi:k 'hɑ:t] schwaches Herz | **11 haunting** ['hɔ:ntɪŋ] Spukerei

"Rafe," I said in a very small voice.

"And you know about the haunting, do you, Rafe?"

"Yes," I said in an even smaller voice.

"You read about it on the Madame Fifi's website?" he asked, with a strange smile.

"Yes, sir," I replied.

Everyone looked at me. They all really wanted to hear the story about the haunting but thanks to me, they didn't get the chance. Gordon just said: "Excellent. Let's go!" – and my popularity score went down again, to -22.

He opened the door and we saw the stone steps that went down into the dark. Down and down we went. At the bottom we heard a loud noise. One of the girls cried out[12] but Gordon told her it was just a passing[13] London Underground train. (OK, it wasn't "one of the girls" who cried out, it was me. Like I say, it was dark …)

Slowly, we started to see the wax figures.

"Cool," we said when we saw the heads on spikes, the murderers[14], the blood … Really scary stuff. Stuff that had *actually happened*[15].

"Now, Rafe …" Gordon said. "I'm sure you can tell us about the famous Temple of Terrors story?"

NO WAY. I shook my head "no". Gordon smiled. "Well, let me tell you then …"

"Over a hundred years ago, two gentlemen are taking a tour around the famous Madame Fifi's House of Wax. With them is a lady and they both want to impress[16] her.

"Do you know this Temple of Terrors?" the first one says. "They say it's very scary."

"Oh yes, very scary," the second man says.

Eleanor (the lady) says: "Oh, Cedric, it sounds terrible."

Both men see their chance to impress their lady friend.

"But I don't believe it," William says.

"Well, William," Cedric says, "let's go down and find out just how scary it is."

And the two men take the stone steps down into the Temple of Terrors.

"Well," William says. He looks around in the dark at the scary wax figures and feels very nervous. "I'm not frightened at all!"

"Frightened? Not me!" Cedric says, when he suddenly needs to use the bathroom.

"So, let's spend[17] the night here!" William says.

"Good idea!" Cedric says.

And so, because the men badly[18] want to impress Eleanor, they both agree[19] to spend the night …

"They couldn't stay the whole night," Gordon continued. "They soon ran out screaming[20], their eyes wide with terror. And the next day, someone found both men at their homes …"

We looked at Gordon in complete silence. "Dead[21]."

→ WB 15/1–4

12 to cry out [kraɪ 'aʊt] aufschreien | **13 passing** ['pɑ:sɪŋ] vorbeifahrend | **14 murderer** ['mɜ:drə] Mörder | **15 stuff that had actually happened** [ˌstʌf ðæt həd ˌæktʃuəli 'hæpnd] Dinge, die tatsächlich passiert sind | **16 to impress sb** [ɪm'pres] jmdn. beeindrucken | **17 to spend** [spend] verbringen | **18 badly** ['bædli] unbedingt | **19 to agree** [ə'gri:] einwilligen | **20 screaming** [skri:mɪŋ] schreiend | **21 dead** [ded] tot

Find more online: c543nu

Unit 2

Let's discover TTS!

1 Basketball Club

2 Dance class

3 Sign Language Club

4 A wall painting in the school building

SPEAKING

1 What you can do at TTS

a) *Look at the quotes in the speech bubbles on page 29. What are they about? Match them to the photos.*

b) *Read the box on the right and then talk about what you can see in the pictures. What is the same or different at your school?*

c) *Your turn: What pictures can you use to present your school?*

Across cultures

Some **subjects** are different in the UK. At TTS, for example, you can take exams in Dance, Drama, Film Studies or Fashion.

But at British schools there's more than just lessons. In the afternoons, clubs offer **additional activities** like sports, birdwatching, cooking or games like chess. Where can you participate in activities like these in Germany?

In Unit 2 you learn

… how to give a presentation about a school club. You learn:

- words do describe school activities
- ways to give extra information in a sentence
- the past progressive
- useful phrases for a presentation

Assembly

A We start school with our tutor at 8:30. Or sometimes we go to the hall for Assembly.

B We love competitions against other schools – well, we love winning.

C Everyone is special and everyone belongs here. We all try to help students with special needs.

D This school is full of art!

E We practise a lot and we sometimes do shows.

LISTENING **2** **This is a fantastic school!** → WB 16/1–2

L 1/19

→ △ 112/1
→ S18–20

a) *Who is Olivia talking to? Take notes about the different parts of her presentation and say what each part is about.*

b) *Choose one of the quotes from A–E. Listen again. What reactions are there from the listeners after the part with that quote?*

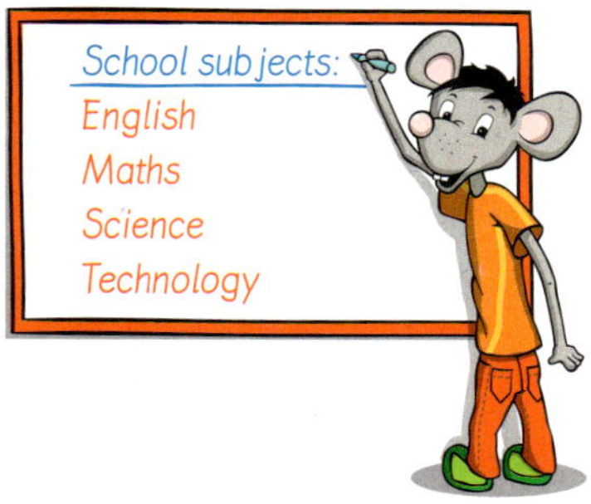

SPEAKING **3** **How to: Talk about a presentation**

You're one of the listeners at Olivia's presentation. What positive feedback can you give her?

Useful phrases

I liked your introduction.
Your presentation was nice / lively / …
First you … / Then you talked about …
That was interesting / surprising / …

L1/20

The queen who loved parties

Luke and Dave are at Luke's house. Luke is telling Dave about his History presentation.

Luke: Listen to this. My presentation is about two queens that lived in Greenwich. Once, there was a queen who loved parties and music and dancing. Her name was Anne. In 1616, her husband, King James, gave her a very special present: a house for her parties! The house had a beautiful view of the Thames. Anne's friends loved to visit her there. The parties which they celebrated were very loud. People say there are ghosts in the house today.

Dave: Anne and her friends?

Luke: Maybe … But the ghosts who live in the house don't come out often.

Dave: And is this the building which they used as a hospital later?

Luke: No, that's a different story. Later, Queen Mary lived in Anne's house. She loved the sea and boats and wanted to build a hospital for sailors. The architect whose design she chose was Christopher Wren. That was in 1692.

Dave: I know that story! When Wren showed her his plans for the first time, she was very upset. The hospital that he wanted to build was between her house and the river. She wanted to see the river and the boats, not a big building!

Luke: That's right! And in those days angry queens cut people's heads off! That's why Wren needed a quick idea. The idea he had was to cut the hospital in half. And he left a space in the middle so the queen kept her view of the river and Wren kept his head!

READING

1 Correct the sentences

Example: The queen who loved parties was Mary.
→ The queen who loved parties was Anne.

1. The parties which they celebrated were quiet.
2. The ghosts who live in the house come out every day.
3. The architect whose design she chose was Christopher Wright.
4. The hospital that he wanted to build was next to her house.

UAGE

2 Find the rule → G6

a) *Look at the text again. Collect the nouns in front of the relative pronouns* ***who, which, that*** *and* ***whose****.*

b) *Check if the nouns are people or things. When do you use which relative pronoun?*

UAGE

3 Match the sentence parts → WB 17/3–4

→ △ 112/2

Example: The king who / that gave his wife a very special present was James.

1. The king
2. The building
3. The queen
4. The river
5. The house
6. The people

who / that

which / that

whose

a) runs through Greenwich is the Thames.
b) went to Anne's parties had a lot of fun.
c) name was Mary loved the sea.
d) ghosts are quiet is a museum now.
e) is by the river was a hospital.
f) gave his wife a very special present was James.

UAGE

4 Contact clauses → G6

a) *Look at the sentences. Is the relative pronoun the subject or the object of the clause?*

1. There are museums **which** have special events for children.
2. It's an event **which** everyone finds exciting.

If the relative pronoun is the object, you don't need it!

→ △ 112/3

b) *Check the sentences. Say where you don't need the relative pronoun.*

1. Children that are interested in history must go there!
2. There are many things that you can do.
3. People who like music can learn songs from Old England.
4. The costumes which you can try on are really cool.
5. And you can make jewellery which they sell at the museum shop later.

UAGE

5 Make one sentence from two → WB 18/5

→ △ 113/4
→ ▲ 113/5

Example: History is a school subject. I really like it.
→ History is a school subject which I really like. / History is a school subject I really like.

1. Last lesson we talked about a famous person. We all know him.
2. First, we looked at a picture. We found it on the school's website.
3. Then we listened to music. He wrote it for Queen Elizabeth I.
4. Finally, we designed a poster. We called it "Meet Thomas Tallis!"

WRITING

6 How to: Write prompt cards

→ △ 113/6
→ S11

Read the skills box. Then look at the text on page 30 again. Add more key words to the prompt card below. Then make a second prompt card about Queen Mary and Christopher Wren.

Who: Anne, …
What: house, …
Where: Thames, …
When: 1616

Writing skills

In a presentation, don't read whole sentences from the page. Use **prompt cards**. On these cards, you write **key words** to help you to remember the main ideas in your presentation. Write important people, events, places, and dates under the headings: **Who** | **What** | **Where** | **When**

LISTENING

7 Gwen's timetable

L1/22
→ △ 114/7

a) *Gwen is a new girl at TTS. She's partially sighted. Listen to her conversation with Holly and Olivia. Why does Gwen need their help?*

b) *Listen again. Which subjects do they talk about? How can teachers and other students help Gwen?*

VOCABULARY

8 School subjects → WB 18/6

→ △ 114/8

a) *Look at Gwen's timetable. Compare it with your timetable.*

Time	Monday	Tuesday	Wednesday	Thursday	Friday
08:30	**Registration**				
08:50	Technology	Science	Maths	RE	English
09:50	Technology	Science	Maths	French	French
10:50	**Break**				
11:10	Maths	Art	Science	English	Humanities
12:10	English	Music	Technology	Humanities	Humanities
13:10	**Lunch**				
14:00	Dance	English	PE	Maths	Dance
15:00	**Registration in tutor group / Assembly**				
15:10	**Home / After-school clubs**				

b) *Write your own timetable in English.*

→ ▲ 114/9

L1/23 ⊙

Everyone was doing a really great job!

Holly wants to join the Eco Club at Thomas Tallis School. On the TTS website, she finds an article about a project the club did last year.

Home | About | New | **Clubs** | Community | Links | Contact | Search

Eco Club

The Wildlife Garden project

It was a beautiful morning, the first day of our Wildlife Garden project, and everyone was really excited to get started. The sun was shining, the birds were singing and the bees were humming. So even the animals were already looking forward to their new home!
It was great to have so much help; the list of jobs was a bit long: put up a sign (Henry), make a bee hotel (Jack), dig a hole (Kate and Filip), take photos (Alice and Rose) …
And everyone was doing a really great job! But then it happened: Sally fell into the pond while she was hanging up a bird house. That's when things started to go wrong. It was one of our funniest projects ever. Just look …!

EAKING **9** What were they doing when Sally fell into the pond? → G7

→ △ 114/10
→ ▲ 115/11

Look at the text and say what the other members of the Eco Club were doing when Sally fell into the pond.

Start like this: Henry **was putting** up a sign.
Alice and Rose **were** …

Do you remember how to make the progressive form of a verb? For the past progressive, look at G7 in the Grammar.

LANGUAGE

10 Match the parts → WB 19/7 → G7

→ △ 115/12
→ ▲ 115/13

Now look at the picture on page 33 again. What happened to the other Eco Club members while they were working on the Wildlife Garden?

1. Henry was putting up a sign
2. Sally fell into the pond
3. Filip and Kate hit a water pipe
4. Alice and Rose were taking photos
5. Jack was making a bee hotel

when
while

a) they were digging a hole.
b) he fell off the ladder.
c) he hit his thumb with the hammer.
d) a fox stole their lunch.
e) she was hanging up a bird house.

We mice were having a picnic **when** a fox **came** round the corner.
We ran into the school **while** the fox **was looking** for food.

SPEAKING

11 A game: What were you doing when ...? → WB 19/8, 20/9

a) *Work with a partner. Think of funny things that you did in your last holidays. (They needn't be true!) Write six sentences in the past progressive and six sentences in the simple past. Number the sentences from 1–6.*

b) *Take turns and throw the dice twice. Choose the sentences that match the numbers on the dice – one sentence in the past progressive and one sentence in the simple past. Then make one sentence with the two and use **while** or **when**.*

MEDIATION

12 A club at a German school → WB 20/10

→ S17

Pia finds a club at her school really interesting and wants to tell Olivia about it. But she doesn't know all the words in English. Help her to describe in her own words what the club is about.

Mediation skills

If you don't know a word in English, try to **describe it in other words** you already know. **Relative clauses** can also help you to describe words!

Example:
"*Hausmeister* – It's a person who looks after the school."

Streitschlichter-AG
Mach dich und andere stark!

In unserer AG lernst du, wie du bei einem Streit zwischen Schülern vermitteln kannst.
Als Streitschlichter hilfst du den Streitparteien, gemeinsam nach einer Lösung zu suchen. Es geht darum, Konflikte durch Reden – und nicht durch Gewalt! – zu lösen.
Lass dich zum Streitschlichter ausbilden und trage zu einem freundlichen Miteinander an unserer Schule bei!

RITING

13 How to: Write a flyer

→ S11

a) *Look at the flyer from the TTS Eco Club. Would you like to join the club? Say why or why not.*

b) *Now read the skills box. Choose* ***one*** *of the clubs on the right. Write and design a flyer for it.*

Maths Club | Singing Club | Tallis TV | Football Club | Science Club

c) *Exchange your flyers with another pair of students and peer-edit each other's work.*

Writing skills

When you write a flyer make sure
- it's easy to read
- it has all the important information about your club:
  the **name** of the club
  what you do
  when you meet (day and time)
  where you meet
  why people should join your club
- you welcome people with a special **welcome message** and a **slogan**!

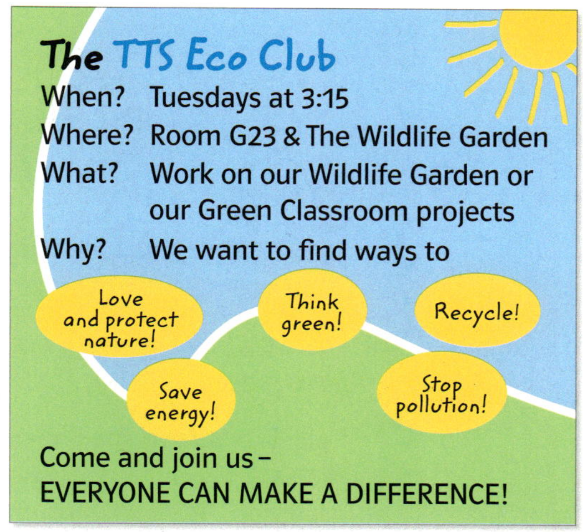

ENING

14 ‹ A song: What a wonderful world › Louis Armstrong

L1/26

a) *Listen to the song and look at the pictures. What is the song about?*

b) *Your turn: What are* ***your*** *ideas for a wonderful world?*

to protect [prəˈtekt] schützen | **nature** [ˈneɪtʃə] Natur | **to recycle** [ˌriːˈsaɪkl] recyceln; wiederverwerten | **to save** [seɪv] sparen | **pollution** [pəˈluːʃn] Verschmutzung | **to make a difference** [ˌmeɪk‿ə‿ˈdɪfrns] etwas ändern; etwas bewegen

The film star → S21–22

SPEAKING

1 Your turn: One day I want to be a/an …

a) *What is your 'dream job'? Why is it so great?*
b) *Talk about the pros and cons of the jobs on the right.*

actor | dancer | pilot | police officer | vet

VIEWING

2 Laura's problem → WB 21/11

2 *Watch the film. What is Laura's dream job? But what is her problem?*

VIEWING

3 Good advice? → WB 21/12

a) *Watch (01:38–04:00) again. What advice do people give Laura? Take notes.*

b) *Talk about the advice for Laura. Here are some ideas:*

A: Polly is a star, so she knows best!
B: Well Marley isn't a star and *his* advice is great too: "Believe in yourself".

c) *Look at the still on the right (04:35). What is Laura thinking at this moment in the film? Look at the phrases.*

d) *Now watch the rest of the film. Why does Laura thank Polly?*

Useful phrases

Don't panic! | Don't be nervous! | Just relax! | I'm sure you're good at … | You're always so confident. | Try again. | Take a deep breath. | Believe in yourself!

SPEAKING

4 What a great film!

In groups of 3–4, talk about something **you** *saw at the cinema – or want to see. These phrases from the film can give you ideas.*

Useful phrases

That was such a great film!
I'm / I was really impressed with …
I just love … He's / She's my favourite actor.
I can't wait for … | I really want to …

How to give a good presentation
→ S14–16

1 What makes a presentation good?

Copy the grid. Then put the tips and phrases from the box under the right headings.

What you talk about	How you present it	How you organise things	What you say
Give facts.	…	…	…
…			

"It's fantastic / really interesting / so much fun because …" | Smile. | Give facts. | Be on time. | "We really want to see you!" | Don't just read from your notes. | "Let's take a look at …" | Add a personal story that is connected to the topic. | Make eye contact with your audience. | "Today, I'd like to …" | Know your facts. | Speak clearly! | "First …, second …, third …" | Introduce yourself. | Don't forget your flyers. | "Do you enjoy / love / want …?" | Give the most important information. | "Hello and welcome to …!"

2 Two presentations
→ WB 22/14

3–4 a) *Watch two presentations. What are they about? Which presentation do you like better?*

b) *Work in groups of four. Each of you chooses one of the headings in Ex. 1. Then watch the presentations again. Focus on your heading and take notes for each film. Add things from each presentation and note down what is missing.*

c) *Talk about your notes. Discuss what makes the presentations good / not so good.*

3 Make a good presentation

Improve Lou's presentation text on the right. You can think of facts that aren't in the text. Then practise your presentation and read it out loud several times.

Hello and welcome to the Drama Club's presentation! Do you enjoy …?

Er – OK, I'm from Drama Club. We meet every week. I wanted to give you a flyer, but – sorry, I forgot it at home. Oh, and what else did I want to tell you? I can't remember …

Join our club!

In this task, work in groups of four. Each group is a school club. At a 'club market', each group does a short presentation (3–5 minutes) about its club. Why is it special? Why is it the best club? You want as many classmates as possible to join **your** club! Each person in your group has a different job to make your presentation great.

Step 1

Which club? → WB 23/16

a) *First, decide together which club your group wants to be. Here are some ideas; maybe you've got ideas of your own.*

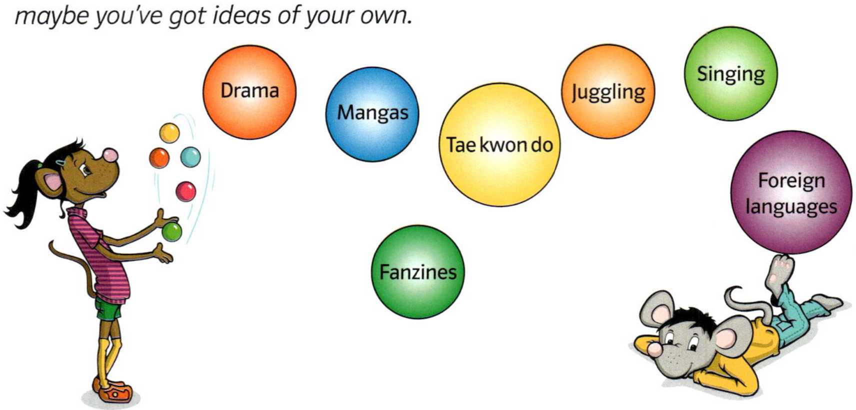

b) *Now choose a time slot for your presentation on the club market's timetable. Your teacher will check that everyone chooses a different time.*

1:15 | 1:20 | 1:25 | 1:30 | 1:35 | 1:40

Step 2

Think of ideas for your club → WB 23/17

a) *What's important to know about your club? What do you do when you meet? Collect information and facts that can interest new members. Answer these questions:*
What | When | Where | Why | Who | ...

b) *Now talk about what makes your club special, what makes it better than the other clubs. Remember, you want new members!*

Step 3

Make your club sound great → WB 24/18

a) *Collect words and phrases which can make your club sound great. Write sentences with them.*

b) *Now think of a slogan for your club.*

Example:
Drama Club: "Once a week you need some drama in your life!"

Look back at the **Skills page** for phrases to make your club sound interesting.

Look back at the **Skills page** for help with presentation skills. **Station 1** is the place to look for help with prompt cards.

Step 4

Pair A: Write your flyer

One pair in your group writes the flyer for your club. Give important information on it, and make it easy to read.

Pair B: Write your prompt cards

The other pair decides what needs to go on the prompt cards for the presentation. Write your prompt cards.

For help with a flyer, look at **Station 2** again.

Step 5

Peer-edit each other's work → WB 24/19

The pair that wrote the prompt cards now checks the flyer; the pair that wrote the flyer checks the prompt cards. Talk about changes in your group.

Step 6

You're on!

a) *Decide together who in your group gives the presentation, and then practise together. Give him / her tips!*

b) *Now give your presentation. Don't forget the flyer!*

Step 7

Which club do YOU want to join? → WB 24/10

a) *As a class, talk about the different presentations.*

b) *Decide for yourself which club* ***you*** *want to join.*

c) *Class activity: Put a flyer for each club on a different table. Then each student goes to the table of the club he / she wants to join. Which club has the most new members?*

Look at **Check-in** and the **Skills page** for giving feedback on a presentation.

S1/17–22
L1/28–33

What a wonderful world

A "Big news today!" Holly said as she walked home from school with Luke and Jay. "Friends of the Earth are having a poster competition and the prize is a day out in London at the Natural History Museum!"

"Cool – they have dinosaurs!" Luke said. "What do you have to do?"

"Design a poster called 'What a Wonderful World' – just listen to the song for ideas," Holly answered.

Luke was excited. "Why don't we do a poster together, Jay?" he asked.

"Maybe …" Jay said, but he wasn't sure. "I know that song," he thought, "and we can make an amazing poster!" But something felt wrong … He really didn't want to share his ideas with anyone else.

When he was home again, he phoned Luke. "I want to enter the competition," he said, "but not together. I want to try on my own."

Luke was very surprised, but he didn't want to show it. "Cool," he said. "Me too! And I'm sure I can win!" Then, after the phone call, he thought to himself: "Just you wait, Jay Azad!"

B That evening, Jay talked to himself while he was writing and drawing his first ideas.

"OK, so on the left side, there's a dirty street with lots of cars and rubbish everywhere, and on the other side we can see the 'wonderful world' with no cars, birds in the trees, flowers everywhere …"

He stopped. It was a bit boring. "I need a big idea to make it more fun," he thought. Suddenly, he noticed a manga magazine which was lying on his bedroom floor.

"Mangas!" he shouted. "That's it!" He was very good at art and started to do some cool manga drawings. But how could he use them on his poster?

C While Jay was drawing, Luke was at home working on his own ideas. He felt very confident. "OK, Jay", he thought. "If you don't want to work with me, fine – because I know I can win!"

"Hey, Irina!" he shouted. "Imagine this … my poster is a manga world. Each character has a different job and they all work together to make the world a cleaner, better place. They have special costumes and names that start with letters that show what they do – Rokuro does recycling, Tomoko looks after the trees, Satoshi cleans the streets … What do you think?"

Irina was quiet for a moment. "It's *great!*" she said finally. "You can win!"

D The next day, Luke and Jay sat together in their Maths class, but they weren't thinking about Maths at all. Luke smiled to himself – he was proud of his brilliant idea! But Jay wasn't happy at all.

When it was time for break, Luke got up and went to get a drink. He left his bag on the table with his exercise book on top. Jay looked at it quickly – and he couldn't believe his eyes! There were little pictures all over it … Mangas!

Jay looked again and laughed – Luke's drawings were really bad! But then he noticed some words too … Bunko – bees,

Fumio – flowers … "That's so clever!" he thought. "That's the big idea I need for my poster – and I'm much better at drawing than Luke!"

Stop and think:
Is Luke right to be angry with Jay?
What should Jay do now?

E After school, the friends were walking home together when Luke decided to make Jay feel nervous.

"My poster is amazing!" he said. "I can't wait to get home and do some more work on it. Is yours finished?"

"Nearly," said Jay. "I just need a bit more time to think of some cool names for my mang…" He stopped. What was he saying?

"No! Not mangas! That's my idea – you can't steal it!" Luke shouted.

"Calm down!" said Olivia. "It's only a competition."

"Yes, a competition which Jay wanted to enter alone!" Luke shouted. He was very angry now. "When he didn't have good ideas, he stole mine!"

"I didn't – I had my own ideas!"

"Did you look in my bag at break time?" Luke asked as he pushed Jay. Jay turned round and hit Luke's arm.

"Stop!" Dave shouted. He stood between the boys and tried to stop the fight. "Are you crazy?! I thought you were friends!"

"But Jay can't just steal my ideas!"

Jay was upset now. "I can't talk to you for another minute," he said. "You idiot!"

F Dave tried again. "Stop, Jay! Listen, Luke – why don't you help each other?"

"I wanted to work together, but he didn't," Luke answered.

Jay turned back. "You can't draw!"

"So what? You think you're special just because you're good at art!" Luke answered. "But where's your big idea? You haven't got one!"

Jay didn't answer. Nobody spoke for a long time. Then at last Jay opened his bag and took out some papers. "I'm sorry!" he said. "Look, I always planned to use mangas. These are the ones I drew during break, after I saw yours. I just didn't have any good ideas, and your idea with the names was so cool. – Come on, let's do a poster together, like you said yesterday."

"I'm not sure," Luke said. He wasn't ready to be friends again and he wanted Jay to know how it felt when your friend didn't want to work with you!

Jay stood next to Luke and gave him his papers. Luke looked at them and saw Tomoko in the trees and Fumio planting flowers – his ideas. But the drawings were just fantastic!

"OK," Luke said at last, "let's try and work together."

"Cool!" Jay answered. "Let's show everyone what a real manga story is!"

SPEAKING

1 Friends? → WB 25/21

a) *Talk about what Jay did and what you think of it. Do you know situations like that?*

b) *Do you like the ending? Say why / why not.*

c) *Say what is good or bad about working together with somebody.*

READING

2 Looking at the story → WB 25/22

→ S7–8

a) *Usually a story has three main parts: beginning, middle and end. Match the parts (A–F) of the story with the three main parts. Which main part says what the story is about? Which part is about a problem? Which part is about the solution?*

b) *Sum up what happens in each part. Use a grid like this for your answers.*

Main part	Letters A–F	What happens?
Beginning: what the story is about	A	…
Middle: …	…	Jay and Luke try to find ideas. …
End: …	…	…

VOCABULARY

3 Inside – outside

a) *In this story we don't only learn what the characters say to other characters, but also what they think or say when they're alone. Go through the story and look for examples. How did you find them? Where did you find the most examples?*

b) *Read the skills box before you look at the story again. Where does the story use language for stronger feelings?*

c) *Now collect different words / phrases for stronger feelings in a mind map.*

→ ▲ 115/14
→ S3

Example: A: What's your favourite club?
B: Drama Club. I **love** acting.

A: Do you like school?
B: I **really like** Maths, but I **absolutely hate** PE.

Vocabulary skills

When you want to **show stronger feelings**, there are special words and phrases you can use like 'really' or 'amazing'. (You can also show stronger feelings when you say things in a **louder voice**.)

→ Solutions p. 241

Can you …

1. give more information about people / things? — The man who / that … | The school which / that … | The queen whose house we visited …
2. say what was happening in the past? — She was eating lunch when her sister called. | They fell over Sherlock while they were playing in the park.
3. talk about lessons and school clubs? — It's really interesting / so much fun because …

GUAGE

1 Relative clauses and contact clauses

a) *Which relative pronoun do you need here?* who / that | which / that | whose

1. Do you like the poster **1** I designed for the competition?
2. I love films **2** are about nature and animals.
3. New students often make friends with people **3** they meet at clubs.
4. There's the teacher **4** lessons I like best.
5. Jamie is a student **5** is really good at sports.

b) *When is a contact clause possible in the sentences in a)?*

GUAGE

2 Past progressive or simple past?

Example: sleep | when | alarm clock ring
→ Dave **was sleeping** when the alarm clock **rang**.

1. wash his face | when | Sid come into bathroom
2. send Jay a text | while | mother make breakfast
3. get his bike | when | father leave the house
4. arrive at school | while | Luke still sleep

RITING

3 School subjects

a) *Look at the pictures. What are the school subjects?*

b) *Which subjects in a) do you like best? Why? Write what is great / interesting / … about it.*

S 1/23–27
L 1/34–38

Horrid[1] Henry's Christmas play[2]

Henry is about 10 years old. He is not a very nice child, so people call him Horrid Henry. Henry doesn't like school, but he has a dream: He wants to be really famous one day. When his teacher tells the class about her plans for a new Christmas play, Henry sees his chance to play the lead[3] – Joseph. But the teacher knows Henry really well and already has other plans …

Horrid Henry sat low down in his chair and watched the clock – it was moving *so* slowly! "Please go faster!" he thought. Only five more minutes until he could go home! Already Henry could taste the crisps that were waiting for him in his bag outside.

Miss Battle-Axe[4] talked on and on about school dinners (yuck[5]), the new drinking fountain blah blah blah, Maths homework blah blah blah, the school Christmas play blah blah … what? Did Miss Battle-Axe say … Christmas play? Horrid Henry sat up.

"This is a new play with singing and dancing," Miss Battle-Axe continued[6]. "And both the older and the younger children are taking part[7] this year."

Singing! Dancing! Showing off[8] in front of the whole school! Years ago, when Henry was still at primary school, he played eighth sheep in the Christmas play and he took the baby from the manger[9] and didn't want to give him back. Henry hoped Miss Battle-Axe didn't remember. Because Henry needed to play the lead this time. Who else could be an all-singing, all-dancing Joseph?

"I want to be Mary!" all the girls shouted.

"I want to be a wise man[10]!" Rude Ralph shouted.

"I want to be a sheep!" Anxious Andrew shouted.

"I want to be Joseph!" Horrid Henry shouted.

"No, me!" Jazzy Jim shouted.

"Me!" Brainy Brian shouted.

"Quiet!" Miss Battle-Axe shouted. "*I'm* the director[11], and *I* decide about who can act each part. Margaret. You are Mary." She gave her a thick[12] script.

Moody Margaret shouted: "I'm so happy! I'm so happy!" All the other girls looked at her angrily.

"Susan, Linda – you're the donkey[13]; cows[14], Fiona and Clare. Blades of grass[15] …" Miss Battle-Axe continued through her list.

"Choose me for Joseph, choose me for Joseph," Horrid Henry prayed[16]. Of course,

1 **horrid** ['hɒrɪd] gemein | 2 **Christmas play** ['krɪsməs pleɪ] Krippenspiel | 3 **the lead** [li:d] Hauptrolle | 4 **Miss Battle-Axe** [mɪs 'bætlæks] Fräulein Streitaxt | 5 **yuck** [jʌk] igitt | 6 **to continue** [kən'tɪnju:] fortfahren | 7 **to take part** [teɪk 'pɑ:t] teilnehmen | 8 **to show off** [ʃəʊ‿'ɒf] angeben | 9 **manger** ['meɪndʒə] Krippe | 10 **wise man** ['waɪz mæn] einer der Heiligen Drei Könige | 11 **director** [dɪ'rektə] Regisseur | 12 **thick** [θɪk] dick | 13 **donkey** ['dɒŋki] Esel | 14 **cow** [kaʊ] Kuh | 15 **blade of grass** [ˌbleɪd‿əv 'grɑ:s] Grashalm | 16 **to pray** [preɪ] beten

the best actor in the school always gets the star part. And the best actor was Henry, wasn't he?

"I'm a sheep, I'm a sheep, I'm a beautiful sheep!" Singing Soraya sang.

"I'm a shepherd[17]!" Jolly Josh smiled.

"I'm an angel[18]," Magic Martha whispered.

"I'm a blade of grass," Weepy William cried[19].

"And Joseph is …"

"Me!" Henry shouted.

"Me!" New Nick, Greedy Graham, Dizzy Dave and Aerobic Al shouted.

"… Peter," Miss Battle-Axe said. "From Miss Lovely's class."

Horrid Henry felt sick[20]. Perfect Peter? His *younger* brother? Perfect Peter gets the star part?

"It's not fair!" Horrid Henry cried.

Miss Battle-Axe looked at him angrily. "Henry, you're …" Miss Battle-Axe looked at her list.

"Please not a blade of grass, please not a blade of grass," Horrid Henry prayed. Miss Battle-Axe always knew how to make him feel *really* silly and small.

"… the innkeeper[21]."

The innkeeper! Horrid Henry sat up and smiled. How silly he was! Of course, the innkeeper was the star part! He already imagined the scene: Henry the innkeeper is washing glasses and pouring out big drinks to all his happy customers[22] and singing a song. He has a nice long argument[23] about why there is no room at the inn, and finally, he has the chance to close the door in Moody Margaret's face. Wow! Maybe he can even sing a second song like 'Ten Green Bottles'. He can sing and dance and his less talented classmates can play the bottles who he can knock off[24] the wall, one by one. What fun!

Miss Battle-Axe gave a page to Henry. "Your script," she said.

→ WB 27/1–4

17 shepherd [ˈʃepəd] Hirte | **18 angel** [ˈeɪndʒl] Engel | **19 to cry** [kraɪ] weinen | **20 He felt sick.** [felt ˈsɪk] Ihm war schlecht. | **21 innkeeper** [ˈɪnkiːpə] Herbergswirt | **22 customer** [ˈkʌstəmə] Kunde/Kundin | **23 argument** [ˈɑːɡjəmənt] Streit | **24 to knock off** [nɒk‿ˈɒf] herunterstoßen

LISTENING

1 Mr Preston's scary story
→ WB 28/1

L 1/39

a) *When Mr Preston reads Dave's travel report, he remembers his own class trip to Wales a long time ago. Listen to the story about Mt Snowdon, a castle[1] and ghosts …*

1. **When** did Mr Preston see the ghosts?
2. **Who** were they?
3. **What** did the ghosts do – or not do?
4. **What** does Dave think about the story?

b) *In class, compare Dave's trip to Wales in Unit 1 with his dad's trip. Which trip is more interesting to you? Say why. (Think of the different activities, different feelings, …)*

c) *Choose one of the two 'ghost scenes' you see in the pictures. Write 6–8 sentences about the ghost in your scene. What do you think is his/her story?*

LANGUAGE

2 Olivia's dream

Last night Olivia had a strange dream. Read her e-mail to Holly. What verbs are missing? Sometimes there's more than one possible answer. Use the simple past.

Holly – I **1** a really strange dream last night …
I **2** at school and **3** the classroom door. But nobody **4** there. Suddenly, I **5** a strange noise outside. So I **6** out to the playground. That's when I **7** something in the air: a UFO! Holly, I **8** sooooo scared! The UFO **9** closer and closer. Then, someone **10** the UFO's door and a green alien **11** out. "Hello Olivia!" he **12**. "But, how do you know my name?!" I **13**. "Oh, it's me. Jay," he said. "I always go to school by UFO." Wasn't that a strange dream? Then, when **14** to school this morning, Jay **15** the first person I **16**! And: He was wearing a GREEN shirt!
xoxo, Olivia ❤

1 **castle** [ˈkɑːsl] Burg; Schloss

EAKING

3 At Greenwich Market → WB 28/2, 29/5

a) *Talk about the scene at Greenwich Market. What was everybody doing? Be creative!*

b) *Use different adjectives to talk about the scene. Here are some ideas:*

funny | good | happy | angry | jealous | tired
bored | boring | interesting | typical | big

Examples: A: The boy's ice cream isn't as big as the girl's.
B: I think the scene with the bird is the funniest! What do you think?

ULARY

4 A flyer for Drama Club → WB 29/6

a) *Which words can you think of for the gaps? Sometimes there's more than one possible answer.*

b) *Do you think the brochure is a good example for this kind of project? Why/Why not? Find five things you can do differently with this flyer.*

We invite all students **1** love theatre to **2** the TTS Drama Club! We **3** every Wednesday at 3:30 in Room 0.4.04. Our next play[2] is William Shakespeare's Romeo and Juliet – and Shakespeare is of course Britain's most **4** writer[3]! But this isn't just a play: This is a musical of 'R&J', so we **5** LOTS of boys and girls **6** can act and **7**! And this isn't a historical 'R&J'! No, we **8** to show the London of TODAY! So, forget **9** costumes like in Shakespeare's days. You can wear your own cool **10**! Also, we always need people who can **11** posters, sell tickets or **12** with the sound. For more **13**, just ask Mr Gibbons **14** teaches Drama in Years 7 and 9.

2 **play** [pleɪ] Theaterstück | 3 **writer** ['raɪtə] Schriftsteller

Find more online: k298fe

London: A special city

London is a huge city, and Greenwich is only a small part of it. On these two pages you can learn more about the British capital and find out what makes it so special.

SPEAKING

1 First facts about London → WB 30/1

a) *What can you find out from the photos? The words on the right can help.*

multi-ethnic city | famous / historical sights | green spaces | royal family | river | underground trains | busy streets | festivals

Example: 1. The Thames goes through the centre of London. It's a big, busy river. You can see famous …

1 The Thames, Big Ben and the London Eye

2 Oxford Street

3 The Tube

4 The Notting Hill Carnival

5 Buckingham Palace

6 Hyde Park

b) *Match the sentence parts to find out more facts about London.*

1. London was originally a Roman town
2. Today London is the
3. It's the capital city of
4. Over eight million people
5. The students in London's schools speak
6. London has got five

a) England and of the UK.
b) international airports.
c) more than 300 different languages.
d) largest city in the European Union (E
e) with the name 'Londinium'.
f) live in London.

c) *Take turns to tell your partner as much as you can about London in one minute.*

WING

2 Royal London → WB 30/2

5

a) *Before you watch: What can you say about the things that Laura is wearing?*

b) *Now watch and choose the correct endings.*

1. Laura's clothes
   a) are for a party.
   b) celebrate royal events.
   c) show what the royal family wear.

2. The Changing of the Guards takes place
   a) in front of Buckingham Palace.
   b) at the Tower of London.
   c) in Hyde Park.

3. Prince Albert was
   a) Queen Victoria's brother.
   b) British.
   c) from Germany.

4. The Royals are part of the British identity
   a) for everyone in the UK.
   b) for some people in the UK.
   c) only for older people.

c) *Your turn: What do you think about royal families? Explain your opinion.*

ENING

3 Young Londoners → WB 30/3

L2/1

a) *A class in London is doing a project about their city. While you listen, work in groups of three. Each group takes different notes under one of these headings.*

b) *Share the information you collected in a) with the other groups with the same question.*

What is good in London?	What is not so good?	How is London different?
– exciting things to do	– expensive	– bigger than other cities
– …	– …	– …

ITING

4 What makes London special?

Talk about what you think makes London a special city. Write your ideas in a mind map.

AKING

5 Your turn: Cities in Germany

Talk about German cities. Compare them with London. What is similar and what is different?

Useful phrases

It's also a Roman town / a capital city / …
It isn't as big / … as London.
There aren't as many …
It has / hasn't got famous sights / a river / …

Find more online: i9c4u3

Unit 3

London is amazing!

A Famous sights: the Houses of Parliament and Big Ben

SPEAKING

1 Talk about places in London

Describe the places in the photos. Say what you can see or do there. Find the places on the map at the back of your book.

LISTENING

2 A video chat with Amir

L2/2

→ S18–20

a) *Jay is having a video chat with Amir, his cousin. Amir lives in Bradford and has plans to see London with Jay. Listen, and say what kind of things each boy is interested in.*

b) *Listen again and take notes about these places.*

Covent Garden | the British Museum | Brick Lane | the London Wall | Shakespeare's Globe

In Unit 3 you learn

… how to discuss plans and how to describe the way people do things. You learn:

- words for things to do and see in London
- the language of plans (*going-to future*)
- word-building with *some, any, every, no*
- words to describe actions (*adverbs*)

Brick Lane: multi-ethnic flair and street art

C The wax figures at Madame Tussauds

Londoners and tourists at Covent Garden

E The Horse Guards at Whitehall

AKING

3 Your turn: Choose your London → WB 31/1

→ △ 116/1

Think about what you already know about London. In groups, take turns to tell each other two things that you would really like to see or do there. Explain why. Use your notes from Ex. 2.

ULARY

4 London vocabulary → WB 31/2

Collect words and names that are useful for your personal vocabulary. Add more words while you work through Unit 3.

L 2/3

It's going to be fun

"It was amazing," Amir tells his aunt. He's staying with the Azads and earlier today Jay took him to the Royal Observatory.

"Good. And what are you two going to do tomorrow?" Mrs Azad asks. "Are you going to see more sights in Greenwich?"

"No, we aren't. We're going to visit the British Museum with Olivia and Holly," Jay tells her. "We met them in Greenwich Park this afternoon, and Olivia is like Amir – she loves museums."

Mrs Azad's face shows that she isn't happy with this plan. But Jay can think fast. "Don't worry," he says. "We aren't going to go alone. Shahid is going to take us." His 18-year-old brother isn't at home at the moment, so Jay must try to persuade him later.

"Oh, is Shahid going to look after you? That's OK then," says Mrs Azad.

"Yes, it's going to be fun. But there's just one thing. The museum is free, but I'm not sure where I'm going to get money for our Oyster cards or for our lunch."

Mrs Azad smiles. "Probably the same place where you *always* get money."

READING

1 What do you think? → WB 32/3

1. What is Mrs Azad's problem with the boys' plan?
2. What is Jay's solution to that problem?
3. Where is Jay going to get money?

Across cultures

The cheapest way to travel by public transport in London is with an **Oyster card**. This is a smartcard you can top up with credit. What's the cheapest way to travel where you live?

LANGUAGE

2 Find the rule for *going to* → WB 32/4, 33/5 → G8

a) *Find phrases with* ***going to*** *in the text. Which part of the time line are they about?*

b) *How do you make* ***going to*** *forms? Write the rule and put it in your folder.*

LANGUAGE

3 Your turn: What are you going to do?

→ △ 116/2
→ S24

a) *First, write down three sentences about your weekend. Walk around and ask a few classmates about their plans.*

b) *Take turns to say what you found out about your classmates' plans.*

What are you going to do next weekend?

On Sunday I'm going to visit my grandma.

JAGE

4 What's going to happen? → WB 33/6

→ △ 116/3

Write about the people in the picture. Find your own verbs.

Start: 1. The old man and woman **are going to sit down.**
2. The man in the wheelchair **is going to** …

KING

5 Play a game: Guess my plans for tomorrow

→ △ 116/4

Think of a place in London but don't say what it is. Your partner must ask questions and guess the activity. Start the questions with "Are you going to …?"

Example: A: Are you going to listen to music?
B: No, I'm not.
A: Are you going to look at animals?
B: Yes, I am.
A: Are you going to visit London Zoo?
B: Yes, I am. That's right.

look at pictures / …

watch football / street shows / …

visit a historical building / …

listen to street musicians

NING

6 How to: Get around by Tube → WB 34/8

L 2/5
→ S18–20

a) *Work with the map of the Tube and DLR at the back of your book. A tourist is at Elephant & Castle station and wants to get to Buckingham Palace. Listen to the dialogue. Which route do you think is best – the man's or the woman's? Why?*

b) *Take turns to describe the routes to the other places above. You can start at Elephant & Castle or go from one sight to another.*

Place / Sight	Station
Buckingham Palace	Victoria
Oxford Street	Oxford Circus
Tower of London	Tower Hill
Transport Museum	Covent Garden
Mudchute Farm	Crossharbour

Useful phrases

You take the … line to … | You change onto the … line. | You go north / south / east / west to … | It's three stops to … | You get off at …

L 2/6

Good idea!

AKING

7 The photo story → WB 34/8

*Imagine you're **one** of the people in the story. What can he / she say about it?*

→ △ 117/5
→ ▲ 117/6

Example: (Jay) I was really hungry. Olivia had a great idea. But then I saw …

UAGE

8 Revision: Comparison of adjectives

*What kind of a food challenge would be the best for **you**? Why? Write about it in 5–6 sentences with different forms of adjectives. The examples can help you.*

Examples: I think the **most important thing** is to find **the best food**!
Healthy food is **better than** … food, but **not as** … **as** …

UAGE

9 Compound words with *some* and *any* → G9

a) *Match the parts.*

1. I'm hungry. I need
2. I've only got £1. I can't buy
3. Are there public toilets
4. Let's watch this guy. He's doing
5. I can't see the show – I'm behind
6. We must go now. We haven't got
7. Where's the Tube station? Does

a) anything expensive.
b) some good tricks.
c) any more time.
d) something to eat.
e) anyone know?
f) someone very tall!
g) anywhere here?

→ △ 117/7
→ ▲ 118/8

b) *Do you remember the rule for **some** and **any** from last year? Explain it.*

UAGE

10 Complete the words → WB 35/9–10, 36/11 → G9

some any every no

→ △ 118/9

Holly: What can we do till we meet Shahid later? Has 1 *body* got a good suggestion?
Jay: It must be 2 *thing* that costs 3 *thing* – we haven't got any money left.
Olivia: Let's just walk around. I'm sure that's fun for 4 *one* new in London like Amir. There are lots of interesting things to see 5 *where* you look. What do you think, Amir?
Amir: Well, if 6 *body* wants to make a different suggestion – yes, I'd like that.
Holly: Is there 7 *where* special you'd like to go or 8 *thing* special you'd like to see?
Amir: Well, 9 *thing* is special for me – it's all amazing. But I'd love to walk near the river.
Jay: Is that OK with 10 *body*? – Great, come on, let's go and find the Thames!

AKING

11 Your turn: Visitors → WB 36/12–13

a) *With a partner, think of where you can go or what you can do with young visitors where you live. Make a list of 4–5 different ideas.*

b) *Present your 'Top 3' to the class.*

Useful phrases

Pros: good for someone who likes history / … | doesn't cost anything | easy to get there by public transport | something everyone enjoys

Cons: (very) expensive | not everyone is into … | boring | too far away | not good in bad weather

L 2/8

They can bite *very* hard

If you don't know London well, a bus tour with a guide can be a good idea. You can see and learn a lot much faster and more easily than if you explore the city alone.

"Now we're going slowly past the Tower of London, one of the city's must-see sights – you can see it clearly on the left. William the Conqueror built the Tower when he became king of England in 1066. In the past it was a castle, a prison and even a royal zoo with big animals like lions and bears! Today it's a must-see sight. Many people come specially to see the Crown Jewels, but the Beefeaters give fantastic tours of the whole Tower – they know its history better than anyone! The Raven Master is a Beefeater too. His job is to look after the ravens carefully and to make sure they stay happily and safely in their home at the Tower. If you visit the Tower, don't go too close to the ravens. They don't always like that – and they can bite *very* hard!"

Across cultures

William the Conqueror and his people came from Normandy in France, so after 1066 many French words became part of the English language. Can you give some examples?

SPEAKING

12 A must-see sight for you too?

Would you like to visit the Tower? Why or why not?

LISTENING

13 Rocky's audio tour

L 2/9–11

a) *Listen once. Who is Rocky? What three topics does he tell you about?*

→ S18–20

b) *Listen again. What does Rocky say about* ***food*****,** ***treasure*** *and* ***ghosts****? Take notes.*

→ S17

c) *Mediation: There's no 'Rocky' audio tour in German, and a young German tourist who doesn't speak English wants to know what Rocky says. Give the main information in German.*

Listening skills

When you listen to information, first just try to understand the **gist** (main ideas). Then listen again for **more information**. Collect **key words and phrases** that help you to remember.

UAGE

14 Find the rule for adverbs → G10–11

a) *What do **adjectives** (slow, clear) describe? What do **adverbs** (slowly, clearly) describe? How do you make adverbs?*

b) *Find adverbs in the text for these adjectives. What can you say about the spelling?*

easy – special – careful – happy

The bus is **slow**. It's going **slowly**.
It's a **clear** view. You can see it **clearly**.

A few adverbs are irregular.

good → well
fast → fast
hard → hard

UAGE

15 Talk about the people in the pictures → WB 36/14

→ △ 118/10
→ △ 119/11

What are they doing, and how are they doing it? What do you think the situation is?

angry – excited – nervous – happy – loud – aggressive – fast – …

Example: 1. He's jumping back **nervously**. Maybe he's scared.

UAGE

16 Adjective or adverb? → WB 37/15

Complete these online comments about two tours in London.

→ △ 119/12
→ ▲ 119/13

A. "It was a 1 (fantastic) tour of the Tower. The Beefeater explained everything 2 (clear) and told us lots of 3 (exciting) stories. After the tour he also gave us some 4 (good) tips about where to eat 5 (good) and 6 (cheap) near the Tower."

B. "I checked the website 7 (careful) and it looked like the 8 (perfect) bus tour. But I was very 9 (disappointed). Most guides work 10 (hard) for their money and are very 11 (nice)! Not our guide. He spoke to us so 12 (rude)! And, the bus went past all the sights *much* too 13 (quick)!"

TING

17 Your turn: Write about a sight / a special place in London → WB 37/16–17

In 6–8 sentences, say what the sight is and where it is. Describe it and say why it's special.

A day out in London
→ S21–22

SPEAKING

1 Warm-up

Write down places / sights you think are symbols of London. Then tell the class.

VIEWING

2 Out and about in London
→ WB 38/18

6 *Watch the film. Which part do **you** really like? Why?*

VIEWING

3 A closer look
→ WB 38/19

Watch again and answer the questions. These ideas can help.

1. Why do you think Jinsoo's sister, Mina, is with the boys?
2. Where did Jinsoo want to go? Why didn't they go there?
3. What was the problem with Mina at Camden Market?

Jinsoo and Mina's dad | adult / child ticket | sightseeing / normal bus | look after | expensive

VIEWING

4 Setting and atmosphere in film scenes

a) *First, read the skills box. Then watch scenes **A** (01:15 – 01:50) and **B** (01:57 – 02:06) again. Say why you think they're important or interesting for the film.*

A

B

b) *In Ex. 2 you named a favourite scene. Now talk about its setting and atmosphere. These words can help:*

cool | crazy | famous | funny | interesting | international | multi-ethnic | lots to see / discover | people everywhere

c) *Write a short description of what Jinsoo, Marley, Nick and Mina could do in a **different** location in London. Look at your lists from Ex. 1 for ideas.*

Film skills

In a film, the viewer needs to know what the film's **setting** is, so the choice of **locations** in a film is important. A famous place like London really needs to *look* like London!

Atmosphere is important too: crowds, places, views, water, things to look at or buy, cool shops … These things can create a special atmosphere for the viewer.

How to find information on the internet → S5, 9

1 Start with the homepage of a famous attraction's website

Most homepages give basic information and also useful links to other pages. Try to answer these questions with the help of the homepage for the Natural History Museum in London. If the answer is not on the page, which 'quick link' do you think can help?

1. Where is the museum?
2. How do I get there?
3. Is it open every day?
4. Are there any special displays at the moment?
5. Must I pay to visit the museum?

NATURAL HISTORY MUSEUM

Home | Visit us | Nature online | Education | Support us | Buy online

Cromwell Road London SW7 5BD UK
Open Monday to Sunday from 10:00 – 17:50 except 24 – 26 December.
Last admission 17:30

Entry is free
There is a charge for some exhibitions.

Quick links:
- Getting here
- Book tickets
- Gallery announcements
- Sign up for news
- Dino Directory

2 Skim and scan internet texts → WB 39/21

a) *Skim the text on the right for the* ***gist****. What is it about? How can the information help visitors?*

b) *Now scan the text for* ***details*** *about animals. Make notes.*

Try to guess new words. Don't worry about words that aren't important.

Home | Visit us | Nature online | Education | Support us | Buy online

The Galleries at the **Natural History Museum** are in four zones. The **Blue Zone** shows you the amazing diversity of life on Earth, from the smallest to the largest animals. This is also where you can find the popular Dinosaurs gallery. In the **Green Zone** you learn about Earth's ecology and how you can help to look after the planet. Visit the **Red Zone** to go back to the beginning of time and find out how and why our planet changes. Also see the minerals and treasures the Earth gives us. In the **Orange Zone** you can explore nature in the Wildlife Garden, which features over 2,000 species. Also, see science in action in the spectacular Darwin Centre.

3 Practise with different websites

Partner A: *Choose a sight in London (an idea from Unit 3 or your own idea).*
Partner B: *Find useful or interesting information about your partner's sight and tell him / her about it.*

Our London tour

For this task, work in small groups. Each group is going to plan and present a different sightseeing tour for a class trip to London. There are three different tour choices:

a tour by bus and boat	a tour by Tube	a tour on foot

Step 1

Tour rules → WB 40/23

a) *First, read the rules in class. Then form groups of 4–5 and choose a tour. Try to have **two** groups for each tour.*

b) *The map below can help you to plan your tour and to get a feeling for distances before you use other maps.*

Rules

- *Your tour starts at **Green Park**.*
- *There must be **enough time** (morning till late afternoon) for everything that you plan to do.*
- *Only **one** stop on your tour costs money. The other sights must be **free**.*
- *You've got sandwiches for **lunch**, so you must plan when and where you can eat them.*

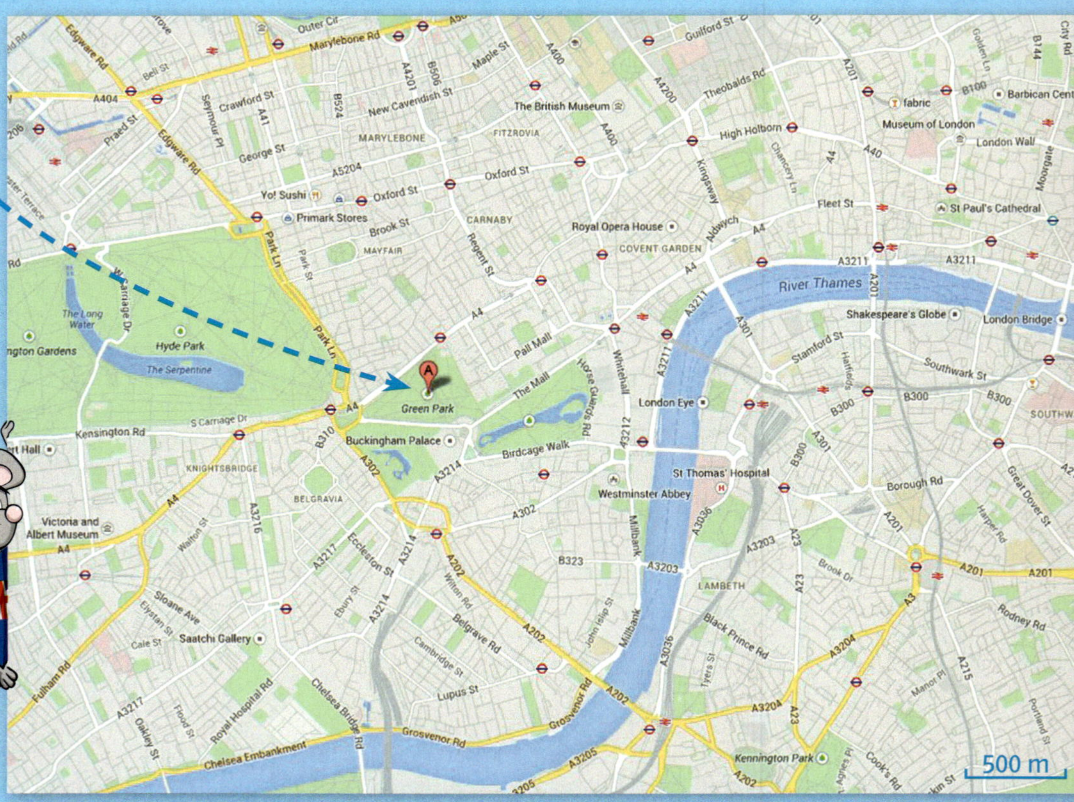

Step 2

Choose the sights on your tour → WB 40/24, 41/25

a) *First think alone for a few minutes about what sights you can visit. Write down your ideas. Then tick (✔) the ones you'd like to visit in one day.*

b) *Share your ideas. What are your group's favourites? Make your decision about the sights. Look at the map again. Are your plans realistic for the time you have and the distance between activities?*

Start: Good idea – but isn't it a bit far / expensive?
I think we've got enough time / money for …

For help with things to do and see in London, look back at **Across Cultures 1**, at pages 50–58 of **Unit 3** and at your **Workbook**.

For help with how to make and discuss suggestions, look again at **Station 2**.

Step 3

Collect information and write a plan

a) *Collect useful information about each of the sights on your list and work out the best route for your tour. Look up the information that you need and make notes.*

b) *Use the information to write a plan for the tour (morning → lunch → afternoon). Make sure it's clear where you're going to go and how you're going to get there.*

Step 4

Prepare your presentation

Decide who is going to talk about what. Think what you want to say and make prompt cards. Also prepare some material about your tour. Maybe these ideas can help:

- a poster of the whole tour
- a tour timetable
- a map with your route / sights

Has your tour got a special name?
I call my tour 'Tony's Top Tube Tour'. That's a tongue-twister *(Zungenbrecher)*.
Try it!

For help with how to find information on the internet, look at the **Skills page** again.

For help with routes on the Tube, look back at **Station 1**.

Step 5

Present your tour in class → WB 41/26

a) *Take turns to present your tours.*

Useful phrases

We'd like to tell you about …
First we're going to …
Then … / After that …
We're / You're going to see / visit …
We can get there easily on foot / by …
It's a fantastic / an amazing …

b) *Take turns to vote for the best tour. Say why you liked that tour best.*

Look back a the **Skills page** in **Unit 2** for help with the presentations.

S 1/31–35
L 2/12–16

I'm a mudlark

Across cultures

Many London visitors don't know that **the Thames** is a river with two faces – one at high tide, one at low tide. Sometimes, it flows out into the sea like a normal river. But every day at high tide, it flows back towards central London. In the heart of the city there can be a difference of seven metres between high and low tides! At low tide, you can see the muddy banks of the river.

A "Number three is the Wobbly Bridge," Jay told his cousin Amir. The four friends were enjoying their own tour of bridges across the Thames. Now they were walking across their third one, the Millennium Footbridge.

"It isn't wobbly any more. That was just a problem when it was new, but people still use the name," explained Olivia.

Before they got very far, Holly noticed Amir's silver bracelet. "Ooh, that's nice!"

"Yeah, let *me* try it on," Jay said.

"Sure, no problem," Amir said. Jay quickly grabbed his cousin's wrist to take the bracelet off. But he wasn't careful enough, dropped it, and the bracelet rolled off the bridge and down into the Thames!

"Jay!" Amir shouted angrily. "That bracelet really meant something to me. And now it's gone!" They all looked down from the bridge. They were lucky. The tide was out and the bracelet was in the mud between the water and the wall.

"Look, there are steps down to the shore," Olivia said. "Come on, let's go and get it. But hm, should we take off our shoes? It's very muddy."

Stop and think:
What could happen next, and why?

B Down on the shore, they found that the mud was very wet. They weren't wearing the right kind of shoes so they needed to walk carefully. They didn't want to fall.

"Hi. Are you looking for this?"

The voice came from a man under the bridge.

"Oh, we didn't see you! Yes, that's my bracelet. Thanks! I'm so happy to get it back," Amir told him.

"No problem," the man smiled. "I didn't think it was a present for me! Nice to meet you all. My name is Mike."

Olivia looked at the bucket and trowel which Mike had with him. "Excuse me, but can you please tell us what you're doing here?" she asked politely.

"I'm a mudlark," he said.

C The friends didn't know about mudlarks, so Mike explained. "In the 19th century many children or old people tried to make a little money from things that fell into the Thames. You know – from boats and ships."

"And bridges too!" Jay added.

"Yes, from bridges too," Mike laughed. "Anyway, when the tide went out the mudlarks looked on the shore for things to sell. They got their name because they worked in the mud. And at that time, the river was *very* dirty, full of all kinds of pollution. Or worse."

"Worse?" Amir wanted to know.

"Well, dead animals washed up all the time. Human bodies too."

"Yuck!" Holly said. "It's nice to know I've got shoes on my feet!"

"Oh, times are different now – don't worry," Mike explained.

"So you're looking for things to sell?" Holly wanted to know.

"No, no. Mudlarks are different now. We look for history in the mud. Just for fun. There are things in the Thames that go back to Roman times, you know."

"Wow, amazing! Listen to that, Olivia!" said Amir. He knew she loved history too.

"Most things aren't as old as that," Mike told them. "But look at this glass in my bucket. OK, it's broken, so it doesn't look very good any more. But it's over 100 years old! And when I hold it in my hand I like to think of the story behind it. Who drank from it? How did it get here?"

Mike also showed the friends the other things in his bucket: an old green bottle, a piece of an 18th-century clay pipe, and part of a lucky-charm bracelet. The friends had no idea there was treasure like this in the Thames! They all wanted to help Mike to look for more things. "OK, but please stay near me," he said.

D At first the four new mudlarks found it hard to see anything in the mud, but Mike showed them the best places to look and they started to notice things more easily. Olivia found a euro coin, Amir found an old key, and Holly found a shoe. And then she found something awful, with hair on it.

"Ugh, a HEAD!!!" she screamed.

Mike laughed. "Well, a head from across the sea!" he laughed, as he pulled a coconut from the mud. Then he said, "Sorry, guys, time to go now. The tide is coming in fast and – hey, where's your friend?"

Suddenly they saw that Jay wasn't with them. He wasn't far away, but the water between them was already near the wall.

"Jay! Look, you're going to be cut off!" Mike shouted. "Come on – quick! We need to get to the steps!"

Stop and think:
What is Jay's problem?
What could happen next?

E After a few dramatic minutes that felt like *hours*, they all got safely to the top of the steps. The friends said thank you and goodbye to Mike. Then it was time to walk along the south side of the river to the London Eye to meet Shahid.

"Mum isn't going to be very happy when she sees our dirty shoes," Jay said to Amir. "Hey, where are you going? That isn't the way to the London Eye!"

Jay, Olivia and Holly watched as Amir ran quickly back onto the bridge and threw something into the river.

"But – that's his bracelet!" Holly said. Jay was surprised too. "The crazy idiot! Why did he do that?"

Olivia just smiled. She understood.

SPEAKING

1 Your reaction → WB 42/27

Talk about what you found interesting about the story: the people, the history, the things in the river?

READING

2 Understanding the text → WB 42/28

a) *Explain the difference between mudlarks in the 19th century and modern mudlarks.*

b) *Why do you think Amir threw his bracelet back into the Thames?*

WRITING

3 One story, three different perspectives

a) *Work in groups of three. In your group, each of you (A, B and C) writes about the main ideas of the story in three different ways:*

A. *Find 6–8* ***key words / phrases*** *from the text. Write down why they're important.*
B. *Tell the* ***main ideas*** *of the story in 6–8 sentences.*
C. *In 6–8 sentences, talk about* ***your reaction*** *to the story.*

b) *Now tell each other your ideas. What ideas are the same or different?*

WRITING

4 What's the story behind it? → WB 42/29

→ 119/14
→ S10–13

Choose ***one*** *thing from Mike's bucket and create a little story about its history. Who did it belong to? How long ago? How did it get into the Thames? Write at least six sentences.*

Useful phrases

The … belonged to a girl / sailor / tourist / …
He / She lived in the 18th / … century.
He / She visited London last year / …
It was for wine / a treasure box / …
It was his / her favourite …
He / She threw it into the river because …
They / … didn't want it any more because …
It broke (into pieces) when …
One day it fell into the river while …

Example:

The wine glass

The wine glass belonged to a family over a hundred years ago. They lived in a house next to the Thames. One day …

7 Mehr zum Thema Thames

→ Solutions p. 241

Can you …

1. talk about your plans? — I'm / We're going to visit London.
2. use compound words with *some* and *any*? — I need something to eat. | Has anybody got anything nice?
3. make adverbs to say how you do things? — You walk very quickly! I can't walk so fast.

1 What are they going to do tomorrow?

Use the clues in the pictures and make sentences about their plans.

Start: 1. The Frasers are going to have …

1  The Frasers

2  Luke and Sherlock

3  Mr and Mrs Azad

4  Holly

5  Amir

6 

Shahid

2 What do these sellers at Camden Market say?

Put in the correct words.

everything | anybody | something | someone | anywhere | somewhere | nothing | everybody

Does [1] want to buy a cool hat? What about you, young man? I can see you're [2] who likes to look cool.

Come on, [3]! If you want [4] good to eat, this is the place to get it!

A book about London in German? I'm sure I've got one [5]. Yes, here you are. Look, [6] is in German.

Great souvenirs! You can't find cheaper ones [7] in London – [8] costs more than £1!

3 Complete the text with the correct adverb forms

The big car takes the star of the new film [1] (fast) and [2] (comfortable) to the cinema in Leicester Square. The people outside the cinema scream [3] (excited) when they see him. He walks [4] (slow) along the red carpet so that everyone can see him [5] (clear) and take photos. Then he stops for an interview. "Where did you learn to act so [6] (good)?" But the film star never answers the question because suddenly the alarm clock rings [7] (loud). Jay sees [8] (sad) that he isn't on the red carpet – he's in bed at home! It was only a dream.

S 1/36–39
L 2/17–20

The copper[1] treasure

Jamie, Ten Tons and Davies are young mudlarks who live in London in the 1850s. One day, they climb aboard a big ship in the River Thames and start to look for things which they can take away and sell for food; they're all hungry. With them is Patty, a woman who doesn't like Ten Tons very much. This is when they find a real treasure … the copper treasure.

We were moving carefully across the decks and looking for bits and pieces. But there wasn't much so we followed Patty down and started to look for spoons[2] and knives[3] and stuff in the cabins.

I could hear Ten Tons two cabins away. He was talking and shouting to himself as usual. Then I saw Patty at the end of the corridor. She was doing well. You could hear the sound of metal things under her skirts[4]. She looked annoyed[5] when she heard Ten Tons, but I didn't say anything. Yes, Ten Tons was a crazy man, but he was *our* crazy man.

I was crazy too – why was I stealing like this? Davies and Ten Tons didn't have parents – they needed to do this to live. But I had a mother and father and a home. I didn't need to do this. The others laughed each time I looked to check that everything was OK. But it was a good thing I checked so often: I looked up again and … and I saw the dock. It was floating past[6].

I thought … what? There was a man with some cows on the river bank … we were on the other side of the river now! He pointed at us and shouted. The ship started to circle and I suddenly understood … Oh no! The anchor[7] was broken and we were floating away[8] from the bank.

"Davies, Tens!" I screamed. "We're moving!"

Ten Tons was up on deck right away. "My God, I've stolen[9] a whole ship this time!" he shouted. Like a captain, he started to march up and down the decks and to give orders[10] to no one. It was so funny! He was very short and he was going up and down the deck like a crazy little engine[11].

Davies came up too. He looked over the side.

"We should[12] get …" he started to say.

Then everything moved. We floated sideways across the river and hit a tugboat[13]. Our ship went up and down and we all fell to the deck floor.

1 copper [kɒpə] Kupfer | **2 spoon** [spu:n] Löffel | **3 knife** [naɪf] Messer | **4 skirt** [skɜ:t] Rock | **5 annoyed** [ə'nɔɪd] verärgert | **6 to float past** [fləʊt 'pɑ:st] vorbeitreiben | **7 anchor** ['æŋkə] Anker | **8 to float away** [fləʊt ə'weɪ] wegtreiben, abtreiben | **9 I've stolen** [aɪv 'stəʊlən] ich habe gestohlen | **10 order** ['ɔ:də] Befehl | **11 engine** ['endʒɪn] Lokomotive; Motor | **12 should** [ʃʊd] sollten | **13 tugboat** ['tʌgbəʊt] Schlepper *(Schiff)*

Davies almost[14] fell into the river. I saw Ten Tons – he was sliding along on his bum[15] and shouting 'Whhhhhooooah!' I held on to the rail[16]. And then we heard a strange sound, like music. I looked along the deck and saw …

The copper! What a sight! It was rolling along the deck and opening itself up into a shining red sheet. It was like a magician[17] who was slowly opening his cape. The ship moved again and the deck turned to one side. The copper was moving faster and faster … and then it crashed into the rail. The rails broke and the copper hung for a moment, right on the edge[18] of the deck. Then there was another movement. It caught[19] the sun, flashed[20] red-golden light[21] at me, went over the edge … and dropped.

I watched it go down. It hummed as it fell. It flashed again in the evening sun and sent a bright[22] red light across the river. Then it hit the water. It was so bright it looked red hot[23]. I was waiting for it to hiss[24]. There was a huge splash in the water … and it was gone. Half a ton or more of new copper, down under the water and lost forever[25].

→ WB 44/1–3

14 **almost** ['ɔ:lməʊst] fast | 15 **bum** [bʌm] Hintern | 16 **rail** [reɪl] Reling | 17 **magician** [mə'dʒɪʃn] Zauberer | 18 **edge** [edʒ] Rand | 19 **to catch** [kætʃ] einfangen | 20 **to flash** [flæʃ] blitzen | 21 **light** [laɪt] Licht | 22 **bright** [braɪt] leuchtend | 23 **red hot** [red 'hɒt] glühend heiß | 24 **to hiss** [hɪs] zischen | 25 **lost forever** [lɒst fə'revə] für immer verloren

Find more online: 34q3y3

Unit 4

Sport is good for you!

B Marathon

A Camel racing

D Rugby

C BMX

LISTENING

1 On the radio

L 2/21 → S18–20

Gwen is preparing for the TTS sports and health project week. She's listening to sports programmes on the radio. Which sports? Three of them are in the photos; which ones?

runner race catch lose match run kick net throw team pass win time racquet court hit score stadium ball pitch goal point

SPEAKING

2 Talk about sports

→ S4

a) *Use the word cloud from Ex. 1 to describe the sports in the photos. Where and why are these sports popular?*

→ △ 120/1

b) *Your turn: Talk about sports you like.*

Vocabulary skills

You can use **word clouds** to show how often a word is in a text. The more often a word is in the text, the bigger it is. You can make word clouds on your computer.

In Unit 4 you learn

… how to talk about sports, about your experiences in the past, and about things which have just happened and are still important now. You learn:

- words for sports
- words for health and accidents
- the language of news reports
- the present perfect

Wheelchair basketball

ENING **3** TTS sport and health projects

L 2/22

a) *Now Olivia is talking to Gwen. Say which sports they're going to use for their projects and why they chose them.*

b) *Make a list of other sports they talk about.*

c) *Why is sport good for your health?*

Across cultures

The **number one sport** in Britain is football, rugby is number two. Other popular team sports in Britain are cricket and hockey. What team sports are popular in Germany and what do you know about them?

ULARY **4** Sports words → WB 45/1–2

Make a grid with words and phrases for the sports you're interested in. (Use a dictionary for help.) Use these four headings:

Sport | Place | Equipment | Team / Individual sport

L 2/23

Have you ever run in a marathon?

"Have you ever seen the London Marathon?" Gwen asked.

"Of course we have!" Holly said. "It starts right here in Greenwich Park."

"I want to run in it," Luke said. "But I've checked: You can't until you're 18."

"But haven't you heard of the *mini* marathon?" Gwen asked.

"No, I haven't," Jay said. "What's that?"

"It's for 11- to 17-year-olds," Gwen explained. "It's just the last part of the race, and it's before the *real* marathon."

"Are you going to run in it?" Olivia asked Gwen. "I know you like running."

"It isn't that easy," Gwen said. "There are teams for different parts of London, and there are trials to find the fastest runners."

"Where are the trials?" Dave asked.

"For the Greenwich team, here in the park, next Saturday," Gwen said.

"Let's do it!" Olivia said. "Who's in?"

"Me," said Gwen. "It was my idea, remember?"

"I'm in too!" Luke said.

Nobody said a word. Then Jay said, "No thanks, I'm out. I've never enjoyed running much. It isn't cool. And Dave has never run in a race. Right, Dave?"

"I've run in races before, but not in a big one like that," Dave said.

Holly said, "I've only ever run in short races too, and I'm not very good at running. But I've got an idea: Why don't you run for charity? People often do charity runs to raise money."

"That's great," Olivia said. "We can ask our parents, teachers and friends to give money. So it's Gwen, Luke and me."

"Er … just one thing," Gwen said. "Can we run together? You know, my eyes …"

"Of course," Olivia said.

"Yeah," Luke said, "we'll be Team Thomas Tallis! The fastest, coolest team in Greenwich. No, in *London*! Look out, here we come!"

READING

1 Are your going to run in it?

a) *Would you like to run in a marathon? Why / Why not?*

b) *Answer these questions:*

1. Say who likes / doesn't like running.
2. What's Holly's idea?
3. Who isn't going to run in the trials for the mini marathon?

Across cultures

The **London Marathon** is one of the world's biggest races, with over 35,000 runners. It starts in Greenwich Park and finishes at Buckingham Palace. Have you ever watched a marathon? What running events are there in your area?

UAGE

2 Find the rule → WB 46/3–4 → G12

a) *There are examples of a new tense in the text, the present perfect. Look at these sentences and the verb forms in the box. What is different between verbs like* **see** *and verbs like* **check***?*

I have run in a race before.
Have you ever watched a marathon?

Infinitive	– Past participle
see	– **seen**
check	– **checked**
hear	– **heard**
enjoy	– **enjoyed**
run	– **run**

There's a list of irregular verbs on page 239.

b) *Now make two sentences like this about Dave.*

He … … . | … he ever … ?

c) *Write down how you make and answer questions in the present perfect.*

UAGE

3 Say who has done what → WB 47/5

→ 120/2

… you ever 1 (be) to London? – No, I …, but my sister 2 (be) there.
… you 3 (hear) of the London Marathon? – Yes, I …, I 4 (watch) it three times.
… your parents ever 5 (run) in a marathon? – No, they …, but my dad 6 (play) in an international tennis match.
… your little brother ever 7 (prepare) a meal? – Yes, he … He always helps in the kitchen.
… your grandma ever 8 (give) you extra pocket money? – No, she …

AKING

4 Your turn: Find somebody who … → WB 47/6, 48/7

→ S24

a) *Write at least three questions for your classmates with* ***Have you ever …?*** *The words on the right can help.*

Examples:
Have you ever seen …?
Have you ever been to …?
Have you ever eaten …?

finished · done · written · fallen · found · broken · asked for · run · been

homework · arm / leg · race · money · book · another country

b) *Ask some of your classmates the questions you wrote.*

c) *Write down what you've found out and tell the class.*

Example: Nicolas and Maria have been to Austria, but Tom and Lara haven't.

L 2/26

Have you been to the doctor's yet?

Gwen: Hi Olivia. Are you still at home?

Olivia: Hi Gwen. Yes, I'm at home. I haven't left for school yet.

Gwen: Good. I've just had an idea. Let's train for the marathon trials. Do you want to go for a run in the park after school today?

Olivia: Great idea, but I've hurt my foot! I think I've twisted my ankle.

Gwen: Oh no! Have you been to the doctor's yet?

Olivia: No, I haven't. I hope it isn't serious. But it hurts when I walk, and I can't run on Saturday with pain like this.

Gwen: But you've already prepared for the trials!

Olivia: I know, it's so unfair! I've done everything I can! I've bought new running shoes, I've stopped eating chocolate, I've found information on the internet about the *best* way to run, I've –

Gwen: Listen, don't worry. I can train with Luke today, and maybe you can join us tomorrow.

Olivia: OK. Have you already asked Luke?

Gwen: No, not yet. I can ask him at school today. See you there.

Olivia: Yeah, see you later. Bye!

READING

5 Questions on the text

1. Why does Gwen call Olivia?
2. What's Olivia's problem?
3. What has Olivia done to prepare for the marathon trials?

LANGUAGE

6 The checklist → G12

Ask and answer questions about what the friends have done or haven't done.

Example: **Has** Gwen **called** Olivia **yet**? – Yes, she **has**.

Things to do	Who?	Done?
1. call Olivia	Gwen	✔
2. make a poster for the charity run	Holly	✘
3. run three miles	Luke	✔
4. read a book about running	Olivia	✔
5. write a chant to cheer the runners	Jay	✘
6. find a good place to watch the marathon	Dave	✘
7. tell their parents about the marathon	Gwen, Luke, Olivia	✔

UAGE

7 What has just happened?

→ △ 120/3
→ ▲ 121/4

Example: Mrs Elliot has just cleaned the windows.

Mrs Elliot – clean ✓

Mr Azad – finish

Luke – come back

Jamie – fall off

Amber – buy

Olivia – tidy

Shahid – write

Lucy – go to

JLARY

8 At the doctor's → WB 48/8–9, 49/10

→ S9

Read Olivia's dialogue with the doctor. Practise your own dialogues with the ideas in the box.

Doctor: So, what's the problem today?
Olivia: I've had an accident and hurt my foot.
Doctor: Can you walk on it?
Olivia: No, I can't.
Doctor: Let me have a look. – Oh yes, you've twisted your ankle.
Olivia: Is it serious, Doctor?
Doctor: No, it isn't. But you need to walk very carefully for a couple of days.
Olivia: Oh no, so I can't run in the marathon trials on Saturday …
Doctor: No, you really shouldn't. Here's a prescription for an ointment. You can put it on your ankle to stop the pain.

Useful phrases

I've hurt my hand / foot / arm / head / shoulder. | I've got a headache / backache / stomachache. | I feel bad / sick and I can't … | I've got a cold / a cough / a fever. | You need to … | You shouldn't … | You can take pills / …

ATION

9 Children and accidents → WB 48/11, 50/12

→ △ 121/5
→ S17

Pia has found a German survey on the internet that Olivia could use for her project. What does the introduction say about German children's health? Tell a partner in English.

Obwohl sie zum größten Teil vermeidbar wären, zählen Unfallverletzungen zu den häufigsten gesundheitlichen Beeinträchtigungen von Kindern und Jugendlichen. Pro Jahr erleiden etwa 15 Prozent der Kinder und Jugendlichen mindestens eine behandlungsbedürftige Unfallverletzung; Jungen sind öfter betroffen als Mädchen. Kleinkinder verletzen sich am häufigsten zu Hause. Ältere Kinder und Jugendliche erleiden Unfälle insbesondere beim Sport und in der Freizeit sowie in der Schule.

L 2/28

An interview with Ayla

Dave and Holly have interviewed Ayla Bayram, a Year 12 student at TTS and the school's best runner.

Dave: Hi Ayla. How are you?

Ayla: I'm fine, thanks.

Holly: Thanks for your time.

Ayla: No problem!

Dave: Er, you had the fastest time in the mini marathon last year. But have you ever run in a *real* marathon?

Ayla: I've never run in a real marathon, no. But two months ago I ran in a half marathon. It was great!

Holly: Are you going to run in this year's mini marathon?

Ayla: I haven't decided yet. But I'm still 17 *this* year, so maybe I should run! – Are *you* going to run?

Holly: Us? Er, no, we aren't. But our friends Luke and Gwen are! Do you have any tips for them?

Ayla: Yes: Always wear *real* running shoes – but never *new* shoes.

Holly: Is there anything else?

Ayla: Oh, and don't run too fast too early; you don't want a cramp!

Dave: Have you ever won any awards?

Ayla: Yes, I have. I won the 'Best Maths Student' award two years ago. But no sports awards – sorry!

Holly: Have you ever had an accident?

Ayla: Oh, I've had *lots* of accidents! Two years ago I had one at the mini marathon: I fell and broke my arm!

Dave: Can you describe how you felt?

Ayla: Well, it was strange: While I was running I felt fine, but *after* the race it really, really hurt.

Dave: Oh, I've never broken anything.

Holly: I have! I fell off a chair and broke my arm when I was a little girl.

Ayla: So you know what it's like. Ouch!

READING **10**

Match the parts

1. Ayla has never run
2. She finished
3. Ayla broke her arm
4. Holly broke her arm
5. Ayla ran
6. Dave has been

a) lucky; he hasn't broken anything yet!
b) when she was just a little girl.
c) in a real marathon before.
d) with the fastest time last year.
e) when she fell two years ago.
f) in a half marathon two months ago.

LANGUAGE **11**

Signal words → WB 50/13, 51/14 → G12

Find these signal words in the text. Which tenses do they go with?

when I was… | last … | never | ever | after | yet | ago

UAGE **12**

Questions and answers

→ △ 121/6

Make questions and answers like the examples. Use the present perfect and simple past.

Examples: **Have** you ever **been** to England? – Yes, I have. I **was** in London last …
Have you ever **seen** a ghost? – No, but I **saw** a famous actor when I …

UAGE **13**

Simple past or present perfect? → WB 51/15

→ △ 122/7
→ ▲ 122/8

Luke wrote his cousin Jan in Cracow an e-mail about a funny basketball game. Put the verbs in the simple past or the present perfect. First look for signal words.

… I've never **1** (see) a basketball game like the one I **2** (see) yesterday. It **3** (be) so embarrassing! First, one reporter almost **4** (become) sick in front of the camera and **5** (go) to find the toilet! "Er, er, we're so sorry: This **6** (never happen) before!" the other reporter **7** (say). After that it **8** (get) worse. Before the game the star player **9** (tell) a reporter: "I **10** (give) the crowd a great show in every game so far, and I can do that in this game too!" He **11** (be) right: Ten minutes later, he **12** (lose) his shorts when a player from the other team **13** (pull) too hard! And then, just when I thought, "I **14** (see) too many embarrassing things today," a strange man **15** (run) onto the court with no clothes on!

KING **14**

How to: Ask interview questions → WB 51/16–17

→ S16

a) *For her health project, Olivia is going to interview Nick Ashton, a member of the Greenwich Rugby Football Club (RFC). Read the internet profile about Nick she found.*

NICK ASHTON: Nick is 21 and joined RFC in 2014. Read about him!

Goals:
– to play for England one day, of course!
– to get through the next season[1] with no broken arms, legs or anything else!

Nick likes … ☺
– getting the ball and sprinting[2] as far as he can (→ see Photo!).
– fast action sports like rugby!

Nick doesn't like… ☹
– all the attention[3] football gets.
– going to the weight room[4] every day. ("But I go anyway; rugby players need their muscles[5]!")

b) *Write questions that Olivia could ask Nick. The phrases can help you.*

c) *Act dialogues in small groups. One is Nick, the others ask interview questions.*

Useful phrases

Have you ever…? | Did you…? | Are you going to…? | What do you do every day / before big games / … | How often do you …? | Describe what you / how you … | Can you please tell me about … | What happened after you …? | Do you have any tips for …?

1 **season** ['si:zn] Saison | 2 **to sprint** [sprɪnt] sprinten | 3 **attention** [ə'tenʃn] Aufmerksamkeit | 4 **weight room** ['weɪt rʊm] Kraftraum | 5 **muscle** ['mʌsl] Muskel

A picnic in the park
→ S21–22

VIEWING

1 Understanding the story so far

8 *Watch (00:00–03:55). Then match the sentences / the sentence parts below.*

1. Marley's ankle hurts.
2. Laura is going to stay with her grandad in Kent
3. Marley wants to watch the football match
4. Marley thinks it's unfair
5. Jinsoo's mum has made 'kimbap'[1].
6. At first, Jinsoo doesn't like the idea

a) but his dad needs his help in the attic.
b) that everyone is going to watch football and he can't.
c) that Alicia is going to come to Kent too.
d) It's typical Korean snack food.
e) and invites her friends to visit her.
f) He thinks he has twisted it.

SPEAKING

2 How's your ankle?

a) *Watch the rest of the film. What does Marley do? The phrases can help you.*

b) *What does Marley's father say at the end? Do you think he's right? Say why / why not. Think about it from Marley's point of view and from Mr Thompson's too. Look at the box again.*

Useful phrases

to fake an injury / a headache / …
to teach somebody a lesson
It's fair / unfair because …
I think / don't think his father is right …
Marley deserves it / doesn't deserve it …

c) *Your turn: Have you ever faked anything? Did you get away with it? Tell the class.*

VOCABULARY

3 The picnic
→ WB 52/18

a) *The friends are having different food for their picnic. Look at the photo and the food words and say what looks good.*

b) *Your turn: In class, talk about **your** 'perfect picnic'. What food from your country / your area / other countries could you have?*

1 **kimbap** ['kɪmbæp] *koreanischer Snack aus Seegras, Reis, Rindfleisch, Käse und Ei* | 2 **cress** [kres] Kresse | 3 **Scotch egg** [skɒtʃ 'eg] *hart gekochtes Ei in Wurstbrät* | 4 **quiche** [kiːʃ] Quiche | 5 **pasta salad** [ˌpæstə 'sæləd] Nudelsalat | 6 **tuna** ['tjuːnə] Thunfisch

How to understand news reports and take notes → S18–20

For the task on pages 78–79, you need to know what the parts of a radio report are and what language is typical for a radio report. This page can help you.

1 A mountain rescue → WB 53/20

L 2/30

a) *Listen to a radio report about an accident in the mountains. Take notes in a grid.*

Time	Place	People	Event

b) *Use your notes and answer the questions.*

1. What was the accident?
2. Why did it happen?
3. What did the mountain rescue team do?
4. Why was the rescue difficult?
5. How serious was the accident?
6. How is the way the news presenter and the reporter speak different to the way the witnesses speak?

2 The language of a radio report → WB 53/21

Read the boxes. Then listen to the report again. Note down which phrases from the bigger box you can hear in the report.

Also, note down ***other*** *interesting or typical phrases for the news presenter, the reporter, the witness. Why do you think they are typical?*

Vocabulary skills

The situations are different, but the **language** of radio reports is often the same:

- **News presenters** and **reporters** stay more formal and use a language of facts.
- An **eyewitness** has just seen something dramatic, strange or maybe scary; the language he / she uses often shows more feelings.

Useful phrases

News reporter at radio station:
Hello / Good morning to all our listeners out there. | We've just received news of … | Now we're going to hear from our reporter at the scene: Can you describe the … / Can you tell us about the … | Stay with us for more …

Reporter at the scene:
What were you doing when …? | Where were you when …? | What have you seen? | Has anyone else …? | What else can you tell us?

Eyewitness at the scene:
I couldn't believe my eyes! | This is strange / dramatic / exciting / …: I've never seen anything like it! | I didn't know what was happening. | I was watching TV when suddenly I heard / saw …

The aliens have landed!

Imagine that aliens have landed on Earth – in Greenwich Park! In this Unit task, you and your group write your own radio report about this strange event. For the report, there are five roles: **three witnesses**; a **reporter** who interviews the witnesses; the **radio news presenter**. Your job is to write – and record – a fun report. Your report should be 3–4 minutes long. Be as creative as possible!

Step 1

The situation → WB 54/22

In groups of five, look at the scenes above. Talk about what you think is happening/has happened in each scene. Look closely at the words in the box. You need them to talk about the pictures.

Martian | Mars | space | spaceship | UFO | light | sky | star | customer | stomachache | human | to land | to invade | to come in peace | to make friends | to get sick on (too much) chocolate | strange-looking | bright | friendly

Examples:

A: In this scene, you can see that the aliens have landed.

B: What's happening at the hospital? Have the aliens eaten too much chocolate?

C: Look at the park scene: It looks like the aliens want to make friends!

Martian [ˈmɑːʃn] Marsmensch | **space** [speɪs] Weltraum | **spaceship** [ˈspeɪsʃɪp] Raumschiff | **light** [laɪt] Licht | **sky** [skaɪ] Himmel | **customer** [ˈkʌstəmə] Kunde / Kundin | **human** [ˈhjuːmən] Mensch | **to invade** [ɪnˈveɪd] eindringen | **in peace** [ɪn ˈpiːs] in Frieden | **to make friends** [meɪk ˈfrendz] Freundschaft schließen | **to get sick on sth** [get ˈsɪk‿ɒn] sich an etw. den Magen verderben | **strange-looking** [ˈstreɪndʒ ˌlʊkɪŋ] seltsam aussehend | **bright** [braɪt] hell

Step 2

Choose roles and form expert groups → WB 54/23

a) *In your group, each of you chooses one of the five roles.*

b) *Form expert groups with all the students who have* ***the same role as you****. In your new group, talk about what kind of things* ***your character*** *should / could say in a radio report. Make notes – and be creative!*

Examples:

A: *(doctor group)* As a doctor, I want to tell the reporter how the aliens are feeling. The people should know that they got sick on chocolate. They don't speak English, but we know they're feeling better; they're smiling now!

B: *(reporter group)* A reporter should ask how the man in his garden felt when he first saw the UFOs. I'm sure it was a big shock! – Oh, and a reporter should ask how the aliens *paid* for their chocolate at the shop!

For typical phrases for reporters and witnesses, have another look at the **Skills page** you've just done. And look back at **Station 3** for interview phrases.

Step 3

Plan and write your report → WB 55/24

a) *Go back to your home group. Each of you is now an expert for one of the roles. Talk about how you all want to put the report together. Think about these points first:*

How should it start? | How should it end: Does the news presenter tell the listeners to listen for more information later? Is the Martians' visit to Earth over? | Which order are the interviews in? | How serious (or silly) should the presenter and the reporter be? | Remember that the presenter needs to say something after every reporter interview.

b) *Now write your report, interview by interview. Each person writes some of it.*

c) *Peer-editing: Trade your part with somebody else and check each other's texts.*

d) *One of you now reads it to the rest of the group. Listen carefully. Does it sound like a radio report? Does it sound interesting enough? Make changes for a better text.*

Step 4

Practice and record your report → WB 55/25

a) *Practice your report a few times, and record yourselves with a smartphone. Does it sound right? Remember: Don't read from the page!*

b) *Now record your final report.*

c) *Play it for the class. Tell the groups what you liked about* ***their*** *reports.*

S 2/6–10
L 2/32–36

Hey, don't call *me* silly!

A In Greenwich, it's almost time for the mini marathon to start …

Gwen: It's too bad Olivia can't join us.

Luke: But she can cheer us on with the others and help us to do well today.

Gwen: Yes, for us *and* for 'See with your Heart'. It means a lot to me, as a partially sighted person.

Luke: Your charity means something to *all* of us, Gwen. – But anyway, remember: You mustn't let go of my hand!

Gwen: Luke, that's *my* line: *I'm* the one who can't see well, remember?

Luke: Oh, sorry. I'm just nervous. Do you think I've trained enough?

Gwen: Well, I have! I did lots of extra training. But I can't speak for *you*.

Luke: Great, that really helps.

Gwen: Don't think so much, silly. Just run. And not too fast too soon!

Luke: Hey, don't call *me* silly – look at *them* in their crazy animal costumes. Can you see them?

Gwen: Er, not very well. But there are always people in fancy dress at events like these. They're running for charity too.

Luke: Oh yes: a pet charity, I'm sure; they've got cat and dog costumes. But how can they *run* in them?!

Gwen: No idea. – But hey, look! There are Holly and Olivia! But hm, where are Dave and Jay?

B A few minutes into the race …

Gwen:
This feels GREAT! My big day, after all that training … Now is the moment – MY moment! I can show them how good I am. Just breathe … run … enjoy it! … But what about Luke? Can he keep up? He didn't do any extra training like me. And *he's* worried about *me*? … Oh, those silly runners in the animal costumes in front of us – they aren't really taking this seriously. … What are they doing? Jumping from right to left and getting in the way. Clowns! … I hope they don't get in *our* way.

C Ten minutes later …

Gwen:
Ouch! What's that?! Oh, my stomach; it *really* hurts. … Oh no, I mustn't stop! I'm running for the charity – *and* for Luke! … I don't want to be the new girl with the funny glasses; I want to be the new girl with fast legs! Oh, but my stomach… Come on, just run! … RUN!

D Not far from the finish line …

Gwen:
I think that stupid cramp is gone. YES! And Luke is still doing fine too. … We're still running fast: I think our time is going to be *really* good. … I want to see our photos on the TTS website! "Gwen Parker, the new running star". Sounds great! – OH NO!!!!!!!!! What's happening?!?! Oh no, I don't want to fall!

E Just after the race …

Luke: Gwen, we did it, WE DID IT!

Gwen: Yes, we did! And it feels GREAT!

Luke: Well, *now* it feels great. But during the race I had a bad cramp. You started too fast for me!

Gwen: *You* had a cramp? Oh, now I feel better.

Luke: I had a cramp and now *you* feel better? I don't understand.

Gwen: Well, I had a cramp too – but I didn't want to tell you; I didn't want to stop the race.

Luke: And I didn't want to tell *you* and hear, "You didn't train enough!"

Gwen: Well, we *both* finished, yippee! And 'See with your Heart' gets some money too!

Luke: Well, they almost *didn't*: That stupid dog and that stupid cat almost ruined everything for us! I couldn't believe my eyes when they pulled out a smartphone and took a selfie. That one boy fell because of them, and we almost fell too!

Gwen: They took a *selfie*? In the middle of the race? Oh, I knew those two were trouble!

Olivia: *(suddenly)* Yes, that's what the race officials thought too so they finally took the dog and the cat out of the race. – Look who I've found!

Luke: Dave and Jay?!?!

Gwen: YOU were the dog and the cat?!?! Aaaargh!!!

Dave: Don't be angry, please! We're really sorry. We only wanted to surprise you.

Jay: Yes, we trained in secret, and ran for the pets' charity!

Gwen: But somebody *fell* because of you two. Luke and I almost fell! I'm sure that boy trained hard. Have you ever thought of that?

Jay: Well, er …

Dave: We said sorry, Gwen.

Gwen: Well, don't tell *me*. Have you told the boy yet?

Dave: Er, no.

Gwen: Well, *tell* him. *(smiling now)* So we can finally forgive you.

Luke: But I'm not sure 'sorry' is enough. How about a present for him?

Olivia: That sounds good. I'm sure we all have nice present ideas.

Gwen: Yes boys, you must do something nice for him. But you can do something nice for me and Luke too. – Luke, where's your phone? Picture time!

Luke: Oh yes – those silly costumes, those faces in the next TTS yearbook! Say CHEESE!

READING

1 Working with the text → WB 56/26

a) *Look at the text and talk about these questions.*

1. What different kinds of text are there in parts A–E?
2. Why do people run in a marathon? Find reasons in the text and say who gives them.
3. What can cause problems in a marathon race?
4. What do we learn about Gwen and Luke's hopes and fears?
5. What can you say about their relationship?

→ △ 123/9

b) *Use the text and the pictures to retell what happened.*

READING

2 What do you think?

a) *Find adjectives to describe Gwen, Luke, Jay and Dave and their actions.*

→ △ 123/10

b) *Find positive and negative things in the story that they did. Use words from a) to discuss what you think about their actions. Here are some ideas:*

Positive	Negative
On the one hand it was **good** that … I think Gwen was **brave** … …	On the other hand it was really **stupid** … But it was also **dangerous** … …

VOCABULARY

3 Looking at spoken language

→ △ 123/11
→ ▲ 123/12

Read the dialogues and Gwen's thoughts out loud. How do Gwen and Luke talk to each other? What language do they use to express their feelings? Collect words and phrases you would like to use again in a mind map.

WRITING

4 Another story → WB 56/27

→ S10–13

*Write about what **isn't** in the story. Choose one of these two topics. You can write a story, a dialogue or a comic. Use your vocabulary from Ex. 2.*

- Just for fun: The race from Jay and Dave's point of view.
- Can you forgive us: Jay and Dave talk to the boy who fell because of them.

→ Solutions p. 241

Can you ...

1. talk about experiences in your life / in somebody else's life?	Have you ever played rugby?
2. talk about things which have (just) happened?	I've hurt my foot!
3. use *just*, *already* and *yet*?	I haven't had my dinner yet.

GUAGE

1 Match the sentence halves.

1. I think you've broken
2. We've been to
3. I've never eaten
4. Jay has just written
5. Holly hasn't finished
6. I've already asked

a) a new chant.
b) in an Indian restaurant.
c) your ankle.
d) Olivia to help me with my project.
e) Buckingham Palace three times.
f) her homework yet.

GUAGE

2 Make dialogues about Luke and Dave

Example: Dave: write | your health report? → Have you already written your report?
Luke: no | have | no time yet → No, I haven't. I haven't had time yet.

1. Luke: find | interesting information on the internet yet?
   Dave: yes | find | yesterday after school.
2. Luke: Jay | draw | new mangas for his report yet?
   Dave: yes | draw | cool new characters at lunch.
3. Dave: see | two new manga comics yet?
   Luke: yes | already finish | one of them.
4. Luke: see | Olivia today?
   Dave: no | but send | text an hour ago.
5. Dave: Holly | write | about guinea pigs?
   Luke: hope not! | write | about guinea pigs last year.

GUAGE

3 BMX: Popular but a bit dirty!

Dave wrote a text for the health project about the history of BMX. Complete his text with the correct verb forms: simple past or present perfect.

The full name of BMX is 'bicycle motocross'. It is a sport that **1** (become) very popular with young people. It **2** (start) with children in the USA in about 1970. At first, the children **3** (use) normal bikes on mud roads; there **4** (be) no special BMX bikes. But then a few bicycle companies **5** (discover) the sport, and the world **6** (have) its first BMX bikes. It's a fast, dangerous sport, and there **7** (be) many serious accidents. That's why many parents are *not* big fans. In one survey with parents last year, BMX **8** (not be) at the top of the list of 'favourite sports'. One mother said: "I **9** (see) dirty football and rugby uniforms, but my children's BMX clothes after a race? They're the worst!"

S 2/11–14
L 3/1–4

The summer[1] table

August was born[2] with a genetic defect and has 'facial issues[3]'. To other people, the highly intelligent boy looks like a monster. Everyone stares at him so he doesn't go to school; his mum teaches him at home. When he is about 10, his parents finally decide to send him to school. On his first day, Auggie has a really hard time. The other children stare at him or ignore him completely. At lunchtime, Auggie feels really bad – his friend Jack Will isn't there, and because of[4] his face, August has problems eating, too. When a girl, Summer, sits down at his table, he is very surprised.

"Hey, is somebody sitting here?"

I looked up, and a girl I never saw before was standing across from my table with a lunch tray[5] full of food. She had long wavy brown hair, and wore a brown T-shirt with a purple peace sign[6] on it.

"Uh, no," I said.

She put her lunch tray on the table, dropped her rucksack on the floor, and sat down across from me. She started to eat the pasta with cheese sauce on her plate.

"Ugh," she said when she took the first bite. "Why didn't I bring a sandwich like you did?"

"Yeah," I said.

"My name is Summer, by the way. What's yours?"

"August."

"Cool," she said.

"Summer!"

Another girl who was carrying[7] a tray came over to the table. "Why are you sitting here? Come back to the table."

"There were too many people," Summer answered her. "Come sit here. There's more room."

The other girl looked confused[8] for a second. I recognized[9] her. She was sitting at another table with some friends a few minutes ago: They were looking at me and she had her hand over her mouth and was whispering. I guess Summer was one of the girls at that table too.

"Don't worry," the girl said and went away.

Summer looked at me, smiled, and took another bite of her pasta.

"Hey, our names match," she said, as she ate.

I guess she noticed that[10] I didn't know what she meant.

"Summer? August?" she said and smiled, her eyes open wide, as she waited for me to understand.

"Oh, yeah," I said after a second.

"We can make this the 'summer only'

1 summer ['sʌmə] Sommer | **2 to be born** [bi 'bɔ:n] geboren werden | **3 facial issues** [ˌfeɪʃl 'ɪʃu:z] Gesichtsprobleme | **4 because of** [bɪ'kɒz‿əv] wegen | **5 tray** [treɪ] Tablett | **6 peace sign** ['pi:s saɪn] Friedenszeichen | **7 to carry** ['kæri] tragen | **8 confused** [kən'fju:zd] verwirrt | **9 to recognize** ['rekəgnaɪz] wiedererkennen | **10 that** [ðæt] dass

lunch table," she said. "Only kids with summer names can sit here. Let's see, is there anyone here named June or July?"

"There's a Maya," I said.

"Technically, May is spring[11]," Summer answered, "but if she wants to sit here, we can make an exception[12]." She said it as if[13] she already had a plan. "There's Julian. That's like the name Julia, which comes from July."

I didn't say anything.

"There's a kid named Reid in my English class," I said.

"Yeah, I know Reid, but how is Reid a summer name?" she asked.

"I don't know," I said. "I just imagine … it's like a reed of grass[14] in summer."

"Yeah, OK," she answered and pulled out her notebook[15]. "And Ms.[16] Petosa could[17] sit here, too. That sounds like the word 'petal[18]', which is a summer thing too, I think."

"She's my tutor," I said.

"I have her for Maths," she answered and made a face[19].

She started to write the list of names on a page of her notebook.

"So, who else?" she said.

When we finished lunch, we had a whole list of names of kids and teachers who could sit at our table if they wanted. Most of the names weren't really summer names, but they were names that had some kind of connection to summer. I even found a way to put Jack Will's name on the list – I suggested that we could put his name into a sentence about summer, like "Jack will go to the beach[20]," and Summer agreed that that was fine.

"But if someone doesn't have a summer name and wants to sit with us," she said very seriously, "they can still sit here if they're nice, OK?"

"OK," I agreed. "Even if it's a winter name."

"Cool," she answered and gave me a thumbs-up.

Summer looked like her name. She had a tan[21], and her eyes were green like the leaves of a tree.

→ WB 58/1–4

11 spring [sprɪŋ] Frühling | **12 exception** [ɪk'sepʃn] Ausnahme | **13 as if** [əz‿'ɪf] als ob | **14 reed of grass** [ˌriːd‿əv 'grɑːs] Schilf | **15 notebook** ['nəʊtbʊk] Notizbuch | **16 Ms.** [mɪz] Frau *(Anrede)* | **17 could** [kʊd] könnte | **18 petal** ['petl] Blütenblatt | **19 to make a face** [meɪk‿ə 'feɪs] das Gesicht verziehen | **20 beach** [biːtʃ] Strand | **21 tan** [tæn] sonnengebräunte Haut

LANGUAGE

1 On tour on a London pedicab[1]

a) *Complete the text. Use adjectives or adverbs.*

The London pedicabs

Do you want to go on a **1** (different) kind of sightseeing tour? Then hop on[2] **2** (quick) and enjoy London's sights and attractions from the backseat[3] of a pedicab. Pedicabs are an **3** (exciting) and environmentally friendly[4] way to travel around the city **4** (easy). Enjoy the view, see all the **5** (famous) sights and get off anywhere you like. Our **6** (friendly) drivers speak three languages and know all the **7** (important) facts and **8** (interesting) stories about London. And, of course, they always drive **9** (slow) and **10** (careful)!

You can start your tour at different places, for example at Covent Garden, with its shops, cafés and restaurants with **11** (fresh) food from all over the world. You want to take a photo or buy something to drink? – No problem. Our drivers work **12** (hard) to make your tour an **13** (amazing) experience. Have a look at Buckingham Palace and the Changing of the Guard. Stop in front of the Houses of Parliament and listen to the sound of Big Ben. You want to know where you can eat **14** (good) and **15** (cheap)? Or where you can buy **16** (cool) clothes? Just ask our drivers!

Tours:

- Mini tour: 1 hour | £50 | 1–2 persons
- Shopping tour: 1 hour | £30 | 1–2 persons

b) *Would you like to see London in a pedicab? Say why/why not.*

c) *Where else could the pedicab tour go? Continue the text. Use adjectives and adverbs.*

LISTENING

2 A radio report: Shopping for souvenirs → WB 59/1–2

L3/5 **a)** *Listen to the radio report and say where the reporter is and what the report is about.*

b) *Listen again. Copy the grid and fill in the missing information.*

	Mr Smith	Amir	American tourist
souvenir			
for			
price			
problem			

c) *What do you think is the best souvenir? What souvenir would you bring? Say why.*

1 **pedicab** ['pedɪkæb] Fahrradtaxi, Fahrradrikscha | 2 **to hop on** [hɒp‿'ɒn] (schnell) einsteigen | 3 **backseat** ['bæksiːt] Rücksitz | 4 **environmentally friendly** [ɪnˌvaɪrənˌmentli 'frendli] umweltfreundlich

ULARY

3 A sports quiz → WB 60/3–4

a) *You and your partner each make notes about one sport that you both like: where people play, what equipment they need, how many players there are in a team, etc. (For new words, use a dictionary.) Don't show each other your notes!*

b) *Write 5–6 quiz questions with the information in your notes.*

Example: Which of these football teams has never won the World Cup?
A. England B. Poland C. Italy

c) *Test your partner with your quiz! Who knows the most about the same sport?*

ADING

4 Are they crazy? → WB 60/5

a) *Skim the text for the gist. Say what it is about in 2–3 sentences.*

BEN NEVIS

You've probably heard of Ben Nevis in Scotland[5]. With its 1344 metres it is the highest mountain in Great Britain. Each year 125,000 people climb this mountain and enjoy the great view from the top. It usually takes a few hours to get to the peak[6]. But if you go up on the first Saturday in September, you can see people who run up or down the mountain. You think they're crazy? Well, they probably are …
They take part in the Ben Nevis race which takes place every year in early September. The race starts and finishes in Fort William. The runners do not only run up the mountain but also back down again – that's a distance of 9.9 miles with a height[7] difference of 1,340 metres. And some runners are really fast. In 1984 Kenny Stuart ran up and down the mountain in 1 hour, 25 minutes and 34 seconds – that's still the record[8] today.
To run up and down the mountain you must be really fit. Only runners with a lot of experience are allowed to take part in the race. For safety reasons[9] the number of runners is limited to[10] 600. The weather can change quickly in the mountains, so the runners must wear waterproofs[11], a hat, gloves and a whistle[12].
But who had this crazy idea anyway? The first person known to run up and down the mountain was William Swan. On September 27 1895 he ran from Fort William to the top of the mountain in 2 hours and 41 minutes. He probably didn't know what he started …

b) *Scan the text. What numbers are there in the text and what do they mean? What does it tell you about 1. safety rules 2. the history of the race? Take notes.*

5 **Scotland** ['skɒtlənd] Schottland | 6 **peak** [pi:k] Gipfel, Bergspitze | 7 **height** [haɪt] Höhe | 8 **record** ['rekɔ:d] Rekord | 9 **safety reasons** ['seɪfti ˌri:zns] Sicherheitsgründe | 10 **limited to** ['lɪmɪtɪd tə] begrenzt auf | 11 **waterproofs** ['wɔ:təpru:fs] Regenkleidung | 12 **whistle** ['wɪsl] Trillerpfeife

Find more online: m2g8ws

English around the world

Many people in different countries around the world speak English. Learn about where and why, and listen to some different kinds of English.

SPEAKING

1 Which countries speak English?

a) *Which countries do you know where the people speak English?*

b) *On a map or in an atlas, show where these countries are.*

c) *Can you think of a time when you spoke English? Where were you and who did you speak to? The phrases can help.*

Useful phrases

I spoke English …
with a friend | with a family member | on video chat | in a chat room | …

I was …
on holiday | at a summer camp | in Germany | in another country | …

VIEWING

2 Speaking English

9

a) *Watch the film. What is it about?*

b) *Does Marley mention any countries you talked about in Ex. 1? Which ones?*

c) *Look at the stills and describe what happens in the two scenes.*

A

B

d) *Watch the film again. Say which statements are right. Correct the wrong ones.*

1. The American man works in England.
2. American English is not exactly the same as British English.
3. You can see English signs in China, India and in some other countries.
4. The South Korean man can't help the Romanian woman.

e) *Act out one of these scenes:*

1. You're on holiday and make a new friend from another country.
2. You help an English-speaking person in your town.

Hi! / Hello! | How are you? | I'm … from … | Where are you from? | Are you here on holiday? | I'm looking for … | Can you …?

ADING **3**

How English became a world language

→ WB 61/1

a) *Before you read: Why do you think so many people in the world speak English?*

b) *Read the text. Make a list of the reasons why so many people speak English today. Only take notes! Then use your notes to explain to your partner why English is so important today.*

More than 400 million people in the world today speak English as their first language, and more than 600 million speak it as a second or official language. The first important reason for this is that from about 1600, British sailors and merchants crossed the sea and started colonies. This went on for many years and the British Empire became huge. For example, Australia was a British colony; India and South Africa too. Today, the British king or queen is still head of state in many countries, e.g. Australia.

There's a second important reason why so many people speak English. After World War II, the USA became a superpower and started to influence the world in many new ways. American rock 'n' roll music and Hollywood films became popular almost everywhere. And later, new technology from America (the PC, the internet, the e-mail) made it possible to communicate in every last corner of the world. In English, of course!

ENING **4**

Where are we from?

→ WB 61/2

L3/7

a) *Listen to four people from different English-speaking regions or countries. Which place is each person from? Which ones did you find easy or difficult to understand? Why?*

b) *Listen again. In which place can you hear these words and expressions? Can you remember what they mean?*

cookie | sunnies | wee | loch | lads and lasses | I'm grand | G'day | candy | movie | What's the craic? |

JLARY **5**

Your turn: English in your language

Collect words in German that are similar to or the same as words in English. Put the words into these categories. (Maybe you can think of more categories too.)

Clothes | Technology | Food | Sport | ...

Find more online: dd832q

Unit 5

Stay in touch

SPEAKING

1 Media and TTS students: A survey

Read what TTS students say about different media in A–E. Which of the activities have you done this week?

VOCABULARY

2 Media collocations

→ △ 124/1

Match these verbs and nouns to make phrases to talk about media.

→ S3

Example: I like to change my profile and post new photos. What about you?

change | post | receive | send | read | talk to | reply to | play | join | check | chat | take part in | write | text | have	profile | photo | text message | forum | social network | video game | video chat | magazine | discussion | each other | friend

In Unit 5 you learn

... how to talk and write about communication in your life. You learn:

- media vocabulary and phrases
- the language of giving and getting advice
- modals and their substitute forms
- writing skills for letters and replies

ENING **3** **More about the survey** → WB 62/1–3

L 3/8–12

a) *Listen and make a list of the media the TTS students use.*

b) *Listen again and take notes. What do the students say about the media?*

Useful phrases

Smartphones / Social networks / ... are great because they're fun / practical / easy to use / ...
... are great for meeting ... / for staying in touch with ... / for sharing information about ...

Which media?	What's positive?	What's not so positive?
smartphone / mobile	texts / easy to stay in touch	texts from parents!
special interest forums	...	...

c) *Your turn: Talk about how you use the different media.*

L3/13 ◎

Dear Ruby

Holly and Olivia have found an interesting problem in the 'agony aunt' pages of their favourite magazine.

Across cultures

In Britain, the advice pages of teen magazines are often very popular. People write to an **agony aunt** for help with their problems. What kind of agony aunts are there in your country?

JUST ASK RUBY!

Dear Ruby,

I'm writing to you because I don't know what to do. Last week I had a big fight with one of my best friends. Before the fight, we spent all our free time together. But now she has made friends with another girl and they're having a lot of fun. I know this because she posts photos of the two of them on the social network site we use. She acts like she's having a much better time without me! Whenever I see these photos, it really hurts my feelings. I'm not jealous, am I? Can you please help? I would really like to hear your advice.

Lauren

Dear Lauren,

You're having a hard time, aren't you? I'm sorry you're feeling so upset. I understand how hard it is to share a friend; it was the same with me when I was young. It doesn't mean you're a jealous person. As a first step, my advice is to be self-critical: Are you overreacting? Maybe the situation isn't as serious as you think. The next step is to talk to your friend in a friendly way and tell her how you feel. Why don't you invite her to your house after school? Or have you tried texting her? Things usually get better as soon as you talk. Another tip: Please stop looking at your social network site until you've talked to her. The photos only make you feel worse!
I hope you two can be friends again very soon.

Ruby

READING

1 Understanding the problem → WB 63/4

→ ▲ 124/2

Answer these questions about Lauren's letter and Ruby's reply.

1. Why is Lauren writing to Ruby?
2. How does Lauren know about her friend's new friend?
3. When does Lauren feel really bad?
4. Compare how her friend acted before the fight and after (in Lauren's opinion).

UAGE

2 Using linking words → WB 63/5–6 → G13

→ △ 124/3
→ S13

Read what different teens say about how they use different social media websites. Put these words in the gaps. There's sometimes more than one correct answer.

after | before | as soon as | until | whenever | like | because

1. I'm careful. I never give my phone number ___ I've met a new friend face-to-face.
2. ___ somebody starts asking too many personal questions, I just block them.
3. ___ you post photos of yourself online, remember: ___ you post them, they're probably on the internet forever!
4. I'm angry with my cousin ___ she posted that awful photo of me at the lake.
5. My friend doesn't even know some of the people on her friends list! It's ___ she doesn't care about real friends, she just wants a long list of 'friends'.
6. I don't get much attention online ___ I don't post pictures of myself very often!

ITING

3 Your turn: Media in your life

Write 5–6 sentences about yourself like the ones you see in Ex. 2. Think about these ideas:

- How much information about yourself do you share online? Why? How often?
- Do you and your friends use media differently? How?

ULARY

4 The right vocabulary for advice → WB 64/7

a) *In the letters on page 92, you see some phrases with 'advice vocabulary' in green. In a grid like this one, match the phrases to the three categories.*

Asking for advice	Giving advice	Showing understanding

b) *Here are some important advice phrases. Think of them as 'building blocks' for your own sentences about advice. Write a sentence with each phrase. You can write about the same problem as on page 92, or about something different.*

→ S3

Useful phrases

My advice is to be self-critical / to see it from the other side / to find a compromise.

Why don't you talk to your friend / invite your friend over / text your friend / …

The next step is to talk to / write to / …

It's always a good idea to talk / try / …

You're having a hard time / trouble with …

I'm sorry you're feeling sad / **you're** having trouble with …

Have you tried talk**ing** to him / text**ing** her?

Stop looking at … / think**ing** about / worry**ing** about / …

LANGUAGE

5 Find the rule: Question tags → WB 64/8 → G14

→ △ 125/4

a) *Look at the examples. What can you say about positive and negative forms?*

You**'re** having a hard time, **aren't** you?
The weather **is** nice today, **isn't** it?
You and Pia **haven't** told our secret, **have** you?
Ben **doesn't** like video games, **does** he?

b) *Make the correct question tags.*

1. That's a cool phone, …?
2. You can pay, …?
3. You aren't online often, …?
4. We need more time for our project, …?
5. She didn't write that awful post, …?
6. Ed hasn't got a new girlfriend, …?

Across cultures

- In English, question tags are a good way to **start a conversation** and to **get feedback**. Example at a football match: "Hey, this is a great game, isn't it?" – "Yeah, it is. Is Manchester City your favourite team too?"
- Also, it's important **to know this difference** with question tags: When it's a *real* question, your voice goes up. When it *isn't*, your voices go down.Just listen to the examples in **Ex. 5 c)**.

L3/16 → ▲ 125/5

c) *Listen to the sentences from b). Are the people sure about the answer or not? Listen again and repeat the sentences.*

LISTENING

6 < A song: Friends > Aura Dione

L3/17 → S9

Free, free to be myself
Free to need some time
Free to need some help
So I'm reaching baby, out
When I'm lonely in the crowd
When the silence[1] gets too loud
I'll be crashing[2] on some couch

And even if I never forget you baby
Tonight I'm gonna let your memory[3] baby
go, oh it's sad I know

But at least[4] I got my friends
Share a raincoat in the wind
They got my back[5] until the end
If I never fall in love again
Well at least I got my friends
Like a lifeboat in the dark
Saving me from the sharks[6]
Even though I got a broken heart
At least I got my friends, got my friends

Text: Aura Dione, Antonina Armato, Tim James, David Jost
© Koolmusic

a) *Which words / lines tell you what kind of a situation the main character is in?*

→ △ 125/6

b) *Your turn: What things are symbols of friendship in the song, and for* ***you****? Why?*

1 silence ['saɪləns] Stille | **2 to crash** [kræʃ] schlafen *(ugs.)* | **3 memory** ['memri] Erinnerung | **4 at least** [ət 'li:st] wenigstens | **5 They got my back** [ðeɪ ˌgɒt maɪ 'bæk] Sie halten mir den Rücken frei; sie passen auf mich auf *(ugs.)* | **6 shark** [ʃɑ:k] Hai

L3/18

Forum? What forum?

Luke: Dad, I wasn't allowed to go over to Jay's house yesterday. But can I … er, what on earth are you doing? There's water everywhere!

Dad: Really? Where?

Luke: Very funny. What's happened?

Dad: There's a problem with one of the pipes. I must fix it before your mum comes home and goes crazy!

Luke: Dad, do you know what you're doing?

Dad: Of course! It's just taking longer than I thought. I had to have a good look at everything first.

Luke: You could look at a forum for help.

Dad: Forum? What forum? You mean on the internet? So I can't fix my own washing machine – is that what you think? I don't need the internet.

Luke: But you're wasting so much time! I *cannot* believe you don't just look online – there's step-by-step advice for everything!

Dad: Well when I was young, I wasn't able to look everything up on the internet. But I still learned to do things my way, step-by-step.

Luke: Your way? Hm …

Dad: I've done this a million times before. You should watch me and learn! – Er, what are you doing with *my* tablet?

Luke: Well I can use it, can't I? Anyway, let's see … hm … Oh yes, look: I've found a great website. Hey, over 1,000 people have given it five stars!

Dad: You shouldn't believe everything you read online, Luke!

Luke: OK, just listen. You see that knob on the right?

Dad: Yes, I think I can reach it.

Luke: You must turn it off, then you …

15 minutes later …

Luke: Yes! It's working! These forums are great! No, please, you needn't say "thanks". Advice is free!

Dad: Fantastic! I fixed it. I told you, didn't I?

Luke: Only because I'm a genius!

Dad: With a *very* big head. Now, may I have my tablet back, please?

READING

7 Luke knows best?

a) *Luke and his dad have different ideas about how to solve the problem. What are they?*

b) *Have you ever had conversations like this one with family or friends? Tell the class.*

SPEAKING

8 The day I fixed my …

Tell your partner about a time when you fixed something. How did you do it?

→ △ 125/7

LANGUAGE

9 Find the rule: *Can* and its substitute forms → G15

a) *In which sentences from the text does* ***can*** *mean the same as the words in sentences A or B on the right?*

b) *Make more sentences for the two meanings of* ***can****.*

A: I'm good at Maths so **I'm able to** help my little brother with his homework.
B: My little brother **isn't allowed to** come into my room.

LANGUAGE

10 Substitute forms: *Be able to, be allowed to* and *have to* → WB 65/9–10

a) *Copy the grid into your folder. Find examples of the three substitute forms in the text and fill in your grid.*

	Present	Past
können		
dürfen		
müssen		

→ △ 126/8–9

b) *What were you not able or not allowed to do in the past? What are you not able or not allowed to do now? Tell your partner.*

Examples: When I was four, I **wasn't able to** swim. Now I can.
When I was ten, I **wasn't allowed to** have my own phone. Now I have one.
When I was five, I **didn't have to** do homework. Now I must.

LANGUAGE

11 *Should, shouldn't* and *could* for advice → WB 66/11–12 → G16

→ ▲ 126/10
→ △ 127/11

Tony is having a very bad day. Look at his problems, then write sentences with advice for him. Use ***should, shouldn't*** *or* ***could****. The ideas on the right can help.*

Example: Oh no, that was my dinner for Lou!
– Maybe you **could** take her to a restaurant.

1. I forgot Lou's birthday yesterday!
2. I've got a new neighbour.
3. I've left my money at home.
4. I want to do something nice for Dad.
5. I want to buy a new phone but haven't got enough money.
6. Someone has stolen my bike!

ask a friend | buy flowers | go to the police | take her to a restaurant ✓ | say hello | take him to a football game | help your parents at home for pocket money

MEDIATION

12 A German survey about young people and media

L 3/20

Listen to part of a radio report about a German media survey. You want to share the most interesting information with your chat friend in Italy. What can you tell him/her in English?

13 Are you media mad?

→ ▲ 127/12

Take the test and find out how media mad you are! Do you agree with your results? Why / why not?

Yes No

You sometimes use the internet, but not often.

You spend a few hours online every day.

You spend much more time online than with other hobbies.

You don't have many apps on your phone.

You check your messages all the time!

You like meeting your friends face-to-face. Texting or e-mailing isn't so important to you.

You have video chats with friends and family who you don't see very often.

Your parents think you spend too much time online or in front of the TV.

Do you ever post photos of yourself online?

Have you ever bought anything online?

You like 'real' shopping in shops better than online shopping.

You download all your music and listen to it on your phone.

You check for messages just two or three times a day.

You like looking at photos of your friends online and you always comment.

You post lots of photos of yourself online so everyone can see.

You love new apps for your phone.

You always compare prices online before you go shopping.

You don't care about video games. Boring!

– You're media mad! You love technology and media and have a lot of fun with it. Too much? Remember that sometimes it's good to go out and do other things with your friends. Try to stay away from your phone or laptop a few hours every day!

! You're clever with media! You know media can help you a lot, e.g. to talk to your friends. You like to be outside and have fun in other ways. But look for *new* ways to use the media too! There are *lots* of things to discover.

? You don't use media very much! You like to be outside, talk to your friends face-to-face, and go to real shops. But maybe your 'media mad' friends could tell you about how much fun media can be and how media can help you. Think about it!

Where's Maisie?

→ S21–22

VIEWING

1 Little dog, big trouble → WB 67/13

a) *Have you ever lost a pet? How did you feel? Tell the class about it.*

10 b) *Watch the film and then talk about the roles of Laura, Nathan and Polly in the story.*

Examples: A: I think Nathan is awful. He's too busy with girls and then …
B: Laura has great friends! They all help …

c) *Now imagine you are Laura. She wants to tell Alicia about what happened with Maisie.*

Start like this: Alicia, I can't believe what Nathan did! He lost Maisie! He was …

SPEAKING

2 Media in the film scenes → WB 67/14–15

Watch the film again. How many different kinds of media can you see in the film? Say how they helped the friends to find Maisie.

SPEAKING

3 Close-ups

a) *First, read the skills box.*

Film skills

In Unit 1 you learned how music can help to show / describe feelings or atmosphere. Another way to do this in films is with **close-ups**: very close shots of a character's face. In this example, the girl isn't sure: Should she give Nathan her phone number, or not?

With the camera so close, you can 'read' the question in her face!

A

B

b) *Look at scenes A and B from the film. What do the two close-ups tell us? The ideas on the right can help you.*

can't believe it | is happy again | loves her dog | wants to look cute / cool for Polly | thinks he's so cool | likes himself a lot | …

How to write a letter and a reply → S10–13

When you write a letter – to an agony aunt, for example – your letter should have different parts. This page shows you how to put a letter and a reply together.

1 The parts of a letter

a) *Read this letter to an agony aunt, and then read the reply. The box on the right shows you which parts of the letters there are. You need to know this for Ex. 2.*

Dear Ruby,

I'm writing to you because I just don't know what to do. I'm 13, and a new friend has invited me to go on holiday with his family this summer, to Spain. They always go to really cool places, and we just go camping. We never have much money. Before I met my friend, camping was fun. But it doesn't sound fun now. My parents say: "No, you can't go." That isn't fair, is it? I feel like I'm missing a lot of fun. I'm angry with my parents. What do you think, Ruby?
Thanks for your help!

Yours, Ben

Begin with a greeting.

The main idea(s): In an advice letter, the main idea is the problem.

Ask for advice.

Say 'Thank you'.

Your name (often with 'Yours')

Dear Ben,

Yes, I understand that a cool holiday in Spain sounds like fun. But my advice is to ask yourself this: Is your friend really a good friend? Do you care about each other? Why don't you ask him to come with your family on a camping trip. If he's a good friend, you can have fun together anywhere, can't you? It needn't be on a beach in Spain.
I hope this advice helps!

Ruby

Begin with a greeting.

The main idea(s): A reply should show understanding / feelings.

Give advice.

Finish your letter.

Name

Look back at the phrases box on p. 93 for the language of advice.

b) *Say what you think about Ben's problem and Ruby's advice.*

2 Write your own letter and reply → WB 68/16–18

a) *Your partner writes a short letter to an agony aunt, and you write another short letter about a* ***different*** *problem. Choose one of the ideas below, or an idea of your own:*

- "My friends say I'm weird because I don't like their music."
- "My two best friends are good at everything and I'm not."

b) *When you're both finished, exchange letters and write a reply to each other with advice.*

Advice letters and replies: Our collection

In this task, you get the chance to talk more about advice for young people's problems. Later, after the different groups have collected and discussed advice for different problems, you're going to write letters and replies for a class advice collection.

Step 1

Choose a topic → WB 69/19

In groups of 4 or 6, choose one of the problems in the list below. Make sure there is at least one group for each question:

A. I want a pet, but my parents say "no".
B. My friends say, "You share too much information about yourself on the internet".
C. My parents never buy cool clothes for me. I look stupid!
D. I never have enough pocket money.
E. I'm only allowed to watch TV or play video games for an hour on weekday evenings. It isn't enough!

Step 2

Pair work: What do you think? → WB 69/20

*Before you talk to your group about advice for your problem, work **with a partner** in your group for a few minutes. Make notes while you talk about these questions:*

- What places / people could the person go to for help?
- What advice could you give?

Example:
A: As soon as I have a problem, I ask somebody in my family, or maybe a friend at the club I go to / on my football team / …
B: I've never written to an agony aunt, but a friend sometimes writes posts in advice forums.
A: And about the problem: Well, the person should … because it's always a good idea to …

Look back at the **Stations** and the **Skills page** for help with advice.

Hey Mick, you always have good advice. What do you think I should do about Lou?

Step 3

Write an 'agony aunt' letter → WB 70/21

a) *Back in your group, discuss the different pairs' ideas about your group's problem. Use your notes from Step 2.*

b) *Now write one letter to an agony aunt about your group's problem. Then put your letter into a class box.*

You know how to write letters. Just look at the **Skills page** again.

Step 4

Exchange questions → WB 70/22

Pick one of the letters from the box. As a group, discuss the problem and write a reply. Everyone in the group should help to check the letter:

- Is the form of the letter correct?
- Is the language for the advice correct?
- Is the advice helpful? How / Why?

Step 5

Present the problem and advice
→ WB 70/23

Tell the class about the problem you chose from the class box and the advice you wrote for that problem. (Speak freely; don't just read from the page!)

The rest of the class should think about these things during the discussion:
- What do you think of the advice?
- Why is it helpful / not so helpful?

Step 6

Organise your letters and replies

As a class, talk about which topics the different problems fit into. Then organise your letters and replies by those topics. Think of how you can make nice pages with pictures, comics, etc.

S 2/19–24
L 3/21–26

It's a disaster!

A Dave's dad, Frank, stopped his car in front of his house. It was raining very hard – he wasn't able to see the house from his car but he was able to see that all the lights were on. The storm was getting worse every minute, with lots of thunder and lightning. He waited for a while and then quickly got out of the car, ran for the house and opened the front door. As he went inside, he nearly fell over all the bags and shoes. "I see Dave's friends are here again!" he thought. He shouted "Hello everyone!" But there wasn't a sound. "Hello-o-o?!" he called again. Nothing. "That's strange," he thought.

Stop and think:
Why do you think the house is so quiet?

He looked in the kitchen – nobody was there. Next, he looked in the living room and saw Gwen, Holly and Olivia. "Hi girls!" he said, but they didn't notice him because they were watching a *loud* music video on Olivia's laptop. Then he saw Jay in the corner.

"How are you, Jay?" he asked, but Jay was busy with text messages and music on his tablet PC. Frank went upstairs. As soon as he opened the door to Dave's bedroom, he saw Dave and Luke. They were sitting on the bed wearing headphones and playing a video game – they didn't notice Frank. "Well, they all look *very* happy to see me, I must say!" he said to himself, as he went back downstairs.

B Jay took off his headphones and tapped the girls' shoulders. "I was thinking," he said. "We should talk about that party we want to have soon."

"Yeah, I was thinking about that too," Olivia answered. "We can have it at my house. My dad and Claire say it's OK. Look, I've already written the invitation."

"Great! Let's post a message with the invitation and tell everyone to go to Olivia's house on –"

"No!" Olivia shouted. "We can't just post the invitation like *that*! A lot of people we don't know could see it and come to my house. No, we can only invite people face-to-face. People we *know*."

"Olivia, it's much quicker by internet," Jay said. "Come on, let's just do it! It's fun! He then grabbed Olivia's laptop.

"Jay, what are you doing?!" Olivia cried.

"I'm going to post it, what do you think?" They all started fighting for the laptop. At first they were laughing and joking, but then the girls saw that Jay was *serious*! They were horrified and tried to push him away from the laptop, but Jay was quicker. "Party on Friday 22nd at my house, 52 Begbie Road. Come and have fun!" it said in the invitation text. But just as Jay was pressing 'post', there was a very loud "BANG!" and everything went black.

C Suddenly, the house became very loud and all the friends started shouting at the same time: "What's happened?" – "I can't see!" – "My computer has crashed!" – "Oh no, we're offline too!" – "I can't find my phone!" – "Help! I don't like the dark!"

Frank shouted, "Calm down, it's only a power cut! Wait a moment while I find some candles."

"Did you really send that message?" whispered Holly. "I don't know, I think so!" Jay said.

"To Olivia's friends?" Holly asked.

"No. To *everyone*! But I'm not sure …" He was really starting to worry now, but he didn't want to tell the girls. Five minutes later, they were all sitting round the kitchen table in candlelight.

"Dad, what do we need candles for?" asked Dave. "Look, our phones have all got torches!"

"Sometimes, the old ways are better!" smiled Frank. "The only problem we have right now," Frank went on, "is that we can't cook – and I'm *really* hungry!"

"How is that a problem?" asked Luke. "Who needs to cook when there are pizza apps?" Dave and Luke started to show Mr Preston fantastic apps for his phone. Mr Preston was impressed! But nobody noticed that Jay wasn't speaking. "What have I done?" he thought to himself. "I was just showing off and I went a bit crazy for a moment. Please tell me the power cut stopped the message." Then he said, "Luke, Dave: Can I borrow a phone? I need to check something and I left mine in the other room." But they were busy with Mr Preston and his new pizza app.

D Frank was still talking about the old days. "When I was young, we *talked* to each other, we didn't text all the time."

"Oh no, he *loves* this topic!" Dave said and, as he spoke, there was a loud CLICK, and all the lights were back on.

The girls ran to the living room and waited nervously to get back online.

"Come on, come on!" Holly said. And suddenly they were online again. They went on to their social network site and … "Fantastic!" shouted Olivia. "The power cut stopped the message! But let's teach Jay a lesson." Gwen and Holly smiled at each other.

E Jay walked slowly back into the living room.

"You're in *big* trouble now!" Olivia said.

"How many messages are there?" he whispered. His face was white. He felt sick. "More than 50!" Holly said. "Listen to these: 'You don't know us but we *love* parties – see you there!', or 'Party? Cool! I love meeting new people!'"

Now Jay felt *really* sick. "It's a disaster!" he said. Holly and Olivia were trying very hard not to laugh.

"What's so funny?" Jay asked.

"Don't worry. The power cut stopped your message. Nobody got it," Olivia said.

"But you're lucky, Jay Azad!" Holly added. "And you *really* should leave the party invitations to us next time!"

"That," said Jay, "is no problem at all!"

READING

1 Understanding the story → WB 71/24-25

a) *Do you think 'It's a disaster!' is a good title for the story? Say why or why not. What ideas for a different story title do you have?*

b) *There are two main characters in this story: One is Frank, and the other is Jay. Find sentences in the text that show how they both feel left out at some point in the story.*

Example: He shouted "Hello everyone!" But there wasn't a sound. (Frank, lines 12-13)

→ △ 127/13
→ S16

c) *Do one of these role plays:*
- *One of you is Frank, the other is Dave's mum. She asks him what happened.*
  Or:
- *One of you is Jay, the other is Olivia. They talk about what happened and what they were feeling. Use ideas from the text.*

WRITING

2 Writing about pros and cons

→ S8

a) *Make a grid with examples of things people can do today with modern technology and examples of things people did or used when Frank was very young. There are a lot of examples in the text, but you can find more and add them to your grid.*

New world	Old world
– watch a video	– use candles
– send text messages	…
…	

→ S13

b) *What are the pros and cons of modern technology? First read the skills box. Then write about the two worlds. The phrases box can help you too.*

Writing skills

Use these words / phrases to link ideas and give information:

When things happen (time):
When my parents were young…, then …, now …, today …, before …, after …, as …, when …

Where things happen (place):
in the house, on my phone/PC, everywhere

Why things happen (reasons):
… because …

What else happens:
and …, or …, but …

How things happen:
easily, carefully, dangerously, more quickly, in a friendly way, without thinking, by internet, face-to-face

Useful phrases

Today we've got … | We can … | It's great that … because … | We weren't able to… before we had … | (Not) everything was …, I think … is better than … | But … can be dangerous. We should …

Unsocial Networking

→ Solutions p. 242

Can you ...

1. talk about media in your life? — I use ... to send / receive / post / chat / play / read / look up / take part in ...
2. link ideas? — I do it when / after / before / because ...
3. give advice to somebody? — Why don't you ...? | You should ... | You could ... | Have you tried ...ing ...?
4. make question tags? — You like texting, don't you? You aren't sad, are you?
5. use substitute forms for modals? — He wasn't allowed / able to come with us. He had to do his History homework.

VOCABULARY

1 How do people use media?

Match the sentence parts and make sentences.

Example: When my grandma wants to chat with her sister, she calls her on the telephone.

1. my dad / want / relax
2. I / want / know / words of a song I've heard
3. my mum / work away from home
4. I / want / tell all my friends how great my holiday is
5. my sister / want / know about the coolest new clothes

a) post / it on my social network profile
b) send / me text messages
c) read / girls' magazines
d) look / it up on the internet
e) watch / football on TV

SPEAKING

2 What can you say to give these people advice?

1. Your brother hurts his foot and doesn't know if it's broken.
2. Your friend missed his favourite TV show.
3. Your sister doesn't know how to fix her bike.
4. Your friend tells you that someone posted really embarrassing photos of her on the internet.
5. Your friend's parents are angry with her: She isn't allowed to use her smartphone for a week.

LANGUAGE

3 Fill in the right forms: *can, be able to, be allowed to, must, have to*

When I was young, we **1** make phone calls from everywhere because there were no mobile phones. Now you **2** use your smartphones nearly everywhere. But you **3** use them at school, are you? There **4** be rules for using them, right? 30 years ago you **5** look for information in books. Today you **6** look things up on the internet. When we were young, we **7** watch TV only sometimes, but today you **8** watch videos online all day.

S 2/25–29
L 3/27–31

Ten-tonne truck

Zoe finds a rat in her room. She wants to train it like she trained her pet hamster (who could break-dance), but she knows she isn't allowed to keep any pets. Raj, a shopkeeper[1] who is the 'agony aunt' of the town, tells her to set Armitage the rat free[2] in the park.

"What am I going to do with him, Raj? I'm not allowed to keep him at home; he's the reason why I was suspended[3] from school. My stepmother hated my hamster, she is *never* going to let me keep a rat."

Raj thought for a moment. "Maybe you should set him free," he finally said.

"Free?" Zoe said, with a tear[4] in her eye.

"Yes. Rats shouldn't be pets …"

"But this little one is so cute …"

"Maybe, but he's going to grow[5]. He can't spend his whole life in your pocket."

"But I love him, Raj, I really do."

"I'm sure you do, Miss Zoe," Raj said. "And if you love him, you should set him free."

So this was goodbye. Zoe knew deep down she would[6] never be able to keep Armitage for long. There were a hundred reasons, but the most important one was: HE WAS A RAT.

Children don't have rats as pets. They have cats and dogs and hamsters and mice and rabbits and tortoises. Some kids even have ponies, but never rats. Rats live underground, not in little girls' bedrooms.

Zoe walked sadly out of Raj's shop. It was true that sometimes he tried to sell his customers[7] a half-eaten chocolate bar, but all the kids in town knew that when they needed advice, he was the best.

And so she had to say goodbye to Armitage. Zoe took the long way back to her flat, through the park. She thought this was the perfect place to set little Armitage free. There were always bits of bread for the ducks – Armitage could[8] eat these. He could drink from the pond and take a bath in it. And maybe there was a squirrel or two he could make friends with.

The little girl carried[9] the little rat in her hand. It was the middle of the afternoon and there were just a few old ladies and their dogs in the park. Armitage wrapped his tail around her thumb – maybe he knew that something was wrong …

Zoe walked as slowly as possible. Finally, she reached the middle of the park. She was looking for a nice quiet place. Then she bent down[10] to the ground slowly and opened her hand. But Armitage didn't move. He just stayed in her hand. It was breaking Zoe's heart …

1 **shopkeeper** [ʃɒp'kiːpə] Ladenbesitzer | 2 **to set sb/sth free** [set 'friː] jmdn./etw. freilassen | 3 **to be suspended** [bi sə'spendɪd] (vorübergehend) der Schule verwiesen werden | 4 **tear** [tɪə] Träne | 5 **to grow** [grəʊ] wachsen | 6 **would** [wʊd] würde | 7 **customer** ['kʌstəmə] Kunde | 8 **could** [kʊd] könnte | 9 **to carry** ['kæri] tragen | 10 **to bend down** [bend 'daʊn] sich bücken

Zoe shook[11] her hand a little, but Armitage only held on tighter[12] to her fingers. She was fighting back tears when she picked the rat up gently[13] and put him carefully on the grass. Once again Armitage didn't move. He just looked up at her sadly. Zoe kissed him gently on his little pink nose.

"Goodbye, little friend," she whispered. "I'm going to miss[14] you."

A tear dropped from her eye.

The little rat turned his little head to one side, like a friend who was trying to understand her. This just made it harder for Zoe.

Finally, Zoe took a big breath and stood up. "Don't look back!" she told herself. But after a few steps she had to look one last time at the place she left him. To Zoe's surprise, Armitage wasn't there.

"He has already run away to the safety of the bushes," she thought. She looked at the grass, but it was long and he was short, and the grass didn't move. Zoe turned round and sadly started to walk home.

She left the park and crossed[15] the road. For a moment, there was no noise of cars, and in the silence, Zoe heard a small 'eek'. She turned round quickly, and in the middle of the road was Armitage.

He was following her!

"Armitage!" she shouted excitedly. He didn't want to be free; he wanted to be with her! She was so happy. Now she didn't have to imagine all kinds of terrible scenes any more: A hungry swan[16] couldn't eat him for dinner, and a ten-tonne truck couldn't run him over[17].

At that moment, she heard a loud thundering noise. Something came along the road towards Armitage, who was still moving slowly to get to Zoe. It was a ten-tonne truck!

Zoe wasn't able to move, she just watched the truck which was speeding[18] closer and closer towards Armitage. How could the driver see a baby rat in the road?

→ WB 73/1–4

11 **to shake** [ʃeɪk] schütteln | **12** **tight** [taɪt] fest | **13** **gently** ['dʒentli] sanft | **14** **to miss sb/sth** [mɪs] jmdn./etw. vermissen | **15** **to cross** [krɒs] überqueren | **16** **swan** [swɒn] Schwan | **17** **to run sth over** [rʌn‿'əʊvə] etw. überfahren | **18** **to speed** [spi:d] rasen

Legende

Diese Symbole und Erklärungen zeigen dir, wie du mit den Hilfen, Aufgaben und Aktivitäten auf den *Diff pool*-Seiten arbeiten kannst.

△ Hilfe zur Unit-Aufgabe | oder eine leichtere Variante der Unit-Aufgabe | oder eine zusätzliche Aufgabe

▲ eine zusätzliche Herausforderung

Unit 1

△ 1 Feelings → Help with Check-in, p. 9/3

How can you feel in these situations? Match the feelings with the sentences. There's often more than one answer.

1. There's a test in English tomorrow.
2. Your team won a football match.
3. You forgot your homework – again.
4. You know all the answers in class today.
5. You're the new student.
6. You're alone, and you don't know what to do.
7. You're at the park and are playing with your friends.
8. You meet your favourite star.
9. You can't find your lucky charm.
10. You have chocolate on your white jeans and everyone can see it.

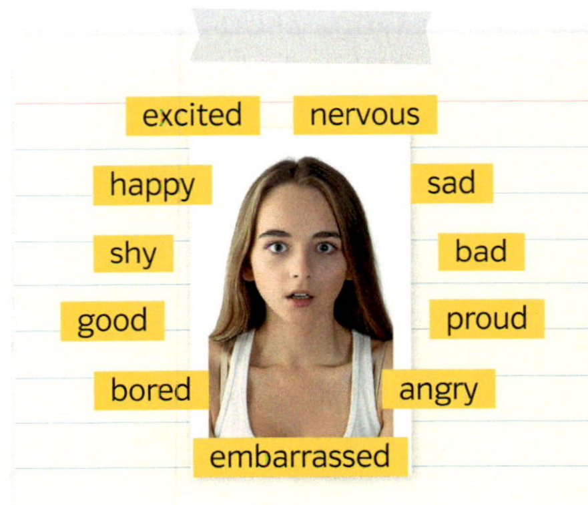

▲ 2 Charity work → After Station 1, p. 10/1

Do you know any children in charity projects? What can ***you*** *do to raise money? Write down some ideas and prepare a short talk for the class.*

△ 3 Irregular simple past forms → Instead of Station 1, p. 10/2 b)

Put in the correct past forms. Use the verbs below.

Two years ago the students **1** (do) fun activities and **2** (get) money for Comic Relief. They **3** (bring) the money to school. Then the school **4** (put) all the money together and **5** (give) it to the charity. Red Nose Day **6** (be) a non-uniform day, so everyone **7** (come) to school in different clothes. But they all **8** (wear) something red. Of course they all **9** (have) red noses too. Some students **10** (take) funny photos for the school website.

got | brought | gave | was | took | wore | had | put | did | came

△ 4 Sounds → After Station 1, p. 11/3

How do you say these simple past forms? Put them in the right box, then read them to your partner. Can you hear the difference?

played | stopped | acted | danced | collected | chased

laughed | watched | wanted | started | looked | turned | jumped

[d]	[t]	[ɪd]
played	stopped	acted

△ 5 The star of the show → Instead of Station 1, p. 11/5

What does Sherlock tell his dog friends the next day? Write the text again in his words, and use the verbs in the simple past below.

Start: I **did** lots of great tricks in the comedy show yesterday.

1. Sherlock does lots of great tricks in the comedy show. 2. First he jumps over a big box. 3. Then he runs around and chases his tail. 4. After that he dances on a skateboard, and when Olivia starts to play the sax he also sings. 5. The people love it. 6. They laugh and clap and give lots of money to Comic Relief. 7. Luke and his friends try to do their best too, but everyone's eyes are on Sherlock. 8. He feels so happy and proud – he is the real star of the show!

was | did ✓ | ran | danced | sang | chased | loved | started

tried | laughed | gave | were | clapped | jumped | felt

△ 6 A report about a special activity → Help with Station 1, p. 12/7

What did these people do to raise money for charity? The words below can help you.

sell old things | flea market

make cakes and biscuits | cake sale

run for charity | find sponsors | pay money per metre

organise talent show | sell tickets | sell drinks

△ 7 What they didn't do and what they did → After Station 2, p. 14/12

Tony was tired last week, but Lou wasn't – so they didn't do things together. What didn't they do? What did they do? Take turns!

Example: You: Tony didn't go skating with Lou, he read a book.
Your partner: Lou didn't read a book, she went skating in the park.

go skating in the park	read a book
swim in the boating lake	watch TV
play tennis with a friend	sleep on the sofa
buy cheese at Greenwich Market	listen to music
prepare dinner for her friends	play a computer game

▲ 8 A perfect day → After Station 2, p. 14/12

Think of something you did on a perfect day. (It needn't be true). Now your partner must find out what it was. He / She can ask questions like these:

Did you do something funny / exciting? Did you do it at home / in the park? Did you do it with friends / parents / alone? Were you nervous / excited / happy?

Think of more questions. Take notes, and then tell your classmates what your partner did on his / her perfect day!

△ 9 The new forms → After Station 3, p. 17/20 b)

Tony and Lou are fighting! What do they say?

Tony: I'm 1 (big) than you, Lou!
Lou: OK, I'm not as 2 (big) as you, but I am 3 (nice).
Tony: Maybe. But I'm 4 (popular) than you!
Lou: Oh no, you aren't. That's because I'm 5 (funny) than you.
Tony: You aren't as 6 (funny) as I am. Your jokes are 7 (bad) than my jokes! And I'm 8 (fast) than you.
Lou: That's because you're 9 (tall). But I'm 10 (intelligent). I can use my skates – and then I'm 11 (fast) than you!

△ 10 Say what's different → Instead of Station 3, p. 17/21

Make sentences with comparisons.

Example: 1. Wales is **smaller than** England.

1. Wales is ___ ___ (small) England.
2. The weather today is ___ ___ (bad) yesterday.
3. Route B is ___ ___ (easy) route A.
4. The courses aren't ___ ___ ___ (expensive) most people think.
5. I'm not ___ ___ ___ (nervous) I was about new challenges.

△ 11 Who's the tallest? → After Station 3, p. 17/22

Find out about your classmates! Choose one of the ideas in the box, find two partners and stand next to each other! Who is taller than you? Who has got the most interesting hobby? When you have got a group, shout "Stop!" and present your group to the class. Find the next group.

tall / short | young / old | boring / interesting hobby | big / small family | long / short way to school | young / old parents | silly / nice brother / sister

▲ 12 The best thing ever → After Station 3, p. 17/22

*Choose two of these things and write a short text about them. Use **than** and **as … as** too. You can start like this: The tastiest meal I ever had was … It was tastier than…*

tasty meal[1] | good film | nice teacher | funny book | exciting holiday | bad joke

△ 13 The secret → Help with Story, p. 20/3 b)

You can use these ideas and phrases to write your scene.

1. Look! I think that window … / … help me up?
2. Hey, here's another … / Do you think it's …? / Shshsh, quiet! / Don't … noise!
3. There's a light[2] …! / I think it's … window! / Let's throw …
4. Who's there? / Oh, it's you! / I heard …
5. We can use this to … / I can climb up, and then I can open …

1 **tasty meal** ['teɪsti 'mi:l] leckeres Essen; leckere Mahlzeit | 2 **light** [laɪt] Licht

Unit 2

△ 1 This is a fantastic school! → After Check-in, p. 29/2

a) *What do you think is important for a good school? Make a list of ten things.*

b) *In groups of three or four, take turns to say an idea on your list. Give yourself one point[1] for each idea on your list when no other student has that same idea. If others in the group have the same idea, nobody gets a point. Who's got the most points?*

△ 2 A school trip which was really cool → After Station 1, p. 31/3

*Do you need **who / that**, **which / that** or **whose**? Put in the right relative pronoun.*

The teacher **1** lessons we like the most is Mrs Jordan. Last year, she took us on a class trip and the coolest place **2** we visited was the Tower of London. Two men **3** costumes were black and red and very funny asked us about our visit. They were 'Beefeaters'[2]. They're the men **4** show the Tower to all the visitors. They told us about the ghosts **5** voices you can hear if you're quiet enough. They're the ghosts of all the people **6** lost their heads in the Tower many, many years ago!

△ 3 Contact clauses → After Station 1, p. 31/4 b)

*Read the sentence pairs. Which sentence in each pair **doesn't** need a relative pronoun?*

1. a) Lots of children that are interested in history go to the museum.
   b) Lots of children that I know go to the museum.
2. a) The art which you can see all around our school gives us lots of ideas!
   b) The art which is all around our school gives us lots of ideas!
3. a) I'm friends with lots of the students who go to Dance class.
   b) I'm friends with lots of the students who I see at Dance class.
4. a) This is a website which I use a lot for my homework.
   b) This is a website which helps me a lot with my homework.
5. a) I think the school trips that we go on are fun.
   b) I think the school trips that help us to understand history are fun.
6. a) Students who walk to school often get there earlier than me!
   b) Students who I see from the car window often get there earlier than me!

1 **point** [pɔɪnt] Punkt | 2 **Beefeater** ['bi:f̩'i:tə] königlicher Leibgardist

△ 4 Make one sentence from two → After Station 1, p. 31/5

Replace[3] the words in blue with a relative pronoun and make a new sentence.

Examples: Last lesson we talked about a famous person. We all know **him**.
→ Last lesson we talked about a famous person **who / that** we all know.
The Cooking Club organises competitions. **They**'re really exciting.
→ The Cooking Club organises competitions **which / that** are really exciting.

1. At TTS, there are lots of clubs and activities. You can do **them** outside.
2. I'm playing tennis with a new friend. **He** can run really fast!
3. Last lesson we watched a film. **It** was really interesting.
4. In Drama Club we learn about different film stars. I like **them** very much.
5. I can show you a cool wall painting. We made **it** yesterday.
6. Do you know the new girl? **She**'s talking to Luke.

▲ 5 Puzzles → After Station 1, p. 31/5

a) *Complete the sentences with **who / that**, **which / that** or **whose**.*

1. It's something ___ has four legs[4] but can't walk.
2. It's something ___ you must break before you can eat it!
3. I'm someone ___ is always cold but I must never feel warm!
4. It's something ___ is yours but your friends use it more than you do!
5. I'm a person ___ chair is a throne[5].
6. It's something ___ is tall when it's new and not so tall when it's old!

b) *Can you guess the answers?*

Answers: a table | an egg | a snowman[6] | your name | a king / a queen | a candle

△ 6 How to: Write prompt cards → Instead of Station 1, p. 32/6

Copy this prompt card about Queen Mary and Christopher Wren and fill in the right information for each heading.

Who:
What:

When:
Where:

Greenwich | cut the hospital in half | hospital between her house and the river | liked the sea | queen was upset | Christopher Wren | wanted a hospital | famous architect | 1692 | Wren had a very good idea | Mary

3 **Replace …** [rɪˈpleɪs] Ersetze … | 4 **leg** [leg] Bein | 5 **throne** [θrəʊn] Thron | 6 **snowman** [ˈsnəʊmæn] Schneemann

△ 7 Gwen's timetable → Help with Station 1, p. 32/7

These pictures can help you to understand what Gwen, Holly and Olivia are talking about.

△ 8 School subjects → Help with Station 1, p. 32/8 a)

These words and phrases can help you to compare your timetable with Gwen's.

Useful phrases

Our school day starts at 7:30 / …
We have … lessons in the afternoon / every day / only on Mondays / Tuesdays / …
There's a break at …
Lunch is from … till …

Gwen and I have the same subjects, but I also have lessons in …
In Maths / History / RE / … we learn / talk about … / we often work on projects.
We have lots of after-school clubs / activities / …

▲ 9 School subjects → After Station 1, p. 32/8 b)

Take turns to describe a lesson that you had last week. Don't say which lesson you're talking about! Your partner must guess the lesson.

Example: Last week I had a lesson in which we built a …

△ 10 The mice's Cooking Club → After Station 2, p. 33/9

What are / were the mice doing in Cooking Club? Put in the correct verb forms.

It's Friday, 10:00
1. I **am** mak**ing** a cheesecake.
2. Tony **is** learn**ing** how to make pizza.
3. Hey Lou, you ___ Tony's cheese!
4. Sophie and Alex **are** prepar**ing** a pie.
5. We ___ for tips on the internet.

Last Friday, 10:00
1. I **was** mak**ing** a cheesecake.
2. Tony ___ how to make pizza.
3. Hey Lou, you **were** eat**ing** Tony's cheese!
4. Sophie and Alex ___ a pie.
5. We **were** look**ing** for tips on the internet.

▲ 11 Act it out and guess! → After Station 2, p. 33/9

One student leaves the classroom. 3–4 other students act an activity ***without*** *words. When the teacher shouts "Stop!", everyone stops. Now the student comes back in and sees the 'frozen'*[1] *students. With yes / no questions, he / she must guess what the others were doing.*

△ 12 When or while? → After Station 2, p. 34/10

Fill the gaps with ***when*** *or* ***while****.*

1. We were watching a film ▬ Mum came home.
2. ▬ I saw my brother, he was buying lots of sweets.
3. I read a whole magazine ▬ I was waiting for the bus.
4. ▬ my dog was sleeping, my cat stole his dinner!
5. Amber was preparing a presentation ▬ her phone rang.
6. ▬ the friends were walking home from school, they discovered a new shop.

▲ 13 A crazy day at home → After Station 2, p. 34/10

Use these photos and write a short story about a crazy day at home. Think of your own crazy ideas too. Use the simple past and the past progressive.

Start like this:
First, breakfast was crazy. While Mum was…, our dog … her breakfast! Then, while Mum and Dad were …, we … in the kitchen. But when …

▲ 14 Write a dialogue → Instead of Story, p. 42/3 c)

After his fight with Jay, Luke talks to his mum. Write their conversation and use words which show that Luke had very strong feelings about what happened.

Start like this: Mum: You look **really** angry, Luke. Is anything wrong?
Luke: I had an **absolutely awful** fight with Jay today …

1 **frozen** [ˈfrəʊzn] *hier:* erstarrt

Unit 3

△ 1 Choose your London → Help with Check-in, p. 51/3

Here are some useful phrases that can help you to discuss where you want to go.

Useful phrases

I'd like to visit … I's free. | I think … is the best place. Let's go there!
We must see …, it's fantastic. | Can we go to …? I hear it's really great.
I'm sure it's fun to …, so I really want to …

△ 2 What are they going to do next week? → After Station 1, p. 52/3

Monday	Tuesday	Wednesday	Thursday	Friday
Amir and Jay – go to the cinema	*Amir – go shopping with Aunt Yasmin, buy a London T-shirt*	*Amir – meet Jay's friends in the afternoon*	*Amir and Shahid – visit Cutty Sark*	*Amir and Jay – have a sleepover at Luke's house*

Amir tells his mum about these plans in an e-mail – what does he write?

Start like this: Dear Mum, I can't call you very often next week because I have so many plans! On Monday, Jay and I are going to go … On Tuesday, Aunt Yasmin is going to …

△ 3 What's going to happen? → Help with Station 1, p. 53/4

These words can help you to write about the people in the picture on p. 53:

open the door | clean the street | take the bus | buy an ice cream | give some money | go to the cinema | play the saxophone

Start: 1. The old man and woman are going to sit down. 2. The man is going to …

△ 4 Guess my plans for tomorrow → Help with Station 1, p. 53/5

What can you do where? These ideas can help you to guess your partner's plans. Match the activities with the right places first.

1. London Dungeon
2. London Eye
3. Royal Observatory
4. Shakespeare's Globe
5. Brick Lane

a) learn about the theatre, watch a Shakespeare play
b) stand on the time line, watch the time ball fall down
c) buy great clothes, see street art
d) get a great view of London
e) hear horror stories, see ghosts

△ 5 The photo story

→ Help with Station 2, p. 55/7

Olivia, Holly, Amir and Jay all have different feelings about the food challenge. These ideas help you to think of something that they might say about it.

Jay	Olivia	Holly	Amir
really like music | fantastic street shows | not so hungry	like a challenge | try something exciting | find cafés boring	doesn't know where the cafés are | try to find something special | everything so expensive	nervous | not know where to look | happy to go with Olivia

▲ 6 A game: Why didn't you buy any food?

→ After Station 2, p. 55/7

One of you is Jay, one of you is Olivia. Olivia starts with the question below. Jay must quickly give three different answers. Olivia chooses one and writes it down. Then it's her turn to answer with three different sentences. Jay chooses one, writes it down and goes on with three different sentences. Go on like this till you have the perfect dialogue.

Start: **Olivia:** Why didn't you buy any food?

I didn't feel hungry any more.
I was watching the street shows and they were great.
I didn't have any money. → What about your pocket money?
Why not? → I forgot it at home.
Maybe someone stole it!
…

△ 7 Compound words with *some* and *any*

→ After Station 2, p. 55/9

a) *Fill the gaps with* ***some*** *or* ***any***.

Jay: Let's buy **1** drinks. I have **2** money left.
Olivia: Oh, no! I don't want **3** drinks, and I'm still hungry. Have you got **4** crisps left, Holly?
Holly: No, sorry. I haven't got **5** crisps, but I've got **6** biscuits.

b) *Complete the words with* ***some*** *or* ***any***.

Amir hasn't bought **1** **thing** for his mum yet, so the friends are looking for souvenir shops. "How much do you want to spend?" Jay wants to know.
"Well, I can't buy **2** **thing** expensive, I've only got a few pounds. But I need **3** **thing** for my mum – maybe there's **4** **thing** in this little shop?" Amir answers.
"I don't think so. Look at the prices! Let's go **5** **where** else," Holly says. "What about Greenwich Market? Or does **6** **one** have a better idea?"

▲ 8 Sherlock, you crazy dog! → After Station 2, p. 55/9

Luke's mum is away at the weekend. She wrote a note for the family – but Sherlock found it and now it's in pieces! Match the parts and write a new note in the right order.

1. You needn't buy
2. Remember: someone must
3. I had to get to the station, so
4. There's something
5. Lots of love for
6. Can someone please
7. I don't want to find
8. Everybody should
9. Hi everyone, I hope

a) clean the windows?
b) in the fridge for you, please check.
c) anything for dinner.
d) clean up a bit.
e) any food on the sofa when I come back.
f) you can manage without me!
g) I didn't do everything before I left.
h) take Sherlock for a walk tomorrow morning.
i) everybody, Mum.

△ 9 Complete the text → Instead of Station 2, p. 55/10

Fill the gaps with these words. Use each word only once.

nothing | everywhere | anybody | someone | something | everybody | everything | nobody | anywhere | anything

Holly: What can we do till we meet Shahid later? Has **1** got a good suggestion?
Jay: It must be **2** that costs **3** – we haven't got any money left.
Olivia: Let's just walk around. I'm sure that's fun for **4** new in London like Amir. There are lots of interesting things to see **5** you look. What do you think, Amir?

Amir: Well, if **6** wants to make a different suggestion – yes, I'd like that.
Holly: Is there **7** special you'd like to go or **8** special you'd like to see?
Amir: Well, **9** is special for me – it's all amazing. But I'd love to walk near the river.
Jay: Is that OK with **10**? – Great, come on, let's go and find the Thames!

△ 10 Adverbs → After Station 3, p. 57/15

Here are some tips for people who visit London. Find the right adverb for each sentence.

Always cross[1] the street **1** (careful). Remember: In England cars drive[2] on the left! Sometimes people in England speak very **2** (fast). You can always ask people to talk **3** (slow) and **4** (clear). They're usually friendly when you ask them **5** (polite). You should try **6** (hard) to understand, but if you have problems, don't react[3] **7** (nervous). When you get back home, you can talk **8** (happy) about the great things you did in London!

1 **to cross** [krɒs] überqueren | 2 **to drive** [draɪv] fahren | 3 **to react** [ri'ækt] reagieren

△ 11 Act it out! → After Station 3, p. 57/15

Write these activities on cards. One of you choooses an activity and acts it without words. The others guess what you're doing, and how.

sing loudly | jump quickly | dance slowly | look around nervously | talk excitedly | walk carefully | write fast | smile happily

△ 12 Adjective or adverb? → After Station 3, p. 57/16

Decide if you need the adjective or the adverb in these sentences.

1. When Amir came to London, he was ___ because he travelled alone. At Victoria Station he looked around ___ to find Jay and his aunt and uncle. (nervous)
2. But he was also ___: Jay always talked so ___ about all the things you can do in London! (excited)
3. Amir, Jay and his aunt and uncle went home by bus. The old London buses are very ___. They travel around the city very ___ so tourists can have a ___ look at all the sights. You can see them very ___ from the top of a real London bus. (slow, good)
4. On the bus, Amir smiled ___. A whole week in London! And he was ___ to see his cousin and his family. (happy)

▲ 13 Adjective or adverb? → After Station 3, p. 57/16

From the two boxes, choose an activity and an adjective. Then write sentences about yourself – and use the adverb form too!

Example: I'm good at sports, but I don't play football very well. I'm nervous before a test, but I don't …

walk to school | do my homework | talk to teachers | dance | sing pop songs | go cycling | …	good | nervous | excited | happy | angry | crazy | loud | slow | fast | …

▲ 14 A treasure in the Thames → Instead of Story, p. 64/4

Think of something the friends find in the Thames: a gold coin, an old ring, a statue, an oil lamp … Tell the story of how they find it, what they do with it, etc.

Unit 4

△ 1 Talk about sports → Help with Check-In, p. 68/2 b)

*Two students made these word clouds. What are their favourite sports? You can use the words to talk about the sports **you** are interested in.*

▲ 2 Have you really done that? → After Station 1, p. 71/3

*Work with a partner. Each of you writes down six very strange or exciting activities. **One** of them must be an activity that you have really done. Exchange your activities and find out which one your partner has done.*

eat worms – take a llama to the park – go water-skiing with my granny – play with a tarantula[1] – sleep in a haunted house[2]

△ 3 Great runners → After Station 2, p. 73/7

Lisa and Mark help to organise the London Marathon; they need great runners. Put the verbs into the present perfect.

Lisa: We need some great runners this year. Mark, **1** (you write an e-mail to) last year's winners?
Mark: Yes, I have. But I **2** (get) answers from everyone yet. What about the German twins[3], Klara and Lena – I **3** (find) some info about them on the internet.
Lisa: **4** (they win) anything yet? I **5** (never hear) of them.
Mark: They **6** (run) in a few important races. Klara **7** (win) one big marathon last year, the Frankfurt City Marathon. Lena **8** (win) yet, but she was 'Best European' in the Hamburg Marathon. They always run together.
Lisa: **9** (you check) if they have a website?
Mark: Of course I have. Here, I **10** (copy) the contact details for you. Let's write them an e-mail. We **11** (not have) famous twins in the Marathon yet, have we?
Lisa: No, it's a good idea to ask them. But wait till I **12** (look) at their website first!

1 **tarantula** [təˈræntjələ] Vogelspinne | 2 **haunted house** [ˌhɔːntɪd ˈhaʊs] Geisterhaus | 3 **twins** [twɪnz] Zwillinge

▲ 4 Write a profile about Brandon → After Station 2, p. 73/7

For a magazine, write a short profile about a rich[4] and famous young actor, Brandon Fairchild. What has he ***already / just / never done****, or* ***not yet done****? What is he* ***going to do*** *in the future? Use the ideas below for the profile, but also add some of your own ideas. Be creative! (Use a dictionary for help with new words.)*

already ✔	buy a cool house in Hollywood / travel around the world in private jet
never ✘	have a famous girlfriend
just ✔	get award[5] for 'Coolest Actor'
not yet ✘	find a new house in London
future plans ✔	buy his own ship / win an Oscar

△ 5 Children and accidents → Help with Station 2, p. 73/9

These words can help you to tell your partner in English about the German survey.

young people | often | get hurt[6]

have accidents | per cent[7] | every year

injury[8] | see a doctor | small children

Remember, your partner only needs to understand **the main ideas**. You needn't try to translate everything word for word!

△ 6 Questions and answers → Help with Station 3, p. 75/12

Here are some ideas for your questions and answers.

Activities:
watch a … / join a …
win an important match / race
play tennis / rugby / handball
run for charity / run for fun
have an accident / a serious injury
finish first / last in a race
enjoy a Sports lesson

When (simple past):
last year / week / month
when I was smaller / a baby / younger
yesterday
in May / January / October / …
When (present perfect):
never / before / yet / ever

4 **rich** [rɪtʃ] reich | 5 **award** [əˈwɔːd] Auszeichnung; Preis | 6 **to get hurt** [ɡetˈhɜːt] sich verletzen | 7 **per cent** [pəˈsent] Prozent | 8 **injury** [ˈɪndʒəri] Verletzung

△ 7 Boys' day! → After Station 3, p. 75/13

Dave and Jay are on the phone. They want to have a picnic in the park with Luke, and then go to the match between Greenwich RFC and Sidcup RFC.

Complete their phone call with the right verb form in the simple past or present perfect. Sometimes you just need a short answer.

Dave: So what's the plan for Saturday, Jay? You **1** (tell) us yet!
Jay: Oh yes, I **2** ! We **3** (talk) about it yesterday in the Maths lesson.
Dave: Really? I can't remember. Sorry! – Anyway, what **4** (you say) yesterday?
Jay: I have tickets for the rugby match between Greenwich and Sidcup! My dad **5** (buy) them as a present for me and two friends!
Dave: Hey, you've got a cool dad. – So when are we going to meet?
Jay: Well, I **6** (think) it would be a good idea to have a picnic in the park first.
Dave: Cool. And what **7** (Luke say) when you **8** (tell) him?
Jay: He thinks it sounds great too. He **9** (already ask) his dad for help with the food. Can you buy some drinks, Dave?
Dave: No problem. My mum **10** (just give) me some extra pocket money because I **11** (do) well in the Maths test last week. So what drinks do we want?
Jay: Just lemonade and water?
Dave: OK. **12** (you ask) the girls if they want to come, Jay?
Jay: The girls?! No, I **13** . It's a *boys'* day, remember? And they **14** (not ask) *us* to come to their sleepover party last weekend, did they?
Dave: No, but who would *want* to be at their sleepover?!

▲ 8 A game: Who is it? → After Station 3, p. 75/13

1. *Choose a famous star, a person in the class or somebody else* ***everybody*** *knows.*
2. *On a card, write five activities this person has already / never done, or did at some time. But don't write his / her name!*
3. *Then collect and shuffle[1] all the cards.*
4. *Take turns to read out the information. The others must guess who it is.*

Example:
- started to play football when he was five
- has played for Schalke and Bayern
- has been a member of the German national football team since[2] 2009
- became the world's best goalkeeper[3] in January 2014
- won the World Cup in 2014

Answer: Manuel Neuer

1 to shuffle [ˈʃʌfl] mischen | **2 since** [sɪns] seit | **3 goalkeeper** [ˈgəʊlˌkiːpə] Torwart

△ 9 The London Mini Marathon → Help with Story, p. 82/1 b)

These words and phrases for the three pictures can help you to retell the story.

When the race started, Gwen was … | Olivia wasn't there, so … | Gwen was a bit worried about … | She told Luke, "Don't …" | Luke saw two people in …

Ten minutes later, she felt … | She told herself … | The two runners in the funny costumes were … | They were getting … | But Luke and Gwen were still …

Suddenly, … pulled out a phone and … chaos … | Another runner … | But Gwen and Luke finished … | Olivia found out that the dog and cat were …

△ 10 What's the person like? → Help with Story, p. 82/2

*Which of these words can you use if you want to say something **positive** about someone? Which ones are **negative**? Make two lists. Some of the words can help you to describe the children and their actions.*

brave | unfriendly | stupid | fast | polite | crazy | clever

careful | helpful | funny | silly | interesting | great

good | boring | confident | friendly | popular | awful | nice

△ 11 Useful phrases from the story → Help with Story, p. 82/3

Complete the phrases; you know them from the story. This can help with your mind map.

1. "My charity does a lot of really important work, so it really ___ to me."
2. "Olivia can't join us. That's ___, isn't it?"
3. "You're silly, not me! So ___ me silly."
4. "This ___ great! After all that training, this is the moment, *my* moment!"
5. "There are so many people here, and it's my first marathon! I'm ___! You too?"

▲ 12 A game: Frozen image[2]! → After Story, p. 82/3

Get together in groups of four or five. Choose a scene from the story and practise a frozen image[4] of that scene. (Practise in another room so your classmates can't see you.) Back in the classroom, the others then shout "One… two… freeze[5]!" and your group does its frozen image. Your classmates must guess the scene and explain how they guessed.

4 **frozen image** [ˌfrəʊzn ˈɪmɪdʒ] erstarrtes Bild | 5 **to freeze** [friːz] erstarren

Unit 5

△ 1 Media collocations → Instead of Check-In, p. 90/2

a) *Write down all the media collocations in the text.*

Tony loves the world of media! He checks his text messages all the time. He loves texting his friends. He sends and receives text messages during lessons too. (Bad boy!) And Tony has joined a popular social network: He's on Mousebook, of course. He regularly posts photos and changes his profile. It's important for Tony to stay in touch with his friends, so he often talks to them on video chat. At weekends, he often plays video games or takes part in discussions. It's easy to forget the time when you're online! Lou isn't so happy about this: Tony doesn't always reply to her text messages quickly enough, and she has to check his profile on Mousebook to see what he's doing!

b) *You can use some of the verbs with more than one noun, e.g., you can **change** your **profile** and you can **check** your **profile** too. How many different media collocations of nouns and verbs can you find?*

▲ 2 Ruby's answer → After Station 1, p. 92/1

*Work with a partner. On little pieces of paper, write down the different bits of advice that Ruby has for Lauren. Then put the pieces of paper face down on the table. Take turns to pick one up and talk about it. Do you think it's good advice? Why/Why not? What other bits of advice do **you** have for Lauren? Talk about them.*

△ 3 Using linking words: Tony and his phone → After Station 1, p. 93/2

Read what Tony's friend Robby says about Tony. Use these words to make one sentence out of the two. There's sometimes more than one way!

after | before | as soon as | whenever | because | when

Example: Tony plays video games too often. He doesn't call me. → **Whenever** Tony plays video games, he doesn't call me.

1. He got a new smartphone for his birthday. We often saw each other before that.
2. Tony can't leave his phone alone for one minute. He's really into texting.
3. I wanted to go to the cinema with him yesterday. He said "yes".
4. At the cinema, someone said, "You must turn off your phone. The film is starting."
5. Tony heard that. He was shocked.
6. Sometimes a phone rings at the cinema. It always makes the other people angry.

△ 4 A game: Who's the fastest? → After Station 1, p. 94/5

1. *Write short positive and negative statements on little pieces of paper.*
   Example: This is a cool T-shirt.
2. *Your teacher then collects the papers.*
3. *Now stand up in two lines. Your teacher reads out a sentence from your list to the first two students in the lines.*
4. *You must complete the sentence with the right question tag.*
   Example: This is a cool T-shirt, **isn't it**?

The student who gives the right answer first joins the queue again; the other student must sit down.

▲ 5 You can hear the difference, can't you? → After Station 1, p. 94/5 c)

You and your partner write six sentences with question tags – three of them must be ***real*** *questions. Take turns to read your sentences to each other. Your partner must listen closely and then answer. Remember: A real question needs a real answer, not just a short answer!*

△ 6 Symbols of friendship → Help with Station 1, 94/6 b)

Here are some phrases and ideas for talking about symbols of friendship.

Useful phrases

A symbol can be **something you do**, like …
when you wear the same clothes / colours | when you have a secret together | when you talk about / help each other with problems | …

A symbol can be **a thing**, like …
a photo together | a mascot keyring[1] / a mascot toy | special words for things | favourite stickers | …

△ 7 The day I fixed my … → Help with Station 2, p. 95/8

Ask yourself these questions before you talk to your partner:

What did you fix? | Did it belong to you or to someone else? | Why did you fix it and not buy a new one? | Where did you look for help / advice? | Did you ask anybody for help? | Was it easy to fix? | How long did it take you? | Does it still work?

1 **mascot keyring** [ˌmæskət ˈkiːrɪŋ] Maskottchen-Schlüsselanhänger

△ 8 The older you are, the more you can do … → Instead of Station 2, p. 96/10 b)

*Look at the list of things Olivia can do now. Say what you think she **wasn't allowed to do** when she was four years old, what she **wasn't able to do**, and what she **didn't have to do** then.*

Examples:

- When Olivia was four, she wasn't able to read a book. Now she can. / Now she loves to read.
- When Olivia was four, she didn't have to …

- go cyling	- help her mum in the kitchen
- read a book	- watch TV in the evening
- go shopping	- make models
- go to school	- join a social network
- do homework	- have a sleepover

△ 9 'Fun' in Scotland … → After Station 2, p. 96/10 b)

Complete Holly and Dave's dialogue with the right forms.

Dave: Hi Holly! Back from Scotland? Did you enjoy your holiday?

Holly: Well, not really. You know I wanted to visit the castle in Edinburgh, but I **1**. My mum said it was too expensive.

Dave: Oh, that's too bad. But you **2** to take some photos of the castle, weren't you?

Holly: Yes, of course. That doesn't cost anything. Amber and I **3** to go shopping on the Royal Mile, so that was good. We went all the way down to Hollyrood House, but we **4** to go inside: "Too expensive", mum said. *Again*.

Dave: When I was in Edinburgh last summer, I didn't want to visit any old castles, but I **5** to visit *lots* of them! My parents *always* take me to museums and castles.

Holly: Well Scotland has lots of beautiful lakes. I'm sure you went swimming, right?

Dave: Wrong! My mum always says, "Forget it, the water is too cold. No swimming!" So no, we **6** to go swimming. We **7** to visit all the different sights.

Holly: Hm, it sounds like you and I **8** to have the best time there. Maybe next time!

▲ 10 Giving and taking advice → After Station 2, p. 96/11

*On cards, write down situations where **you** might need advice. (The ideas on the right can help you.) Put them face down on the table, between you and your partner. Take turns to choose a card, read the situation to your partner, and say what advice you have for him / her.*

- not good at school
- trouble with teacher
- fight with friend
- not enough pocket money
- small room
- …

△ 11 You could do that, but I think you should …

→ After Station 2, p. 96/11

Read these situations and decide what advice you want to give. Do you need ***could*** *or* ***should****? (Remember, there's a difference! Check G16 for help.)*

1. Oh no. I left my smartphone at home! (use mine)
2. This phone doesn't work at all. (buy a new one)
3. Do you like this photo? I want to post it. (not post private photos)
4. My computer has been so slow! (let me check it)
5. Hmm, 'World of Heroes' or 'Super Talents' – which game is better? (try both)
6. Susan is still angry because I sent her that text. (tell her you're sorry)
7. I think my profile is boring. (write something interesting / exciting)

▲ 12 Media mad

→ After Station 2, p. 97/13

When you read a flow chart, always start at the top and work down, step by step. First read the text in the middle box in the first line, and then decide if you must follow the red (= no) or green (= yes) flash. Are you surprised abour your results?

Work with a partner. Choose a box for your partner (e.g. 'five / four' is the box with "You don't care about video games"). Your partner must find the box and comment on it. Then it's his / her turn.

Example: A: Two / two. "You check your messages all the time!"
B: I don't know. When I'm bored I often check them. But when I'm with my friends, I don't do that. What about you?

△ 13 Writing a dialogue

→ Help with Story, p. 104/1 c)

Here are some ideas to help you write your dialogue.

Mrs Preston: When did you get … | Was anybody … ? | Didn't you ask them what… | What happened when … | That sounds like a lot of fun, but …

Mr Preston: When I got home, I wasn't able … | I was angry because… | I found some candles and thought … | The kids used their smartphones to …

Jay: I was thinking about the party we wanted to have and … | It takes so long to write … | I'm sorry, I wasn't thinking when I … | I was so worried when…

Olivia: Don't you know how dangerous it is to … ? | Why didn't you wait for … ? | We were really lucky that … | I think next time you should … | But it's OK, don't worry …

Vocabulary

S1 Vokabelheft

Führe ein dreispaltiges Vokabelheft, in dem du auch neue Vokabeln notieren kannst, die nicht in der Wortliste stehen. Die erste Spalte ist für die englische Vokabel bestimmt, die zweite für die Übersetzung und die dritte für Beispielsätze oder alles, was dir hilft, dir die Bedeutung zu merken, z. B. Bilder, *mind maps*, Beziehungen zu anderen Wörtern, auch in anderen Sprachen.

S2 Vokabelkartei

Es lohnt sich, eine Vokabelkartei anzulegen, um Vokabeln zu lernen. Sie besteht aus Karteikarten für die Vokabeln und einem Karton mit fünf Fächern für die Karten.
Schreibe das englische Wort auf die Vorderseite der Karteikarte und die deutsche Bedeutung auf die Rückseite. Zusätzlich kannst du weitere Merkhilfen notieren. Stelle zunächst alle Karten ins erste Fach.
Übe jeden Tag fünf bis zehn Minuten, und zwar so: Nimm eine Karte nach der anderen heraus und überprüfe, ob du die Übersetzung weißt (deutsch – englisch, englisch – deutsch). Wenn ja, stellst du die Karte ins zweite Fach. Mache weiter, bis das erste Fach leer ist. Das zweite Fach bearbeitest du dann genauso, allerdings nicht jeden Tag, sondern nur einmal in der Woche, das dritte Fach alle zwei Wochen usw.

S3 Wörter im Zusammenhang

Wörter sind die Bausteine der Sprache. Du musst sie natürlich lernen und jedes für sich verstehen. Zur Beherrschung einer Sprache gehört aber auch zu wissen, welche Kombinationen dieser Bausteine möglich sind. Deshalb ist es wichtig, mit den Wörtern schon die richtigen Kombinationen mitzulernen. Schreibe Wörter möglichst immer in typischen Zusammenhängen auf.

Mit Verben kannst du passende Ergänzungen mitlernen, z. B.:

*to **read** a book, a magazine, a comic, a manga*
*to **write** a letter, an e-mail, an invitation, a blog*
*to **go** swimming, shopping, home, away, to the cinema*

Du solltest auch wissen, wann bestimmte grammatische Formen auf bestimmte Wörter folgen. Schreibe dir passende Beispiele zusammen mit der Vokabel auf, z. B.:

*I **would like to** swim, **to** read, **to** go shopping*
*I **like** swimm**ing**, read**ing**, go**ing** shopping*

Welche die richtigen Präpositionen sind, muss man in jeder Sprache auswendig lernen. Notiere auch dafür Beispiele und lerne sie, z.B.:

*The party is **on Friday**, **at seven**, **at the weekend**.*
*My house is **in Dover Street**. We're **on the road to London**.*
*London is **on the Thames**.*

S4 Methoden

Du hast schon mehrere Methoden gelernt, wie du dir Vokabeln besser einprägen kannst:

- Klebezettel mit englischen Wörtern an die entsprechenden Gegenstände in deinem Zimmer kleben
- Wörter als Bildwörter oder mit passenden Bildern aufmalen
- Wörter zusammen mit anderen, die zu einem Thema gehören, in *mind maps* anordnen
- Wörter pantomimisch darstellen und gegenseitig erraten lassen
- Wörter aussprechen, zusammen mit ihrer Übersetzung und vielleicht einem Beispielsatz aufnehmen und immer wieder anhören
- Wörter mit ähnlichen Wörtern in anderen Sprachen notieren
- Wörter, die miteinander in Beziehung stehen, zusammen notieren, z. B. verwandte Wörter, Gegensatzpaare, zusammengehörige Paare

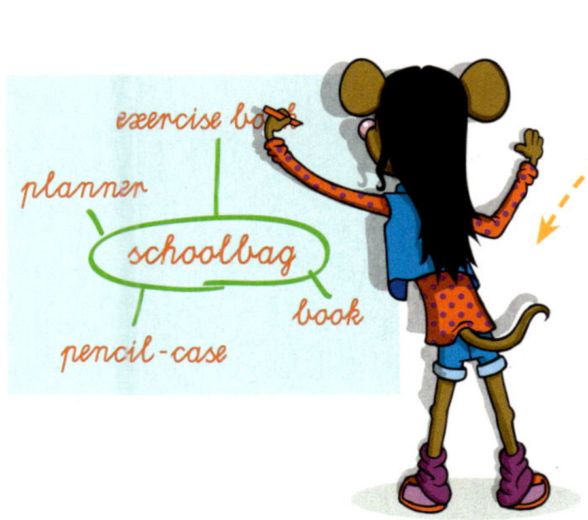

Reading

S5 Schnelllesetechniken

Normalerweise denkst du während des Lesens nicht darüber nach, wie du dabei vorgehst. Wenn du aber eine Aufgabe zu einem Text bekommst oder eine bestimmte Information suchst, liest du bewusster und gezielter. Diese Techniken helfen dir, wenn die Zeit begrenzt ist.

Skimming („den Rahm abschöpfen“)	Scanning („maschinell durchsuchen“)
Wenn du danach gefragt wirst, worum es in einem Text geht, sollst du ihn nicht einfach nacherzählen, sondern nur das Wichtigste *(gist)* zusammenfassen. Dazu kannst du den ganzen Text überfliegen und darauf achten, ob bestimmte Wörter *(key words)* oder Personen häufiger vorkommen. Auch die Überschrift oder Bilder können dir helfen einzuschätzen, was wichtig ist und was nicht. Diese Art des Schnelllesens nennt man *skimming*.	Wenn du nach bestimmten Einzelheiten *(details)* in einem Text gefragt wirst, musst du ihn überfliegen und die Stellen mit der wichtigen Information finden. Dazu suchst du gezielt nach passenden Stichwörtern *(key words)*. Sie zeigen an, welche Teile du genauer lesen solltest, um die gesuchte Information zu bekommen. Diese Art des Überfliegens nennt man auch *scanning*.

S6 Wichtige Inhalte von Texten herausfinden

Wenn du einen Text liest, solltest du danach immer folgende Fragen beantworten können:

Who …?
Wer ist beteiligt?

What …?
Was geschieht?

When …?
Wann?

Where …?
Wo?

Dazu kannst du Schnelllesetechniken anwenden, Markierungen im Text machen und dir Fragen und Anmerkungen notieren (S8). Wenn du den Text noch genauer liest, kannst du weitere Fragen beantworten, z. B. Warum geschieht etwas? Wenn es eine Geschichte ist, wer erzählt sie? Für wen wurde der Text geschrieben (Adressat)?

S7 Gliederung als Hilfe

Um einen Text besser zu verstehen, kann es dir helfen, ihn in mehrere Abschnitte zu gliedern. Orientiere dich dabei z. B. an Absätzen und inhaltlichen Punkten, die du dir markiert hast. Überlege anschließend, was in den einzelnen Teilen jeweils das Wichtigste ist und formuliere passende Überschriften. Dies erleichtert es dir, Zusammenfassungen von Texten zu geben oder *Mediation*-Aufgaben zu lösen.

A Henry hopes to play the lead
B Henry is disappointed
C Henry sees the positive side of things

S8 Textbearbeitung mit Markierungen und Notizen

Im geliehenen Buch darfst du das zwar nicht, aber auf Kopien oder in Arbeitsheften solltest du dir angewöhnen, wichtige Stellen in Texten zu markieren und Randnotizen zu machen (z. B. Fragen oder Anmerkungen). Verwende am besten verschiedene Farben: Markiere z. B. wichtige inhaltliche Punkte grün und Informationen zu den Personen blau. Wörter, die du nachschlagen musst, solltest du auch hervorheben. Unterstreiche sie beispielsweise und notiere die richtige Übersetzung am Rand. So fällt dir das erneute Lesen leichter.

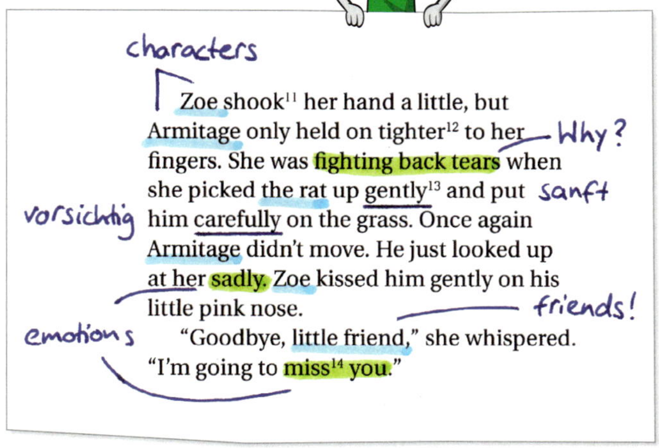

Zoe shook[11] her hand a little, but Armitage only held on tighter[12] to her fingers. She was fighting back tears when she picked the rat up gently[13] and put him carefully on the grass. Once again Armitage didn't move. He just looked up at her sadly. Zoe kissed him gently on his little pink nose.

"Goodbye, little friend," she whispered. "I'm going to miss[14] you."

S9 Umgang mit neuen Wörtern

Viele Wörter kannst du schon verstehen, obwohl du sie noch nicht gelernt hast.

1. **Ähnlichkeit mit Wörtern, die du schon kennst**
   Oft haben verwandte Wörter den gleichen Stamm, aber andere Vorsilben oder Endungen. Wenn du z. B. *happy* schon kennst, wirst du *unhappy* sicher auch verstehen. Englische Wörter haben oft keine Endungen, aber es gibt sie in verschiedenen Wortarten. Wenn du also das Wort *guide* als Nomen kennst, kannst du dir bestimmt denken, was das Verb *to guide* oder die Zusammensetzung *travel guide bedeutet*.

2. **Ähnlichkeit mit Wörtern, die du aus einer anderen Sprache kennst**
   Viele englische Wörter gibt es genauso oder ähnlich auch im Deutschen, z. B. *computer, hobby* oder *pony*. Manchmal hilft dir auch ein Wort, das du aus einer anderen Sprache kennst (Französisch, Latein, …) ein englisches Wort zu verstehen, z. B. weil es ähnlich geschrieben wird oder ähnlich klingt.

3. **Verstehen der Wörter im Zusammenhang**
   Manchmal kannst du dir anhand eines Bildes oder einer Überschrift denken, was ein Wort in einem Text bedeutet. Und wenn du alle Wörter in einem Satz verstehst außer einem, kann dieses oft nur eine bestimmte Bedeutung haben. Was bedeutet z. B. *return* in diesem Satz?
   My dog ran away, and I was really happy when he ***returned*** *after three days.*

Und wenn du doch im Wörterbuch nachschlagen musst, helfen dir die Tipps auf S. 21.

Writing

S10 Planung deines Textes

Überlege, für wen dein Text bestimmt ist (Adressat) und welchen Zweck er erfüllen soll. Vor dem Schreiben machst du dir am besten einen Plan: Notiere in Stichwörtern, was in der Einleitung, dem Hauptteil und dem Schluss deines Textes stehen soll. So vergisst du nichts Wichtiges und findest auch leichter eine schöne Einleitung und einen guten Schluss.

S11 Textsorten und ihre Besonderheiten

Du kennst schon einige wichtige Textsorten und ihre Haupteigenschaften:

E-mail, letter, postcard, invitation	Achte auf die richtige Anrede für den Adressaten, z. B. *Dear …*, Grußformeln am Schluss, z. B. *Yours/Love/Best wishes*, und beachte die Höflichkeitsregeln. Denke bei einem Brief an die Angabe der Empfänger- und Absenderadresse und an das Datum.
Story	Wenn du eine Geschichte vervollständigen sollst, muss dein Teil zum vorgegebenen Text passen. Vermeide also inhaltliche Widersprüche. Außerdem sollten die Erzählperspektive und die Erzählzeit nicht wechseln. Meistens sind Geschichten im *past tense* geschrieben. Gestalte deine Geschichten sprachlich abwechslungsreich und schmücke sie aus.
Dialogue	Wenn du einen Dialog, z. B. für eine Filmszene, schreibst, denke daran, dass du echte mündliche Sprache verwendest, also z. B. *short forms, question tags*, verstärkende Ausdrücke usw.
Report	Bei einem Bericht ist die Vollständigkeit und Verständlichkeit der sachlichen Informationen das Wichtigste. Er wird im *past tense* geschrieben.
Prompt cards	Wenn du dich auf eine Präsentation vorbereitest, notiere auf Karteikarten nur Stichwörter, die dich an die einzelnen Punkte des Vortrags erinnern. Schreibe z. B. wichtige Namen, Ereignisse, Orte und Daten unter die Überschriften *Who, What, Where, When*.
Flyer	Ein Flyer sollte gut lesbar sein (Schriftart- und größe) und alle wichtigen Informationen enthalten: *Who?, What?, When?, Where?, Why?* Formuliere außerdem einen ansprechenden Slogan.
Diary entry	Ein Tagebucheintrag erzählt und kommentiert vergangene und erwartete Ereignisse aus der ganz persönlichen Sicht einer Person und ist normalerweise nicht für andere Leser bestimmt.

S12 Überarbeitung deines Textes

Wenn du einen Entwurf erstellt hast, liest du ihn am besten noch einmal gründlich durch. Meistens entdeckst du so noch einige Fehler und kannst holprige Formulierungen verbessern. Nimm dabei eine Checkliste zur Hilfe (siehe rechts), damit du nichts Wichtiges vergisst. Es ist auch eine gute Übung, die Texte mit einem Partner zu tauschen.

Checkliste

Rechtschreibung:
- Wörter richtig geschrieben?
- Am Satzanfang groß?
- Getrennt oder zusammen?

Grammatik:
- Richtige Zeitformen?
- Richtige Formenbildung?

Inhalt:
- Alle wesentlichen Punkte enthalten?
- Keine inhaltlichen Fehler?
- Zusammenhänge erkennbar und logisch?

S13 Sprachliche Verbesserungen

Je größer dein Wortschatz wird, desto mehr Möglichkeiten eröffnen sich dir beim Schreiben von Texten.
Einzelne Sätze kannst du genauer und interessanter gestalten, indem du z. B. Nomen durch Adjektive oder durch weitere Nomen näher beschreibst. Verben kannst du durch adverbiale Bestimmungen ergänzen. Vergleiche die unterschiedliche Information in den beiden folgenden Sätzen:

A *I went to the shop.*

B *I went to the big pet shop in Greenwich with my sister last Saturday.*

Deinen gesamten Text kannst du flüssiger gestalten, indem du die Sätze miteinander verknüpfst. So werden logische Zusammenhänge klarer und der Text liest sich leichter. Vergleiche die beiden folgenden Textausschnitte. Der erste wirkt durch die unverbundenen Hauptsätze abgehackt. Der zweite enthält auch Satzgefüge aus Haupt- und Nebensätzen, die mit Hilfe von Bindewörtern *(linking words)* logische Zusammenhänge herstellen. Außerdem geben die vielen Adjektive und Adverbien genauere Informationen und machen den Text interessanter.

A *I went to the shop. I wanted a guinea pig. We looked at all the guinea pigs. I didn't like them. We wanted to leave.*
A girl came in with a box. She brought back a guinea pig.
It was cute! I bought it. I'm happy.

B *I went to the big pet shop in Greenwich with my sister last Saturday* ***because*** *I wanted to buy a nice guinea pig. We looked at all the guinea pigs,* ***but*** *I didn't like them.* ***Just when*** *I wanted to leave, a girl came in with a box. She brought back a guinea pig* ***which*** *was really cute.* ***So*** *I bought it* ***and*** *I'm very happy now.*

Speaking

S14 Sprechen üben

Sprechen lernt man nur durch Sprechen. Du solltest dir angewöhnen, im Englischunterricht immer englisch zu sprechen, ob mit deiner Lehrerin/deinem Lehrer oder in der Partner- und Gruppenarbeit. Um Sprechen zu üben, solltest du allerdings viel mehr sprechen als nur im Unterricht. Vielleicht üben deine Freunde, Eltern oder Geschwister mit dir?

Eine Voraussetzung für das richtige Sprechen ist natürlich, dass du übst, die englischen Wörter richtig auszusprechen. Beim Lernen mit dem Buch kann dir die Lautschrift dabei helfen. Sage sie dir immer wieder laut vor. Einfacher und einprägsamer ist es natürlich, die Vokabeln richtig ausgesprochen anzuhören und nachzusprechen. Hilfsmittel dafür sind Audio-CDs mit den Schülerbuchtexten, Lernsoftware oder Online-Wörterbücher, in denen du jedes Wort anklicken und anhören kannst.

They thought of the three thousand thankful thieves.

Why work with vocabulary when you can visit a wonderful village world?

Übe schwierig auszusprechende Laute, die anders sind als im Deutschen, z. B. das stimmhafte oder stimmlose *th* oder das *w* im Kontrast zum *v* oder ein stimmhaftes *d* oder *g* am Wortende. Dazu kannst du (lustige) Sätze erfinden, sie dir immer wieder vorsprechen und dabei das Tempo steigern, bis die Aussprache zuverlässig klappt.

She wanted her bag back and said what a nice hat she had.

Wenn du ganze Texte hörst, bekommst du ein Gefühl dafür, wie die Wörter im Textzusammenhang ausgesprochen werden. Die Aussprache unterscheidet sich manchmal stark von der Aussprache der Einzelwörter. Aufeinander treffende Laute werden z. B. häufig miteinander verbunden.

This is the end of the story. They know over a hundred different stories.

Du hast auch schon gehört, wie die Betonung die Aussprache beeinflussen kann, wenn jemand besonders starke Gefühle ausdrücken will. Das kannst du auch üben.

It's **so** unfair! Why doesn't anyone **ever** ask **me** what I'm feeling?

S15 Gesprochene Sprache

Auch beim Sprechen kommt es auf die Situation und deinen Gesprächspartner an, wie du dich ausdrückst. Denke z. B. auch an Höflichkeitsregeln.
In der gesprochenen Sprache ist es normal, dass Pausen, unvollständige Sätze, Wiederholungen oder Füllwörter vorkommen:

- Während bei Gleichaltrigen ein *Hi!* als Begrüßung ausreicht, ist Lehrpersonen oder fremden Erwachsenen gegenüber ein *Good morning! / Good morning …* eher angemessen.
- Statt *I want …* sagst du höflicher *I would like …* oder *Could I please have …?*
- Entscheidungsfragen beantwortest du mit Kurzantworten, nicht einfach mit *Yes* oder *No: Yes, I do. No, I'm not.*

***Well, I – I** really don't know. It's – **er**, maybe you want to …?*

Es ist wichtig, einem Dialogpartner immer das Gefühl zu geben, dass er einbezogen wird. Dazu dienen *feedback phrases*, Nachfragen und *question tags*.

*Then we went to the city farm, Mudchute, **you know**. And there was this cute little pig – **you saw it too, didn't you? Guess what Linda did when she saw it!***

S16 Mündliche Aufgaben und ihre Besonderheiten

Es ist viel wichtiger, dass du regelmäßig länger zusammenhängend sprichst, als dass jedes Wort perfekt ausgesprochen und die Grammatik absolut korrekt ist. Wie wäre es, wenn jeder in deiner Klasse in einer Englischstunde eine Minute lang Englisch über ein selbst gewähltes Thema spricht? Hier findest du ein paar Tipps für bestimmte mündliche Aufgaben:

Interview	Sei höflich, aber scheue dich nicht nachzufragen, wenn du etwas nicht sofort verstehst. Achte bei der Fragestellung auf die richtige Zeitform und das richtige Hilfsverb. Antworte auch in der passenden Zeitform.
Asking/ Showing the way	Auch hier ist Höflichkeit wichtig und ganz bestimmte Vokabeln wie *go down X Street, go straight on, go past/turn left/right into Y Lane, it's on the left / right / opposite Z.*
Role play	Versetze dich in deine Rolle und versuche nachzufühlen, was die Person weiß und was sie denkt und fühlt. Verwende typische Merkmale der gesprochenen Sprache und unterstütze deine Worte mit Mimik und Gestik.
Presentation	Bereite deine Präsentation gut vor. Recherchiere die Fakten gründlich. Überlege, was dir wichtig ist und was du sagen möchtest. Besorge Material, das du zeigen willst, und bereite es so auf, dass es gut aussieht und verständlich ist. Mache dir einen Ablaufplan. Schreibe dir Notizen auf *prompt cards*. Versuche frei zu sprechen und nicht abzulesen. Übe deine Präsentation vorher und stoppe die Zeit, die du brauchst.

Mediation

S17 Bearbeitung von Mediationsaufgaben

Mediation ist die Übertragung wichtiger Informationen aus einem gesprochenen oder geschriebenen Text in eine andere Sprache, z.B. aus dem Englischen ins Deutsche oder umgekehrt. Das machst du, wenn du einen Text für jemanden zusammenfassen sollst, der die Sprache des Ausgangstexts nicht versteht. Gelegentlich kann es auch sein, dass du dolmetschen musst, also zwischen Gesprächspartnern vermittelst, die nicht dieselbe Sprache sprechen. Ganz wichtig: Es geht bei der *Mediation* niemals um eine wörtliche Übersetzung *(translation)*!

Lies dir die *Mediation*-Aufgabe gut durch und beachte besonders folgende Dinge:

Adressat:
Für wen ist die Information bestimmt?
--> Je nachdem, wer die Person ist und wie viel sie schon weiß, sprichst du sie unterschiedlich an.

Zweck:
Wozu benötigt die Person die Information?
--> Du musst nur die Informationen wiedergeben, die für den Adressaten in der jeweiligen Situation wichtig sind. Alles andere kannst du weglassen. Es kann aber auch vorkommen, dass du Dinge zusätzlich erklären musst.

Beispiel: Dein Ausgangstext ist die Infobroschüre eines Museums, die alle Öffnungszeiten und Eintrittspreise enthält. Wenn dein Gegenüber dich fragt, ob das Museum heute geöffnet ist, musst du nicht unbedingt sagen, wann es sonst noch geöffnet oder geschlossen ist. Will die Person den Eintrittspreis wissen, kommt es auf ihr Alter an und darauf, ob sie allein oder mit einer Gruppe unterwegs ist.

Einen schriftlichen Ausgangstext kannst du in Ruhe durchlesen und die wichtigen Informationen auswählen. Dabei helfen dir alle Techniken, die auf S. 158 / 159 unter *Reading* beschrieben sind. Formuliere die entsprechenden Inhalte so, dass der Adressat sie gut verstehen kann.
Bei einer Dolmetscheraufgabe wird eine echte mündliche Gesprächssituation simuliert. Deshalb musst du schneller reagieren, um möglichst viel von dem sinngemäß wiederzugeben, was die Gesprächspartner zueinander sagen.

Wenn dir ein Wort in der Zielsprache nicht einfällt, umschreibe es mit anderen Worten *(paraphrasing)*. Beachte bei der schriftlichen und mündlichen Bearbeitung von *Mediation*-Aufgaben außerdem die Tipps unter *Writing* und *Speaking* (siehe S. 160–163)

Listening

S18 Hörverstehen üben

Grundsätzlich ist es zur Übung immer sinnvoll, viele echte englische Texte anzuhören, z. B. Nachrichten oder Kindersendungen in Radio und Fernsehen oder Hörbücher. Dabei ist es nicht schlimm, wenn du nicht jedes Wort verstehst. Dir wird außerdem auffallen, wie unterschiedlich die Aussprache des Englischen je nach Herkunft des Sprechers sein kann.

S19 Techniken des Hörverstehens

Analog zum Lesen gibt es auch beim Hörverstehen unterschiedliche Techniken. Beim *Listening for gist* geht es darum, das Wichtigste in einem Hörtext zu erkennen und zusammenzufassen. Beim *Listening for detail* hingegen sollst du einem Hörtext bestimmte Einzelheiten entnehmen.

Listening for gist	Listening for detail
Welche Wörter und Themen kommen mehrmals vor und spielen deshalb vermutlich eine wichtige Rolle? Höre besonders auf diese und fasse die wichtigsten Inhalte des Textes zusammen.	Nach welchen bestimmten Einzelheiten im Text wirst du gefragt? Höre besonders auf Wörter, die du in der Antwort erwartest, und die Informationen dazu.

Auch beim Hörverstehen hilft eine Tabelle wie beim Leseverstehen. Du kannst darin während des Hörens deine Notizen machen.

Who ...?	What ...?	When ...?	Where ...?

S20 Typische Hörverstehenssituationen

Manchmal hilft dir beim Hörverstehen auch die Kenntnis von typischen Textsorten und Situationen. Wenn du die Textsorte des Hörtextes kennst, überlege dir, worauf es beim Telefonieren, beim Dolmetschen, bei Präsentationen, Durchsagen, Radio- oder Fernsehsendungen ankommt und welche Themen jeweils zu erwarten sind. Gelegentlich geben dir auch Bilder Hinweise zur entsprechenden Situation: Wenn z. B. bestimmte Personen oder Orte dargestellt sind, kannst du leichter einschätzen, worum es in dem Hörtext geht. Achte beim Hören auf Geräusche sowie Stimme und Tonfall des Sprechers. In echten Gesprächssituationen oder Filmen können dir auch Gestik und Mimik das Verständnis erleichtern.

Film skills/Viewing

S21 Inhalt und Gliederung

Ein Film ist auch eine Art Text. Deshalb lassen sich viele ähnliche Fragen dazu stellen:

- Worum geht es?
- Wird eine Geschichte erzählt?
- Welche Personen spielen mit?
- Welches sind die Hauptpersonen?
- Was passiert in welcher Reihenfolge?
- Wann und wo passiert es?
- Welche Gliederung und welche Themen sind zu erkennen?
- Aus wessen Sicht wird die Geschichte erzählt?
- Wer hat den Film gemacht, für welches Publikum und wozu?

Das Anschauen und Verstehen eines Films verlangt dir jedoch nicht nur das Verständnis der Sprache ab, sondern du musst auch auf viele weitere Dinge achten.

S22 Wichtige filmische Aspekte

Wie stellen die Schauspieler den Charakter der Personen dar, die sie verkörpern? Wie drücken sie Gefühle aus?

--> Achte vor allem auf Sprache, Mimik und Gestik. Aber auch Kleidung oder Frisuren können eine Rolle spielen.

Wie werden Handlungsort und -zeit dargestellt *(setting)*?

--> Achte auf Landschaften, Gebäude und Innenräume, Kleidung und Gegenstände.

Wie wird eine bestimmte Atmosphäre geschaffen *(atmosphere)*?

--> Achte auf Licht, Farben, Musik, Geräusche.

Wie unterstützt die Musik den Inhalt des Films?

--> Beachte, wann welche Musik ertönt und wann sie wechselt.

Wie helfen bestimmte Kameraeinstellungen den Inhalt deutlicher darzustellen *(shot)*?

--> Achte z. B. auf Nahaufnahmen *(close-ups)*.

Wie wird Spannung erzeugt *(suspense)*?

--> Achte auf Vorandeutungen, Musik, Licht, Geräusche und natürlich die Gestik und Mimik der Schauspieler.

Mit der Zeit wirst du weitere filmische Mittel kennen lernen, die bestimmte Wirkungen auf den Zuschauer erzeugen.

Kooperative Lernformen

Hier findest du die Erklärung für einige ausgewählte Methoden der kooperativen Arbeit.

S23 Think – Pair – Share

1. *Think:* Du sammelst still mögliche Lösungen zu der Aufgabe. Du kannst deine Ideen in Stichpunkten notieren.
2. *Pair:* Zusammen mit deinem Partner besprichst du leise deine gesammelten Ideen.
3. *Share:* Im Klassengespräch meldet ihr euch und teilt euren Mitschülern die Ergebnisse eurer Partnergespräche mit.

Variante: *Placemat* in Vierergruppen

S24 Milling around (Marktplatz)

Du gehst durch das Klassenzimmer, erfragst von deinen Mitschülern bestimmte Informationen und gibst auch selbst Auskunft. Versuche mit möglichst vielen Mitschülern zu sprechen und verschiedene Informationen zu sammeln. Ihr könnt auch ein Signal vereinbaren, zu dem ihr eure Gesprächspartner wechselt.

S25 Inside outside circle (Kugellager)

1. Bildet zwei Stuhlkreise, einen inneren und einen äußeren.
2. Setzt euch in den Stuhlkreisen so hin, dass immer ein Schüler des äußeren und des inneren Stuhlkreises sich gegenüber sitzen.
3. Stellt euch gegenseitig eure Fragen und beantwortet diese.
4. Rutscht im inneren oder äußeren Kreis nach dem Ende der Gesprächsrunde einen Platz weiter und beginnt ein Gespräch mit einem neuen Mitschüler.

S26 Bus stop (Lerntempoduett)

Sobald du deine Aufgabe fertig bearbeitet hast, gehst du zu einem vereinbarten Treffpunkt, dem *bus stop*. Dort wartest du auf den nächsten Mitschüler, der fertig ist, und zusammen besprecht und vergleicht ihr eure Lösungen. Anschließend verlasst ihr den *bus stop* und bearbeitet die nächste Aufgabe.

S27 Gallery walk (Museumsgang)

1. *Group work:* In der Gruppe erarbeitet ihr ein Thema und haltet euer Ergebnis, z. B. auf einem Poster, fest.
2. *Gallery walk:* Es werden neue Gruppen gebildet. In jeder Gruppe ist ein Schüler jeder Ausgangsgruppe. Jede Gruppe betrachtet die verschiedenen Ergebnisse der Gruppenarbeiten. Jeder präsentiert nun in der neuen Gruppe das Ergebnis seiner Ausgangsgruppe.

Grammar

Liebe Schülerin, lieber Schüler,
jede Sprache besteht aus bestimmten Bausteinen und funktioniert nach bestimmten Regeln. Die Bausteine sind z. B. einzelne Wörter (Vokabeln). Die Regeln für ihre Zusammensetzung nennt man Grammatik. Diese musst du außer den Vokabeln lernen, damit du dich verständigen kannst und damit es nicht zu Missverständnissen kommt.

Jedes Grammatikkapitel (**G**) behandelt Themen, die auf bestimmten Seiten vorne in den *Units* vorkommen (z. B. Seiten 10–11). Erklärungen, Bilder und Tabellen helfen dir, …
- die Grammatik zu verstehen,
- beim Nachholen, wenn du ein paar Stunden gefehlt hast,
- bei den Hausaufgaben,
- beim Wiederholen,
- bei der Vorbereitung auf Tests und Klassenarbeiten

Regeln sind mit einem blauen Punkt (o) gekennzeichnet.
Ein Ausrufezeichen (!) bedeutet, dass du hier besonders aufpassen musst. Mit kleinen Aufgaben (**Test yourself**) kannst du überprüfen, ob du alles verstanden hast.
Die Lösungen findest du ab Seite 242.

Hier ist eine Liste aller grammatischen Begriffe aus diesem Buch in alphabetischer Reihenfolge zum Nachschlagen. Links findest du den englischen Begriff, in der Mitte ein Beispiel und rechts den deutschen Ausdruck.

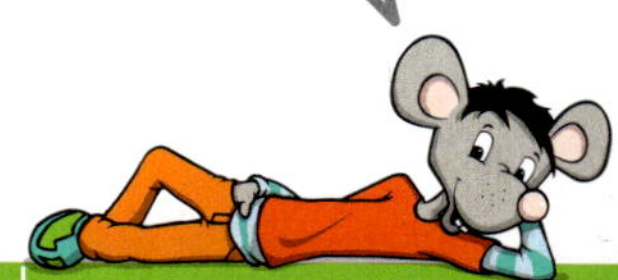

Grammatical terms

English term		Example	*Deutsche Bezeichnung*
adjective	G4, G5	exciting, easy, young	*Adjektiv*
comparison of adjectives	G4	After the adventure course I was **more confident**.	*Steigerung der Adjektive*
comparisons with adjectives	G5	Wales is**n't as big as** England or Scotland, but it's **bigger than** Northern Ireland.	*Vergleiche mit Adjektiven*
adverb of manner	G10	The Raven Master's job is to look after the ravens **carefully**.	*Adverb der Art und Weise*
comparison of adverbs	G11	Our guides know London's history **better** than anyone.	*Steigerung der Adverbien*
compounds of some, any, every and no	G9	Listen, **everybody**. What can we do for lunch? Are there any cafés **anywhere** near here?	*Zusammensetzungen mit* some, any, every *und* no

English term		Example	*Deutsche Bezeichnung*
defining relative clause contact clause	G6 G6b	My presentation is about two queens **that lived in Greenwich**. Christopher Wren is **an architect we** talked about in our Art lesson.	*notwendiger Relativsatz* *notwendiger Relativsatz ohne Relativpronomen*
going-to future	G8	Jay and Amir **are going to visit** the British Museum.	*Futur mit* going to
modal auxiliary substitute form	G15, G16 G15	can, can't, must, needn't, mustn't, should(n't), could When I was ten, I **wasn't allowed to** have my own smartphone.	*Modalverb, modales Hilfsverb* *Ersatzform*
past participle	G12	Gwen and Luke have already **prepared** for the trials. Olivia has **hurt** her foot.	*Partizip Perfekt*
past progressive	G7	Jack **was making** a bee hotel when he hit his thumb.	*Verlaufsform der Vergangenheit*
present perfect simple	G12	**Have** you ever **seen** the London Marathon?	*einfache Form des Perfekts*
question tag	G14	You're having a hard time, **aren't you**?	*Bestätigungsfrage, Frageanhängsel*
simple past irregular verb regular verb negating statements questions	G1–G3 G1 G1 G2 G3	Lenny Henry **started** Comic Relief in 1985. came, had, met, wore answered, played, watched The man **didn't break** any shop windows. Did the police arrest the man? What did he take from the shop?	*einfache Form der Vergangenheit* *unregelmäßiges Verb* *regelmäßiges Verb* *Aussagesätze verneinen* *Fragen*
subordinate clauses of comparison, time, reason	G13	The girl wrote to an agony aunt **because** she had a problem. **Before** we had an argument, we spent all our free time together.	*Nebensätze des Vergleichs (Komparativsätze), der Zeit (Temporalsätze), des Grundes (Kausalsätze)*

Unit 1

G1 Two years ago we raised lots of money.

Die einfache Form der Vergangenheit

The simple past

Seiten 10–12

Lenny Henry **started** Comic Relief in 1985 to help people in Africa. On the first Red Nose Day in 1988 people **wore** red noses, **did** fun activities to raise money and **watched** a big comedy show on TV. That **was** many years ago, but today people still do the same things.

Das simple past *verwendest du, um über eine Handlung oder ein Ereignis zu sprechen, das in der Vergangenheit liegt und abgeschlossen ist. Du findest es oft in Berichten und Geschichten.*

- *Bei der Bildung des* simple past *unterscheidest du zwischen regelmäßigen und unregelmäßigen Verben. Anders als bei den Gegenwartsformen sind sie in allen Personen gleich.*
- *Das* simple past *von* ***regelmäßigen Verben*** *bildest du aus der* ***Grundform des Verbs + -ed****. Doch bevor du* -ed *anhängst, musst du folgende Besonderheiten bei der Schreibweise beachten:*

normal	*stummes -e*	*einfacher Konsonant*	*y nach Konsonant*
play – play**ed**	like – lik**ed**	plan – plan**ned**	try – tr**ied**

- *Beachte, dass* -ed *auf drei verschiedene Weisen ausgesprochen wird. Sprich …*

[d] *nach Vokalen gefolgt von stimmhaften Konsonanten:*	love – lov**ed**, organise – organis**ed**
[t] *nach stimmlosen Konsonanten:*	help – help**ed**, like – lik**ed**
[ɪd] *nach* [t] *oder* [d]:	need – need**ed**, paint – paint**ed**

- *Bei unregelmäßigen Verben musst du die Formen des* simple past *auswendig lernen.*

come – came [keɪm]
do – did [dɪd]
go – went [went]
get – got [gɒt]
give – gave [geɪv]

have – had [hæd]
make – made [meɪd]
put – put [pʊt]
see – saw [sɔː]
take – took [tʊk]

! *Das Verb* be *hat im* simple past *zwei Formen:*
I / He / She / It **was** … [wɒz]
We / You / They **were** … [wɜː]
Die verneinten Formen lauten **wasn't** *und* **weren't**.

Auf Seite 239 findest du weitere unregelmäßige Verben. Im Dictionary *erkennst du sie am* *.

- *Im Englischen verwendest du das* simple past, *um eine abgeschlossene Handlung der Vergangenheit wiederzugeben. Im Deutschen kannst du dafür das Präteritum (z. B. er spielte, er ging) oder aber das Perfekt (z. B. er hat gespielt, er ist gegangen) verwenden. Vergleiche:*

Zeitangaben wie yesterday, last week / month / year, in 1985 *oder* two years ago *können dir den Gebrauch des* simple past *signalisieren.*

Letztes Jahr **haben** wir viel Geld **gesammelt**. – Last year we **raised** lots of money.

Test yourself *Complete the e-mail. Use the verbs in the simple past.*

Dear Olivia,
Thank you for your e-mail and the photos. I like them a lot.
You (want) to know about our charity event. Well, last month we (organise) an event in the park and we (plan) lots of activities. First there (be) games for students, parents and teachers. After that we (sell) cakes. In the afternoon the students in Year 7 (do) some really cool tricks. And then it (be) the turn of the students in Year 8. They (create) a comedy show. The girls (want) to look funny so they (paint) their faces and (wear) some funny costumes too. In the evening the school band (sing) in the park – lots of people (come) to listen. Michael (be) the real star of their show. He (do) some cool moves!
We (raise) 400 euros in just one day!
Write soon.
Pia

G2 How did they know?

Seiten 13–15

Fragen in der einfachen Form der Vergangenheit
Questions in the simple past

Policeman:	**Where were** you last Saturday evening?
Man:	Last Saturday evening? Let me think … Oh yes. On Saturday evening I was at the cinema.
Policeman:	**What** time **did** the film **finish**?
Man:	At about 10 p.m.
Policeman:	**Did** you **go** home right away?
Man:	Well, … **no, I didn't**. I walked along Trafalgar Road before I went home.
Policeman:	Um, … Trafalgar Road?

Bei Fragen unterscheidest du zwischen Entscheidungsfragen und Ergänzungsfragen. ***Entscheidungsfragen*** *beantwortest du im Deutschen mit* ***„ja" oder „nein"***. ***Ergänzungsfragen enthalten ein Fragewort*** (what, who, where, when, why, how).

- *Du kennst schon die Fragebildung im* simple present:

(Fragewort)	do / does	*Subjekt*	*Vollverb*	*restlicher Satz*	*Antwort*
	Do	**you**	**go**	shopping at the market?	– Yes, I **do**.
When	**do**	**you**	**go**	shopping at the market?	– I usually go there in the mornings.
	Does	**Olivia**	**go**	shopping on Sundays?	– No, she **doesn't**.
Why	**does**	**Olivia**	**go**	shopping on Saturdays?	– Because she's got time then.

- *Im* **simple past** *hat das Hilfsverb* do *nur eine Form, nämlich* **did**. *Nach dem Subjekt folgt die* ***Grundform des Vollverbs****, weil das Hilfsverb bereits die Vergangenheit ausdrückt.*

(Fragewort)	did	*Subjekt*	*Vollverb*	*restlicher Satz*	*Antwort*
	Did	the police	**arrest**	the man?	– Yes, they **did**.
	Did	the man	**take**	any money?	– No, he **didn't**.
What	**did**	he	**take**	from the shop?	– He took some T-shirts, sports shoes and a bike.

- *Enthält die Frage eine Form von* be, *verwendest du im* simple past *bei* I / he / she / it **was** *und bei* we / you / they **were**.

(Fragewort)	was / were	*Subjekt*	*restlicher Satz*	*Antwort*
	Was	the man	in Trafalgar Road last Saturday?	– Yes, he **was**.
	Were	there	any photos of him in Trafalgar Road?	– No, there **weren't**.
Where	**were**	you	yesterday evening?	– I was at the cinema.
Who	**was**		with you?	– My friend was with me.

! *Wenn* who *oder* what *Subjekt des Fragesatzes sind, darfst du das Hilfsverb* did *nicht verwenden. Die Fragebildung funktioniert dann genauso wie im Deutschen:*
Who phoned the police? – *Wer rief die Polizei an?*
What happened on 4th September? – *Was geschah am 4. September?*

Du brauchst ein ‚not' in deiner Frage? Kein Problem! Es schließt sich direkt an das Hilfsverb bzw. die Form von be *an:* Why did**n't** you go home after the film?, Why were**n't** you at home?

Test yourself *Work in pairs. After somebody broke into a sports shop in Trafalgar Road, the police got a tip from an anonymous caller. Write down four questions that the police asked the caller. Then give them to your partner to answer.* Example:

Policeman: What did the man look like?
Caller: He had brown hair and big ears.

G3 The police didn't know what the man looked like.

Seiten 13–15

Aussagesätze in der einfachen Form der Vergangenheit verneinen
Negating statements in the simple past

Yesterday evening a man broke into a sports shop in Trafalgar Road. He came in through the door, so he **didn't break** any shop windows. He took ten pairs of expensive sports shoes, some T-shirts and a bike. He **didn't take** any money or computers. Luckily, there **weren't** any people in the shop.

Mit didn't, wasn't / weren't *kannst du sagen, dass jemand etwas nicht gemacht hat oder etwas nicht geschehen ist.*

- *Aussagesätze im* simple present *kennst du schon. Du verneinst sie, indem du ein Hilfsverb einsetzt und es verneinst:*
  I / You / We / They **don't** like dogs.
  He / She / It **doesn't** like dogs.

- *Im* **simple past** *hat das verneinte Hilfsverb* do *nur eine Form, nämlich* **didn't**. *Danach folgt die* **Grundform des Vollverbs**, *weil das Hilfsverb bereits die Vergangenheit ausdrückt.*

+	−
The man **took** a bike.	The man **didn't take** any money.
The shoes **looked** nice.	The shoes **didn't look** cheap.
He **did** judo on Friday.	He **didn't do** any other sport.

- *Ist im Satz eine Form von* be *vorhanden, verwendest du bei* I / he / she / it **wasn't** *und bei* we / you / they **weren't**.

+	−
The man **was** young.	The man **wasn't** old.
There **were** people in the street.	There **weren't** any people in the shop.

- *Sätze mit modalen Hilfsverben* (can, can't, must, mustn't, needn't) *kannst du noch nicht in der Vergangenheit verwenden. Das lernst du erst in* **Unit 5 / G15**.

Test yourself *Complete the article. Use the verbs in the simple past.*

8th September

Man arrested

Greenwich. On 4th September a young man (break into) a sports shop in Trafalgar Road. Yesterday the police (arrest) him. They (not know) what he (look) like at first. But then they (get) an anonymous phone call. The caller (not give) them much information, but she (give) them an address in Greenwich. When the police (get to) the house, two women (be) there but the man (not be). So they (wait) till he (come) home and then they (arrest) him – he (not try) to run away. The police (find) the sports shoes and the T-shirts in the loft, but they (not find) the bike.

G4 An adventure course helps students to be more confident.

Seiten 16–17

Steigerung der Adjektive

Comparison of adjectives

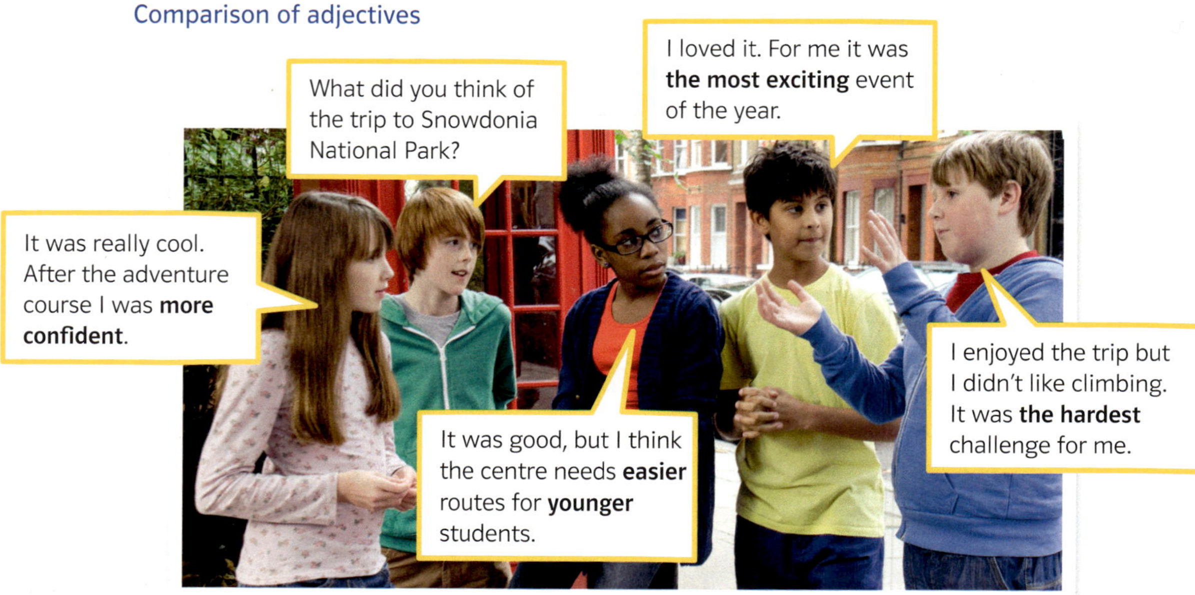

Du verwendest Adjektive und ihre Steigerungsformen, um Lebewesen und Sachen näher zu beschreiben und um sie miteinander zu vergleichen.

- *Es gibt zwei Möglichkeiten Adjektive zu steigern. Welche du benötigst, hängt von der Anzahl der Silben ab, die die Grundform des Adjektivs (Positiv) hat.*
- ***Einsilbige Adjektive** und **zweisilbige Adjektive**, die **auf -y** enden, steigerst du, indem du **-er** (1. Steigerung / Komparativ) bzw. **-est** (2. Steigerung / Superlativ) an die Grundform des Adjektivs anhängst.*

- *Fast alle anderen* **zweisilbigen Adjektive** *sowie* **alle Adjektive mit mehr als zwei Silben** *steigerst du, indem du* **more** *(1. Steigerung / Komparativ) bzw.* **most** *(2. Steigerung / Superlativ)* **vor** *die* **Grundform** *des Adjektivs setzt.*

	Grundform	1. Steigerung	2. Steigerung	Besonderheiten
	einsilbige Adjektive			
Endungen -er, -est	hard	harder	the hardest	–
	big	bigger	the biggest	*Endkonsonant wird nach kurzem Vokal verdoppelt*
	nice	nicer	the nicest	*stummes -e am Ende des Adjektivs fällt weg*
	zweisilbige Adjektive auf -y			
	easy	easier	the easiest	*y wird zu i, wenn das Adjektiv auf Konsonant + -y endet (außer: shy)*
	funny	funnier	the funniest	
	andere zweisilbige Adjektive sowie mehrsilbige Adjektive			
more, most	awful	more awful	the most awful	–
	interesting	more interesting	the most interesting	–

❗ *Beachte, dass* **zweisilbige Adjektive**, *die* **auf -le, -ow oder -er** *enden, mit -er / -est gesteigert werden:*
simple *(einfach)* – simpler – the simplest *(e am Ende des Adjektivs fällt weg)*
narrow *(eng, schmal)* – narrower – the narrowest
clever *(klug, schlau)* – cleverer – the cleverest

❗ *Einige wenige Adjektive werden unregelmäßig gesteigert. Diese musst du auswendig lernen:*
bad – worse – the worst
good – better – the best

Test yourself a) *Copy the grid into your exercise book and fill it in.*

Grundform	1. Steigerung	2. Steigerung
big		
		the worst
	happier	
important		

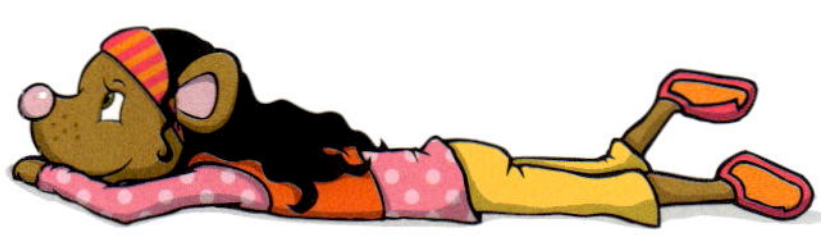

b) *Write sentences and describe the pictures.*

Luke is tall.
Holly is … .
But Olivia is the … of the three.

The red car is … .
The blue … .
But … .

Hook Lane is … .
King's Street is … .
But London Road … .

Luke has got a … .
Holly's idea is … .
But Dave has got … .

G5 Outdoor activities are as important as lessons in the classroom.

Seiten 16–17

Gleich oder verschieden: Vergleiche mit Adjektiven
The same or different: Making comparisons with adjectives

DID YOU KNOW …?

1. Wales is part of the UK. It is**n't as big as** England or Scotland, but it's **bigger than** Northern Ireland.
2. Mount Snowdon (1,085 m) is the highest mountain in Wales. But it is**n't higher than** Ben Nevis (1,343 m) in Scotland.
3. The River Severn (362 km) is the longest river in the UK. It is **as long as** the River Neckar in Germany.

Vergleiche mit Adjektiven benutzt du, um Lebewesen oder Sachen miteinander zu vergleichen.

- *Wenn die Lebewesen oder Sachen in Bezug auf eine Eigenschaft* ***gleich*** *sind, benutzt du* **as + *Grundform* + as***:*
  The River Severn is **as long as** the River Neckar. *… genauso/so lang wie …*

- *Wenn die Lebewesen oder Sachen in Bezug auf eine Eigenschaft* **verschieden** *sind, benutzt du entweder* **not as + *Grundform* + as** *oder* ***1. Steigerung*** **+ than***:*
  Wales is**n't as big as** England. *... nicht so groß wie ...*
  Wales is **bigger than** Northern Ireland. *... größer als ...*
  Is climbing **more dangerous than** gorge scrambling? *... gefährlicher als ...*

! *Verwechsle nicht* **than** *(als) und* **then** *(dann)!*

Test yourself *Write sentences and compare the rivers, cities, mountains and regions.*

big small short high long

Rhine: 1,233 km
Spree: 400 km
Oder: 854 km

Düsseldorf: 590,000
Stuttgart: 590,000
Cologne: 1 million

Brocken: 1,141 m
Feldberg: 1,493 m
Großer Arber: 1,455 m

the Saarland: 2,570 km²
Hesse: 21,100 km²
Saxony: 18,415 km²

Unit 2

G6 The queen who loved parties

Notwendige Relativsätze
Defining relative clauses

Seiten 30–31

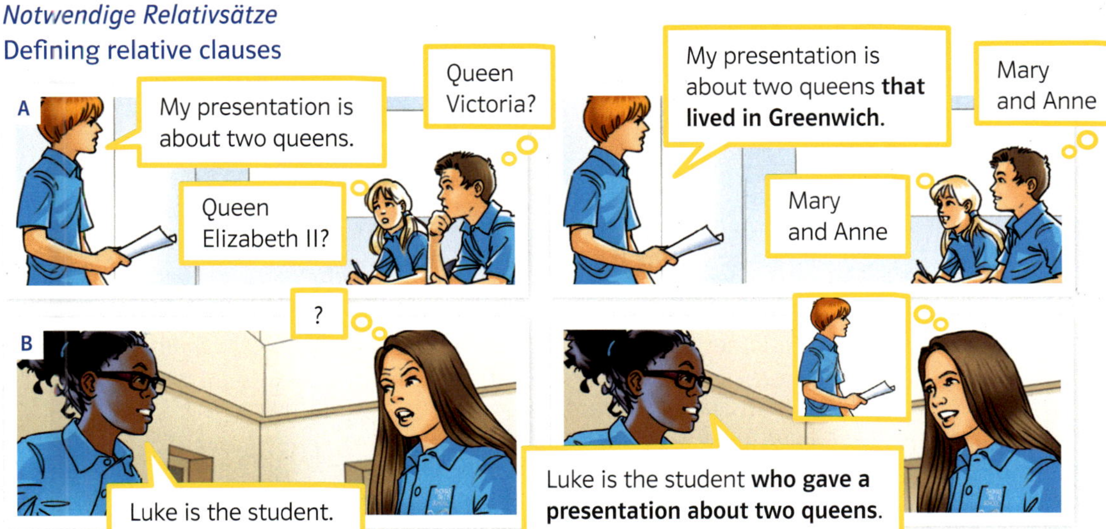

Relativsätze sind Nebensätze, die ein Nomen (Bezugswort) näher beschreiben oder definieren. Notwendige Relativsätze werden deshalb so genannt, weil der Hauptsatz ohne die im Relativsatz enthaltene Information nicht eindeutig (A) oder nicht verständlich wäre (B):

- *Relativsätze leitest du durch ein **Relativpronomen** ein. Du verwendest …*

who *für Personen*

which *für Sachen*

that *für Personen oder Sachen*

- *Das Relativpronomen **whose** (dt. deren, dessen) benutzt du, um Besitz oder Zugehörigkeit auszudrücken.*
- *Das **Relativpronomen** steht meist direkt nach dem **Bezugswort** und leitet den Relativsatz ein. Danach folgt die **notwendige Information**.*
  My presentation is about **two queens**. They **lived in Greenwich**.
  My presentation is about **two queens** **who / that** **lived in Greenwich**.
  In meinem Vortrag geht es um zwei Königinnen, die in Greenwich lebten.

! *Im Gegensatz zum Deutschen trennst du solche notwendigen Relativsätze nicht durch Kommas vom Hauptsatz ab.*

- *Relativpronomen können Subjekt oder Objekt des notwendigen Relativsatzes sein:*

a) ***Relativpronomen als Subjekt***

- *Die Relativpronomen **who**, **which** und **that** darfst du **nie weglassen**, wenn sie Subjekt im Relativsatz sind.*

Hauptsätze	*Hauptsatz + Relativsatz*
Anne was **a queen**. She loved parties.	Anne was **a queen** **who / that** loved parties.
Do you know **the big building**? It's across the river.	Do you know **the big building** **which / that** is across the river?
That's the **woman**. Her husband gave her a house for parties.	That's the **woman** **whose** husband gave her a house for parties.

b) ***Relativpronomen als Objekt***

- *Die Relativpronomen **who**, **which** und **that** kannst du **weglassen**, **wenn** sie **Objekt** im Relativsatz sind. Das erkennst du am **neuen Subjekt** nach dem Relativpronomen. Solche Relativsätze nennt man* contact clauses*, weil sie ohne Relativpronomen in direktem Kontakt zum Hauptsatz stehen.*

Hauptsätze	*Hauptsatz + Relativsatz*
Christopher Wren was **an architect**. We talked about him in Art.	Christopher Wren was **an architect** **(who / that) we** talked about in Art.
The hospital was near the river. Wren built it.	**The hospital** **(which / that) Wren** built was near the river.
The architect was Christopher Wren. Mary chose his design.	**The architect** **whose** design **Mary** chose was Christopher Wren.

Test yourself **a)** *Complete the dialogues. Use the correct relative pronoun.*

1. Dave: Have you got any music … people listened to at Anne's parties? You can use it in your presentation.
   Luke: Yes, I have. But I'm not sure. I don't like the songs … they played in the 17th century.
   Dave: Well, don't worry about that. Luke, what's that under the table?
   Luke: Oh, thanks, Dave. This is the photo of the Queen's House … I'm looking for.

2. Jay: Who was Christopher Wren?
   Olivia: He was the famous architect … designs you can see in London.
   Jay: Really?
   Olivia: Yes, he was the man … designed the Royal Naval College, the Royal Observatory, St Paul's Cathedral and many other buildings.
   Jay: Cool! Those are all buildings … I know.

b) *Which of the sentences in a) can you use without the relative pronoun?*

G7 What were they doing when Sally fell into the pond?

Seiten 33–34

Die Verlaufsform der Vergangenheit

The past progressive

Das **past progressive** *ist eine Zeitform der Vergangenheit. Damit beschreibst du nicht das Ergebnis einer Handlung (→ G1), sondern den* ***Verlauf einer Handlung zu einem bestimmten Zeitpunkt in der Vergangenheit****. Du kennst auch schon das* present progressive*, mit dem du ausdrückst, dass eine Handlung jetzt gerade im Verlauf ist.*

- *Mit dem* past progressive *kannst du drei verschiedene Situationen beschreiben:*

a) *Die Handlung befand sich zu einem bestimmten Zeitpunkt in der Vergangenheit noch im Verlauf, sie war also noch nicht abgeschlossen:*

9:30 10:30	At 10 o'clock yesterday Kate and Filip **were digging** a hole.
	*Gestern um 10 Uhr **hoben** Kate und Filip **gerade** ein Loch **aus**.*

b) *Eine Handlung befand sich noch im Verlauf, als eine neue Handlung oder ein neues Ereignis einsetzte. Diese(s) steht im* **simple past***:*

simple past	Jack **was making** a bee hotel when he **hit** his thumb.
past progressive	*Jack **baute gerade** ein Bienenhaus, als er sich auf den Daumen **schlug**.*

c) *Zwei Handlungen befanden sich gleichzeitig im Verlauf:*

	While the girls **were taking** photos, Filip and Kate **were digging** a hole.
	*Während die Mädchen **gerade** Fotos machten, **hoben** Filip und Kate ein Loch **aus**.*

- *Du bildest das* past progressive *aus der Vergangenheitsform von* **be (was/were)** *und dem* **present participle** *(= Verb + -ing).*

Aussage:	Henry **was putting up** a sign when he fell off his ladder.
Verneinung:	Kate and Filip **weren't taking** photos.
Ergänzungsfrage:	What **was** Jack **doing** when he hit his thumb?
Entscheidungsfrage mit Kurzantwort:	**Was** Jack **making** a bee hotel when he hit his thumb? – Yes, he **was**. / No, he **wasn't**.

! *Das* past progressive *gibt es im Deutschen nicht. Du kannst es mit „gerade dabei sein, etwas zu tun" wiedergeben. Sieh dir dazu die Übersetzungen in a) – c) noch einmal an.*

Test yourself *What were the students doing at 4 p.m. yesterday? Work in pairs and make dialogues. Use the past progressive.*

Jay – Dance class

Luke – Football Club

Holly – Sign Language Club

Olivia – Netball Club

A: Was Luke playing basketball at 4 o'clock yesterday?
B: No, he wasn't. He was playing football with his friends.

Unit 3

G8 It's going to be fun.

Das Futur mit going to

The going-to future

Seiten 52–53

Mit dem going-to future *drückst du feststehende Pläne und Absichten für die nahe Zukunft aus. Du verwendest es auch, wenn es bereits jetzt deutliche Anzeichen dafür gibt, wie die Zukunft werden wird:* A visit to London **is going to be** fun.

- *Das* going-to future *bildest du aus einer* ***Form von* be (am/is/are) + going to + *Grundform des Verbs*:**

Aussage:	The boys **are going to visit** the British Museum with Olivia and Holly.
Verneinung:	Jay **isn't going to go** alone.
Ergänzungsfrage:	What **are** you **going to do** tomorrow, Amir?
Entscheidungsfrage mit Kurzantwort:	**Are** you **going to see** more sights in Greenwich? – Yes, I **am**. / No, I**'m not**.

! *Um etwas Zukünftiges auszudrücken, kannst du im Deutschen neben dem Futur oft auch das Präsens verwenden. Im Englischen geht das nicht. Vergleiche:*
We**'re going to visit** London next week.
*Wir **werden** nächste Woche London **besuchen**.*
*Wir **besuchen** nächste Woche London.*

Wörter wie tomorrow *und* next week *können dir den Gebrauch des* going-to future *anzeigen.*

Test yourself *What are/aren't the people going to do tomorrow? Look at the pictures and write sentences.*

Jay

Amir

Olivia and Holly

Shahid

Mrs Azad

Mr Azad

G9 It's something important.

Seiten 54–55

Zusammensetzungen mit some, any, every *und* no

The compounds of *some, any, every* and *no*

Listen, **everybody**. What can we do for lunch? Are there any cafés **anywhere** near here?

Follow me, there's a great place **somewhere** around the corner here.

Mit den Zusammensetzungen von some, any, every *und* no *kannst du allgemein über Dinge, Menschen und Orte sprechen.*

- *Das kennst du schon:*
  Some *benutzt du in positiven Aussagen:* Jay has got **some** money.
  oder in höflichen Bitten, Angeboten oder Vorschlägen, wenn du eine positive Antwort erwartest: Can you give me **some** money, please? – Yes, sure.

  Any *benutzt du in Fragen und zur Verneinung:*
  Are there **any** cheap cafés near here? – No, there are**n't any** cheap cafés near here.

- *Für* some *und* any *gibt es Zusammensetzungen mit* -body/-one *(„jemand"),* -thing *(„etwas") und* -where *(„irgendwo"). Du verwendest sie auf die gleiche Weise wie* some *und* any.

Somebody *und* someone *bzw.* anybody *und* anyone *sind bedeutungsgleich.*

***Zusammensetzungen mit* some**	
somebody / someone:	I can't see the show – **someone** tall is standing in front of me.
something:	I'm hungry. I need **something** to eat.
somewhere:	I know a good café. It's **somewhere** near Covent Garden.
***Zusammensetzungen mit* any**	
anybody / anyone:	Did you ask **anyone**?
anything:	He hasn't got **anything**!
anywhere:	Are there any cheap cafés **anywhere**?

- *Auch von* no *und* every *gibt es Zusammensetzungen mit* -body/-one, -thing *und* -where. *Sie drücken jeweils das Gegenteil aus:*

***Zusammensetzungen mit* every**	⟷	***Zusammensetzungen mit* no**
Everybody likes London.		Olivia bets **nobody** can beat her.
jeder, alle		*niemand, keiner*
Everything is OK.		The British Museum costs **nothing**.
alles		*nichts*
There are people **everywhere**.		There's **nowhere** to sit.
überall		*nirgends, nirgendwo*

! *Beachte den Unterschied zwischen* everybody/-one *und* anybody/-one*:*
Everybody in my class likes London. *(ausnahmslos) Jeder …*
Anybody can visit Tate Britain. It's free. *Jeder (x-beliebige) …*
Mit anybody/-one *ist keine bestimmte Person gemeint, sondern jeder x-beliebige. In dieser Bedeutung kann es auch in positiven Aussagesätzen und* if*-Sätzen verwendet werden.*

Nobody *und* no one *sind bedeutungsgleich. Beachte aber, dass* no one *nicht zusammengeschrieben wird.*

! Everybody/-one *und* anybody/-one *sind Singularformen. Die dazugehörigen Pronomen und Possessivbegleiter stehen aber meist im Plural:*
Everybody pays for **their** own Oyster card.
Anybody at the Tube station can tell you where you can buy an Oyster card if you ask **them**.

Test yourself *Complete the dialogue.*

Amir: Listen, (*alle*). I want to buy a little present for my aunt to say 'thank you'. Is there a good shop (*irgendwo*)?
Olivia: What are you thinking of?
Amir: Well, it must be (*etwas*) special, but it mustn't be (*nichts*) expensive.
Jay: (*Alles*) is expensive in London!
Holly: That's not true! I know a good shop where (*nichts*) costs more than £10.
Amir: OK. Let's go there and see if we can find (*etwas*) for her.

G10 Now we're going slowly past the Tower of London.

Seiten 56–57

Adverbien der Art und Weise
Adverbs of manner

Welcome to the Tower of London!
Many people come here **specially** to see the Crown Jewels. You too, I guess. But let me tell you about the ravens first. Look, there's the Raven Master! His job is to look after the ravens **carefully**.

Mit Adverbien bestimmst du ein Verb näher. Du beschreibst also, wie etwas getan wird. Zur Erinnerung: Mit Adjektiven beschreibst du ein Nomen näher.

- *Die meisten Adverbien bildest du aus dem* **Adjektiv** ***und*** *der Endung* **-ly** ***oder*** **-ally**. *Adverbien stehen in der Regel am Satzende, jedoch vor einer Orts- und Zeitangabe.*

***Adjektiv* + -ly:**	The bus is going **slowly** past the Tower of London. You can see the Tower of London **clearly** on the left.
***Adjektiv auf* -ic + -ally:**	The Beefeaters explain the history of the Tower **fantastically**. "Help!" shouted the little boy **dramatically** when the ravens came near.

! *Beachte folgende Rechtschreibregeln:*
a) *Endet das Adjektiv auf* -y, *wird* y *zu* i: angry → angr**i**ly, happy → happ**i**ly;
außer: shy → shyly.
b) *Endet das Adjektiv auf* -le, *fällt* e *weg*: comfortable → comfortably, terrible → terribly

! *Merke dir folgende Ausnahmen:*

good → well — The guide gave us some tips about where to eat **well**.
fast → fast — The Tube takes you very **fast** through London.
hard → hard — Ravens can bite very **hard**.

! *Wenn* **feel** *oder eine* **Form von be** *das einzige Verb im Satz ist, benutzt du kein Adverb, sondern ein* **Adjektiv**, *z.B.:* The guide is **nice**.

Test yourself *Read the tips and complete the sentences. Do you need an adjective or an adverb?*

Tips for London visitors

1. Buy an Oyster card and travel by public transport (cheap) and (comfortable).
2. Stand on Westminster Bridge and take (fantastic) photos of Big Ben.
3. On a (nice) day, take a picnic with you and have lunch in one of London's (great) parks.
4. Go to the British Museum and learn about money, animals and ships. It's (free)!
5. Visit Madame Tussauds. The museum shows famous people very (realistic).
6. If you're in London for a day or two only, take a sightseeing bus. Most guides know London and its history (good).

G11 You can see London faster and more easily with a guide.

Seiten 56–57

Steigerung der Adverbien

The comparison of adverbs

EXPLORE LONDON BY BUS

Only £16

Buy a ticket for one of our sightseeing buses and you can see London **faster** and **more easily** than if you explore alone. Our guides know London's history **better** than anyone.

Mit den Steigerungsformen der Adverbien kannst du Vorgänge vergleichen.

- **Einsilbige Adverbien** *steigerst du auf* **-er** *(1. Steigerung / Komparativ) bzw.* **-est** *(2. Steigerung / Superlativ).*
- *Alle* **Adverbien**, *die* **auf -ly** *enden* **oder mehrsilbig** *sind, steigerst du mit* **more** *(1. Steigerung / Komparativ) bzw.* **most** *(2. Steigerung / Superlativ).*

	Grundform	1. Steigerung	2. Steigerung
	einsilbige Adverbien		
Endungen -er, -est	(run) fast	faster	fastest
	(try) hard	harder	hardest
	(jump) high	higher	highest
	(go) near	nearer	nearest
	Adverbien auf -ly sowie mehrsilbige Adverbien		
more, most	(finish) easily	more easily	most easily
	(do) quickly	more quickly	most quickly
	(talk) interestingly	more interestingly	most interestingly
	(sit) comfortably	more comfortably	most comfortably

❗ *Beachte, dass die Formen von* **early earlier** *und* **earliest** *lauten, obwohl* early *auf* -ly *endet.*

❗ *Merke dir folgende Ausnahmen:*

badly – worse – worst   well – better – best
much – more – most   little – less – least

Test yourself *Look at the table and make comparisons.*

Example: A lion runs **faster** than a bear. A horse runs **fastest**.

animal	run fast	eat little	sleep long	weigh much
horse	70 km/h	6 kg	4 h	400 kg
bear	50 km/h	40 kg	6 h (in summer)	380 kg
lion	60 km/h	10 kg	13 h	180 kg
pig	45 km/h	1,5 kg	13 h	100 kg
cat	45 km/h	250 g	15 h	4 kg

Unit 4

G12 Have you ever run in a marathon?

Die einfache Form des Perfekts

The present perfect simple

Seiten 70–75

Mit dem present perfect simple *verbindest du die Vergangenheit mit der Gegenwart.*

- *Mit dem* present perfect simple *kannst du verschiedene Situationen beschreiben:*

  a) *Mit* Have you ever … *fragst du, ob jemand etwas schon ein- oder mehrmals gemacht hat.*

Have you ever …? ***In den Antworten auf die Frage findest du oft eines dieser Signalwörter:* never, before, only ever, … times.**	**Has** Jay **ever run** in a marathon? – No, he **hasn't**. He **has never run** one mile.
	Have Dave and Holly **ever run** in big races? – No, Dave **hasn't run** in big races **before**. And Holly **has only ever run** in short races.
	Have the Elliots **ever watched** the London Marathon? – Yes, they **have**. They**'ve watched** it **three times**.

b) *Mit dem* present perfect simple *kannst du sagen, dass eine Handlung bereits, gerade erst oder noch nicht abgeschlossen wurde:*

already *(schon, bereits)*	Olivia **has already prepared** for the trials.
just *(gerade erst, eben)*	Gwen **has just had** an idea.
not yet *(noch nicht)*	The girls **haven't left** for school **yet**.

Die Signalwörter never, only ever, already *und* just *stehen direkt nach dem Hilfsverb.*

c) *Außerdem kannst du ausdrücken, dass eine Handlung irgendwann in der Vergangenheit stattfand und das Ergebnis dieser Handlung bis in die Gegenwart spürbar bzw. sichtbar ist:*

I**'ve hurt** my foot. It hurts when I walk.
Olivia **has bought** new running shoes. They're still clean.

- *Du bildest das* present perfect simple *aus einer Form von* **have (have/has)** *und dem* **past participle**.

Das past participle *von regelmäßigen Verben entspricht ihrer Form im* simple past *(→G1). Die Formen von unregelmäßigen Verben musst du lernen. Du findest sie in der 3. Spalte auf den Seiten 239–240.*

Aussage:	I**'ve run** in races before, but not in a big race like a marathon.
Verneinung:	Jay **hasn't run** one mile.
Ergänzungsfrage:	Who **has heard** of the mini marathon?
Entscheidungsfrage mit Kurzantwort:	**Has** Dave ever **run** in race? – Yes, he **has**. / No, he **hasn't**.

! *Beachte die Unterschiede zum Deutschen:*

a) *Das* present perfect simple *bildest du immer mit* have / has + past participle. *Vergleiche:*
I'**ve hurt** my foot. = Ich **habe** mir den Fuß **verletzt.**
I **haven't left** yet. = Ich **bin** noch nicht **losgegangen**.

b) *Auch in Sätzen, die das* present perfect simple *beinhalten, gilt im Englischen die Regel* ***S – V – O***. *Das* ***Objekt*** *steht also nach der Verbform.*
Olivia **has hurt** **her foot**.
Olivia **hat** sich **den Fuß** **verletzt**.

! *Anders als im Deutschen sind das* simple past (→G1) *und das* present perfect simple *nicht beliebig austauschbar, um Handlungen oder Ereignisse in der Vergangenheit zu beschreiben. Das* **present perfect simple** *verwendest du, um zu sagen, dass etwas stattgefunden hat. Wenn du genau berichtest, wann und unter welchen Umständen etwas stattgefunden hat, verwendest du das* **simple past**.

I'**ve** already **run** in a marathon.

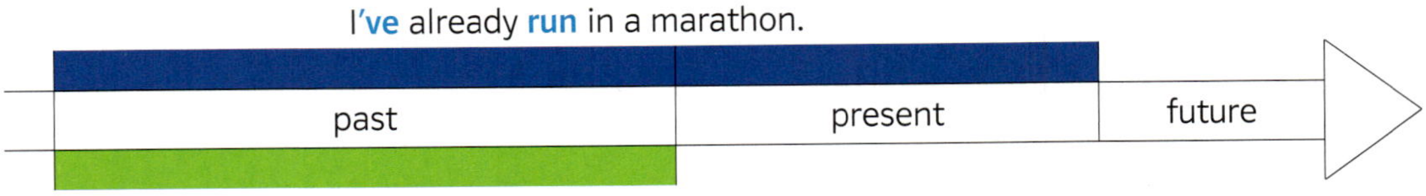

My dad **ran** in a marathon when he was 20.

Test yourself **a)** *You and your classmates are talking about Sports Day. Make questions and write them in your exercise book.*

Have you …	(prepare)	eating healthy food?
	(buy)	a name for your team yet?
	already (start)	your foot while you were playing sports?
	ever (hurt)	for Sports Day yet?
	(find)	new sports shoes yet?

b) *Work in small groups. Ask and answer the questions from a).*

Example:
Sabrina: Have you prepared for Sports Day yet?
Martin: Yes, I have. I've already run around the park three times.
Ella: Yes, I have. I went jogging yesterday.

Unit 5

G13 I'm writing to you because I need your advice.

Seiten 92–93

Nebensätze der Zeit, des Grundes und des Vergleichs
Subordinate clauses of time, reason and comparison

Du kannst Nebensätze verwenden, wenn du deiner Hauptaussage zusätzliche Informationen hinzufügen möchtest. Mit den aus Haupt- und Nebensatz entstehenden Satzgefügen stellst du logische Verbindungen her. Sie sind stilistisch eleganter als hintereinander gereihte Hauptsätze.

a) *Nebensätze der Zeit (= Temporalsätze):*

after ***(nachdem)***	**After** I spoke to my friend, I felt much better.
as soon as ***(sobald)***	Things often get better **as soon as** you talk to somebody about it.
before ***(bevor, ehe, vor)***	**Before** they had an argument, Lauren spent a lot of her free time with her friend.
until ***(bis)***	Never give your address **until** you've really met your new friend face-to-face.
when ***(wenn)***	Ask your parents, older sister or brother **when** you need advice.
whenever ***(jedes Mal, wenn)***	**Whenever** you want to put photos of other people online, ask them first.

b) *Nebensätze des Grundes (= Kausalsätze):*

because ***(weil)***	Lauren wrote to an agony aunt **because** she had a problem.

c) *Nebensätze des Vergleichs (= Komparativsätze):*

like ***(als ob)***	My friend acts **like** she's having a much better time without me.

! *Beachte, dass die Satzstellung im Deutschen anders ist als im Englischen. Im Englischen bleibt die Reihenfolge **Subjekt** – **Verbform** – **Objekt** sowohl im Haupt- als auch Nebensatz immer erhalten. Vergleiche:*
After **I** **spoke** to my friend, **I** **felt** much better.
Nachdem **ich** mit meinem Freund **gesprochen hatte**, **fühlte** **ich** mich besser.

! *Wenn du dir die Beispiele in a) – c) einmal genauer anschaust, wirst du feststellen, dass Nebensätze sowohl nach dem Hauptsatz als auch vor dem Hauptsatz stehen können. Steht der **Hauptsatz vor** dem **Nebensatz**, setzt du **kein Komma**, weil die Konjunktion die Sätze trennt. Steht der **Nebensatz vor** dem **Hauptsatz**, trennst du beide durch **ein Komma**.*

Test yourself *Read the posts of some* TeenLife *readers. Complete the sentences with the correct linking word. Add commas where you need them.*

Joe: I like your magazine … it's always got interesting news on my favourite stars in it.
Ginny: I buy *TeenLife* … I get my pocket money from my parents. I love it!
Michael: The concert photos are fantastic. When I look at them it's … I'm there.
Lisa: … I read Ruby's advice I think she really understands our problems.
Sheila: … I tried the make-up which came with the magazine last week I'm not going to buy *TeenLife* again! It looked awful on my face.

G14 You watched the match last night, didn't you?

Seite 92, 94

Bestätigungsfragen
Question tags

Bestätigungsfragen sind kurze Fragen am Ende eines Aussagesatzes. Sie entsprechen dem deutschen „nicht wahr?", „oder?" bzw. „stimmt's?" und kommen häufig im mündlichen Sprachgebrauch vor.

- *Du bildest Bestätigungsfragen, indem du das **Hilfsverb** des Hauptsatzes **mit anderer Polung** wiederholst – bejahte Hauptsätze verneinst du; verneinte Hauptsätze bejahst du.*

present progressive	You**'re** having a hard time**, aren't you?**
past progressive	Many players **were** playing badly**, weren't they?**
past perfect simple	You**'ve never** seen a match live in the stadium before**, have you?**
going-to future	Jay **isn't** going to watch a match live**, is he?**

- *Wenn ein **Name das Subjekt im Hauptsatz** ist, benutzt du **in der Bestätigungsfrage** immer das passende **Personalpronomen**, z.B.:* **Jay** isn't going to watch a match live, is **he**?

- *Enthält der Hauptsatz eine **Form von** **be** **oder** **can**, so steht diese ebenso in der Bestätigungsfrage.*

***Form von* be**	Luke **is** an Arsenal fan, **isn't he?**
***Modalverb* can**	Jay is good at dancing, but he **can't** play football well, **can he?**

! *Beachte den folgenden Unterschied beim Verb* be *in der 1. Person Singular:*
Luke: I'**m** late for football practice, **aren't I**?

- *Steht im Hauptsatz kein Hilfsverb, sondern nur ein **Vollverb*** (knows, talked, …)*, verwendest du eine **Form von** **do**. Die Zeitform richtet sich nach dem Hauptsatz.*

simple present	Luke **knows** a lot about football, **doesn't he?**
simple past	We **talked** about this in PE, **didn't we?**

! *Denke daran, die Bestätigungsfrage durch Komma vom Hauptsatz abzutrennen! Steigt die Intonation in der Bestätigungsfrage, handelt es sich um eine echte Frage. Fällt die Intonation, kennt der Sprecher bereits die Antwort.*

! *Ist* have *die einzige Verbform im Hauptsatz, handelt es sich um ein Vollverb und muss in der Bestätigungsfrage durch* do *ersetzt werden. Ist es Teil einer zusammengesetzten Form, ist es ein Hilfsverb und wird in die Bestätigungsfrage übernommen:*

simple present	We often **have** a little party after the match, **don't we?**
simple past	The team **had** a lot of bad luck, **didn't they?**
present perfect simple	They'**ve** just had a bad day, **haven't they?**

! *Apostroph +* s *kann für* is *oder* has *stehen. Vergleiche:*
Luke'**s** a good football player, **isn't** he?
Luke'**s** never been more than ten minutes late, **has** he?

Test yourself *Complete the dialogues. Add the correct question tags. Remember to look at the subject and verb form carefully.*

1. Olivia: Miss Brown played an interesting song in class today, …?
   Holly: Its title was *Life before media technology*, …?
   Jay: Yes, and it's a really cool song, …?
   Holly: Well, yeah. I liked it.
2. Luke: We're going to work on our media project this afternoon, …?
   Dave: Of course. Let's meet in front of the school after lessons and go to my house.
   Luke: Good idea. With Jamie and Irina it's always very noisy at our house, …?

Dave: That's true! If we concentrate, perhaps we can finish the project today.
Luke: I'm not sure. We haven't worked on this kind of project before, …? So we don't really know how long it's going to take us, …?
Dave: That's right. But you've already collected some ideas, …?
Luke: Well, erm …

G15 I wasn't allowed to go over to Jay's house yesterday.

Seite 95-96

Modalverben und ihre Ersatzformen
Modals and their substitute forms

Luke: Let's look for help on the internet.
Dad: Well when I was young, I **wasn't able to** look everything up on the internet. But I still learned to do things my way.

Die Modalverben can, may, can't, mustn't, must *und* needn't *kannst du nur im* simple present *verwenden. Ihre Ersatzform verwendest du vor allem für alle anderen Zeitformen.*

	Modalverb	*Ersatzform im* simple present	*Ersatzform im* simple past
Erlaubnis / Verbot be allowed to	can	Olivia **is allowed to** use her parents' computer when she likes.	She **was allowed to** play a game on it last weekend.
	can't / mustn't	You **aren't allowed to** chat with your friends all day.	In my last school we **weren't allowed to** use computers just for fun.
	may	**Am** I **allowed to** use your tablet, Dad?	**Were** you **allowed to** use your dad's tablet when you were younger?
(Un)Fähigkeit be able to	can	Luke **is able to** help his dad with the washing machine.	He **was able to** find help on the internet.
	can't	Luke and Jamie **aren't able to** swim very fast.	When the boys were four, they **weren't able to** swim.
(keine) Notwendigkeit have to	must	I **have to** show Dad this advice. Mrs Elliot **has to** do the washing.	He **had to** ask somebody for help. She **had to** do the shopping yesterday.
	needn't	You **don't have to** look for the phone number. I've got it. Mr Elliot **doesn't have to** work in the evenings.	We **didn't have to** wait long until the man came to fix the pipe. He **didn't have to** pay for Luke's advice.

Test yourself *Complete Luke's message. Use the substitute forms in the simple past.*

> Hi,
> Guess what. When I came home from school, there was water everywhere on the kitchen floor. Something was wrong with the washing machine and Dad (musste) fix it before Mum came home. Dad had no idea what he was doing … But I (durfte) use his tablet and check for advice in a forum. I (konnte) find a great website quickly. It was very helpful. All we (mussten) do was turn the knob off. So we (konnten) solve the problem in 20 minutes and Mum (konnte) use the washing machine when she came home.
> See you at school on Monday.
> Luke

G16 You could look at a forum for help.

Seite 95-96

Die Modalverben should, shouldn't *und* could
The modals *should, shouldn't* and *could*

Have you got a problem? Well, you **could** look at a forum for help. But you **shouldn't** believe everything you read online.

Mit den Modalverben should, shouldn't *und* could *kannst du jemandem etwas vorschlagen oder raten.*

- *Die Modalverben* should, shouldn't *und* could *fu… die du schon kennst: Du verwendest sie im* simple present, *sie sind in allen Personen gleich und nach ihnen folgt immer ein Vollverb in der Grundform. Vergleiche:*

Mr Elliot **could look** for help on the internet.	*Herr Elliot **könnte** im Internet nach Hilfe **suchen**.*
They **should ask** their parents for advice.	*Sie **sollten** ihre Eltern um Rat **fragen**.*
You **shouldn't try** to fix everything yourself.	*Du **solltest nicht versuchen**, alles selbst zu reparieren.*

Test yourself *What should, could or shouldn't they do? Give advice.*

1. Olivia: In netball I pushed a girl while we were playing. She fell and hurt her hand.
2. Jay: I've ruined Dave's book.
3. Holly: Mr Fluff often explores under my bed. It's difficult to get him out when he needs to go to bed.
4. Dave: Last weekend I pulled out some flowers in Granny's garden. I thought they were weeds[1].

Vocabulary

Im ***Vocabulary*** findest du alle wichtigen englischen Wörter und Redewendungen aus *Green Line* 2. Sie stehen in der Reihenfolge, in der sie im Buch vorkommen. Diese Wörter solltest du lernen und anwenden können. Andere nützliche Wörter und Begriffe (z. B. Arbeitsanweisungen), die du **nicht** auswendig lernen musst, findest du ab S. 236. Das *Vocabulary* ist in drei Spalten aufgeteilt:

- Links stehen die englischen Wörter und Sätze. In Klammern ist die Lautschrift aufgeführt. Sie zeigt dir, wie du das Wort oder den Satz aussprichst. Die Erklärung der Lautschrift findest du am Ende dieser Seite.
- In der Mitte steht die deutsche Übersetzung.
- Rechts findest du Beispielsätze, Erklärungen, Bilder oder Hinweise auf Besonderheiten.

In *Green Line* findest du manchmal neue Wörter in Fußnoten unten auf einer Seite. Auch diese helfen dir, die Texte zu verstehen. Du musst sie aber nicht lernen.

Auf das *Vocabulary* folgt das ***Dictionary (English – German, German – English)***. Falls du ein Wort vergessen hast, kannst du in diesen alphabetischen Wortlisten nachsehen.

Englische Begriffe wie *e-mail*, *cool* oder *cornflakes*, die du auch im Deutschen verwendest, stehen nicht im *Vocabulary*. Du kannst ihre Aussprache und Übersetzung aber im *Dictionary* nachschlagen. Das gleiche gilt für Wörter, die auf Englisch und Deutsch fast gleich geschrieben und ausgesprochen werden, wie z. B. *park* oder *partner*.

Abkürzungen und Zeichen

pl	Mehrzahl (Plural)	↔	ist das Gegenteil von
sg	Einzahl (Singular)	→	ist verwandt mit
ugs	umgangssprachlich	=	entspricht
5	In dieser Übung kommen die Wörter vor.	*Fr./Lat.*	verwandte Wörter in anderen Fremdsprachen
!	Achtung!		

Englische Laute

Mitlaute (Konsonanten)

[b]	**b**ed	[p]	**p**icture
[d]	**d**ay	[r]	**r**ed
[ð]	**th**e	[s]	**s**ix
[f]	**f**amily	[ʃ]	**sh**e
[g]	**g**o	[t]	**t**en
[ŋ]	morni**ng**	[tʃ]	**ch**air
[h]	**h**ouse	[v]	**v**ideo
[j]	**y**ou	[w]	**w**e, **o**ne
[k]	**c**an, mil**k**	[z]	ea**s**y
[l]	**l**etter	[ʒ]	revi**si**on
[m]	**m**an	[dʒ]	pa**g**e
[n]	**n**o	[θ]	**th**ank you

Selbstlaute (Vokale)

[ɑː]	c**ar**	[i]	happ**y**
[æ]	**a**pple	[iː]	t**ea**cher
[e]	p**e**n	[ɒ]	d**o**g
[ə]	**a**gain	[ɔː]	b**a**ll
[ɜː]	g**ir**l	[ʊ]	b**oo**k
[ʌ]	b**u**t	[u]	Jan**u**ary
[ɪ]	**i**t	[uː]	t**oo**, tw**o**

Doppellaute

[aɪ]	**I**, m**y**
[aʊ]	n**ow**, m**ou**se
[eɪ]	n**a**me, th**ey**
[eə]	th**ere**, p**air**
[ɪə]	h**ere**, id**ea**
[əʊ]	hell**o**
[ɔɪ]	b**oy**
[ʊə]	s**ure**

[ː]	der vorangehende Laut ist lang, z. B. *you* [juː]
[‿]	der Bindebogen zeigt, dass zwei Wörter in der Aussprache verbunden werden
[ˈ]	die folgende Silbe trägt den Hauptakzent
[ˌ]	die folgende Silbe trägt den Nebenakzent

Unit 1 My friends and I

Check-in

past [pɑ:st]	Vergangenheit	'Today' is now, 'yesterday' is the *past.*
feeling ['fi:lɪŋ]	Gefühl	*feeling* → to feel
that [ðæt]	der; dem; den; die; das *(Relativpronomen)*	
caught on camera [ˌkɔ:t‿ɒn 'kæmrə]	ertappt; mit der Kamera festgehalten	
embarrassing [ɪm'bærəsɪŋ]	peinlich	In the photo Jay is wearing an *embarrassing* outfit.
to **end up** [ˌend‿'ʌp]	enden; landen	
yearbook ['jɪəbʊk]	Jahrbuch	A book with information about events and students at the school.
round of boxing [ˌraʊnd‿əv 'bɒksɪŋ]	Boxrunde	
nose [nəʊz]	Nase	They look funny with their red *noses.*
eye [aɪ]	Auge	
lovebirds *(pl)* ['lʌvˌbɜ:dz]	Turteltauben	
to **lie** [laɪ]	lügen	The camera never *lies*!
trip [trɪp]	Trip; Reise; Ausflug; Fahrt	Let's go on a fun *trip* at the weekend!
guy [gaɪ]	Typ; Kerl; *(Pl.)* Leute	Our new classmate is a really cool *guy.*
2 **himself** [hɪm'self]	(er) selbst; sich (selbst)	You mustn't help him. He wants to do everything *himself.*
3 **shy** [ʃaɪ]	schüchtern	Are you *shy*? – Yes, I am. That's why I don't like parties.
embarrassed [ɪm'bærəst]	verlegen	*embarrassed* → embarrassing *Fr.* embarrassé/-e
proud (of) ['praʊd‿əv]	stolz (auf)	Jay is *proud of* himself because he is good at singing.
American [ə'merɪkən]	Amerikanisch; amerikanisch; aus Amerika; Amerikaner/-in	Yearbooks are an *American* tradition.
report [rɪ'pɔ:t]	Bericht; Meldung	Who can write the *report* about the class trip?
during *(+ noun)* ['djʊərɪŋ]	während *(+ Nomen)*	Don't eat *during* lessons.
highlight ['haɪlaɪt]	Highlight; Höhepunkt	

Describing a person's character

He**'s** a very **shy** person. It isn't easy for him to give presentations.	schüchtern
She's good at lots of things so she**'s** always **confident** that she can do almost anything.	zuversichtlich; selbstbewusst
He**'s** so **brave**. He's never scared.	tapfer; mutig
She**'s** a **nice / friendly / unfriendly / funny** person.	nett / freundlich / unfreundlich / lustig
He**'s lucky** because he**'s happy**.	Glück haben / glücklich sein

Describe a person to your partner. Who is it?

Station 1: I love Red Nose Day

	(the) best [best]	(der/die/das) Beste	I always try to do *my best* when there's a class test.
	ago [ə'gəʊ]	vor *(zeitlich)*	! *Ago* steht meistens am Satzende: I did my homework two days *ago*.
	to **raise money** [ˌreɪz 'mʌni]	Geld sammeln	Charities *raise money*.
	in need [ɪn 'ni:d]	bedürftig; in Not	*in need* → to need
	also ['ɔ:lsəʊ]	auch	I like football and I *also* like basketball. = I like football and I like basketball too.
	that's how [ðæts 'haʊ]	so	Look at Luke. *That's how* you play football – he's good!
	noticeboard ['nəʊtɪsbɔ:d]	schwarzes Brett	Olivia saw a Red Nose Day poster on the school *noticeboard*.
	month [mʌnθ]	Monat	day – week – *month* – year
	in the end [ˌɪn ði‿'end]	schließlich; zum Schluss	
	real [rɪəl]	echt; richtig; wirklich	Not everything you see on TV is *real*. *real* → really
	collection [kə'lekʃn]	Kollektion; Sammlung	*collection* → to collect *Fr.* collection *(f)*
	I can't wait till next time. [aɪ kɑ:nt ˌweɪt tɪl nekst 'taɪm]	Ich kann es bis zum nächsten Mal kaum erwarten.	
2	**non-** [nɒn]	nicht-	Red Nose Day is a *non*-uniform day.
5	**the next day** [ðə ˌnekst 'deɪ]	am nächsten Tag	What did Luke tell his friends *the next day*?
	yesterday ['jestədeɪ]	gestern	*yesterday* – today – tomorrow
6	**pyjamas** *(pl)* [pɪ'dʒɑ:məz]	Schlafanzug; Pyjama	Do you wear *pyjamas* in bed? 
	to **enjoy** [ɪn'dʒɔɪ]	genießen; sich freuen an	The party was great. I really *enjoyed* it.
	comment ['kɒment]	Kommentar	This is a serious problem, so I don't need your funny *comments*!

	to **turn off** [ˌtɜ:n‿ˈɒf]	abschalten; ausschalten	Please *turn off* the TV. It's time to go to bed.
	hard [hɑ:d]	hart; schwer; schwierig	I find German *hard*.
	for ... [fɔ:; fə]	... lang	Sherlock can swim *for* 30 minutes.
	to **think of** [ˈθɪŋk‿əv]	(sich) ausdenken; sich etwas einfallen lassen	Can you *think of* other things to do at the weekend?
7	**nervous** [ˈnɜ:vəs]	nervös; aufgeregt	I felt *nervous* before the class test. *Fr.* nerveux/nerveuse
8	**sale** [seɪl]	Verkauf	*sale* → to sell
	to **keep going** [ˌki:p ˈgəʊɪŋ]	aufrechterhalten	A quick answer *keeps* the conversation *going*.

Station 2: How did they know?

	coach [kəʊtʃ]	Reisebus	A big bus (for holidays or long trips). 
	someone [ˈsʌmwʌn]	jemand	*someone* = somebody
	missing [ˈmɪsɪŋ]	fehlend; verschwunden	What's the *missing* word? "I really ... you."
	solution [səˈlu:ʃn]	Lösung	Let's find a *solution* for your problem. *Fr.* solution *(f)*
	anonymous [əˈnɒnɪməs]	anonym	
	police [pəˈli:s]	Polizei	! The *police* <u>are</u> looking for a dangerous man. *Fr.* police *(f)*
	to **arrest** [əˈrest]	festnehmen; verhaften	The police *arrested* two men. *Fr.* arrêter
	what the man looked like [ˌwɒt ðə mæn ˈlʊkt laɪk]	wie der Mann aussah	I didn't see the man. I don't know *what he looks like*.
	taxi [ˈtæksi]	Taxi	
	driver [ˈdraɪvə]	Fahrer/-in	! My uncle is <u>a</u> taxi *driver*. = Mein Onkel ist Taxifahrer.
	mechanic [məˈkænɪk]	Mechaniker/-in; Kfz-Mechaniker/-in	
	farmer [ˈfɑ:mə]	Farmer/-in; Landwirt/-in	*farmer* → farm
	postman [ˈpəʊstmən]	Briefträger	
	clue [klu:]	Hinweis; Spur	The man's name is the *clue*.
13	**friendly** [ˈfrendli]	freundlich; nett	I always try to be *friendly* to everyone. *friendly* → friend
14	**all day** [ɔ:l ˈdeɪ]	den ganzen Tag	What did you do *all day* on Saturday?
15	**singer** [ˈsɪŋə]	Sänger/-in	Jay thinks he's a *singer*. *singer* → to sing
16	**dream** [dri:m]	Traum	In my *dream* I was James Bond.

Station 3: Everyone can enjoy a challenge

challenge ['tʃælɪndʒ]	Herausforderung	
course [kɔ:s]	Kurs	They organise sports *courses* for school groups. *Lat.* cursus *(m)*
mountain ['maʊntɪn]	Berg	
forest ['fɒrɪst]	Wald	There are lots of trees in a *forest*. *Fr.* forêt *(f)*
adventure [əd'ventʃə]	Abenteuer	*Adventure* stories tell about exciting events.
confident ['kɒnfɪdnt]	selbstsicher; selbstbewusst	*Lat.* confidens
walking ['wɔ:kɪŋ]	Wandern	! Wenn man *-ing* an ein Verb anhängt, wird es zum Hauptwort (Nomen): walk – *walking*, climb – climbing
climbing ['klaɪmɪŋ]	Klettern	! Achtung Aussprache.
gorge scrambling ['gɔ:dʒ ˌskræmblɪŋ]	Schluchtenklettern	
route [ru:t]	Strecke; Route	*Fr.* route *(f)*
than [ðæn]	als *(bei Vergleichen)*	Her English is better *than* her French.
the worst [ðə 'wɜ:st]	der/die/das schlimmste; der/die/das schlechteste	*the worst* ↔ the best

Outdoor activities

to **play** football / tennis	Fußball / Tennis spielen
to **go** skating / swimming / climbing / gorge scrambling	inlineskaten / schwimmen / schluchtenklettern gehen
to **ride** your bike / a horse	Fahrrad fahren / reiten
to **run**	laufen; rennen
to **go for a walk** in a park / in a forest / in the mountains	im Park / im Wald / in den Bergen spazieren gehen
to **climb** a mountain	einen Berg besteigen
to **do** gorge scrambling / mountain climbing	schluchtenklettern / bergsteigen

Tell your partner what you'd like to do in your holidays.

18	**separate** ['seprət]	separat; getrennt; verschieden	Wales is a *separate* country. *Lat.* separatus/-a/-um
	Celtic ['keltɪk; 'seltɪk]	keltisch	*Fr.* celtique
	Welsh [welʃ]	walisisch; Walisisch; Waliser/-in	*Welsh* people are from Wales. Some of them still speak *Welsh*.
22	**low** [ləʊ]	niedrig	

tall [tɔ:l]	groß; hoch	Olivia is *taller* than Lucy.
high [haɪ]	hoch; groß	*high* ↔ low

Comparing things

Tony: My house is **big**.
Lou: My sister's house is **bigger**.
Tony: I think my house is **the biggest**.

Lou: Your joke is **good**. But my joke is **better**.
Tony: No, my joke is **the best**.

Lou: Football is **exciting**, but tennis is **more exciting**, and inline skating is **the most exciting** sport.

Compare the things in your schoolbag with a partner's things.

Story: It was amazing

amazing [ə'meɪzɪŋ]	unglaublich; toll; erstaunlich	That's an *amazing* story!
planet ['plænɪt]	Planet	
sheep, sheep *(pl)* [ʃi:ɔ]	Schaf	
sign [saɪn]	Zeichen; Schild	In Wales the *signs* are in Welsh. ***Lat.*** signum *(nt)*
road [rəʊd]	Straße	I live in King's *Road*.
soon [su:n]	bald	in a short time from now; a short time later
field [fi:ld]	Feld; Spielfeld; Wiese; Weide; Acker	On farms there are *fields*.
Welcome! ['welkəm]	Willkommen!	
instructor [ɪn'strʌktə]	Lehrer/-in; Betreuer/-in	An *instructor* shows you how to do things. ***Lat.*** instructor *(m)*
few [fju:]	wenige	! He's got a *few* friends. = … ein paar Freunde. He's got *few* friends. = … wenige Freunde.
meal [mi:l]	Mahlzeit; Essen	Lunch is a *meal*.
a bit [ə 'bɪt]	ein bisschen; ein wenig	

	cold [kəʊld]	kalt	The nights in Wales were a bit *cold*.
	torch [tɔ:tʃ]	Fackel; Taschenlampe	
	to **go for a walk** [ˌgəʊ fər‿ə 'wɔ:k]	spazieren gehen	It's nice today. Let's *go for a walk*.
	the dark [ðə 'dɑ:k]	Dunkelheit	in *the dark* = im Dunkeln
	noise [nɔɪz]	Lärm; Geräusch	What all the *noise*? I can't sleep!
	dark [dɑ:k]	dunkel	*dark* → the dark
	night walk ['naɪt wɔ:k]	Nachtwanderung	
	against [ə'genst]	gegen	It was *against* the rules.
	to **be asleep** [ˌbi ə'sli:p]	schlafen	*to be asleep* = to sleep
	to **tiptoe** ['tɪptəʊ]	auf Zehenspitzen gehen	They *tiptoed* back to their rooms.
	cloudy ['klaʊdi]	bedeckt; bewölkt	On a *cloudy* night you can't see the stars.
	battery ['bætri]	Batterie; Akku	*Fr.* batterie *(f)*
	no idea [ˌnəʊ‿aɪ'dɪə]	keine Ahnung	Which is the right way? – I have *no idea*!
	locked [lɒkt]	abgeschlossen	*locked* ↔ open
	trouble ['trʌbl]	Ärger; Probleme; Schwierigkeiten	We didn't want *trouble* with our teacher.
	secret ['si:krət]	Geheimnis	Don't tell the others, it's a *secret*. *Fr.* secret *(m)*
	memory ['memri]	Erinnerung; Gedächtnis	We all have great *memories* of our school trip. ***Lat.*** memoria *(f)*
4	**travel report** [ˌtrævl rɪ'pɔ:t]	Reisebericht	Do you like Dave's *travel report* about the class trip?

Skills: How to use a dictionary

1	**electronic** [ˌelek'trɒnɪk]	elektronisch	Do you use an *electronic* dictionary?
	search [sɜ:tʃ]	Suche; Such-	Write the word in the *search* box.
	meaning ['mi:nɪŋ]	Bedeutung; Sinn	What's the *meaning* of 'to describe'?

Unit task: Our travel report

	spaceship ['speɪsʃɪp]	Raumschiff	In science fiction stories there are often *spaceships*.
	beginning [bɪ'gɪnɪŋ]	Anfang; Beginn	*beginning* ↔ end

Action UK! The new boy

1	to **sneak around** [ˌsni:k‿ə'raʊnd]	herumschleichen	
	lemon ['lemən]	Zitrone	

	surprising [sə'praɪzɪŋ]	überraschend	*surprising* → surprise
2	**filmmaker** ['fɪlmˌmeɪkə]	Filmemacher/-in	A *filmmaker* makes films.
	mood [mu:d]	Stimmung; Laune	Can you describe the *mood* in that scene?
	unfriendly [ʌn'frendli]	unfreundlich	*unfriendly* ↔ friendly
	hurt [hɜ:t]	verletzt	He made some really unfriendly comments and now I feel *hurt*.
	aggressive [ə'gresɪv]	aggressiv	! Achtung Aussprache. *Fr.* agressif/agressive
	scary ['skeəri]	unheimlich; gruselig; beängstigend	*scary* → to be scared

Unit 2 Let's discover TTS!

Check-in

	to **discover** [dɪ'skʌvə]	entdecken	The students *discover* Thomas Tallis School.
	painting ['peɪntɪŋ]	Malerei; Gemälde	*painting* → to paint 
	assembly [ə'sembli]	Versammlung; Morgenappell	
	hall [hɔ:l]	Halle; Saal	In the *hall*, the students meet for Assembly.
	competition [ˌkɒmpə'tɪʃn]	Wettbewerb; Turnier	There's a painting *competition* at our school this year. *Fr.* compétition *(f)*
	to **belong (to)** [bɪ'lɒŋ (tə)]	gehören (zu)	
	with special needs [wɪð ˌspeʃl 'ni:dz]	behindert	Students *with special needs* belong to TTS too.
	art [ɑ:t]	Kunst	Not every painting is *art*! *Lat.* ars *(f)*
1	**subject** ['sʌbdʒɪkt]	Schulfach	What *subjects* do you like?
	exam [ɪg'zæm]	Examen; Prüfung	An *exam* is an important test *Fr.* examen *(m)*
	drama ['drɑ:mə]	Theater; Drama	 In *Drama* class, you can learn how to be an actor.
	studies *(pl)* ['stʌdiz]	Studium; Lernen; Arbeit für die Schule	My favourite subject is Film *Studies*. *Lat.* studēre
	fashion ['fæʃn]	Mode	In *Fashion* lessons you learn about clothes.

to **offer** ['ɒfə]	anbieten	Can I *offer* you something to drink? *Fr.* offrir
additional [ə'dɪʃnl]	zusätzlich	
birdwatching ['bɜ:dˌwɒtʃɪŋ]	Vogelbeobachtung	*Birdwatching* is an additional activity at TTS.
chess [tʃes]	Schach	
2 **fantastic** [fæn'tæstɪk]	fantastisch; großartig	*fantastic* = great *Fr.* fantastique
reaction [ri'ækʃn]	Reaktion	
3 **positive** ['pɒzətɪv]	positiv	Give *positive* feedback and be friendly when your feedback isn't so *positive*.
introduction [ˌɪntrə'dʌkʃn]	Einführung; Einleitung; Vorstellung	the *introduction* of a presentation = the first part of a presentation
lively ['laɪvli]	lebendig	Holly's presentation was interesting and *lively*.

Station 1: The queen who loved parties

queen [kwi:n]	Königin	Elizabeth II is the *Queen* of England.
who [hu:]	der; dem; den; die *(Relativpronomen)*	Pia is the girl *who* comes from Germany.
history ['hɪstri]	Geschichte	*Lat.* historia *(f)*
husband ['hʌzbənd]	Ehemann	My dad is my mum's *husband*.
beautiful ['bju:tɪfl]	schön; hübsch; wunderbar	
view [vju:]	Aussicht; Sicht; Ausblick; Blick	Anne's house had a beautiful *view* of the Thames.
which [wɪtʃ]	der; die; das; dem; den *(Relativpronomen)*	The subject *which* I like most is English.
ghost [gəʊst]	Geist	Sometimes there are stories of *ghosts* in old houses. 
as [æz; əz]	als	
hospital ['hɒspɪtl]	Hospital; Krankenhaus	Later they used the house as a *hospital*. *Fr.* hôpital *(m)*
to **build, built** [bɪld; bɪlt]	bauen	
architect ['ɑ:kɪtekt]	Architekt/-in	Which *architect* built the museum? *Lat.* architectus *(m)*
whose [hu:z]	dessen; deren *(Relativpronomen)*	
design [dɪ'zaɪn]	Design; Gestaltung; Entwurf	

	to **choose, chose** [tʃuːz; tʃəʊz]	auswählen; wählen	Christopher Wren was the architect whose design Anne *chose*.
	upset [ʌpˈset]	aufgebracht; bestürzt	Why are you so *upset*? – My brother lost my phone!
	to **cut, cut (off)** [kʌt kʌt (ɒf)]	schneiden; abschneiden	Anne wanted to *cut off* Wren's head.
	that's why [ðæts ˈwaɪ]	deshalb	Luke hurt his hand. *That's why* he didn't do his homework.
	to **leave, left** [liːv; left]	verlassen; lassen; abfahren	
	space [speɪs]	Raum; Fläche; Platz; Ort	Please leave some *space* for my picture on the wall.
3	**wife, wives** *(pl)* [waɪf, waɪvz]	Ehefrau	Mr and Mrs Preston are husband and *wife*.
	by the river [baɪ ðə ˈrɪvə]	am Fluss	Christopher Wren built the hospital *by the river*.
4	to **be interested in** [bi‿ˈɪntrəstɪd‿ɪn]	interessiert sein an; sich interessieren für	Are you *interested in* history?
	to **try on** [traɪ‿ˈɒn]	anprobieren	That's a nice T-shirt. Why don't you *try* it *on*, Olivia?
5	**finally** [ˈfaɪnli]	schließlich; endlich; zum Schluss; letztlich	first – then – *finally* ***Lat.*** finis *(m)*
	to **design** [dɪˈzaɪn]	entwerfen; gestalten	*to design* → design
7	**partially sighted** [ˌpɑːʃəli ˈsaɪtɪd]	sehbehindert	Gwen is the new girl who is *partially sighted*.
8	**registration** [ˌredʒɪsˈtreɪʃn]	Anwesenheitskontrolle	*Registration* is before lessons.
	Technology [tekˈnɒlədʒi]	Technik; Computerunterricht	
	Science [saɪəns]	Naturwissenschaften	***Lat.*** scientia *(f)*
	Maths [mæθs]	Mathematik; Mathe	***Fr.*** maths *(f) (pl)*
	RE *(= Religious Education)* [ˌɑːrˈiː; rɪˌlɪdʒəs‿edʒʊˈkeɪʃn]	Religion *(Schulfach)*	
	French [frenʃ]	französisch; Französisch	
	Humanities *(pl)* [hjuːˈmænətiz]	Sozialwissenschaften	***Lat.*** humanitas *(f)*
	PE *(= Physical Education)* [ˌpiːˈiː; ˌfɪzɪkl‿edʒʊˈkeɪʃn]	Sportunterricht	In *PE* you do lots of sport.

Subjects at school

English	Englisch	**Music**	Musik
German	Deutsch	**Humanities**	Sozialwissenschaften
French	Französisch	**Technology**	Technik
Maths	Mathe	**Science**	Naturwissenschaften
PE	Sport	**RE**	Religion
Art	Kunst		

Make you own fantasy timetable and compare it with your partner's.

Station 2: Everyone was doing a really great job!

	to **join** [dʒɔɪn]	beitreten; sich anschließen; verbinden	Let's *join* the Computer Club!
	Eco [ɪkəʊ]	Öko-	
	article ['ɑːtɪkl]	Artikel; Bericht *(in einer Zeitschrift, Zeitung)*	On the TTS website there are lots of *articles* about clubs. *Fr.* article *(m)*
	wildlife ['waɪldlaɪf]	Tierwelt *(in freier Wildbahn)*	The Eco Club did a *wildlife* project.
	to **get started** [ˌget 'stɑːtɪd]	anfangen	*to get started* = to start
	sun [sʌn]	Sonne	
	to **shine, shone** [ʃaɪn; ʃɒn]	scheinen; glänzen	The sun is *shining* – let's go swimming.
	bee [biː]	Biene	
	to **hum** [hʌm]	summen	
	to **look forward to** [ˌlʊk 'fɔːwəd tə]	sich freuen auf	I'm *looking forward to* my grandma's visit next week.
	to **put up, put up** [ˌpʊt‿'ʌp; ˌpʊt‿'ʌp]	aufstellen; errichten	*to put up* → to put
	hotel [həʊ'tel]	Hotel	
	to **dig, dug** [dɪg; dʌg]	graben	
	hole [həʊl]	Loch	They dug a *hole* in the garden.
	pond [pɒnd]	Teich	
	to **hang up, hung up** [ˌhæŋ‿'ʌp; ˌhʌŋ‿'ʌp]	aufhängen	You can *hang up* a bird house in your garden.
	bird [bɜːd]	Vogel	
	ever ['evə]	jemals	It was our funniest project *ever*!
9	**member** ['membə]	Mitglied	Dave is a *member* of the Preston family. *Fr.* membre *(m)*
10	**pipe** [paɪp]	Rohr; Rohrleitung	He broke a *pipe* and now there's water everywhere!
	to **fall off, fell off** [ˌfɔːl‿'ɒf; ˌfel‿'ɒf]	herunterfallen; hinunterfallen	

	ladder ['lædə]	Leiter	 Be careful! Don't fall off the *ladder*.
	fox [fɒks]	Fuchs	
	to **steal, stole** [sti:l; stəʊl]	stehlen	A fox *stole* the students' lunch.
	thumb [θʌm]	Daumen	
	hammer ['hæmə]	Hammer	She hit her thumb with the *hammer*.
	corner ['kɔ:nə]	Ecke	Most rooms have four *corners*.
13	to **welcome** ['welkəm]	willkommen heißen	Let's go and *welcome* our new classmates.

Action UK! The film star

1	**one day** [wʌn 'deɪ]	eines Tages	Jay wants to be a famous singer *one day*.
	actor ['æktə]	Schauspieler	*actor* → to act ***Lat.*** actor *(m)*
	dancer ['dɑ:nsə]	Tänzer/-in	*dancer* → to dance
	pilot ['paɪlət]	Pilot/-in	
	police officer [pə'li:s‿ɒfɪsə]	Polizeibeamter	

Jobs

Who?		**What he / she does, and where**
actor	Schauspieler/-in	to act, to sing, to dance, to speak, drama
architect	Architekt/-in	to plan, to design, to build
coach	Trainer/-in	sport, dancing
dancer	Tänzer/-in	to dance, drama, music
driver	Fahrer/-in	to drive a car / taxi
farmer	Bauer/Bäuerin	to work on a farm, to look after the animals
instructor	Betreuer/-in	to look after people in a course
police officer	Polizist/-in	to arrest somebody
postman/ postwoman	Postbote/Postbotin; Briefträger/-in	to bring mail
sailor	Matrose/Matrosin	to work on a ship
singer	Sänger/-in	to sing, song, music
teacher	Lehrer/-in	to work at school, to help students
vet	Tierarzt/Tierärztin	to work in a surgery, to help pets / farm animals

Which jobs do you like and why?

3	**advice** [əd'vaɪs]	Rat; Ratschlag	What *advice* can you give me?
	to **panic** ['pænɪk]	panisch werden	Don't *panic*! ***Fr.*** paniquer
	to **relax** [rɪ'læks]	sich entspannen; sich ausruhen; sich beruhigen	Just *relax*!
	Take a deep breath. [ˌteɪk‿ə ˌdiːp 'breθ]	Atme(t) tief ein.	
	to **thank** [θæŋk]	danken	*to thank* → Thank you.
4	**such** [sʌtʃ]	solch; solche/-r/-s	It was *such* a good film!
	impressed [ɪm'prest]	beeindruckt	The friends were *impressed* with Jay's dancing and singing.

Skills: How to give a good presentation

1	**fact** [fækt]	Fakt; Tatsache	I know a lot of *facts* about King James and his wife Anne. ***Lat.*** factum *(nt)*
	on time [ɒn 'taɪm]	pünktlich	Be *on time*. = Don't be late.
	take a look at [ˌteɪk‿ə 'lʊk‿æt]	einen Blick werfen auf	Let's *take a look at* this design.
	to **be connected** [bi kə'nektɪd]	zusammenhängen; in Zusammenhang stehen	
	topic ['tɒpɪk]	Thema	This story is connected with the *topic* of my presentation.
	contact ['kɒntækt]	Kontakt	
	audience ['ɔːdiəns]	Publikum	Make eye contact with your *audience* during a presentation.

Unit task: Join our club!

juggling ['dʒʌglɪŋ]	Jonglieren	
foreign language [ˌfɒrɪn 'læŋgwɪdʒ]	Fremdsprache	A lot of British students learn French as their first *foreign language*.
fanzine [fæn'ziːn]	Fanzeitschrift	
life, lives *(pl)* [laɪf, laɪvz]	Leben	*life* → to live

Story: What a wonderful world

wonderful ['wʌndəfl]	wunderbar	*wonderful* = great = fantastic
news *(sg)* [njuːz]	Nachricht(en); Neuigkeit(en)	! That's good *news*. = Das ist eine gute Nachricht.
earth [ɜːθ]	Erdboden; Erde; die Erde	
dinosaur ['daɪnəsɔː]	Dinosaurier	
to **have to** ['hæv tə]	müssen	They *have to* make a poster for the competition.

to **share** [ʃeə]	teilen	Jay doesn't want to *share* his ideas with Luke.
anyone else [ˌeniwʌn ˈels]	jemand anderes	Don't tell the story to *anyone else*.
to **enter** [ˈentə]	hineingehen; betreten; eintreten; *hier:* mitmachen	He *entered* the competition. The teacher *entered* the room.
on my own [ˌɒn maɪ ˈəʊn]	allein; für mich	If you're *on your own*, you're alone.
side [saɪd]	Seite	
dirty [ˈdɜːti]	dreckig; schmutzig	I can't wear this T-shirt because it's *dirty*.
to **notice** [ˈnəʊtɪs]	bemerken; wahrnehmen	Did you *notice* anything strange about the woman?
to **lie, lay** [laɪ; leɪ]	liegen	My phone is *lying* on the table.
could [kʊd]	könnte/-n	
moment [ˈməʊmənt]	Moment; Augenblick	! Achtung Betonung.
class [klɑːs]	*hier:* Unterricht	In *class*, sometimes you work on your own, sometimes with your classmates.
break [breɪk]	Pause	After the first two lessons we always have *break*.
quickly [ˈkwɪkli]	schnell	Jay looked at the exercise book *quickly*.
He couldn't believe his eyes. [hi ˌkʊdnt bɪˌliːv hɪz‿aɪz]	Er traute seinen Augen nicht.	*I couldn't believe my eyes* when I got a dog for my birthday.
flower [flaʊə]	Blume	
clever [ˈklevə]	schlau; klug	What a *clever* idea!
yours [jɔːz]	dein/-er/-e/-es; eure/-r/-s; Ihr/-e	This is my drawing. Is that one *yours*?
nearly [ˈnɪəli]	fast; annähernd	My presentation is *nearly* finished.
to **calm down** [ˌkɑːm ˈdaʊn]	sich beruhigen	! Das „l" in *calm* wird nicht ausgesprochen.
mine [maɪn]	mein/-er/-e/-es	*mine* ↔ yours
to **push** [pʊʃ]	stoßen; schieben; schubsen	He *pushed* me – and I fell over. That wasn't nice!
to **turn (a)round** [ˌtɜːn‿(ə)ˈraʊnd]	(sich) umdrehen; wenden	When they heard a voice behind them, they *turned (a)round*.
arm [ɑːm]	Arm	
fight [faɪt]	Kampf; Streit	
idiot [ˈɪdiət]	Idiot/-in	! Achtung Betonung.
to **turn back** [tɜːn ˈbæk]	umkehren; zurückgehen	*to turn back* → to turn (a)round → to turn off
nobody [ˈnəʊbədi]	niemand	
ready [ˈredi]	fertig; bereit	Let's get *ready* for school now.
to **plant** [plɑːnt]	pflanzen; anpflanzen	Let's *plant* some flowers in the garden.
3 **strong** [strɒŋ]	stark	
absolutely [ˌæbsəˈluːtli]	absolut; völlig	***Lat.*** absolutus/-a/-um
to **hate** [heɪt]	hassen; nicht mögen	*to hate* ↔ to love

Feelings and reactions

She **feels nervous / embarrassed / hurt** because …	nervös / verlegen / verletzt
I'**m impressed / surprised**.	beeindruckt / überrascht
He'**s in an aggressive mood**.	in aggressiver Stimmung

Draw a face. Can your partner guess what feeling it shows?

Check-out

1	**nature** ['neɪtʃə]	Natur	I only watch films about *nature*. *Lat.* natura *(f)*
	to **make friends** [ˌmeɪk 'frendz]	Freundschaft schließen	I *made* lots of *friends* at my new school.
2	**alarm clock** [ə'lɑːm ˌklɒk]	Wecker	

Across cultures 1 London: A special city

	huge [hjuːdʒ]	riesig; riesengroß; gewaltig	Berlin is a big city. London is a *huge* city.
	capital ['kæpɪtl]	Hauptstadt	London is the *capital* of England. *Lat.* capitalis
1	**multi-ethnic** [ˌmʌlti'eθnɪk]	Vielvölker-; international	London is a *multi-ethnic* city.
	sight [saɪt]	Sehenswürdigkeit; Anblick	A *sight* is an interesting thing to see in a city.
	underground ['ʌndəgraʊnd]	U-Bahn	Let's go by *underground*.
	the **Tube** [ðə 'tjuːb]	die Londoner U-Bahn	Another name for the London underground is *the Tube*.
	carnival ['kɑːnɪvl]	Karneval	What costume do you want to wear at the *carnival*?
	originally [ə'rɪdʒnli]	ursprünglich	
	Roman ['rəʊmən]	Römer/-in; römisch	London was originally a *Roman* town. *Lat.* Romanus/-a/-um
	airport ['eəpɔːt]	Flughafen	London has got five *airports*. *Fr.* aéroport *(m)*
	million ['mɪljən]	Million	1,000,000
	large [lɑːdʒ]	groß; riesig	London is the *largest* city in the EU.
	bell [bel]	Glocke	
2	**guard** [gɑːd]	Wache; Wächter/-in	There are always *guards* in front of Buckingham Palace.
	identity [aɪ'dentəti]	Identität	*Fr.* identité *(f)*

Unit 3 London is amazing!

Check-in

	flair [fleə]	Flair; Atmosphäre	Brick Lane has a multi-ethnic *flair*.
	wax figure ['wæks ˌfɪgə]	Wachsfigur	At Madame Tussauds you can see *wax figures* of famous people.

Station 1: It's going to be fun

	to **stay with** ['steɪ wɪð]	wohnen bei	Amir is *staying with* the Azads.
	this afternoon [ðɪs ɑ:ftənu:n]	heute Nachmittag	yesterday afternoon – *this afternoon* – tomorrow afternoon
	18-year-old [ˌeɪti:n 'jɪər‿ˌəʊld]	18-jährig	My sister is 18. I've got an *18-year-old* sister.
	to **persuade** [pə'sweɪd]	überreden	Jay wants to *persuade* his brother to come with them. ***Lat.*** persuadēre
	probably ['prɒbəbli]	möglicherweise; wahrscheinlich	
1	to **travel** ['trævl]	fahren; reisen	This year I'd like to *travel* to England.
	public transport *(nc pl)* [ˌpʌblɪk 'trænspɔ:t]	öffentliche Verkehrsmittel	*public transport* = the Underground, buses, trains
	smartcard ['smɑ:tkɑ:d]	Chipkarte	
	to **top up** [tɒp‿'ʌp]	aufladen	Jay *topped up* his Oyster card yesterday. Now he must *top up* his phone too.
	credit ['kredɪt]	Guthaben	I must top up my phone. There's no *credit* on it.
4	**wheelchair** ['wi:ltʃeə]	Rollstuhl	 *wheelchair* → chair
5	**zoo** [zu:]	Zoo; Tierpark	There are lots of animals in a *zoo*.
	musician [mju:'zɪʃn]	Musiker/-in	*musician* → music ***Fr.*** musicien *(m)*/musicienne *(f)*
6	to **get around** [ˌget‿ə'raʊnd]	*hier:* sich fortbewegen	What's the best way to *get around* London? – By Tube.
	to **change (onto)** [tʃeɪndʒ ('ɒntʊ)]	umsteigen (in)	To get to Buckingham Palace from here, you *change onto* the Victoria line.
	north [nɔ:θ]	Norden; Nord-	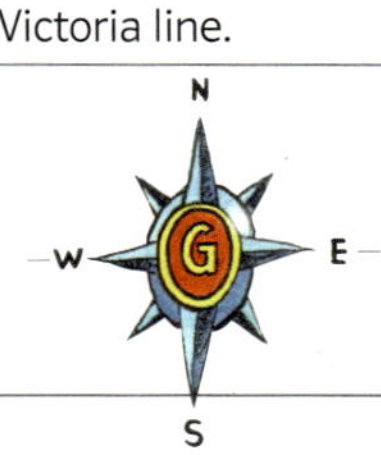
	south [saʊθ]	Süden; Süd-	

stop [stɒp]	Haltestelle; Halt	The next *stop* is Elephant & Castle. *stop* → to stop
to **get off, got off (a bus/ train)** [ˌget_ˈɒf; ˌgɒt_ˈɒf]	aussteigen (aus einem Bus/ Zug)	Let's *get off* the Underground and take the bus.

Station 2: Good idea!

to **deal, dealt (with)** [diːl; delt (wɪð)]	sich befassen (mit); umgehen (mit)	We've got a problem so let's *deal with* it.
a while [ə ˈwaɪl]	eine Weile	*a while* = a little time
to **mean, meant** [miːn; ment]	meinen; bedeuten	You think the new boy is strange? What do you *mean*? I think he's nice.
girlfriend [ˈgɜːlfrend]	Freundin *(in einer Paarbeziehung)*	Shahid has a *girlfriend*.
souvenir [ˌsuːvnˈɪə]	Souvenir; Andenken	I'd like to buy a *souvenir* of London.
anywhere [ˈeniweə]	irgendwo; überall (egal, wo)	Are there any souvenir shops *anywhere*?
everybody [ˈevribɒdi]	jeder; alle	all the people
... where to go. [ˌweə tə ˈgəʊ]	... wohin ich gehen kann.	I don't know *where to go*.
to **follow** [ˈfɒləʊ]	folgen; hinterhergehen; befolgen	The bird is *following* the man. 
I bet [aɪ ˈbet]	ich wette	
to **beat, beat** [biːt; biːt]	schlagen; besiegen	I bet nobody can *beat* Arsenal this year!
one *(sg)*/**ones** *(pl)* [wʌn/wʌnz]	eine/-r/-s	Wenn du im Englischen ein Nomen nicht wiederholen möchtest, kannst du es durch *one*/*ones* ersetzen: This sandwich is big, that *one* is bigger.
11 **pro** [prəʊ]	Argument dafür	*Lat.* pro
con [kɒn]	Argument dagegen	*Lat.* contra
far [fɑː]	weit	Is Big Ben *far* from Buckingham Palace?

Station 3: They can bite very hard

to **bite, bit** [baɪt; bɪt]	beißen	Does your dog *bite*? It looks a bit scary!
hard [hɑːd]	*hier:* stark	In tennis you must hit the ball *hard*.
tour [tʊə]	Tour; Fahrt; Rundgang	
guide [gaɪd]	Führer/-in; Reiseführer	A person or a book that gives you information (e.g. about a city or a museum). *Fr.* guide *(m) (f)*
to **become, became** [bɪˈkʌm, bɪˈkeɪm]	werden	William the Conqueror *became* king of England in 1066.
castle [ˈkɑːsl]	Schloss; Burg	! Das „t" in *castle* wird nicht gesprochen.

	prison ['prɪzn]	Gefängnis	*Fr.* prison *(f)*
	lion [laɪən]	Löwe	 *Fr.* lion *(m)*
	bear [beə]	Bär	
	crown jewels [ˌkraʊn 'dʒu:əlz]	Kronjuwelen	The Tower is a museum where you can see the *Crown Jewels*.
	Beefeater ['bi:fˌi:tə]	königlicher Leibgardist	
	raven ['reɪvn]	Rabe	
	raven master ['reɪvn ˌmɑ:stə]	Herr der Raben	The *raven master* looks after the ravens in the Tower.
	careful ['keəfl]	vorsichtig; sorgfältig	
	safe [seɪf]	sicher; ungefährlich	*safe* ↔ dangerous
	close [kləʊs]	nahe	Don't go too *close* to the ravens.
13	**audio tour** ['ɔ:diəʊ ˌtʊə]	Audioführung	! Achtung Aussprache. *Fr.* audio-; *Lat.* audire
	treasure ['treʒə]	Schatz	Just look and you can find real *treasures* in the Thames.
15	to **jump back** [ˌdʒʌmp‿'bæk]	zurückspringen; *hier:* zurückschrecken	My mum *jumps back* when she sees a mouse.

Action UK! A day out in London

	a day out in … [ə ˌdeɪ‿'aʊt ɪn]	ein Tag in …	What would you like to do on *a day out in* London?
2	**out and about** [ˌaʊt‿ən‿ə'baʊt]	unterwegs	
3	**adult** ['ædʌlt]	Erwachsene/-r	*adult* ↔ child
	sightseeing ['saɪtsi:ɪŋ]	Sightseeing-; Besichtigungs-	
	normal ['nɔ:ml]	normal	Is it better to take the sightseeing bus or the *normal* one?
4	**choice** [tʃɔɪs]	Wahl; Auswahl	*choice* → to choose *Fr.* choix *(f)*
	location [ləʊ'keɪʃn]	Handlungsort; Lage; Standort	The *location* of the film is a famous street in London. *Lat.* locus *(m)*
	crowd [kraʊd]	Menschenmenge	A lot of people all together in one place.

Out and about in the city

to **take** the bus / the Underground	den Bus / die U-Bahn nehmen
to **go for a walk** in the streets / in a park / along the river	in den Straßen / im Park / am Fluss entlang spazieren gehen
to **sit** in a café / restaurant	in einem Café / Restaurant sitzen
to **have** lunch / dinner	zu Mittag / zu Abend essen
to **go** shopping / to the cinema	einkaufen / ins Kino gehen
to **visit** a sight / a tourist attraction / a museum / a historical building / the zoo	eine Sehenswürdigkeit / eine Touristenattraktion / ein Museum / ein historisches Gebäude / den Zoo besichtigen; besuchen
to **see** famous people / the sights / lots of interesting things	berühmte Leute / die Sehenswürdigkeiten / viele interessante Dinge sehen
to **listen** to street musicians / an audio tour	Straßenmusikern / einer Audioguide-Führung zuhören
to **watch** a football game / a street show	ein Fußballspiel / eine Straßenshow ansehen

What would you like to do in London?

Skills: How to find information on the internet

1	**attraction** [ə'trækʃn]	Attraktion; Sehenswürdigkeit	The London Eye is one of the city's most popular *attractions*.
	basic ['beɪsɪk]	grundlegend; Grund-	In the first two years of English you learn a lot of *basic* words.
	display [dɪ'spleɪ]	Ausstellung	The Natural History Museum has a great *display* with strange animals at the moment.

Unit task: Our London tour

on foot [ɒn 'fʊt]	zu Fuß	by car/train/bus, *but: on foot*
distance ['dɪstns]	Distanz; Entfernung	What's the *distance* from here to there? *Fr.* distance *(f)*
realistic [ˌrɪə'lɪstɪk]	realistisch	Are your plans *realistic*?
material [mə'tɪəriəl]	Material	

Story: I'm a mudlark

mudlark ['mʌdlɑ:k]	*jemand, der im Schlamm nach Sachen sucht, die er dann verkaufen kann*	
high tide ['haɪ ˌtaɪd]	Flut	
low tide ['ləʊ ˌtaɪd]	Ebbe	The River Thames has two faces – one at high tide, one at *low tide.*
to **flow out** [fləʊ‿'aʊt]	hinausfließen	Rivers *flow out* into the sea.
towards [tə'wɔ:dz]	in Richtung; auf … zu; darauf zu	Look, that man is coming *towards* us.
central ['sentrl]	zentral; Zentral-	*central* → centre ***Lat.*** centrum *(nt)*
heart [hɑ:t]	Herz; *hier:* Zentrum	the *heart* of London = the centre of London
metre ['mi:tə]	Meter	
muddy ['mʌdi]	schlammig	
bank [bæŋk]	Ufer	A river has two *banks.*
wobbly ['wɒbli]	wackelig	
bridge [brɪdʒ]	Brücke	A *bridge* goes over a river. 
silver ['sɪlvə]	Silber	
to **grab** [græb]	greifen; ergreifen; schnappen	Holly *grabbed* her bag and left the house quickly.
wrist [rɪst]	Handgelenk	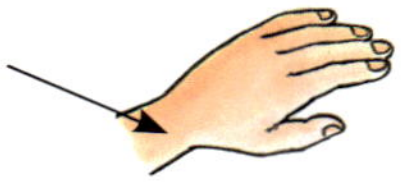
to **drop** [drɒp]	fallen (lassen)	Jay *dropped* Amir's bracelet.
to **roll off** [rəʊl]	hinunterrollen; herunterrollen	The bracelet *rolled* off the bridge.
It's gone. [ɪts 'gɒn]	Es ist weg.	
down [daʊn]	nach unten; herunter; hinunter	They looked *down* from the bridge.
to **be lucky** [bi‿'lʌki]	Glück haben	I'*m lucky.* = Ich habe Glück. I'm happy. = Ich bin glücklich.
mud [mʌd]	Schlamm	*mud* → muddy → mudlark
shore [ʃɔ:]	Ufer; Küste	*shore* = bank
wet [wet]	nass	
bucket ['bʌkɪt]	Eimer	
trowel ['traʊəl]	kleiner Spaten	

	century ['senʃri]	Jahrhundert	We live in the 21st *century*.
	anyway ['eniweɪ]	trotzdem; jedenfalls; sowieso	
	pollution [pə'lu:ʃn]	Verschmutzung	*Pollution* made the river dirty.
	dead [ded]	tot	
	to **wash up** [ˌwɒʃ‿'ʌp]	angespült werden	Dead animals *washed up* on the river banks.
	all the time [ˌɔ:l ðə 'taɪm]	die ganze Zeit	I use my phone almost *all the time*.
	human body [ˌhju:mən 'bɒdi]	menschlicher Körper	
	clay pipe ['kleɪ paɪp]	Tonpfeife	
	at first [ət 'fɜ:st]	zuerst; zunächst	*At first* Luke didn't like Jay very much, but then they became good friends.
	key [ki:]	Schlüssel	
	to **scream** [skri:m]	schreien; kreischen	Holly *screamed* because she found something awful.
	coconut ['kəʊkənʌt]	Kokosnuss	
	dramatic [drə'mætɪk]	dramatisch	*dramatic* → drama *Fr.* dramatique
	hour [aʊə]	Stunde	There are 24 *hours* in a day. ***Lat.*** hora *(f)*
	to **be surprised** [bi sə'praɪzd]	überrascht sein	They *were surprised* about all the 'treasure' in the mud!
2	**modern** ['mɒdn]	modern	Smartphones are *modern* technology. *Fr.* moderne

Water words

sea – river – lake – pond	Meer – Fluss – See – Teich
high tide – low tide – wave	Flut – Ebbe – Welle
to flow out – to flow towards … – to wash up	hinausfließen – in Richtung … fließen – anspülen
bank – shore	Ufer
bridge	Brücke
mud – muddy – wet	Schlamm – schlammig – nass
ship – boat	Schiff – Boot

Check-out

3	**comfortable** ['kʌmftəbl]	komfortabel; bequem	This sofa is really *comfortable*.
	carpet ['kɑ:pɪt]	Teppich	

Unit 4 Sport is good for you!

Check-in

	experience [ɪk'spɪəriəns]	Erfahrung	What interesting *experiences* can you tell us about?
	health [helθ]	Gesundheit	*health* → healthy
	accident ['æksɪdnt]	Unfall	My sister had a bike *accident*. *Fr.* accident *(m)*
	camel racing ['kæml ˌreɪsɪŋ]	Kamelrennen	Is *camel racing* really a sport?
	marathon ['mærəθn]	Marathon	
1	**radio** ['reɪdiəʊ]	Radio	! Achtung Aussprache. *Fr.* radio *(f)*
	programme ['prəʊgræm]	Programm; Sendung	There's an interesting *programme* about camel racing on TV now. *Fr.* programme *(m)*
	runner ['rʌnə]	Läufer/-in	*runner* → to run
	race [reɪs]	Wettlauf; Rennen	Can we watch the bike *race* on TV, Mum?
	net [net]	Netz	For tennis, you need a *net*. 
	to **lose, lost, lost** [lu:z; lɒst; lɒst]	verlieren	Our team *lost* again!
	match [mætʃ]	Spiel; Match	a game (of football/…)
	racquet ['rækɪt]	Schläger	
	court [kɔ:t]	Spielfeld	! a tennis *court* – a football field
	to **pass** [pɑ:s]	zupassen; zuspielen	
	to **kick** [kɪk]	schießen; treten	'Pass' means to throw or *kick* the ball to another player in the same team.
	stadium ['steɪdiəm]	Stadion	
	score [skɔ:]	Punktestand; Spielstand	At the end of the match the *score* was 2-2.
	point [pɔɪnt]	Punkt	That's right. One *point* for your team.
	to **catch, caught, caught** [kætʃ; kɔ:t; kɔ:t]	fangen	*to catch* a ball ↔ to throw a ball
	pitch [pɪtʃ]	Spielfeld; Platz	You play rugby on a *pitch*.
2	**the … the** [ðə … ðə]	je … desto	*The* quicker you are with your homework, *the* earlier you can meet your friends.
4	**equipment** [ɪ'kwɪpmənt]	Ausstattung; Ausrüstung	*equipment* = things you need for sports activities

	individual [ˌɪndɪ'vɪdʒuəl]	individuell; einzeln	Do you do an *individual* sport or a team sport? *Lat.* individuus/-a/-um

Station 1: Have you ever run in a marathon?

	right here [ˌraɪt 'hɪə]	genau hier	The marathon starts *right here*.
	until [ʌn'tɪl]	bis; erst wenn	You can't run in a marathon *until* you're 18.
	11-year-old [ɪˌlevn'jɪərəʊld]	11-Jährige/-r	The mini marathon is for *11-* to *18-year-olds*.
	running ['rʌnɪŋ]	Laufen; Rennen	Gwen loves *running*.
	trial [traɪəl]	Qualifikation	There are *trials* in sports to find the best runners or players.
	Who's in? [hu:z‿'ɪn]	Wer macht mit?; Wer ist dabei?	
	to **be in** [bi‿'ɪn]	dabei sein; mitmachen	Are you going to run? Well, I'*m in*, and I hope you are too!
	run [rʌn]	Rennen; Lauf	*a run* → to run → runner
	to **look out** [ˌlʊk‿'aʊt]	aufpassen	*Look out*, everyone! I'm going to win this race!
1	**area** ['eəriə]	Areal; Gebiet; Fläche	What sports events are there in your *area*?
2	**before** [bɪ'fɔ:]	schon einmal; vorher; zuvor	Have you been here *before*? Or is this your first trip?
4	**leg** [leg]	Bein	

Parts of the body

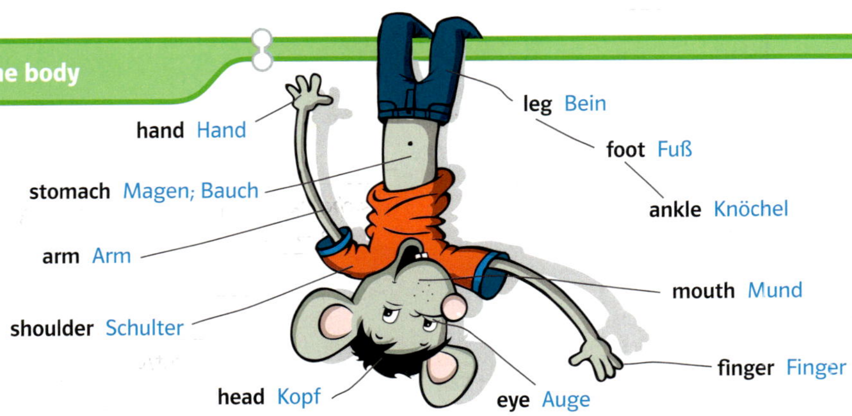

Read the English words to your partner in a different order. Can he/she point to the right part of his/her body?

Station 2: Have you been to the doctor's yet?

doctor ['dɒktə]	Arzt/Ärztin	! Beachte den Unterschied: Have you seen the *doctor* yet? Have you been to the *doctor's* yet? *doctor's* ist die Abkürzung für *doctor's surgery*. *Fr.* docteur *(m)*
yet [jet]	schon; noch	Have you asked your parents about the party *yet*?

	to **leave, left, left** [li:v; left; left]	losgehen	
	not ... yet [nɒt 'jet]	noch nicht	The friends have*n't* left for the marathon *yet*.
	to **train** [treɪn]	trainieren	Luke plays football. He *trains* every day.
	to **hurt, hurt, hurt** [hɜ:t; hɜ:t; hɜ:t]	verletzen; weh tun	I *hurt* my leg last month, and it still *hurts* now.
	to **twist your ankle** [ˌtwɪst jɔ:r‿'æŋkl]	sich den Knöchel verrenken	
	pain [peɪn]	Schmerz	I've got a really bad *pain* in my left foot.
	unfair [ʌn'feə]	unfair	*unfair* ↔ fair
	Bye! [baɪ]	Tschüss!	*bye* ↔ hello
6	**mile** [maɪl]	Meile *(brit. Längenmaß)*	1 *mile* = 1,609 metres
	chant [tʃɑ:nt]	Sprechgesang	***Lat.*** cantare
	to **cheer** [tʃɪə]	anfeuern; jubeln; zujubeln	Jay is writing a chant to *cheer* the runners in the marathon.
8	to **have a look (at)** [ˌhæv‿ə 'lʊk]	anschauen	Let's *have a look* at it. = Let's look at it.
	shouldn't ['ʃʊdnt]	sollte(n) nicht	Olivia *shouldn't* run in the marathon with ankle problems.
	prescription [prɪ'skrɪpʃn]	Rezept *(für Arzneimittel)*	***Lat.*** praescribere
	ointment ['ɔɪntmənt]	Salbe	The doctor gave Olivia a prescription for an *ointment*.
	shoulder ['ʃəʊldə]	Schulter	
	headache *(no pl)* ['hedeɪk]	Kopfschmerzen; Kopfweh	! *headache* steht immer im Singular: I've got a bad *headache*. *headache* → head
	backache ['bækeɪk]	Rückenschmerzen; Rückenweh	
	stomachache ['stʌməkeɪk]	Bauchschmerzen; Bauchweh	
	to **feel sick** [ˌfi:l 'sɪk]	Übelkeit verspüren; sich schlecht fühlen	I *feel sick*. = Mir ist schlecht/übel.
	cold [kəʊld]	Erkältung	
	cough [kɒf]	Husten	
	fever ['fi:və]	Fieber	People with a cold often have a cough and a *fever*. ***Fr.*** fièvre *(f)*
	pill [pɪl]	Pille; Tablette	The doctor wrote a prescription for some *pills*.

Health

to **have an accident**	einen Unfall haben
to **call the emergency service**	den Rettungsdienst rufen
to **hurt your foot / arm / leg / …**	sich den Fuß / Arm / das Bein / … verletzen
to **twist your ankle**	sich den Knöchel verrenken
to **feel a pain in …**	Schmerzen haben in / an …
to **get a prescription**	ein Rezept bekommen
to **put ointment on …**	… einsalben
to **take pills**	Tabletten nehmen
to **have a headache / backache / stomachache**	Kopfweh / Rückenweh / Bauchweh haben
to **feel bad / sick**	sich schlecht / krank fühlen
to **catch a cold / cough / fever**	eine Erkältung / Husten / Fieber bekommen

With a partner, make more doctor dialogues as on p. 73.

Station 3: An interview with Ayla

	should [ʃʊd]	sollte; solltest; sollten; solltet	In a race you *should* wear real running shoes, an you *shouldn't* run too fast.
	cramp [kræmp]	Krampf	
	award [ə'wɔ:d]	Auszeichnung; Preis	Ayla has won a Maths *award* but no sports *award*.
	… what it's like [ˌwɒt‿ɪts 'laɪk]	… wie das ist	Do you know *what it's like* when you break something?
13	**almost** ['ɔ:lməʊst]	fast; beinahe	It's *almost* 8 o'clock! You're late for school.
	player ['pleɪə]	Spieler/-in; Mitspieler/-in	*player* → to play
	so far [ˌsəʊ 'fɑ:]	bis jetzt	The players have given the people a great show *so far*.

Action UK! A picnic in the park

1	**attic** ['ætɪk]	Dachboden	
	Korean [kə'ri:ən]	koreanisch; Koreanisch; Koreaner/-in	There was *Korean* food at the picnic.
2	to **fake** [feɪk]	vortäuschen; fälschen	
	injury ['ɪndʒəri]	Verletzung	Who faked an *injury* in the film?
	to **teach somebody a lesson** [ˌti:tʃ‿ə 'lesn]	jmdm. eine Lehre/Lektion erteilen	That wasn't a nice thing to do. Let's *teach him a lesson*.
	to **teach, taught, taught** [ti:tʃ; tɔ:t; tɔ:t]	unterrichten; lehren; beibringen	*to teach* → teacher

to **deserve** [dɪ'zɜːv]	verdienen	The others are angry with you, but you *deserved* it. You tricked them!
point of view [ˌpɔɪnt‿əv 'vjuː]	Standpunkt; Ansicht; Perspektive	Who's right and who's wrong from your *point of view*?
to **get away with** [ˌget‿ə'weɪ wɪð]	davonkommen mit	Marley didn't *get away with* it.

Skills: How to understand news reports and take notes

1	**rescue** ['reskjuː]	Rettung	Here is a report about a *rescue* in the mountains.
	difficult ['dɪfɪklt]	schwierig	*difficult* ↔ easy *Fr.* difficil/-e; ***Lat.*** difficilis/-e
	witness ['wɪtnəs]	Zeuge/Zeugin	The police is looking for *witnesses* for the accident.
2	**eyewitness** ['aɪwɪtnəs]	Augenzeuge/Augenzeugin	The reporter is talking to an *eyewitness* in front of the camera.
	station ['steɪʃn]	Sender	What's your favourite radio *station*?
	listener ['lɪsənə]	Zuhörer/-in	*listener* → to listen
	to **receive** [rɪ'siːv]	empfangen; erhalten; bekommen	A formal word for 'to get'. *Fr.* recevoir; ***Lat.*** recipere
	scene [siːn]	Schauplatz	The reporter was trying to get to the *scene* of the accident.

Unit task: The aliens have landed!

to **land** [lænd]	landen	Do you believe that aliens have ever *landed* on Earth?
to **record** [rɪ'kɔːd]	aufnehmen; aufzeichnen	Let's *record* the scene with a camera.
assistant [ə'sɪstnt]	Assistent/-in; Verkäufer/-in	! Achtung Schreibung und Aussprache.
to **end** [end]	enden; beenden	*to end* ↔ to start *to end* → end
over ['əʊvə]	vorüber; vorbei	School is *over* at 3:15.

Story: Hey, don't call me silly!

to **let go (of)** [ˌlet 'gəʊ (əv)]	loslassen	Don't *let go of* my hand, Gwen!
silly ['sɪli]	Dummkopf	
fancy dress ['fænsi dres]	Verkleidung; Kostüm	
to **breathe** [briːð]	atmen	
to **keep up, kept, up, kept up (with)** [ˌkiːp‿'ʌp; ˌkept‿'ʌp; ˌkept‿'ʌp (wɪð)]	mithalten (mit); Schritt halten (mit)	Can Luke *keep up with* Gwen? = Is Luke fast enough?

	to **be worried** [bi ˈwʌrid]	beunruhigt sein; besorgt sein	Don't *be worried* = Don't worry
	to **get in the way** [ˌget͜ ɪn ðə ˈweɪ]	stören; im Weg stehen	The people in the costumes shouldn't *get in the way* of the runners.
	stomach [ˈstʌmək]	Magen; Bauch	*Fr.* estomac *(m)* 
	glasses *(pl)* [ˈglɑːsɪz]	Brille	! *glasses* steht immer im Plural: My *glasses* are broken. I need new ones.
	finish line [ˈfɪnɪʃ ˌlaɪn]	Ziellinie	At the end of a run there's always a *finish line*.
	stupid [ˈstjuːpɪd]	dumm; blöd	The *stupid* cat and dog almost ruined the race for Gwen and Luke.
	to **be gone** [biː ˈgɒn]	verschwunden sein; weg sein	Near the end of the race, Gwen's cramp *was gone*.
	We did it! [ˌwiː ˈdɪd͜ ɪt]	Wir haben es geschafft!	*Luke and Gwen did it!*
	both [bəʊθ]	beide	Luke and Gwen *both* finished the race.
	to **ruin** [ˈruːɪn]	ruinieren; zerstören	Jay and Dave almost *ruined* the race for Luke and Gwen.
	official [əˈfɪʃl]	Schiedsrichter/-in	In a race there are always *officials*.
	to **surprise** [səˈpraɪz]	überraschen	*to surprise* → surprise
	in secret [ɪn ˈsiːkrət]	heimlich	Jay and Dave trained *in secret*. No one knew about it. *in secret* → a secret
	because of [bɪˈkɒz͜ əv]	wegen	My feet really hurt *because of* my new shoes.
	to **forgive, forgave, forgiven** [fəˈgɪv; fəˈgeɪv; fəˈgɪvn]	vergeben; verzeihen	Can Gwen *forgive* them?
1	**reason** [ˈriːzn]	Grund	Why did you do it? What was the *reason*? *Fr.* raison *(f)*
	to **cause** [kɔːz]	verursachen	What or who *caused* the accident?
	hope [həʊp]	Hoffnung	*hope* → to hope
	fear [fɪə]	Angst; Furcht; Befürchtung	The feeling you have when you are scared.
	relationship [rɪˈleɪʃnʃɪp]	Beziehung	Is the *relationship* between you and your neighbours a good one?
2	**On the one hand ..., (but) on the other hand ...** [ɒn ðə ˈwʌn ˌhænd ... (bʌt) ɒn ði͜ ˈʌðə ˌhænd ...]	Einerseits ..., (aber) andererseits ...	*On the one hand* he'd like to be a better runner, *but on the other hand* he doesn't want to train very hard.

Positive and negative words

	+	−
What you think of something:	easy, good, great, interesting, useful; *stronger words:* amazing, fantastic, perfect	bad, boring, dangerous, difficult; *stronger words:* awful, scary
What you think of a person:	beautiful, creative, cute, fair, friendly, fun, funny, good, polite, popular	aggressive, boring, rude, silly, stupid, unfair, unfriendly
How a person feels:	confident, good, happy, lucky	bad, embarrassed, lonely, sad, shy, unhappy, unlucky

Which of the words are opposites? Write them down together.

Check-out

3	**bicycle motocross** [ˌbaɪsɪkl 'məʊtəʊkrɒs]	Fahrradmotocross	The word 'bike' is short for *'bicycle'*.

Across cultures 2 English around the world

1	**summer camp** ['sʌmə kæmp]	Sommerferienlager	I only spoke English when I was at *summer camp* last year.
2	to **mention** ['menʃn]	erwähnen	Did I *mention* that I have a cool new phone? *Fr.* mentionner
	statement ['steɪtmənt]	Aussage; Behauptung; Erklärung	to make a *statement* = to say something
	exactly [ɪg'zæktli]	genau	I don't understand. What *exactly* do you mean? ***Lat.*** exactus/-a/-um
	as [æz]	wie	My favourite music is not the same *as* yours.
	South Korean [ˌsaʊθ kə'riːən]	Südkoreaner/-in; südkoreanisch; Südkoreanisch	
	Romanian [rʊ'meɪniən]	Rumäne/Rumänin; rumänisch; Rumänisch	
3	**first language** [ˌfɜːst 'læŋgwɪdʒ]	Muttersprache	My *first language* is German.
	official language [əˌfɪʃl 'læŋgwɪdʒ]	Amtssprache	In India, English is an *official language*.
	merchant ['mɜːtʃənt]	Kaufmann, Händler	A *merchant* sells and buys things.
	to **cross** [krɒs]	überqueren; kreuzen	You need to *cross* the street to get to the shoe shop.
	colony ['kɒləni]	Kolonie	Many years ago, Germany had *colonies* too. *Fr.* colonie *(f)*; ***Lat.*** colonia *(f)*

	for example [fər‿ɪg'zɑ:mpl]	zum Beispiel	I speak four languages, *for example* English and French.
	head of state [ˌhed‿əv 'steɪt]	Staatsoberhaupt	The British queen is *head of state* in Australia.
	superpower ['su:pəˌpaʊə]	Supermacht	Will China and India be the next *superpowers*?
	to **influence** ['ɪnfluəns]	beeinflussen	The USA has *influenced* the world in different ways. ! Im Englischen verwendet man für „USA" immer die Einzahl (The USA has …), im Deutschen aber die Mehrzahl (Die USA haben …).
	technology [tek'nɒlədʒi]	Technologie	
	to **communicate** [kə'mju:nɪkeɪt]	kommunizieren; sich verständigen	An easy way to *communicate* with people is to speak to them. ***Lat.*** communicare
4	**region** ['ri:dʒn]	Region; Gegend	What *region* in Germany do you come from? ***Lat.*** regio *(f)*
	expression [ɪk'spreʃn]	Ausdruck; Wendung; Äußerung	We often use English *expressions* in German. ***Lat.*** expressio *(f)*

Unit 5 Stay in touch

Check-in

	to **stay in touch (with)** [ˌsteɪ ɪn 'tʌtʃ (wɪð)]	in Kontakt bleiben (mit)	E-mails are a good way to *stay in touch* with your friends.
	media ['mi:diə]	Medien	Radio, TV and the internet are all *media*. ***Fr.*** médias *(f) (pl)*; ***Lat.*** medium *(nt)*
	letter ['letə]	Brief	 ***Lat.*** littera *(f)*
	interest ['ɪntrəst]	Interesse	*interest* → interesting → be interested
	paradise ['pærədaɪs]	Paradies	***Fr.*** paradis *(m)*
	print [prɪnt]	gedruckt; Druck-	
	for [fɔ:; fə]	wegen	I buy print magazines *for* the posters.
	social network [ˌsəʊʃl 'netwɜ:k]	soziales Netzwerk	You can chat with all kinds of people in *social networks*.
	nasty ['nɑ:sti]	garstig; gemein	*nasty* ↔ nice
	cyber bully [ˌsaɪbə 'bʊli]	*jemand, der andere in sozialen Netzwerken belästigt oder mobbed*	*Cyber bullies* write nasty comments in social networks.
2	to **change** [tʃeɪndʒ]	wechseln; (sich) ändern	I *changed* my phone number. A stupid cyber bully was sending me nasty texts. ***Fr.*** changer
	to **post** [pəʊst]	online stellen; posten	Have you *posted* the photos of the class trip?

to **take part (in)** [ˌteɪk ˈpɑːt (ɪn)]	teilnehmen (an)	Let's *take part in* the new Drama Club at school.
to **text** [tekst]	eine SMS schicken	*to text* → text message
discussion [dɪˈskʌʃn]	Diskussion	*discussion* → to discuss
3 **practical** [ˈpræktɪkl]	praktisch	Smartphones are *practical* to stay in touch with friends. *Fr.* pratique
mobile [ˈməʊbaɪl]	Handy; Mobiltelefon	*mobile* = phone

Media collocations

to check	checken, überprüfen	my e-mails / my profile / my friend's profile	meine E-Mails / mein Profil / das Profil meines Freundes
to change	ändern	my profile	mein Profil
to post to share	posten; hochladen teilen	photos / information about …	Fotos / Informationen über …
to read / to write / to reply to	lesen / schreiben / antworten auf	texts / text messages / e-mails	SMS-Nachrichten / E-Mails
to send / to receive	senden / empfangen	texts / text messages / e-mails / photos / information	SMS-Nachrichten / E-Mails / Fotos / Informationen
to chat with to text to stay in touch with	chatten mit eine SMS schreiben in Kontakt bleiben mit	a friend	einem Freund
to join to take part in	beitreten teilnehmen an	a discussion / a social network / a forum	einer Diskussion / einem sozialen Netzwerk / einem Forum
to have to take part in	führen teilnehmen an	a discussion / a video chat	eine Diskussion / einen Videochat einer Diskussion / einem Videochat
to play	spielen	video games	Computerspiele

Station 1: Dear Ruby

agony aunt [ˈæɡəniˌɑːnt]	Kummerkastentante	Lauren didn't want to talk about her problem with her friends or her family. So she wrote a letter to her favourite magazine's *agony aunt*.
teen [tiːn]	Jugend-	*teen* → teenager

	... what to do. ['wɒt tə du:]	... was ich tun soll.	I don't know *what to do*.
	to **spend, spent, spent** [spend; spent; spent]	verbringen *(Zeit)*	 She *spends* all her free time with her dog.
	the two of them [ðə 'tu:‿əv ðəm]	beide	My brothers sent me a photo of *the two of them*.
	site [saɪt]	Webseite	
	to **act like** ['ækt laɪk]	tun als ob	My sister often *acts like* a baby.
	whenever [wen'evə]	wann immer; jedes Mal, wenn; so oft	*Whenever* I ask my brother for something, he says "no".
	self-critical ['self‚krɪtɪkl]	selbstkritisch	The agony aunt's advice is to be *self-critical*. I think she's right.
	to **overreact** [‚əʊvəri'ækt]	überreagieren	I know you're angry with him, but don't *overreact* and say bad things about him, OK?
	as soon as [əz 'su:n‿əz]	sobald	Things usually get better *as soon as* you talk to the person you're fighting with.
	to **make somebody do something** [meɪk]	jmdn. dazu bringen, etw. zu tun	My friend's texts *make* me *feel bad*.
1	**opinion** [ə'pɪnjən]	Meinung	In my *opinion* ... = I think ... ***Lat.*** opinio *(f)*
2	**face-to-face** [‚feɪstə'feɪs]	*hier:* persönlich; von Angesicht zu Angesicht	It's fun to meet people *face-to-face* and not just in social networks. 
	to **block** [blɒk]	blockieren; abblocken	You can *block* messages from people you don't like.
	forever [fə'revə]	für immer; ewig	Photos that you post on the internet never go away. They can stay there *forever*.
	to **care (about)** ['keər‿ə‚baʊt]	wichtig nehmen; sich kümmern (um); sich interessieren (für)	If you *care about* something then it's important to you.
	attention [ə'tenʃn]	Aufmerksamkeit; Beachtung	***Fr.*** attention *(f)*; ***Lat.*** attentio *(f)*
	myself [maɪ'self]	ich/mir/mich (selbst); selber	*myself* → yourself → himself
4	**understanding** [‚ʌndə'stændɪŋ]	Verständnis	What can you say to show *understanding*?
	compromise ['kɒmprəmaɪz]	Kompromiss	It isn't always easy to find a *compromise*. ***Fr.*** compromis *(m)*
	to **worry** ['wʌri]	sich Sorgen machen	Don't *worry* about your friend. Everything is OK now.
5	**up** [ʌp]	hinauf; nach oben	She looked *up* and down the street.
6	**friendship** ['frendʃɪp]	Freundschaft	I've got lots of friends. I think *friendship* is very important.

Station 2: Forum? What forum?

to **be allowed to (do sth)** [bi‿ə'laʊd tə]	dürfen	Students *aren't allowed to* use mobiles at school.
to **go over to** [ˌɡəʊ 'əʊvə tə]	hinübergehen zu; zu jmdm. nach Hause gehen	Come on, let's *go over* to your house.
What on earth ...? [ˌwɒt:‿ɒn‿'ɜ:θ]	Was um alles in der Welt ...?	*What on earth* is this?
to **fix** [fɪks]	reparieren; befestigen	My bike is broken. Can you *fix* it?
to **go crazy** [ˌɡəʊ 'kreɪzi]	ausflippen; durchdrehen; verrückt werden	I think I'm *going crazy*: I don't understand the Maths homework at all!
to **take, took, taken** [teɪk; tʊk; 'teɪkn]	dauern; (Zeit) brauchen	It *takes* two hours to get to London by train.
washing machine ['wɒʃɪŋ məˌʃi:n]	Waschmaschine	*washing machine* → to wash 
to **waste** [weɪst]	verschwenden	You're *wasting* your time, Dad!
cannot ['kænɒt]	kann nicht; können nicht	*cannot* = can't
step-by-step [ˌstepbaɪ'step]	Schritt-für-Schritt-	On the internet, there's *step-by-step* advice for everything.
to **be able to (do sth)** [bi‿'eɪbl tə]	fähig sein zu; können; dürfen	When my grandma lived in the next town, we *were able to* see her often. Now she lives in another town.
still [stɪl]	dennoch	I don't have any money, but I'm *still* going to go to London.
I've done this a million times before. [ˌaɪv dʌn ðɪs ə ˌmɪljən taɪmz bɪ'fɔ:]	Ich habe das schon eine Million Mal gemacht.	
knob [nɒb]	Griff	Cupboard doors often have *knobs*.
to **reach** [ri:tʃ]	erreichen; dran kommen	My mum put the chocolate on top of the cupboard so my little sister can't *reach* it.
to **work** [wɜ:k]	*hier:* funktionieren	Is the washing machine *working* again?
genius ['dʒi:niəs]	Genie	*Fr.* génie *(m)*
With a very big head! [ˌwɪð ə ˌveri bɪɡ 'hed]	Und ein Angeber!	
may [meɪ]	(vielleicht) können; dürfen	! Wenn du auf Englisch nach etwas fragst oder um etwas bittest, beginne deine Frage mit *may*: *May* I take another piece of cake, please?
13 **mad** [mæd]	verrückt	My parents think that I'm media *mad*.
result [rɪ'zʌlt]	Ergebnis; Resultat	Have we got the test *results* yet? Who got the most points? *Fr.* résultat *(m)*
to **(e-)mail** ['i:meɪl]	mailen; per E-Mail schicken	Could you *e-mail* me your part of the class project? I can *mail* you my part too.
to **download** [ˌdaʊn'ləʊd]	herunterladen *(aus dem Internet)*	

to **comment (on)** ['kɒment‿(ɒn)]	kommentieren	Please don't *comment* on my test results; I didn't do very well at all! *to comment* → a comment
to **stay away from** [ˌsteɪ‿ə'weɪ frəm]	fernbleiben von; meiden	*Stay away from* too much chocolate. It isn't good for your health.
in other ways [ɪn‿'ʌðə weɪz]	auf andere Weise	I don't need my phone all the time. I can have fun *in other ways* too.

Skills: How to write a letter and a reply

1	**camping** ['kæmpɪŋ]	Camping; Zelten	We go *camping* every year!
	to **miss** [mɪs]	verpassen; versäumen	Hey, you *missed* a great party! Where were you?
	Yours ... [jɔːz]	Viele Grüße ... *(am Ende von Briefen und Mails)*	! You can end a letter or e-mail like this.
	to **begin, began, begun** [bɪ'gɪn; bɪ'gæn; bɪ'gʌn]	beginnen; anfangen	How do you *begin* a letter or e-mail?
	beach [biːtʃ]	Strand	
2	**weird** [wɪəd]	merkwürdig; seltsam; sonderbar	*weird* = strange

Unit task: Advice letters and replies: Our collection

chance [tʃɑːns]	Chance; Gelegenheit; Möglichkeit	Give me another *chance*, please!
weekday ['wiːkdeɪ]	Wochentag	On *weekday* mornings I usually go to school.
to **do about** ['duː‿əˌbaʊt]	unternehmen wegen	What can I *do about* my teacher? I don't think she likes me.

Story: It's a disaster!

disaster [dɪ'zɑːstə]	Desaster; Katastrophe; Unglück	Frank's day was a *disaster*. ***Fr.*** désastre *(m)*
to **rain** [reɪn]	regnen	It's *raining*! 
light [laɪt]	Licht; Lampe	At night you need *light*.
to **be on** [bi‿'ɒn]	an sein; laufen	The race *is on*.
thunder *(no pl)* ['θʌndə]	Donner	In a storm there's usually *thunder* and lightning.

lightning *(no pl)* ['laɪtnɪŋ]	Blitz	
to **get out of** [get ˌɛʊt ̮əv]	aussteigen	He *got out of* the car quickly and ran to the house.
front door [ˌfrʌnt 'dɔ:]	Haustür	Every house has a *front door*.
upstairs [ʌp'steəz]	nach oben; im Obergeschoss; oben	
headphones *(pl)* ['hedfəʊnz]	Kopfhörer	 Take my *headphones* and listen to this!
downstairs [ˌdaʊn'steəz]	nach unten; im Untergeschoss; unten	*downstairs* ↔ upstairs
to **tap** [tæp]	antippen	Jay *tapped* Olivia's shoulder.
to **cry** [kraɪ]	schreien; rufen	*to cry* = to shout ***Fr.*** crier
to **fight, fought, fought** [faɪt; fɔ:t; fɔ:t]	kämpfen; (sich) streiten	My brother and I often *fight*.
to **joke** [dʒəʊk]	scherzen	Don't worry, I'm only *joking*! *to joke* → a joke ***Lat.*** iocus *(m)*
to **press** [pres]	drücken; pressen	***Fr.*** presser
to **go black** [ˌgəʊ 'blæk]	schwarz werden	After the bang everything *went black*.
to **crash** [kræʃ]	abstürzen	Has your computer ever *crashed*?
power cut ['paʊə ˌkʌt]	Stromausfall	
round [raʊnd]	um … herum	Five minutes later they all sat *round* the table.
candlelight *(no pl)* ['kændlaɪt]	Kerzenlicht	
only ['əʊnli]	einzige/-r/-s	I'm the *only* girl in my tutor group without glasses.
right now [ˌraɪt 'naʊ]	jetzt gleich; sofort; gerade	*Right now* I don't have any problems.
to **cook** [kʊk]	kochen	Have you ever *cooked* an Indian curry?
to **show off** [ʃəʊ ̮'ɒf]	angeben	My brother always *shows off* with his expensive smartphone.
to **borrow** ['bɒrəʊ]	(sich) ausleihen	Can I *borrow* this t-shirt? – OK, but please remember to give it back.
1 to **feel left out** [ˌfi:l left ̮'aʊt]	sich ausgeschlossen fühlen	Did Frank *feel left out*?
2 to **link** [lɪŋk]	verbinden	

Dictionary

In dieser alphabetischen Wortliste findest du das gesamte Vokabular von *Green Line* 1 und 2.
Namen stehen in einer extra Liste am Ende des ***Dictionary***.
Einträge, die aus mehreren Wörtern bestehen, kannst du meist unter verschiedenen Stichwörtern nachschlagen. So ist z.B. *at home* unter *at* und unter *home* eingetragen.
Die Fundstellen stehen immer hinter dem jeweiligen Wort und zeigen dir an, wo es zum ersten Mal vorkommt, z.B.:
accident ['æksɪdnt]] Unfall **II U4,** 69 kommt zum ersten Mal vor in Band II, Unit 4, Seite 69
U = Unit, AC = Across cultures
Die mit * gekennzeichneten Verben sind unregelmäßig.
Die mit ° gekennzeichneten Vokabeln sind rezeptiv.

A

a [ə] ein/-e **I**
a bit [ə 'bɪt] ein bisschen; ein wenig **II U1**, 18
a couple of [ə 'kʌpl͜əv] ein paar **I**
a few [ə 'fju:] ein paar; wenige; einige **I**
a girl from Germany [ə ˌgɜ:l frəm 'dʒɜ:məni] ein Mädchen aus Deutschland **I**
a group of three [ə ˌgru:p͜əv 'θri:] eine Dreiergruppe **I**
a little [ə 'lɪtl] ein wenig; etwas **I**
a lot [ə 'lɒt] viel **I**
a lot of [ə 'lɒt͜əv] viel/-e; eine Menge **I**
a lot to learn [ə ˌlɒt tə 'lɜ:n] viel zu lernen **I**
a.m. [ˌeɪ'em] vormittags *(Uhrzeit)* **I**
*to be **able** to (do sth) [bi͜ˈeɪbl tə] fähig sein zu; können; dürfen **II U5**, 95
aboard [ə'bɔ:d] an Bord **I**
about [ə'baʊt] ungefähr; circa; etwa **I**
out and **about** [ˌaʊt͜ən͜ə'baʊt] unterwegs **II U3**, 58
about [ə'baʊt] über; von **I**
What **about** ...? ['wɒt͜əˌbaʊt] Wie wär's mit ...?; Was ist mit ...? **I**
What is ... **about**? [ˌwɒt͜ɪz ...͜ə'baʊt] Worum geht es in/im ...? **I**
above [ə'bʌv] oben **°II U3**, 53
absolutely [ˌæbsə'lu:tli] absolut; völlig **II U2**, 42
accident ['æksɪdnt] Unfall **II U4**, 69
across [ə'krɒs] auf der anderen Seite von; über; hinüber; herüber; quer durch **I**
Across cultures [əˌkrɒs 'kʌltʃəz] Interkulturelles **I**
to **act** [ækt] spielen *(Theater)* **I**
to **act** like ['ækt laɪk] tun als ob **II U5**, 92
to **act** out [ækt 'aʊt] nachspielen **°II AC2**, 88
acting a scene [ˌæktɪŋ͜ə 'si:n] eine Theaterszene spielen **I**
action ['ækʃn] Handlung; Action; Aktion **I**
activity [æk'tɪvəti] Aktivität **I**
actor ['æktə] Schauspieler **II U2**, 36
to **add** [æd] hinzufügen; ergänzen **I**
additional [ə'dɪʃnl] zusätzlich **II U2**, 28
address [ə'dres] Adresse **I**
adjective ['ædʒɪktɪv] Adjektiv; Eigenschaftswort **°II U1**, 16
adult ['ædʌlt] Erwachsene/-r **II U3**, 58
adventure [əd'ventʃə] Abenteuer **II U1**, 16
adverb ['ædvɜ:b] Adverb **°II U3**, 51
advice [əd'vaɪs] Rat; Ratschlag **II U2**, 36
after ['ɑ:ftə] nach *(zeitlich)* **I**
after all [ˌɑ:ftər͜'ɔ:l] doch; schließlich; immerhin **I**
after that [ˌɑ:ftə 'ðæt] danach **I**
afternoon [ˌɑ:ftə'nu:n] Nachmittag **I**
this **afternoon** [ðɪs 'ɑ:ftənu:n] heute Nachmittag **II U3**, 52
again [ə'gen] wieder; noch einmal; noch mal **I**
against [ə'genst] gegen **II U1**, 19
aggressive [ə'gresɪv] aggressiv **II U1**, 24
ago [ə'gəʊ] vor *(zeitlich)* **II U1**, 10
agony aunt ['ægəni͜ˌɑ:nt] Kummerkastentante **II U5**, 92
to **agree** (with) [ə'gri:] einer Meinung sein (mit); zustimmen **°II U5**, 97
airport ['eəpɔ:t] Flughafen **II AC1**, 48
alarm clock [ə'lɑ:m ˌklɒk] Wecker **II U2**, 43
alien ['eɪliən] Außerirdische/-r; außerirdisches Wesen **I**
all [ɔ:l] alle/-s; ganz **I**
after **all** [ˌɑ:ftər͜'ɔ:l] doch; schließlich; immerhin **I**
all day [ˌɔ:l 'deɪ] den ganzen Tag **II U1**, 14
all night [ˌɔ:l 'naɪt] die ganze Nacht **I**
all over [ˌɔ:l͜'əʊvə] überall (in) **I**
all the time [ˌɔ:l ðə 'taɪm] die ganze Zeit **II U3**, 62
at **all** [ət͜'ɔ:l] überhaupt **I**
all of them ['ɔ:l͜əv ˌðem] alle **I**
bowling **alley** ['bəʊlɪŋ͜ˌæli] Bowlingbahn **I**
*to be **allowed** to (do sth) [bi͜ə'laʊd tə] dürfen **II U5**, 95
almost ['ɔ:lməʊst] fast; beinahe **II U4**, 75
alone [ə'ləʊn] allein; ohne fremde Hilfe **I**
along [ə'lɒŋ] entlang **I**
alphabet ['ælfəbet] Alphabet **I**
alphabetical [ˌælfə'betɪkl] alphabetisch **°II U1**, 21
already [ɔ:l'redi] schon; bereits **I**
also ['ɔ:lsəʊ] auch **II U1**, 10
always ['ɔ:lweɪz] immer; ständig **I**
amazing [ə'meɪzɪŋ] unglaublich; toll; erstaunlich **II U1**, 18
American [ə'merɪkən] Amerikanisch; amerikanisch; aus Amerika; Amerikaner/-in **II U1**, 9
an [ən] ein/-e **I**
and [ænd; ənd] und **I**
angry ['æŋgri] wütend; zornig; verärgert; böse **I**
animal ['ænɪməl] Tier **I**
ankle ['æŋkl] Fußgelenk; Fußknöchel **II U4**, 72
to twist your **ankle** [ˌtwɪst jɔ:r͜'æŋkl] sich den Knöchel verrenken **II U4**, 72
anonymous [ə'nɒnɪməs] anonym **II U1**, 13
another [ə'nʌðə] ein/-e andere/-r/-s; noch ein/-e; ein/-e andere/-r/-s **I**
answer ['ɑ:nsə] Antwort **I**
short **answer** [ˌʃɔ:t͜'ɑ:nsə] Kurzantwort **I**
to **answer** ['ɑ:nsə] antworten; beantworten **I**
to **answer** the phone [ˌɑ:nsə ðə 'fəʊn] einen Anruf entgegennehmen **I**
answering machine ['ɑ:nsrɪŋ məˌʃi:n] Anrufbeantworter **I**
any ['eni] irgendein/-e/-er; irgendwelche **I**
not **any** more [ˌnɒt͜eni 'mɔ:] nicht mehr **I**
not ... **any** [nɒt ... eni] kein/-e **I**
anyone else [ˌeniwʌn 'els] jemand anderes **II U2**, 40
Anything else? [ˌeniθɪŋ͜'els] Sonst noch etwas? **I**
not ... **anything** [ˌnɒt 'eniθɪŋ] nichts **I**
anyway ['eniweɪ] trotzdem; jedenfalls; sowieso **II U3**, 62
anywhere ['eniweə] irgendwo; überall (egal, wo) **II U3**, 54
app [æp] App **II U5**, 97
apple ['æpl] Apfel **I**
April ['eɪprəl] April **I**
architect ['ɑ:kɪtekt] Architekt/-in **II U2**, 30
How **are** you? [ˌhaʊ͜'ɑ: jə] Wie geht es dir?; Wie geht es euch?; Wie geht es Ihnen? **I**

area ['eəriə] Areal; Gebiet; Fläche **II U4**, 70
arm [ɑ:m] Arm **II U2**, 41
around [ə'raʊnd] um … herum; umher **I**
to turn **around** [ˌtɜ:n_(ə)'raʊnd] (sich) umdrehen; wenden **II U2**, 41
to **arrest** [ə'rest] festnehmen; verhaften **II U1**, 13
Art [ɑ:t] Kunstunterricht **I**
art [ɑ:t] Kunst **II U2**, 29
article ['ɑ:tɪkl] Artikel; Bericht *(in einer Zeitschrift, Zeitung)* **II U2**, 33
as [æz; əz] als **II U2**, 30
as … **as** [əz … əz] so … wie **I**
as [æz] während; indem **I**; wie **II AC2**, 88
as soon **as** [əz 'su:n_əz] sobald **II U5**, 92
to **ask** [ɑ:sk] fragen; bitten **I**
Ask about … ['ɑ:sk_əˌbaʊt] Frage/Fragt nach … **I**
to **ask** for ['ɑ:sk fə] fragen nach; bitten um **I**
*to be **asleep** [ˌbi ə'sli:p] schlafen **II U1**, 19
*to fall **asleep** [ˌfɔ:l_ə'sli:p] einschlafen **I**
assembly [ə'sembli] Versammlung; Morgenappell **II U2**, 29
assistant [ə'sɪstnt] Assistent/-in; Verkäufer/-in **II U4**, 78
at [æt; ət] in; auf; bei; an; um *(bei Uhrzeitangaben)* **I**
at 7:30 [ət ˌsevn_'θɜ:ti] um halb acht **I**
at all [ət_'ɔ:l] überhaupt **I**
at first [ət 'fɜ:st] zuerst; zunächst **II U3**, 63
at home [ət 'həʊm] zu Hause **I**
at last [ət 'lɑ:st] endlich; schließlich **I**
at least [ət 'li:st] mindestens; wenigstens °**II U3**, 63
at the back of [ət ðə 'bæk_əv] hinten; am Ende; im hinteren Teil °**II U3**, 50
at the moment [ət ðə 'məʊmənt] im Moment; gerade **I**
at the same time [ət ðə ˌseɪm 'taɪm] zur selben Zeit; gleichzeitig **I**
at the weekend [ət ðə ˌwi:k'end] am Wochenende **I**
atlas ['ætləs] Atlas **II AC2**, 88
atmosphere ['ætməsfɪə] Atmosphäre; Stimmung °**II U3**, 58
attention [ə'tenʃn] Aufmerksamkeit; Beachtung **II U5**, 93
attic ['ætɪk] Dachboden **II U4**, 76
attraction [ə'trækʃn] Attraktion; Sehenswürdigkeit **II U3**, 59
audience ['ɔ:diəns] Publikum **II U2**, 37
audio ['ɔ:diəʊ] Audio-; Hör- **I**
audio tour ['ɔ:diəʊ ˌtʊə] Audioführung **II U3**, 56
audio-visual effect [ˌɔ:diəʊvɪʒuəl ɪ'fekt] audiovisueller Effekt °**II U1**, 24
August ['ɔ:gəst] August **I**
aunt [ɑ:nt] Tante **I**
agony **aunt** ['ægəni_ɑ:nt] Kummerkastentante **II U5**, 92
award [ə'wɔ:d] Auszeichnung; Preis **II U4**, 74
away [ə'weɪ] weg **I**
right **away** [ˌraɪt_ə'weɪ] sofort; gleich **I**
*to run **away** [ˌrʌn_ə'weɪ] wegrennen **I**
*to throw **away** [ˌθrəʊ_ə'weɪ] wegwerfen **I**
awful ['ɔ:fl] schrecklich; furchtbar **I**

B

baby ['beɪbi] Baby; Säugling **I**
back to **back** [ˌbæk tʊ 'bæk] Rücken an Rücken **I**
at the **back** of [ət ðə 'bæk_əv] hinten; am Ende; im hinteren Teil °**II U3**, 50
back [bæk] zurück **I**
to turn **back** [tɜ:n 'bæk] umkehren; zurückgehen **II U2**, 41
backache ['bækeɪk] Rückenschmerzen; Rückenweh **II U4**, 73
background ['bækgraʊnd] Hintergrund **I**
bacon ['beɪkn] Schinkenspeck; Speck **I**
bad [bæd] schlecht; böse; schlimm *(ugs.)* **I**
Too **bad**! [ˌtu: 'bæd] Zu dumm!; Schade! **I**
badminton ['bædmɪntən] Badminton **I**
bag [bæg] Tasche; Tüte **I**
baked beans *(pl)* [ˌbeɪkt 'bi:nz] weiße Bohnen in Tomatensoße **I**
ball [bɔ:l] Ball **I**
banana [bə'nɑ:nə] Banane **I**
Bang! [bæŋ] Peng! **II U5**, 102
bank [bæŋk] Ufer **II U3**, 62
snack **bar** ['snæk ˌbɑ:] Café; Imbissstube **I**
bargain ['bɑ:gɪn] Schnäppchen **I**
to **bark** [bɑ:k] bellen **I**
basic ['beɪsɪk] grundlegend; Grund- **II U3**, 59
basketball ['bɑ:skɪtbɔ:l] Basketball **I**
bath [bɑ:θ] Bad; Badewanne **I**
bathroom ['bɑ:θrʊm] Bad; Badezimmer **I**
battery ['bætri] Batterie; Akku **II U1**, 19
*to **be** [bi:] sein **I**
*to **be** able to (do sth) [bi_'eɪbl tə] fähig sein zu; können; dürfen **II U5**, 95
*to **be** about [bi:_ə'baʊt] sich handeln um **I**
*to **be** allowed to (do sth) [bi_ə'laʊd tə] dürfen **II U5**, 95
*to **be** asleep [ˌbi ə'sli:p] schlafen **II U1**, 19
*to **be** connected [bi kə'nektɪd] zusammenhängen; in Zusammenhang stehen **II U2**, 37
*to **be** gone [bi: 'gɒn] verschwunden sein; weg sein **II U4**, 81
*to **be** good at [bi: 'gʊd_ət] gut sein in **I**
*to **be** in [bi_'ɪn] dabei sein; mitmachen **II U4**, 70
*to **be** in the way [bi:_ɪn ðə 'weɪ] im Weg sein/stehen **I**
*to **be** interested in [bi_'ɪntrəstɪd_ɪn] interessiert sein an; sich interessieren für **II U2**, 31
*to **be** into [bi:_'ɪntə] mögen; stehen auf **I**
*to **be** jealous (of) [bi: 'dʒeləs] eifersüchtig sein (auf); neidisch sein (auf) **I**
*to **be** late [bi: 'leɪt] zu spät dran sein; zu spät kommen **I**
*to **be** lucky [bi_'lʌki] Glück haben **II U3**, 62
*to **be** on [bi_'ɒn] an sein; laufen **II U5**, 102
*to **be** right [bi 'raɪt] recht haben **I**
*to **be** scared (of) [bi: 'skeəd_əv] Angst haben (vor) **I**
*to **be** sorry [bi: 'sɒri] leid tun **I**
*to **be** surprised [bi sə'praɪzd] überrascht sein **II U3**, 63
*to **be** unlucky [bi:_ʌn'lʌki] Pech haben **I**
*to **be** up to [bi_'ʌp tə] vorhaben °**II U1**, 24
*to **be** worried [bi 'wʌrid] beunruhigt sein; besorgt sein **II U4**, 80
*to **be** worth [bi: 'wɜ:θ] wert sein **I**
*to **be** wrong [bi: 'rɒŋ] unrecht haben; sich irren **I**
Be careful! [bi: 'keəfl] Vorsicht!; Pass/Passt auf! **I**
Be polite. [bi: pə'laɪt] Sei/Seid höflich. **I**
Here you **are**. [ˌhɪə ju_'ɑ:] Bitte schön. **I**
How **are** you? [ˌhaʊ_'ɑ: jə] Wie geht es dir?; Wie geht es euch?; Wie geht es Ihnen? **I**
How much **is/are** …? [ˌhaʊ 'mʌtʃ_ɪz/ɑ:] Wie viel (kostet/kosten) …? **I**
I'**m** from … [ˌaɪm frɒm] Ich bin aus … **I**
Is this how you (do) …? [ɪz 'ðɪs haʊ jʊ ˌdu:] Machst du so …? **I**
beach [bi:tʃ] Strand **II U5**, 99
baked **beans** *(pl)* [ˌbeɪkt 'bi:nz] weiße Bohnen in Tomatensoße **I**
bear [beə] Bär **II U3**, 56
*to **beat** [bi:t] schlagen; besiegen **II U3**, 54
beautiful ['bju:tɪfl] schön; hübsch; wunderbar **II U2**, 30
because [bɪ'kɒz] weil; da **I**
because of [bɪ'kɒz_əv] wegen **II U4**, 81
*to **become** [bɪ'kʌm] werden **II U3**, 56
bed [bed] Bett **I**
*to go to **bed** [ˌgəʊ tə 'bed] ins Bett gehen **I**
bedroom ['bedrʊm] Schlafzimmer **I**
bee [bi:] Biene **II U2**, 33
Beefeater ['bi:fˌi:tə] königlicher Leibgardist **II U3**, 56
before [bɪ'fɔ:] schon einmal; vorher; zuvor **II U4**, 71
before [bɪ'fɔ:] vor *(zeitlich)*; bevor **I**
*to **begin** [bɪ'gɪn] beginnen; anfangen **II U5**, 99
beginning [bɪ'gɪnɪŋ] Anfang; Beginn **II U1**, 22
behind [bɪ'haɪnd] hinter **I**
to **believe** [bɪ'li:v] glauben **I**
He couldn't **believe** his eyes. [hi ˌkʊdnt bɪˌli:v hɪz_'aɪz] Er traute seinen Augen nicht. **II U2**, 40
bell [bel] Glocke **II AC1**, 48
to **belong** (to) [bɪ'lɒŋ (tə)] gehören (zu) **II U2**, 29
below [bɪ'ləʊ] unterhalb; unten **I**

(the) **best** [best] (der/die/das) Beste **II U1**, 10
best [best] beste/-r/-s; am besten **I**
I **bet** [aɪ 'bet] ich wette **II U3**, 54
better ['betə] besser; lieber **I**
between [bɪ'twi:n] zwischen **I**
bicycle motocross [ˌbaɪsɪkl 'məʊtəʊkrɒs] Fahrradmotocross **II U4**, 83
big [bɪg] groß **I**
bike [baɪk] Fahrrad **I**
bilingual [baɪ'lɪŋgwl] zweisprachig °**II U1**, 21
bird [bɜ:d] Vogel **II U2**, 33
birdwatching ['bɜ:dˌwɒtʃɪŋ] Vogelbeobachtung **II U2**, 28
birthday ['bɜ:θdeɪ] Geburtstag **I**
Happy **Birthday**! [ˌhæpi 'bɜ:θdeɪ] Alles Gute zum Geburtstag!; Herzlichen Glückwunsch zum Geburtstag! **I**
biscuit ['bɪskɪt] Keks **I**
a **bit** [ə 'bɪt] ein bisschen; ein wenig **II U1**, 18
*to **bite** [baɪt] beißen **II U3**, 56
black [blæk] schwarz **I**
*to go **black** [ˌgəʊ 'blæk] schwarz werden **II U5**, 102
building **block** ['bɪldɪŋ blɒk] Baustein °**II U5**, 93
to **block** [blɒk] blockieren; abblocken **II U5**, 93
*to **blow** out [ˌbləʊ‿'aʊt] ausblasen; auspusten **I**
blue [blu:] blau **I**
BMX [ˌbi:em'eks] BMX **II U4**, 68
boat [bəʊt] Boot **I**
boating lake ['bəʊtɪŋ ˌleɪk] See zum Rudern **I**
human **body** [ˌhju:mən 'bɒdi] menschlicher Körper **II U3**, 62
bonfire ['bɒnfaɪə] Lagerfeuer; Freudenfeuer **I**
book [bʊk] Buch **I**
exercise **book** ['eksəsaɪz ˌbʊk] Übungsheft **I**
bored [bɔ:d] gelangweilt **I**
boring ['bɔ:rɪŋ] langweilig **I**
to **borrow** ['bɒrəʊ] (sich) ausleihen **II U5**, 103
both [bəʊθ] beide **II U4**, 81
bottle ['bɒtl] Flasche **I**
bowl [bəʊl] Schale; Schälchen; Schüssel **I**
bowling alley ['bəʊlɪŋ‿æli] Bowlingbahn **I**
box [bɒks] Box; Kasten; Schachtel; Kiste **I**
boxing ['bɒksɪŋ] Boxen **II U1**, 8
round of **boxing** [ˌraʊnd‿əv 'bɒksɪŋ] Boxrunde **II U1**, 8
boy [bɔɪ] Junge **I**
cabin **boy** ['kæbɪn ˌbɔɪ] Schiffsjunge **I**
bracelet ['breɪslət] Armband **I**
brave [breɪv] mutig; tapfer **I**
bread [bred] Brot **I**
break [breɪk] Pause **II U2**, 40
half-term **break** [ˌhɑ:ftɜ:m 'breɪk] Halbjahresferien **I**
lunch **break** ['lʌnʃbreɪk] Mittagspause **I**
*to **break** [breɪk] brechen; zerbrechen **I**
broken ['brəʊkn] gebrochen; kaputt **I**
breakfast ['brekfəst] Frühstück **I**
*to have **breakfast** [ˌhæv 'brekfəst] frühstücken **I**
Take a deep **breath**. [ˌteɪk‿ə ˌdi:p 'breθ] Atme(t) tief ein. **II U2**, 36
to **breathe** [bri:ð] atmen **II U4**, 80
bridge [brɪdʒ] Brücke **II U3**, 62
*to **bring** [brɪŋ] bringen; mitbringen **I**
British ['brɪtɪʃ] britisch; Brite/Britin **I**
brochure ['brəʊʃə] Broschüre; Prospekt **I**
broken ['brəʊkn] gebrochen; kaputt **I**
brother ['brʌðə] Bruder **I**
brown [braʊn] braun **I**
bucket ['bʌkɪt] Eimer **II U3**, 62
*to **build** [bɪld] bauen **II U2**, 30
building ['bɪldɪŋ] Gebäude **I**
building block ['bɪldɪŋ blɒk] Baustein °**II U5**, 93
cyber **bully** [ˌsaɪbə 'bʊli] *jemand, der andere in sozialen Netzwerken belästigt oder mobbed* **II U5**, 91
*to give the **bumps** [ˌgɪv ðə 'bʌmps] hochleben lassen **I**
burger ['bɜ:gə] Hamburger **I**
bus [bʌs] Bus **I**
bus station ['bʌs ˌsteɪʃn] Busbahnhof **I**
busy ['bɪzi] belebt; beschäftigt **I**
but [bʌt] aber **I**
*to **buy** [baɪ] kaufen **I**
buyer ['baɪə] Käufer/-in **I**
by *(bike)* [baɪ] mit *(dem Fahrrad)* **I**
by the river [baɪ ðə 'rɪvə] am Fluss **II U2**, 31
Bye! [baɪ] Tschüss! **II U4**, 72

C

cabin boy ['kæbɪn ˌbɔɪ] Schiffsjunge **I**
café ['kæfeɪ] Café **I**
cafeteria [ˌkæfə'tɪəriə] Cafeteria **I**
cake [keɪk] Kuchen; Torte **I**
(phone) **call** ['fəʊn ˌkɔ:l] Anruf; Telefonanruf **I**
to **call** [kɔ:l] nennen; anrufen; rufen **I**
caller ['kɔ:lə] Anrufer/-in **I**
to **calm** down [ˌkɑ:m 'daʊn] sich beruhigen **II U2**, 41
camel racing ['kæml ˌreɪsɪŋ] Kamelrennen **II U4**, 68
camera ['kæmrə] Fotoapparat; Kamera **II U1**, 8
caught on **camera** [ˌkɔ:t‿ɒn 'kæmrə] ertappt; mit der Kamera festgehalten **II U1**, 8
summer **camp** ['sʌmə kæmp] Sommerferienlager **II AC2**, 88
camping ['kæmpɪŋ] Camping; Zelten **II U5**, 99
can [kæn] Dose; Büchse **I**
can [kæn; kən] können; dürfen **I**
can't [kɑ:nt] kann nicht; können nicht **I**
Can you name …? ['kæn jʊ ˌneɪm] Kannst du … nennen? **I**
candle ['kændl] Kerze **I**
candlelight *(no pl)* ['kændlaɪt] Kerzenlicht **II U5**, 103
cannot ['kænɒt] kann nicht; können nicht **II U5**, 95
capital ['kæpɪtl] Hauptstadt **II AC1**, 48
capital letter [ˌkæpɪtl 'letə] Großbuchstabe **I**
captain ['kæptɪn] Kapitän/-in; Mannschaftsführer/-in **I**
car [kɑ:] Auto **I**
card [kɑ:d] Karte; Spielkarte **I**
prompt **card** ['prɒmpt kɑ:d] Stichwortkarte; Rollenkarte °**II U2**, 32
to **care** (about) ['keər‿əˌbaʊt] wichtig nehmen; sich kümmern (um); sich interessieren (für) **II U5**, 93
careful ['keəfl] vorsichtig; sorgfältig **II U3**, 56
Be **careful**! [bi: 'keəfl] Vorsicht!; Pass/Passt auf! **I**
carnival ['kɑ:nɪvl] Karneval **II AC1**, 48
carpet ['kɑ:pɪt] Teppich **II U3**, 65
carrot ['kærət] Karotte; Möhre **I**
castle ['kɑ:sl] Schloss; Burg **II U3**, 56
cat [kæt] Katze **I**
*to **catch** [kætʃ] fangen **II U4**, 68
category ['kætəgri] Kategorie; Klasse °**II AC2**, 89
caught on camera [ˌkɔ:t‿ɒn 'kæmrə] ertappt; mit der Kamera festgehalten **II U1**, 8
to **cause** [kɔ:z] verursachen **II U4**, 82
to **celebrate** ['seləbreɪt] feiern **I**
Celtic ['keltɪk; 'seltɪk] keltisch **II U1**, 16
cent [sent] Cent *(Währung)* **I**
central ['sentrl] zentral; Zentral- **II U3**, 62
centre ['sentə] Zentrum; Center **I**
community **centre** [kə'mju:nəti ˌsentə] Gemeindezentrum **I**
leisure **centre** ['leʒə ˌsentə] Freizeitzentrum **I**
tourist information **centre** [ˌtʊərɪst ɪnfə'meɪʃn ˌsentə] Touristeninformation **I**
century ['senʃri] Jahrhundert **II U3**, 62
cereal *(no pl)* ['sɪəriəl] Frühstückszerealie; Getreideprodukt *(z. B. Cornflakes oder Müsli)* **I**
chair [tʃeə] Stuhl; Sessel **I**
challenge ['tʃælɪndʒ] Herausforderung **II U1**, 16
chance [tʃɑ:ns] Chance; Gelegenheit; Möglichkeit **II U5**, 100
change [tʃeɪndʒ] Änderung; Veränderung; Wechsel °**II U2**, 39
to **change** [tʃeɪndʒ] wechseln; (sich) ändern **II U5**, 90
to **change** (onto) [tʃeɪndʒ ('ɒntʊ)] umsteigen (in) **II U3**, 53
chant [tʃɑ:nt] Sprechgesang **II U4**, 72
character ['kærəktə] Charakter; Figur **I**

charity ['tʃærɪti] Wohltätigkeitsverein; wohltätige Zwecke; Wohlfahrt **I**
charity shop ['tʃærɪti ʃɒp] Second-Hand-Laden **I**
lucky **charm** [ˌlʌki 'tʃɑ:m] Glücksbringer; Talisman **I**
to **chase** [tʃeɪs] jagen; nachjagen **I**
chat room ['tʃæt rʊm] Chatroom **II AC2**, 88
video **chat** ['vɪdiəʊ ˌtʃæt] Videochat **II U3**, 50
to **chat** [tʃæt] plaudern; chatten *(sich online unterhalten)* **I**
cheap [tʃi:p] billig; preiswert **I**
to **check** [tʃek] überprüfen; prüfen; kontrollieren **I**
Check-in ['tʃekɪn] Einchecken **I**
checklist ['tʃeklɪst] Checkliste °**II U4**, 72
Check-out ['tʃekaʊt] Auschecken **I**
to **cheer** [tʃɪə] anfeuern; zujubeln; jubeln **II U4**, 72
cheese [tʃi:z] Käse **I**
chess [tʃes] Schach **II U2**, 28
chicken ['tʃɪkɪn] Huhn; Hähnchen **I**
chicken tikka masala [ˌtʃɪkɪn ˌtɪkə mə'sɑ:lə] *indisches Hühnchengericht* **I**
child, **children** *(pl)* ['tʃaɪld; 'tʃɪldrən] Kind **I**
only **child** ['əʊnli ˌtʃaɪld] Einzelkind **I**
chips *(pl) (BE)* [tʃɪps] Pommes frites **I**
chocolate ['tʃɒklət] Schokolade **I**
choice [tʃɔɪs] Wahl; Auswahl **II U3**, 58
*to **choose** [tʃu:z] auswählen; wählen **II U2**, 30
Choose … [tʃu:z] Wähle/Wählt … aus. **I**
Christmas ['krɪsməs] Weihnachten **I**
church [tʃɜ:tʃ] Kirche **I**
cinema ['sɪnəmə] Kino **I**
circle ['sɜ:kl] Kreis; Ring **I**
city ['sɪti] Stadt; Großstadt **I**
to **clap** [klæp] klatschen **I**
Clap your hands. [ˌklæp jɔ: 'hændz] Klatsch/Klatscht in die Hände. **I**
class [klɑ:s] Klasse; Schulklasse **I**; Unterricht **II U2**, 40
class display ['klɑ:s dɪˌspleɪ] Ausstellung in der Klasse **I**
class poster ['klɑ:s ˌpəʊstə] Klassenposter **I**
classmate ['klɑ:smeɪt] Klassenkamerad/-in; Mitschüler/-in **I**
classroom ['klɑ:srʊm] Klassenzimmer **I**
contact **clause** ['kɒntækt ˌklɔ:z] *Relativsatz ohne Relativpronomen* °**II U2**, 31
defining relative **clause** [dɪˌfaɪnɪŋ 'relətɪv ˌklɔ:z] notwendiger Relativsatz °**II U2**, 30
clay pipe ['kleɪ paɪp] Tonpfeife **II U3**, 63
to **clean** [kli:n] säubern; reinigen **I**
to **clear** out [ˌklɪər‿'aʊt] ausräumen; entrümpeln **I**
clear [klɪə] klar; deutlich **I**
clever ['klevə] schlau; klug **II U2**, 41
click [klɪk] Klicken; Klick **II U5**, 103

to **climb** [klaɪm] klettern; besteigen; steigen **I**
climbing ['klaɪmɪŋ] Klettern **II U1**, 16
clock [klɒk] Uhr **I**
alarm **clock** [ə'lɑ:m ˌklɒk] Wecker **II U2**, 43
o'**clock** [ə'klɒk] Uhr *(Zeitangabe bei vollen Stunden)* **I**
to **close** [kləʊz] schließen; zumachen **I**
close [kləʊs] eng; knapp **I**; nahe **II U3**, 56
Look **closely** … [ˌlʊk 'kləʊsli] Schau(t) genau … °**II U4**, 78
That was **close**! [ˌðæt wəz 'kləʊs] Das war knapp! **I**
close-up ['kləʊsʌp] Nahaufnahme °**II U5**, 98
clothes *(pl)* [kləʊðz] Kleider; Kleidung **I**
word **cloud** ['wɜ:d ˌklaʊd] Wörterwolke °**II U4**, 68
cloudy ['klaʊdi] bedeckt; bewölkt **II U1**, 19
clown [klaʊn] Clown **II U4**, 80
club [klʌb] Klub; Verein; AG **I**
Cooking **Club** ['kʊkɪŋ ˌklʌb] Koch-AG **I**
clue [klu:] Hinweis; Spur **II U1**, 13
coach [kəʊtʃ] Trainer/-in **I**; Reisebus **II U1**, 13
coconut ['kəʊkənʌt] Kokosnuss **II U3**, 63
coffee ['kɒfi] Kaffee **I**
coin [kɔɪn] Münze **I**
coke ['kəʊk] Cola **I**
cold [kəʊld] Erkältung **II U4**, 73
cold [kəʊld] kalt **II U1**, 18
to **collect** [kə'lekt] sammeln **I**
collection [kə'lekʃn] Kollektion; Sammlung **II U1**, 10
collocation [ˌkɒlə'keɪʃn] Wortverbindung °**II U5**, 90
colony ['kɒləni] Kolonie **II AC2**, 89
colour ['kʌlə] Farbe **I**
What **colour** is …? [ˌwɒt 'kʌlər‿ɪz] Welche Farbe hat …? **I**
colourful ['kʌləfl] farbenfroh; bunt **I**
*to **come** [kʌm] kommen **I**
*to **come** down [ˌkʌm 'daʊn] herunterkommen **I**
Come on! [ˌkʌm‿'ɒn] Komm schon!; Komm jetzt! **I**
comedian [kə'mi:diən] Komiker/-in; Comedian **II U1**, 10
comedy show ['kɒmədi ˌʃəʊ] Comedy Show **II U1**, 10
comfortable ['kʌmftəbl] komfortabel; bequem **II U3**, 65
comic ['kɒmɪk] Comicheft **II U4**, 82
comment ['kɒment] Kommentar **II U1**, 12
to **comment** (on) ['kɒment‿(ɒn)] kommentieren **II U5**, 97
to **communicate** [kə'mju:nɪkeɪt] kommunizieren; sich verständigen **II AC2**, 89
communication [kəˌmju:nɪ'keɪʃn] Kommunikation °**II U5**, 90
community centre [kə'mju:nəti ˌsentə] Gemeindezentrum **I**
comparative [kəm'pærətɪv] Komparativ °**II U1**, 16

to **compare** (with/to) [kəm'peə] vergleichen (mit) **I**
comparison [kəm'pærɪsn] Vergleich °**II U3**, 55
competition [ˌkɒmpə'tɪʃn] Wettbewerb; Turnier **II U2**, 29
Complete … [kəm'pli:t] Vervollständige/Vervollständigt … **I**
compound word ['kɒmpaʊnd wɜ:d] Kompositum *(zusammengesetztes Wort)* °**II U3**, 55
compromise ['kɒmprəmaɪz] Kompromiss **II U5**, 93
computer [ˌkəm'pju:tə] Computer **I**
con [kɒn] Argument dagegen **II U3**, 55
confident ['kɒnfɪdnt] selbstsicher; selbstbewusst **II U1**, 16
*to be **connected** [bi kə'nektɪd] zusammenhängen; in Zusammenhang stehen **II U2**, 37
contact ['kɒntækt] Kontakt **II U2**, 37
contact clause ['kɒntækt ˌklɔ:z] *Relativsatz ohne Relativpronomen* °**II U2**, 31
contest ['kɒntest] Wettkampf; Wettbewerb **I**
conversation [ˌkɒnvə'seɪʃn] Konversation; Gespräch; Unterhaltung **I**
to **convince** [kən'vɪns] überzeugen °**II U2**, 38
to **cook** [kʊk] kochen **II U5**, 103
cooker ['kʊkə] Herd **I**
cooking ['kʊkɪŋ] Kochen **I**
Cooking Club ['kʊkɪŋ ˌklʌb] Koch-AG **I**
*to leave it to **cool** [ˌli:v‿ɪt tə 'ku:l] kalt stellen **I**
cool [ku:l] cool; super **I**
to **copy** ['kɒpi] abschreiben; kopieren **I**
corner ['kɔ:nə] Ecke **II U2**, 34
Correct … [kə'rekt] Korrigiere/Korrigiert … **I**
correct [kə'rekt] richtig; korrekt **I**
*to **cost** [kɒst] kosten **I**
costume ['kɒstju:m] Kostüm **I**
cough [kɒf] Husten **II U4**, 73
could [kʊd] könnte/-n **II U2**, 40
to **count** (on) ['kaʊnt‿ɒn] zählen (auf) **I**
country, **countries** *(pl)* ['kʌntri; 'kʌntriz] Land **I**
a **couple** of [ə 'kʌpl‿əv] ein paar **I**
course [kɔ:s] Kurs **II U1**, 16
of **course** [əv 'kɔ:s] natürlich; selbstverständlich **I**
court [kɔ:t] Spielfeld **II U4**, 68
cousin ['kʌzn] Cousin/Cousine **I**
cramp [kræmp] Krampf **II U4**, 74
to **crash** [kræʃ] abstürzen **II U5**, 103
crazy ['kreɪzi] verrückt **I**
*to go **crazy** [ˌgəʊ 'kreɪzi] ausflippen; durchdrehen; verrückt werden **II U5**, 95
cream [kri:m] Creme; Sahne **I**
ice **cream** [ˌaɪs 'kri:m] Eis; Eiscreme **I**
to **create** [kri'eɪt] schaffen; erschaffen; erfinden **I**
creative [kri'eɪtɪv] kreativ **I**

credit ['kredɪt] Guthaben **II U3**, 52
cricket ['krɪkɪt] Cricket **II U4**, 69
crisp *(BE)* [krɪsp] Kartoffelchip **I**
to cross [krɒs] überqueren; kreuzen **II AC2**, 89
*to keep your fingers **crossed** [ˌki:p jɔ: ˌfɪŋgəz 'krɒst] die Daumen drücken **I**
crowd [kraʊd] Menschenmenge **II U3**, 58
crown jewels [ˌkraʊn 'dʒu:əlz] Kronjuwelen **II U3**, 56
to cry [kraɪ] schreien; rufen **II U5**, 102
CU *(= See you)* ['si: ju] Bis dann!; Bis … **I**
culture ['kʌltʃə] Kultur **I**
Across **cultures** [əˌkrɒs 'kʌltʃəz] Interkulturelles **I**
cupboard ['kʌbəd] Küchenschrank; Schrank **I**
curry ['kʌri] Curry *(Gewürz oder Gericht)* **I**
custard ['kʌstəd] Vanillesoße; Vanillepudding **I**
*to cut (off) [kʌt (ɒf)] schneiden; abschneiden **II U2**, 30
cute [kju:t] niedlich; süß **I**
cyber bully [ˌsaɪbə 'bʊli] *jemand, der andere in sozialen Netzwerken belästigt oder mobbed* **II U5**, 91
cycling ['saɪklɪŋ] Radfahren **I**

D

dad [dæd] Papa **I**
to dance [dɑ:ns] tanzen **I**
I like singing and **dancing**. [ˌaɪ laɪk ˌsɪŋɪŋ‿ənd 'dɑ:nsɪŋ] Ich singe und tanze gern. **I**
dancer ['dɑ:nsə] Tänzer/-in **II U2**, 36
dangerous ['deɪndʒrəs] gefährlich **I**
the dark [ðə 'dɑ:k] Dunkelheit **II U1**, 18
dark [dɑ:k] dunkel **II U1**, 18
date [deɪt] Datum **I**
day [deɪ] Tag **I**
all **day** [ˌɔ:l 'deɪ] den ganzen Tag **II U1**, 14
one **day** [wʌn 'deɪ] eines Tages **II U2**, 36
a **day** out in … [ə ˌdeɪ‿'aʊt ɪn] ein Tag in … **II U3**, 58
the next **day** [ðə ˌnekst 'deɪ] am nächsten Tag **II U1**, 11
dead [ded] tot **II U3**, 62
*to deal (with) [di:l] sich befassen mit; umgehen mit **II U3**, 54
Dear … [dɪə] Lieber …; Liebe … *(Anrede in Briefen)* **I**
December [dɪ'sembə] Dezember **I**
to decide [dɪ'saɪd] (sich) entscheiden **I**
*to make a decision [ˌmeɪk‿ə dɪ'sɪʒn] eine Entscheidung treffen °**II U3**, 61
deck [dek] Deck **I**
to decorate ['dekəreɪt] dekorieren; verzieren; schmücken **I**
decorations *(pl)* [ˌdekə'reɪʃnz] Dekoration; Schmuck **I**
defining relative clause [dɪˌfaɪnɪŋ 'relətɪv ˌklɔ:z] notwendiger Relativsatz °**II U2**, 30
to describe [dɪ'skraɪb] beschreiben **I**
description [dɪ'skrɪpʃn] Beschreibung °**II U3**, 58
to deserve [dɪ'zɜ:v] verdienen **II U4**, 76
design [dɪ'zaɪn] Design; Gestaltung; Entwurf **II U2**, 30
to design [dɪ'zaɪn] entwerfen; gestalten **II U2**, 31
detail ['di:teɪl] Detail; Einzelheit °**II U3**, 59
diagram ['daɪəgræm] Diagramm **I**
dialogue ['daɪəlɒg] Dialog; Gespräch **I**
dice [daɪs] Würfel °**II U2**, 34
Roll two **dice**. [ˌrəʊl ˌtu: 'daɪs] Würfle/Würfelt mit zwei Würfeln. **I**
throw the **dice** twice [ˌθrəʊ ðə daɪs 'twaɪs] würfle zweimal °**II U2**, 34
dictionary ['dɪkʃnri] Wörterbuch **I**
difference ['dɪfrəns] Unterschied **I**
different ['dɪfrnt] anders; unterschiedlich; verschieden **I**
difficult ['dɪfɪklt] schwierig **II U4**, 77
*to dig [dɪg] graben **II U2**, 33
dinner ['dɪnə] Abendessen **I**
dinosaur ['daɪnəsɔ:] Dinosaurier **II U2**, 40
direction [dɪ'rekʃn] Richtung **I**
dirty ['dɜ:ti] dreckig; schmutzig **II U2**, 40
disappointed [ˌdɪsə'pɔɪntɪd] enttäuscht **I**
disaster [dɪ'zɑ:stə] Desaster; Katastrophe; Unglück **II U5**, 102
to discover [dɪ'skʌvə] entdecken **II U2**, 28
to discuss [dɪ'skʌs] diskutieren **I**
discussion [dɪ'skʌʃn] Diskussion **II U5**, 90
display [dɪ'spleɪ] Ausstellung **II U3**, 59
class **display** ['klɑ:s dɪˌspleɪ] Ausstellung in der Klasse **I**
distance ['dɪstns] Distanz; Entfernung **II U3**, 60
*to do [du:] machen; tun **I**
*to **do** about ['du:‿əˌbaʊt] unternehmen wegen **II U5**, 100
*to **do** our hair [ˌdu:‿aʊə 'heə] uns frisieren; unsere Haare machen **I**
Don't translate … [ˌdəʊnt trænz'leɪt] Übersetze/Übersetzt nicht … **I**
Don't worry! [ˌdəʊnt 'wʌri] Keine Sorge! **I**
We **did** it! [ˌwi: 'dɪd‿ɪt] Wir haben es geschafft! **II U4**, 81
doctor ['dɒktə] Arzt/Ärztin **II U4**, 72
dog [dɒg] Hund **I**
to walk the **dog** [ˌwɔ:k ðə 'dɒg] den Hund ausführen; mit dem Hund spazieren gehen **I**
I'm dog-tired. [ˌaɪm ˌdɒg'taɪəd] Ich bin hundemüde. **I**
door [dɔ:] Tür **I**
front **door** [ˌfrʌnt 'dɔ:] Haustür **II U5**, 102
down [daʊn] nach unten; herunter; hinunter **II U3**, 62
*to come **down** [ˌkʌm 'daʊn] herunterkommen **I**
*to go **down** [ˌgəʊ 'daʊn] hinuntergehen; nach unten gehen; entlanggehen **I**
to note **down** [ˌnəʊt 'daʊn] notieren; aufschreiben °**II U2**, 37
*to sit **down** [ˌsɪt 'daʊn] sich hinsetzen; sich setzen **I**
*to write **down** [ˌraɪt 'daʊn] aufschreiben **I**
to download [ˌdaʊn'ləʊd] herunterladen *(aus dem Internet)* **II U5**, 97
downstairs [ˌdaʊn'steəz] nach unten; im Untergeschoss; unten **II U5**, 102
draft [drɑ:ft] Entwurf; Konzept **I**
drama ['drɑ:mə] Theater; Drama **II U2**, 28
dramatic [drə'mætɪk] dramatisch **II U3**, 63
*to draw [drɔ:] zeichnen **I**
drawing ['drɔ:ɪŋ] Zeichnung **I**
dream [dri:m] Traum **II U1**, 15
fancy dress ['fænsi dres] Verkleidung; Kostüm **II U4**, 80
drink [drɪŋk] Getränk **I**
*to drink [drɪŋk] trinken **I**
driver ['draɪvə] Fahrer/-in **II U1**, 13
to drop [drɒp] fallen (lassen) **II U3**, 62
during *+ noun* ['djʊərɪŋ] während *(+ Nomen)* **II U1**, 9
DVD [ˌdi:vi:'di:] DVD **I**

E

e.g. *(= for example)* [ˌi:'dʒi:] z.B. *(= zum Beispiel)* **I**
each [i:tʃ] jede/-r/-s **I**
each other [ˌi:tʃ‿'ʌðə] einander; sich; sich gegenseitig **I**
each [i:tʃ] pro Person; pro Stück **I**
early ['ɜ:li] früh **I**
to earn [ɜ:n] verdienen **I**
earth [ɜ:θ] Erdboden; Erde; die Erde **II U2**, 40
What on **earth** …? [ˌwɒt:‿ɒn‿'ɜ:θ] Was um alles in der Welt …? **II U5**, 95
east [i:st] Osten; Ost- **I**
Easter ['i:stə] Ostern **I**
easy ['i:zi] einfach; leicht **I**
*to eat [i:t] essen; fressen **I**
Eco [ɪkəʊ] Öko- **II U2**, 33
audio-visual effect [ˌɔ:diəʊvɪʒuəl ɪ'fekt] audiovisueller Effekt °**II U1**, 24
egg [eg] Ei **I**
eight [eɪt] acht **I**
electronic [ˌelek'trɒnɪk] elektronisch **II U1**, 21
eleven [ɪ'levn] elf **I**
what else [ˌwɒt‿'els] was sonst; was noch **I**
e-mail ['i:meɪl] E-Mail **I**
to e-mail ['i:meɪl] mailen; per E-Mail schicken **II U5**, 97
embarrassed [ɪm'bærəst] verlegen **II U1**, 9
embarrassing [ɪm'bærəsɪŋ] peinlich **II U1**, 8
end [end] Ende; Schluss **I**
in the **end** [ˌɪn ði‿'end] schließlich; zum Schluss **II U1**, 10
to end [end] enden; beenden **II U4**, 79
to **end** up [ˌend‿'ʌp] enden; landen **II U1**, 8

ending ['endɪŋ] Ende; Schluss *(einer Geschichte)* **I**
English ['ɪŋglɪʃ] englisch, Englisch; aus England; Engländer/-in **I**
English-speaking ['ɪŋglɪʃˌspi:kɪŋ] englischsprachig **I**
I'm **English**. [aɪm‿'ɪŋglɪʃ] Ich bin Engländer/-in. **I**
to **enjoy** [ɪn'dʒɔɪ] genießen; sich freuen an **II U1**, 12
enough [ɪ'nʌf] genug; genügend **I**
to **enter** ['entə] hineingehen; betreten; eintreten; *hier:* mitmachen **II U2**, 40
equipment [ɪ'kwɪpmənt] Ausstattung; Ausrüstung **II U4**, 69
er [ɜ:] äh **I**
escalator ['eskəleɪtə] Rolltreppe **I**
etc. *(= et cetera)* [ɪt'setrə] usw. *(= und so weiter)* °**II U5**, 101
euro ['jʊərəʊ] Euro *(Währung)* **I**
even ['i:vn] sogar; selbst **I**
evening ['i:vnɪŋ] Abend **I**
in the **evenings** [ɪn ði‿'i:vnɪŋz] abends **I**
event [ɪ'vent] Ereignis; Veranstaltung **I**
ever ['evə] jemals **II U2**, 33
every ['evri] jede/-r/-s **I**
everybody ['evribɒdi] jeder; alle **II U3**, 54
everyone ['evriwʌn] jeder; alle **I**
everything ['evriθɪŋ] alles **I**
everywhere ['evriweə] überall **I**
exactly [ɪg'zæktli] genau **II AC2**, 88
exam [ɪg'zæm] Examen; Prüfung **II U2**, 28
example [ɪg'zɑ:mpl] Beispiel **I**
for **example** [fər‿ɪg'zɑ:mpl] zum Beispiel **II AC2**, 89
to **exchange** [ɪks'tʃeɪndʒ] austauschen °**II U2**, 35
excited [ɪk'saɪtɪd] aufgeregt; begeistert **I**
exciting [ɪk'saɪtɪŋ] spannend; aufregend **I**
Excuse me … [ɪk'skju:z mi] Entschuldigung!; Entschuldigen Sie! **I**
exercise ['eksəsaɪz] Übung; Aufgabe **I**
exercise book ['eksəsaɪz ˌbʊk] Übungsheft **I**
expensive [ɪk'spensɪv] teuer **I**
experience [ɪk'spɪəriəns] Erfahrung **II U4**, 69
expert ['ekspɜ:t] Experte/Expertin °**II U4**, 79
to **explain** [ɪk'spleɪn] erklären **I**
to **explore** [ɪk'splɔ:] auf Entdeckungsreise gehen; sich umschauen; erkunden; erforschen **I**
to **express** [ɪk'spres] ausdrücken °**II U4**, 82
expression [ɪk'spreʃn] Ausdruck; Wendung; Äußerung **II AC2**, 89
extra ['ekstrə] extra; zusätzlich **I**
eye [aɪ] Auge **II U1**, 9
He couldn't believe his **eyes**. [hi ˌkʊdnt bɪˌli:v hɪz‿'aɪz] Er traute seinen Augen nicht. **II U2**, 40
eyewitness ['aɪwɪtnəs] Augenzeuge/Augenzeugin **II U4**, 77

F

face [feɪs] Gesicht **I**
Put … **face** down. [pʊt ˌfeɪs 'daʊn] Lege/Legt … umgedreht hin. **I**
face-to-face [ˌfeɪstə'feɪs] *hier:* persönlich; von Angesicht zu Angesicht **II U5**, 93
fact [fækt] Fakt; Tatsache **II U2**, 37
fair [feə] gerecht; fair **I**
to **fake** [feɪk] vortäuschen; fälschen **II U4**, 76
*to **fall** [fɔ:l] fallen; hinfallen **I**
*to **fall** asleep [ˌfɔ:l‿ə'sli:p] einschlafen **I**
*to **fall** off [ˌfɔ:l‿'ɒf] herunterfallen; hinunterfallen **II U2**, 34
*to **fall** over [ˌfɔ:l‿'əʊvə] hinfallen; umkippen **I**
family ['fæməli] Familie **I**
family tree ['fæməli ˌtri:] Stammbaum **I**
famous ['feɪməs] berühmt **I**
fan [fæn] Fan; Anhänger/-in **II U4**, 83
fancy dress ['fænsi dres] Verkleidung; Kostüm **II U4**, 80
fantastic [fæn'tæstɪk] fantastisch; großartig **II U2**, 29
fantasy ['fæntəsi] Fantasie; Traum- **I**
fanzine [fæn'zi:n] Fanzeitschrift **II U2**, 38
far [fɑ:] weit **II U3**, 55
so **far** [ˌsəʊ 'fɑ:] bis jetzt **II U4**, 75
farm [fɑ:m] Farm; Bauernhof **I**
farmer ['fɑ:mə] Farmer/-in; Landwirt/-in **II U1**, 13
fashion ['fæʃn] Mode **II U2**, 28
fast [fɑ:st] schnell **I**
father ['fɑ:ðə] Vater **I**
favourite ['feɪvrɪt] Lieblings- **I**
My **favourite** … [maɪ 'feɪvrɪt] Mein/e Lieblings … **I**
What's your **favourite** …? ['wɒts jə ˌfeɪvrɪt] Was ist dein/-e Lieblings…? **I**
fear [fɪə] Angst; Furcht; Befürchtung **II U4**, 82
February ['februri] Februar **I**
feedback ['fi:dbæk] Feedback; Rückmeldung **II U2**, 29
*to **feel** [fi:l] fühlen; sich fühlen **I**
*to **feel** left out [ˌfi:l left‿'aʊt] sich ausgeschlossen fühlen **II U5**, 104
*to **feel** sick [ˌfi:l 'sɪk] Übelkeit verspüren; sich schlecht fühlen **II U4**, 73
feeling ['fi:lɪŋ] Gefühl **II U1**, 9
festival ['festɪvl] Festival; Fest **I**
fever ['fi:və] Fieber **II U4**, 73
few [fju:] wenige **II U1**, 18
a **few** [ə 'fju:] ein paar; wenige; einige **I**
science fiction [ˌsaɪəns 'fɪkʃn] Science-Fiction *(Zukunftsdichtung)* **II U1**, 22
field [fi:ld] Feld; Spielfeld; Wiese; Weide; Acker **II U1**, 18
fifteen [ˌfɪf'ti:n] fünfzehn **I**
fight [faɪt] Kampf; Streit **II U2**, 41

*to **fight** [faɪt] kämpfen; (sich) streiten **II U5**, 102
figure ['fɪgə] Figur; Gestalt **II U3**, 51
wax **figure** ['wæks ˌfɪgə] Wachsfigur **II U3**, 51
to **fill** in [ˌfɪl‿'ɪn] ausfüllen °**II U5**, 96
film [fɪlm] Film **I**
filmmaker ['fɪlmˌmeɪkə] Filmemacher/-in **II U1**, 24
final ['faɪnl] endgültig °**II U4**, 79
finally ['faɪnli] schließlich; endlich; zum Schluss; letztlich **II U2**, 31
*to **find** [faɪnd] finden; herausfinden **I**
*to **find** out [ˌfaɪnd‿'aʊt] herausfinden **I**
fine [faɪn] gut; in Ordnung; schön **I**
I'm **fine**. [ˌaɪm 'faɪn] Mir geht's gut. **I**
finger ['fɪŋgə] Finger **I**
*to keep your **fingers** crossed [ˌki:p jɔ: ˌfɪŋgəz 'krɒst] die Daumen drücken **I**
finish line ['fɪnɪʃ ˌlaɪn] Ziellinie **II U4**, 81
to **finish** ['fɪnɪʃ] beenden; enden; fertigstellen; aufhören **I**
finished ['fɪnɪʃt] fertig °**II U5**, 99
fireworks *(pl)* ['faɪəwɜ:ks] Feuerwerk **I**
first [fɜ:st] zuerst; als Erstes; erste/-r/-s **I**
at **first** [ət 'fɜ:st] zuerst; zunächst **II U3**, 63
first language [ˌfɜ:st 'læŋgwɪdʒ] Muttersprache **II AC2**, 89
fish, **fish** (pl) [fɪʃ] Fisch **I**
to **fit** [fɪt] passen °**II U5**, 101
*to **get fit** [ˌget 'fɪt] in Form kommen; fit werden **I**
five [faɪv] fünf **I**
to **fix** [fɪks] reparieren; befestigen **II U5**, 95
flair [fleə] Flair; Atmosphäre **II U3**, 51
flat [flæt] Wohnung **I**
flea market ['fli: ˌmɑ:kɪt] Flohmarkt **I**
floor [flɔ:] Fußboden **I**
to **flow out** [fləʊ‿'aʊt] hinausfließen **II U3**, 62
flower [flaʊə] Blume **II U2**, 41
flyer ['flaɪə] Flyer **I**
to **focus** (on) ['fəʊkəs‿ɒn] sich konzentrieren (auf) °**II U2**, 37
folder ['fəʊldə] Ordner; Mappe **I**
to **follow** ['fɒləʊ] folgen; hinterhergehen; befolgen **II U3**, 54
food [fu:d] Essen; Lebensmittel **I**
foot, feet (pl) [fʊt; fi:t] Fuß **I**
on **foot** [ɒn 'fʊt] zu Fuß **II U3**, 60
football ['fʊtbɔ:l] Fußball **I**
for [fɔ:; fə] wegen **II U5**, 91
for example [fər‿ɪg'zɑ:mpl] zum Beispiel **II AC2**, 89
for … [fɔ:; fə] … lang **II U1**, 12
foreign language [ˌfɒrɪn 'læŋgwɪdʒ] Fremdsprache **II U2**, 38
forest ['fɒrɪst] Wald **II U1**, 16
forever [fə'revə] für immer; ewig **II U5**, 93
*to **forget** [fə'get] vergessen **I**
*to **forgive** [fə'gɪv] vergeben; verzeihen **II U4**, 81

form [fɔ:m] Form I
negative **form** ['negətɪv ˌfɔ:m] verneinte Form I
past **form** ['pɑ:st fɔ:m] Vergangenheitsform °II U1, 10
possessive **form** [pəˌsesɪv 'fɔ:m] Possessivform I
short **form** ['ʃɔ:t fɔ:m] Kurzform I
to **form** [fɔ:m] formen; bilden °II U4, 79
formal ['fɔ:ml] formal; formell; förmlich °II U4, 77
forum ['fɔ:rəm] Forum II U5, 90
to look **forward** to [ˌlʊk 'fɔ:wəd tə] sich freuen auf II U2, 33
four [fɔ:] vier I
Four and six is ten. [ˌfɔ:r‿ənd ˌsɪks‿ɪz 'ten] Vier plus sechs ist zehn. I
fox [fɒks] Fuchs II U2, 34
free [fri:] frei; kostenlos I
free time [ˌfri: 'taɪm] Freizeit I
French [frenʃ] französisch; Französisch II U2, 32
frequently asked [ˌfri:kwəntli‿'ɑ:skt] häufig gefragt I
fresh [freʃ] frisch I
Friday ['fraɪdeɪ] Freitag I
fridge [frɪdʒ] Kühlschrank I
friend [frend] Freund/-in I
*to make **friends** [ˌmeɪk 'frendz] Freundschaft schließen II U2, 43
That's what **friends** are for. [ˌðæts wɒt 'frendz‿ɑ: ˌfɔ:] Dafür sind Freunde da. I
friendly ['frendli] freundlich; nett II U1, 14
friendship ['frendʃɪp] Freundschaft II U5, 94
from [frɒm; frəm] aus; von I
from … to [frəm … tə] von … bis I
Where … **from**? [ˌweə … 'frɒm] Woher …? I
front door [ˌfrʌnt 'dɔ:] Haustür II U5, 102
in **front** of [ɪn 'frʌnt‿əv] vor I
fruit [fru:t] Frucht; Obst I
full (of) [fʊl‿əv] voll (von) I
fun [fʌn] Freude; Spaß I
*to have **fun** [ˌhæv 'fʌn] Spaß haben; sich amüsieren I
It's **fun**. [ɪts 'fʌn] Es macht Spaß. I
fun [fʌn] lustig; witzig; fröhlich I
funny ['fʌni] lustig; witzig I
future ['fju:tʃə] Zukunft °II U3, 51

G

gallery walk ['gæləri ˌwɔ:k] Museumsrundgang; Vernissage I
game [geɪm] Spiel I
guessing **game** ['gesɪŋ ˌgeɪm] Ratespiel °II U1, 13
gap [gæp] Lücke; Spalt; Abstand I
garage ['gærɑ:ʒ] Garage I
garden ['gɑ:dn] Garten I
genius ['dʒi:niəs] Genie II U5, 95

German ['dʒɜ:mən] deutsch; Deutsch; aus Deutschland; Deutsche/-r I
*to **get** [get] holen; bringen; bekommen; besorgen; kaufen I
*to **get** around [ˌget‿ə'raʊnd] *hier:* sich fortbewegen II U3, 53
*to **get** away with [ˌget‿ə'weɪ wɪð] davonkommen mit II U4, 76
*to **get** fit [ˌget 'fɪt] in Form kommen; fit werden I
*to **get** in the way [ˌget‿ɪn ðə 'weɪ] stören; im Weg stehen II U4, 80
*to **get** into [ˌget‿'ɪntə] einsteigen; hineingelangen I
*to **get** off (a bus/train) [ˌget‿'ɒf] aussteigen (aus einem Bus/Zug) II U3, 53
*to **get** on people's nerves [ˌget‿ɒn sʌmbɒdiz 'nɜ:vz] jemandem auf die Nerven gehen I
*to **get** out of [get ˌaʊt‿əv] aussteigen II U5, 102
*to **get** started [ˌget 'stɑ:tɪd] anfangen II U2, 33
*to **get** there ['get ðeə] hinkommen I
*to **get** to ['get tə] kommen zu; kommen nach; erreichen I
*to **get** up [ˌget‿'ʌp] aufstehen *(aus dem Bett)* I
Time to **get** up! [ˌtaɪm tə ˌget‿'ʌp] Es ist Zeit aufzustehen! I
ghost [gəʊst] Geist II U2, 30
girl [gɜ:l] Mädchen I
a **girl** from Germany [ə ˌgɜ:l frəm 'dʒɜ:məni] ein Mädchen aus Deutschland I
girlfriend ['gɜ:lfrend] Freundin *(in einer Paarbeziehung)* II U3, 54
gist [dʒɪst] das Wesentliche °II U3, 56
*to **give** [gɪv] geben; schenken I
*to **give** the bumps [ˌgɪv ðə 'bʌmps] hochleben lassen I
glass [glɑ:s] Glas I
glasses *(pl)* ['glɑ:sɪz] Brille II U4, 80
glove [glʌv] Handschuh I
*to **go** [gəʊ] gehen; fahren I
*to **go** black [ˌgəʊ 'blæk] schwarz werden II U5, 102
*to **go** crazy [ˌgəʊ 'kreɪzi] ausflippen; durchdrehen; verrückt werden II U5, 95
*to **go** down [ˌgəʊ 'daʊn] hinuntergehen; nach unten gehen; entlanggehen I
*to **go** for a walk [ˌgəʊ fər‿ə 'wɔ:k] spazieren gehen II U1, 18
*to **go** on [ˌgəʊ‿'ɒn] weitergehen; weitermachen; weiterführen; fortfahren I
*to **go** over to [ˌgəʊ 'əʊvə tə] hinübergehen zu; zu jmdm. nach Hause gehen II U5, 95
*to **go** shopping [ˌgəʊ 'ʃɒpɪŋ] einkaufen gehen I
*to **go** swimming [ˌgəʊ 'swɪmɪŋ] Schwimmen gehen I

*to **go** to bed [ˌgəʊ tə 'bed] ins Bett gehen I
*to **go** together [ˌgəʊ tə'geðə] zueinander passen; zueinander gehören I
*to **go** with ['gəʊ wɪð] passen zu; gehören zu I
*to **go** wrong [ˌgəʊ 'rɒŋ] schiefgehen I
*to let **go** (of) [ˌlet 'gəʊ (əv)] loslassen II U4, 80
It's **gone**. [ɪts 'gɒn] Es ist weg. II U3, 62
goal [gəʊl] Tor; Ziel I
*to be **gone** [bi: 'gɒn] verschwunden sein; weg sein II U4, 81
good [gʊd] gut I
*to be **good** at [bi: 'gʊd‿ət] gut sein in I
Good morning. [ˌgʊd 'mɔ:nɪŋ] Guten Morgen. I
goodbye [gʊd'baɪ] auf Wiedersehen I
gorge scrambling ['gɔ:dʒ ˌskræmblɪŋ] Schluchtenklettern II U1, 16
to **grab** [græb] greifen; ergreifen; schnappen II U3, 62
grammar ['græmə] Grammatik °II U2, 33
grandad ['grændæd] Opa I
grandma ['grænmɑ:] Oma I
grandparents *(pl)* ['grænˌpeərənts] Großeltern I
granny ['græni] Oma I
great [greɪt] großartig; toll; super I
It's **great** for … [ɪts 'greɪt fə] Es ist super zum/für … I
… is a **great** sport. [ɪz‿ə 'greɪt ˌspɔ:t] … ist ein toller Sport. I
green [gri:n] grün I
Greenwich Mean Time *(= GMT)* [ˌgrenɪdʒ 'mi:n ˌtaɪm] westeuropäische Zeit I
greeting ['gri:tɪŋ] Gruß I
grey [greɪ] grau I
grid [grɪd] Gitter; Tabelle; Raster I
group [gru:p] Gruppe; Klasse I
a **group** of three [ə ˌgru:p‿əv 'θri:] eine Dreiergruppe I
tutor **group** ['tju:tə ˌgru:p] Klasse *(in einer englischen Schule)* I
guard [gɑ:d] Wache; Wächter/-in II AC1, 49
to **guess** [ges] raten; erraten; vermuten I
guessing game ['gesɪŋ ˌgeɪm] Ratespiel °II U1, 13
guide [gaɪd] Führer/-in; Reiseführer II U3, 56
guinea pig ['gɪni: ˌpɪg] Meerschweinchen I
guy [gaɪ] Typ; Kerl; *(Pl.)* Leute II U1, 9

H

*to do our **hair** [ˌdu: ˌaʊə 'heə] uns frisieren; unsere Haare machen I
half, halves *(pl)* (of) [hɑ:f; hɑ:vz] die Hälfte I
half [hɑ:f] halb I
half past [ˌhɑ:f 'pɑ:st] halb *(bei Uhrzeitangaben)* I
half-sister ['hɑ:fˌsɪstə] Halbschwester I

half-term break [ˌhɑ:ftɜ:m 'breɪk] Halbjahresferien I
hall [hɔ:l] Halle; Saal **II U2**, 29
hammer ['hæmə] Hammer **II U2**, 34
hand [hænd] Hand I
Clap your **hands**. [ˌklæp jɔ: 'hændz] Klatsch/Klatscht in die Hände. I
On the one **hand** …, (but) on the other **hand** … [ɒn ðə‿'wʌn ˌhænd … (bʌt) ɒn ði‿'ʌðə ˌhænd …] Einerseits …, (aber) andererseits … **II U4**, 82
*to **hang** up [ˌhæŋ‿'ʌp] aufhängen **II U2**, 33
to **happen** ['hæpn] geschehen; passieren I
happy ['hæpi] glücklich; froh; fröhlich I
Happy Birthday! [ˌhæpi 'bɜ:θdeɪ] Alles Gute zum Geburtstag!; Herzlichen Glückwunsch zum Geburtstag! I
hard [hɑ:d] hart; schwer; schwierig **II U1**, 12; *hier:* stark **II U3**, 56
hat [hæt] Hut I
to **hate** [heɪt] hassen; nicht mögen **II U2**, 42
*to **have** [hæv] haben I
*to **have** a look (at) [ˌhæv‿ə 'lʊk] anschauen **II U4**, 73
*to **have** breakfast [ˌhæv 'brekfəst] frühstücken I
*to **have** fun [ˌhæv 'fʌn] Spaß haben; sich amüsieren I
*to **have** got [hæv 'gɒt] besitzen; haben I
*to **have** to ['hæv tə] müssen **II U2**, 40
*to **have** *(a sweet)* [hæv] *(ein Bonbon)* nehmen; *(ein Bonbon)* essen I
he [hi:] er I
head [hed] Kopf I
head of state [ˌhed‿əv 'steɪt] Staatsoberhaupt **II AC2**, 89
With a very big **head**! [ˌwɪð ə ˌveri bɪg 'hed] Und ein Angeber! **II U5**, 95
headache *(no pl)* ['hedeɪk] Kopfschmerzen; Kopfweh **II U4**, 73
heading ['hedɪŋ] Überschrift; Titel I
headphones *(pl)* ['hedfəʊnz] Kopfhörer **II U5**, 102
health [helθ] Gesundheit **II U4**, 69
healthy ['helθi] gesund I
*to **hear** [hɪə] hören I
I **hear** … [aɪ 'hɪə] Ich habe gehört, dass … I
heart [hɑ:t] Herz; *hier:* Zentrum **II U3**, 62
*to learn … by **heart** [ˌlɜ:n baɪ 'hɑ:t] auswendig lernen I
Hello. [hel'əʊ] Hallo. I
*to say **hello** (to) [ˌseɪ hel'əʊ tə] grüßen; Grüße ausrichten (an) I
help [help] Hilfe I
to **help** [help] helfen I
helpful ['helpfl] hilfsbereit; hilfreich I
helpless ['helpləs] hilflos I
her [hɜ:] ihr/-e; sie I
here [hɪə] hier I
right **here** [ˌraɪt 'hɪə] genau hier **II U4**, 70
Here you are. [ˌhɪə ju‿'ɑ:] Bitte schön. I
Here's … [hɪəz] Hier ist … I
Hey! [heɪ] Hi.; He!; Hallo. I
Hi. [haɪ] Hi.; Hallo. I
high [haɪ] hoch; groß **II U1**, 17
high tide ['haɪ ˌtaɪd] Flut **II U3**, 62
highlight ['haɪlaɪt] Highlight; Höhepunkt **II U1**, 9
him [hɪm] ihn; ihm I
himself [hɪm'self] er/sich (selbst); selber **II U1**, 8
his [hɪz] sein/-e I
historical [hɪ'stɒrɪkl] historisch; geschichtlich I
history ['hɪstri] Geschichte **II U2**, 30
*to **hit** [hɪt] schlagen; treffen I
hobby, **hobbies** *(pl)* ['hɒbi; 'hɒbiz] Hobby I
hockey [hɒki] Hockey **II U4**, 69
*to **hold** [həʊld] halten; festhalten I
hole [həʊl] Loch **II U2**, 33
holiday ['hɒlədeɪ] Urlaub; Feiertag I
holidays (pl) ['hɒlədeɪz] Ferien I
home [həʊm] Zuhause; Heim I
at **home** [ət 'həʊm] zu Hause I
home [həʊm] nach Hause I
homepage ['həʊmpeɪdʒ] Homepage I
homework ['həʊmwɜ:k] Hausaufgabe(n) I
hope [həʊp] Hoffnung **II U4**, 82
to **hope** [həʊp] hoffen I
hopeful ['həʊpfl] hoffnungsvoll I
horrified ['hɒrɪfaɪd] entsetzt I
horse [hɔ:s] Pferd I
hospital ['hɒspɪtl] Hospital; Krankenhaus **II U2**, 30
hotel [həʊ'tel] Hotel **II U2**, 33
hour [aʊə] Stunde **II U3**, 63
house [haʊs] Haus I
how [haʊ] wie I
How many …? [ˌhaʊ 'meni] Wie viele …? I
How are you? [ˌhaʊ‿'ɑ: jə] Wie geht es dir?; Wie geht es euch?; Wie geht es Ihnen? I
How much (is/are) …? [ˌhaʊ 'mʌtʃ‿ɪz/ɑ:] Wie viel (kostet/kosten) …? I
How old are you? [haʊ‿'əʊld‿ə ju:] Wie alt bist du?; Wie alt sind Sie? I
How to … ['haʊ tə] Wie man … I
Is this **how** you (do) …? [ɪz 'ðɪs haʊ jʊ ˌdu:] Machst du so …? I
that's **how** [ðæts 'haʊ] so **II U1**, 10
to **hug** [hʌg] umarmen I
huge [hju:dʒ] riesig; riesengroß; gewaltig **II AC1**, 48
to **hum** [hʌm] summen **II U2**, 33
human body [ˌhju:mən 'bɒdi] menschlicher Körper **II U3**, 62
Humanities *(pl)* [hju:'mænətiz] Sozialwissenschaften **II U2**, 32
hungry ['hʌŋgri] hungrig I
to **hurry** ['hʌri] eilen; sich beeilen I
*to **hurt** [hɜ:t] verletzen; weh tun **II U4**, 72
hurt [hɜ:t] verletzt **II U1**, 24
husband ['hʌzbənd] Ehemann **II U2**, 30

I

I [aɪ] ich I
I don't know! [ˌaɪ ˌdəʊnt 'nəʊ] Ich weiß (es) nicht! I
I don't like … [aɪ 'dəʊnt laɪk] Ich mag … nicht.; Ich mache … nicht gern. I
I hear … [aɪ 'hɪə] Ich habe gehört, dass … I
I like … [aɪ 'laɪk] Mir gefällt …; Ich mag … I
I love you. [aɪ 'lʌv ju] Ich liebe dich.; Ich mag dich. I
I love … [aɪ 'lʌv] Ich liebe …; Ich mag … total gern. I
I'd like to … *(= I would like to)* [aɪd 'laɪk tə] Ich möchte …; Ich würde gern … I
I'm (not) scared of … [ˌaɪm (nɒt) 'skeəd‿əv] Ich habe (keine) Angst vor … I
I'm dog-tired. [ˌaɪm ˌdɒg'taɪəd] Ich bin hundemüde. I
I'm English. [aɪm‿'ɪŋglɪʃ] Ich bin Engländer/-in. I
I'm fine. [ˌaɪm 'faɪn] Mir geht's gut. I
I'm from … [ˌaɪm frɒm] Ich bin aus … I
I'm sorry! [ˌaɪm 'sɒri] Tut mir leid! I
I'm … [aɪm] Ich bin … I
ice [aɪs] Eis I
ice cream [ˌaɪs 'kri:m] Eis; Eiscreme I
ice rink ['aɪs ˌrɪŋk] Eisbahn; Schlittschuhbahn I
idea [aɪ'dɪə] Idee; Einfall I
no **idea** [ˌnəʊ‿aɪ'dɪə] keine Ahnung **II U1**, 19
identity [aɪ'dentəti] Identität **II AC1**, 49
idiot ['ɪdiət] Idiot/-in **II U2**, 41
if [ɪf] wenn; falls; ob I
to **imagine** [ɪ'mædʒɪn] sich (etwas) vorstellen I
important [ɪm'pɔ:tnt] wichtig I
impressed [ɪm'prest] beeindruckt **II U2**, 36
to **improve** [ɪm'pru:v] sich verbessern; verbessern I
in [ɪn] in; im; rein; herein I
in front of [ɪn 'frʌnt‿əv] vor I
in need [ɪn 'ni:d] bedürftig; in Not **II U1**, 10
in secret [ɪn 'si:krət] heimlich **II U4**, 81
in the end [ˌɪn ði‿'end] schließlich; zum Schluss **II U1**, 10
in the evenings [ɪn ði‿'i:vnɪŋz] abends I
in the mornings [ˌɪn ðə 'mɔ:nɪŋz] morgens; vormittags I
in the photo(s) [ˌɪn ðə 'fəʊtəʊ(z)] auf dem Foto/den Fotos I
in the street [ˌɪn ðə 'stri:t] in der Straße; auf der Straße I
Indian ['ɪndiən] Inder/-in; indisch I

individual [ˌɪndɪ'vɪdʒuəl] individuell; einzeln **II U4**, 69
infinitive [ɪn'fɪnətɪv] Infinitiv **I**
to **influence** ['ɪnfluəns] beeinflussen **II AC2**, 89
information *(no pl)* [ˌɪnfə'meɪʃn] Information; Informationen **I**
injury ['ɪndʒəri] Verletzung **II U4**, 76
inline skating ['ɪnlaɪn ˌskeɪtɪŋ] Inlineskatefahren **I**
inside [ˌɪn'saɪd] innen; im Innern; hinein; nach drinnen; in; drin **I**
instruction [ɪn'strʌkʃn] Instruktion; Anweisung **I**
instructor [ɪn'strʌktə] Lehrer/-in; Betreuer/-in **II U1**, 18
interest ['ɪntrəst] Interesse **II U5**, 90
to **interest** ['ɪntrəst] (sich) interessieren °**II U2**, 38
*to be **interested** in [biˌ'ɪntrəstɪdˌɪn] interessiert sein an; sich interessieren für **II U2**, 31
interesting ['ɪntrəstɪŋ] interessant **I**
international [ˌɪntə'næʃnl] international **I**
internet ['ɪntənet] Internet **I**
interview ['ɪntəvju:] Interview; Befragung **I**
to **interview** ['ɪntəvju:] interviewen; befragen **I**
into ['ɪntə] in; in … hinein **I**
*to be **into** [bi:ˌ'ɪntə] mögen; stehen auf **I**
You're **into** … ['jɔ:rˌɪntə] Du magst …; Du stehst auf … **I**
Introduce … [ˌɪntrə'dju:s] Stelle/Stellt … vor. **I**
introduction [ˌɪntrə'dʌkʃn] Einführung; Einleitung; Vorstellung **II U2**, 29
invitation [ˌɪnvɪ'teɪʃn] Einladung **I**
to **invite** [ɪn'vaɪt] einladen **I**
irregular [ɪ'regjələ] unregelmäßig **I**
Is this how you (do) …? [ɪz 'ðɪs haʊ jʊ ˌdu:] Machst du so …? **I**
it [ɪt] es **I**
It's fun. [ɪts 'fʌn] Es macht Spaß. **I**
It's great for … [ɪts 'greɪt fə] Es ist super zum/für … **I**
It's your turn. [ˌɪts 'jɔ: tɜ:n] Du bist dran. **I**
It's …/They're … [ɪts/ðeə] Es kostet …/ Sie kosten … **I**
its [ɪts] sein/-e; ihr/-e **I**

J

January ['dʒænjuri] Januar **I**
*to be **jealous** (of) [bi: 'dʒeləs] eifersüchtig sein (auf); neidisch sein (auf) **I**
jelly ['dʒeli] Tortenguss; Götterspeise; Wackelpudding; Gelee **I**
crown **jewels** [ˌkraʊn 'dʒu:əlz] Kronjuwelen **II U3**, 56
jewellery ['dʒu:əlri] Schmuck **I**
job [dʒɒb] Arbeit; Aufgabe; Job **I**
mouth **jogging** ['maʊθ ˌdʒɒgɪŋ] Training für den Mund **I**
to **join** [dʒɔɪn] beitreten; sich anschließen; verbinden **II U2**, 33
joke [dʒəʊk] Witz **I**
to **joke** [dʒəʊk] scherzen **II U5**, 102
juggling ['dʒʌglɪŋ] Jonglieren **II U2**, 38
juice [dʒu:s] Saft **I**
July [dʒʊ'laɪ] Juli **I**
to **jump** [dʒʌmp] springen **I**
to **jump** back [ˌdʒʌmpˌ'bæk] zurückspringen; *hier:* zurückschrecken **II U3**, 57
to **jump** the queue [ˌdʒʌmp ðə 'kju:] sich vordrängeln **I**
June [dʒu:n] Juni **I**
just [dʒʌst] gerade; nur; einfach **I**

K

*to **keep** [ki:p] behalten; aufbewahren; halten **I**
*to **keep** going [ˌki:p 'gəʊɪŋ] aufrechterhalten **II U1**, 12
*to **keep** up (with) [ˌki:pˌ'ʌp (wɪð)] mithalten (mit); Schritt halten (mit) **II U4**, 80
*to **keep** your fingers crossed [ˌki:p jɔ: ˌfɪŋgəz 'krɒst] die Daumen drücken **I**
key [ki:] Schlüssel **II U3**, 63
key word ['ki: wɜ:d] Stichwort; Schlüsselbegriff **I**
to **kick** [kɪk] schießen; treten **II U4**, 68
kind [kaɪnd] Art; Sorte **I**
king [kɪŋ] König **I**
kitchen ['kɪtʃɪn] Küche **I**
knob [nɒb] Griff **II U5**, 95
*to **know** [nəʊ] kennen; wissen **I**
I don't **know**! [ˌaɪ ˌdəʊnt 'nəʊ] Ich weiß (es) nicht! **I**
You **know** how to … [ju: 'nəʊ ˌhaʊ tə] Du weißt, wie man …; Ihr wisst, wie man … **I**
Korean [kə'ri:ən] koreanisch; Koreanisch; Koreaner/-in **II U4**, 76
South **Korean** [ˌsaʊθ kə'ri:ən] Südkoreaner/-in; südkoreanisch; Südkoreanisch **II AC2**, 88

L

ladder ['lædə] Leiter **II U2**, 34
lake [leɪk] See **I**
boating **lake** ['bəʊtɪŋ ˌleɪk] See zum Rudern **I**
lamb [læm] Lamm; Lämmchen **I**
land [lænd] Land **I**
to **land** [lænd] landen **II U4**, 78
language ['læŋgwɪdʒ] Sprache **I**
first **language** [ˌfɜ:st 'læŋgwɪdʒ] Muttersprache **II AC2**, 89
foreign **language** [ˌfɒrɪn 'læŋgwɪdʒ] Fremdsprache **II U2**, 38
official **language** [əˌfɪʃl 'læŋgwɪdʒ] Amtssprache **II AC2**, 89
laptop ['læptɒp] Laptop **II U5**, 97
large [lɑ:dʒ] groß; riesig **II AC1**, 48
lassi ['lʌsi] Lassi **I**
last [lɑ:st] letzte/-r/-s **I**
at **last** [ət 'lɑ:st] endlich; schließlich **I**
late [leɪt] spät; zu spät **I**
*to be **late** [bi: 'leɪt] zu spät dran sein; zu spät kommen **I**
later ['leɪtə] später **I**
to **laugh** [lɑ:f] lachen **I**
*to **learn** [lɜ:n] lernen **I**
*to **learn** … by heart [ˌlɜ:n baɪ 'hɑ:t] auswendig lernen **I**
a lot to **learn** [ə ˌlɒt tə 'lɜ:n] viel zu lernen **I**
at **least** [ət 'li:st] mindestens; wenigstens °**II U3**, 63
*to **leave** [li:v] verlassen; lassen; abfahren **II U2**, 30; losgehen **II U4**, 72
*to **leave** a message [ˌli:vˌə 'mesɪdʒ] eine Nachricht hinterlassen **I**
*to **leave** it to cool [ˌli:vˌɪt tə 'ku:l] kalt stellen **I**
*to **leave** space [li:v 'speɪs] Platz lassen **I**
left [left] linke/-r/-s; links **I**
on the **left** [ɒn ðə 'left] auf der linken Seite; links **I**
left [left] übrig **I**
leg [leg] Bein **II U4**, 71
leisure ['leʒə] Freizeit; Freizeit- **I**
leisure centre ['leʒə ˌsentə] Freizeitzentrum **I**
lemon ['lemən] Zitrone **II U1**, 24
lemonade [ˌlemə'neɪd] Limonade **I**
lesson ['lesn] Unterrichtsstunde; Schulstunde; Unterricht **I**
*to **let** [let] lassen **I**
*to **let** go (of) [ˌlet 'gəʊ (əv)] loslassen **II U4**, 80
Let's … [lets] Lass/Lasst uns … **I**
letter ['letə] Buchstabe **I**; Brief **II U5**, 91
capital **letter** [ˌkæpɪtl 'letə] Großbuchstabe **I**
to **lie** [laɪ] lügen **II U1**, 9
*to **lie** [laɪ] liegen **II U2**, 40
life, **lives** *(pl)* [laɪf, laɪvz] Leben **II U2**, 39
lifeboat ['laɪfbəʊt] Rettungsboot **I**
lifebuoy ['laɪfbɔɪ] Rettungsring **I**
light [laɪt] Licht; Lampe **II U5**, 102
lightning *(no pl)* ['laɪtnɪŋ] Blitz **II U5**, 102
to **like** [laɪk] mögen; gern haben **I**
would **like** [wʊd 'laɪk] würde/-st/-n/-t gern; hätte/-st/-n/-t gern **I**
I don't **like** … [aɪ 'dəʊnt laɪk] Ich mag … nicht.; Ich mache … nicht gern. **I**
I **like** singing and dancing. [ˌaɪ laɪk ˌsɪŋɪŋˌ ənd 'dɑ:nsɪŋ] Ich singe und tanze gern. **I**
I **like** … [aɪ 'laɪk] Mir gefällt …; Ich mag … **I**

I'd **like** to … *(= I would like to)* [aɪd ˈlaɪk tə] Ich möchte …; Ich würde gern … I
Would you **like** …? [ˌwʊd jʊ ˈlaɪk] Möchtest du …?; Möchten Sie …?; Möchtet ihr …? °II U4, 70
like [laɪk] wie I
like that [laɪk ˈðæt] so I
like this [laɪk ˈðɪs] so I
line [laɪn] Zeile; Linie I
finish **line** [ˈfɪnɪʃ ˌlaɪn] Ziellinie II U4, 81
time **line** [ˈtaɪm ˌlaɪn] Zeitstrahl I
link [lɪŋk] Link; Verbindung II U3, 59
to **link** [lɪŋk] verbinden II U5, 104
linking word [ˈlɪŋkɪŋ ˌwɜːd] Bindewort I
lion [laɪən] Löwe II U3, 56
list [lɪst] Liste I
to **listen** (to) [ˈlɪsn] zuhören; anhören I
Listen again. [ˌlɪsn‿əˈgen] Hör/Hört noch einmal zu. I
to **listen** for [ˈlɪsn fə] horchen auf I
listener [ˈlɪsənə] Zuhörer/-in II U4, 77
listening [ˈlɪsnɪŋ] Hören I
little [ˈlɪtl] klein I
a **little** [ə ˈlɪtl] ein wenig; etwas I
to **live** [lɪv] wohnen; leben I
lively [ˈlaɪvli] lebendig II U2, 29
living room [ˈlɪvɪŋ rʊm] Wohnzimmer I
location [ləʊˈkeɪʃn] Handlungsort; Lage; Standort II U3, 58
locked [lɒkt] abgeschlossen II U1, 19
locker [ˈlɒkə] Schließfach; Spind I
loft [lɒft] Dachboden I
LOL (= laughing out loud) [lɒl] LOL II U1, 8
Londoner [ˈlʌndənə] Londoner/-in I
lonely [ˈləʊnli] einsam I
long [lɒŋ] lang I
look [lʊk] Blick I
*to have a **look** (at) [ˌhæv‿ə ˈlʊk] anschauen II U4, 73
*to take a **look** at [ˌteɪk‿ə ˈlʊk‿æt] einen Blick werfen auf II U2, 37
to **look** [lʊk] schauen; sehen; aussehen I
Look! [lʊk] Schau/Schaut mal! I
to **look** after [ˌlʊk‿ˈɑːftə] aufpassen auf; hüten; sich kümmern um I
to **look** at [ˈlʊk‿ət] anschauen; ansehen I
to **look** for [ˈlʊk fɔː] suchen nach I
to **look** forward to [ˌlʊk ˈfɔːwəd tə] sich freuen auf II U2, 33
to **look** out [ˌlʊk‿ˈaʊt] aufpassen II U4, 70
to **look** up [ˌlʊk‿ˈʌp] nachschlagen; nachschauen I
Look closely … [ˌlʊk ˈkləʊsli] Schau(t) genau … °II U4, 78
what the man **looked** like [ˌwɒt ðə mæn ˈlʊkt laɪk] wie der Mann aussah II U1, 13
*to **lose** [luːz] verlieren II U4, 68
a **lot** [ə ˈlɒt] viel I
a **lot** of [ə ˈlɒt‿əv] viel/-e; eine Menge I
lots (of) [ˈlɒts‿əv] viel/-e; jede Menge I
loud [laʊd] laut I

Love … [lʌv] Liebe Grüße *(am Briefende)*; Herzliche Grüße *(am Briefende)* I
to **love** [lʌv] lieben; gern mögen I
would **love** [wʊd ˈlʌv] würde/-st/-n/-t sehr gern; hätte/-st-/-n/-t sehr gern I
I **love** you. [aɪ ˈlʌv ju] Ich liebe dich.; Ich mag dich. I
I **love** … [aɪ ˈlʌv] Ich liebe …; Ich mag … total gern. I
lovebirds *(pl)* [ˈlʌvˌbɜːdz] Turteltauben II U1, 9
low [ləʊ] niedrig II U1, 17
low tide [ˈləʊ ˌtaɪd] Ebbe II U3, 62
lucky … [ˈlʌki] … der/die Glückliche I
*to be **lucky** [bi‿ˈlʌki] Glück haben II U3, 62
lucky charm [ˌlʌki ˈtʃɑːm] Glücksbringer; Talisman I
… is/are **lucky**. [ɪz/ɑː ˈlʌki] … hat/haben Glück. I
lunch [lʌnʃ] Mittagessen I
lunch break [ˈlʌnʃbreɪk] Mittagspause I

M

machine [məˈʃiːn] Automat; Maschine; Apparat; Gerät I
answering **machine** [ˈɑːnsrɪŋ məˌʃiːn] Anrufbeantworter I
washing **machine** [ˈwɒʃɪŋ məˌʃiːn] Waschmaschine II U5, 95
mad [mæd] verrückt II U5, 97
magazine [ˌmægəˈziːn] Zeitschrift I
to **mail** [ˈiːmeɪl] mailen; per E-Mail schicken II U5, 97
main [meɪn] Haupt- I
*to **make** [meɪk] machen; tun; bilden; *hier:* ergeben I
*to **make** a decision [ˌmeɪk‿ə dɪˈsɪʒn] eine Entscheidung treffen °II U3, 61
*to **make** a wish [ˌmeɪk‿ə ˈwɪʃ] sich etwas wünschen I
*to **make** friends [ˌmeɪk ˈfrendz] Freundschaft schließen II U2, 43
*to **make** money [ˌmeɪk ˈmʌni] Geld verdienen I
*to **make** notes [ˌmeɪk ˈnəʊts] Notizen machen I
*to **make** somebody do something [meɪk] jmdn. dazu bringen, etw. zu tun II U5, 92
*to **make** sure [ˌmeɪk ˈʃɔː] sich versichern I
*to **make** trouble [ˌmeɪk ˈtrʌbl] Ärger machen; in Schwierigkeiten bringen I
man, **men** *(pl)* [mæn; men] Mann I
what the **man** looked like [ˌwɒt ðə mæn ˈlʊkt laɪk] wie der Mann aussah II U1, 13
manga [ˈmæŋgə] Manga *(japanischer Comic)* II U2, 38
mango [ˈmæŋgəʊ] Mango I
many [ˈmeni] viele I
How **many** …? [ˌhaʊ ˈmeni] Wie viele …? I
map [mæp] Stadtplan; Landkarte I

mind **map** [ˈmaɪnd mæp] Wörternetz *(eine Art Schaubild)* I
marathon [ˈmærəθn] Marathon II U4, 68
March [mɑːtʃ] März I
market [ˈmɑːkɪt] Markt I
flea **market** [ˈfliː ˌmɑːkɪt] Flohmarkt I
raven **master** [ˈreɪvn ˌmɑːstə] Herr der Raben II U3, 56
match [mætʃ] Spiel; Match II U4, 68
to **match** [mætʃ] zuordnen; passen zu; entsprechen I
mate [meɪt] Schiffsoffizier; Maat I
material [məˈtɪəriəl] Material II U3, 61
Maths [mæθs] Mathematik; Mathe II U2, 32
May [meɪ] Mai I
may [meɪ] (vielleicht) können; dürfen II U5, 95
maybe [ˈmeɪbi] vielleicht I
me [miː] ich; mich; mir I
meal [miːl] Mahlzeit; Essen II U1, 18
ready **meal** [ˌredi ˈmiːl] Fertiggericht I
*to **mean** [miːn] bedeuten; meinen II U3, 54
meaning [ˈmiːnɪŋ] Bedeutung; Sinn II U1, 21
mechanic [məˈkænɪk] Mechaniker/-in; Kfz-Mechaniker/-in II U1, 13
media [ˈmiːdiə] Medien II U5, 91
mediation [ˌmiːdiˈeɪʃn] Sprachmittlung I
*to **meet** [miːt] treffen; sich treffen I
member [ˈmembə] Mitglied II U2, 33
memory [ˈmemri] Erinnerung; Gedächtnis II U1, 19
to **mention** [ˈmenʃn] erwähnen II AC2, 88
merchant [ˈmɜːtʃənt] Kaufmann; Händler II AC2, 89
message [ˈmesɪdʒ] Botschaft; Nachricht I
*to leave a **message** [ˌliːv‿ə ˈmesɪdʒ] eine Nachricht hinterlassen I
*to take a **message** [ˌteɪk‿ə ˈmesɪdʒ] eine Nachricht entgegennehmen; jmdm. etw. ausrichten I
text (**message**) [ˈtekst ˌmesɪdʒ] SMS; Kurznachricht I
metre [ˈmiːtə] Meter II U3, 62
middle [ˈmɪdl] Mitte I
mile [maɪl] Meile *(brit. Längenmaß)* II U4, 72
milk [mɪlk] Milch I
million [ˈmɪljən] Million II AC1, 48
I've done this a **million** times before. [ˌaɪv dʌn ðɪs ə ˌmɪljən taɪmz bɪˈfɔː] Ich habe das schon eine Million Mal gemacht. II U5, 95
mind map [ˈmaɪnd mæp] Wörternetz *(eine Art Schaubild)* I
mine [maɪn] mein/-er/-e/-es II U2, 41
mini [mɪni] Mini- II U4, 70
minute [ˈmɪnɪt] Minute I
to **miss** [mɪs] verpassen; versäumen II U5, 99
missing [ˈmɪsɪŋ] fehlend; verschwunden II U1, 13
What is **missing**? [ˌwɒt‿ɪz ˈmɪsɪŋ] Was fehlt? I

mistake [mɪ'steɪk] Fehler **I**
mobile ['məʊbaɪl] Handy; Mobiltelefon **II U5**, 91
modal ['məʊdl] Modalverb °**II U5**, 91
model ['mɒdl] Modell; Tonmodell; Model **I**
modern ['mɒdn] modern **II U3**, 64
moment ['məʊmənt] Moment; Augenblick **II U2**, 40
at the **moment** [ət ðə 'məʊmənt] im Moment; gerade **I**
Monday ['mʌndeɪ] Montag **I**
on **Mondays** [ɒn 'mʌndeɪz] montags **I**
money ['mʌni] Geld **I**
*to make **money** [ˌmeɪk 'mʌni] Geld verdienen **I**
pocket **money** ['pɒkɪt ˌmʌni] Taschengeld **I**
to raise **money** [ˌreɪz 'mʌni] Geld sammeln **II U1**, 10
monster ['mɒnstə] Monster; Ungeheuer **I**
month [mʌnθ] Monat **II U1**, 10
mood [mu:d] Stimmung; Laune **II U1**, 24
more [mɔ:] mehr; weitere **I**
not any **more** [ˌnɒt‿eni 'mɔ:] nicht mehr **I**
more … than ['mɔ: ðən] mehr … als **I**
morning ['mɔ:nɪŋ] Morgen; Vormittag **I**
in the **mornings** [ˌɪn ðə 'mɔ:nɪŋz] morgens; vormittags **I**
Good **morning**. [ˌgʊd 'mɔ:nɪŋ] Guten Morgen. **I**
(the) **most** [ðə 'məʊst] der/die/das meiste; die meisten **I**
mother ['mʌðə] Mutter **I**
to **motivate** ['məʊtɪveɪt] motivieren **I**
bicycle **motocross** [ˌbaɪsɪkl 'məʊtəʊkrɒs] Fahrradmotocross **II U4**, 83
mountain ['maʊntɪn] Berg **II U1**, 16
mouse (sg), mice (pl) [maʊs; maɪs] Maus/Mäuse **I**
mouth [maʊθ] Mund **I**
mouth jogging ['maʊθ ˌdʒɒgɪŋ] Training für den Mund **I**
move [mu:v] Bewegung **I**
to **move** [mu:v] (sich) bewegen **I**
Mr ['mɪstə] Herr *(Anrede)* **I**
Mrs ['mɪsɪz] Frau *(Anrede)* **I**
much [mʌtʃ] viel **I**
mud [mʌd] Schlamm **II U3**, 62
muddy ['mʌdi] schlammig **II U3**, 62
mudlark ['mʌdlɑ:k] *jemand, der im Schlamm nach Sachen sucht, die er dann verkaufen kann* **II U3**, 62
multi-ethnic [ˌmʌlti'eθnɪk] Vielvölker-; international **II AC1**, 48
mum [mʌm] Mama **I**
museum [mju:'zi:əm] Museum **I**
music ['mju:zɪk] Musik **I**
musician [mju:'zɪʃn] Musiker/-in **II U3**, 53
must [mʌst] müssen **I**
mustn't ['mʌsnt] nicht dürfen **I**
my [maɪ] mein/-e **I**
My favourite … [maɪ 'feɪvrɪt] Mein/e Lieblings … **I**
My name is … [maɪ 'neɪm‿ɪz] Ich heiße … **I**
myself [maɪ'self] ich/mir/mich (selbst); selber **II U5**, 93

N

name [neɪm] Name **I**
name day ['neɪm ˌdeɪ] Namenstag **I**
My **name** is … [maɪ 'neɪm‿ɪz] Ich heiße … **I**
What's your **name**? [ˌwɒts jə 'neɪm] Wie heißt du?; Wie heißen Sie? **I**
to **name** [neɪm] nennen; benennen **I**
Can you **name** …? ['kæn jʊ ˌneɪm] Kannst du … nennen? **I**
nasty ['nɑ:sti] garstig; gemein **II U5**, 91
national ['næʃnl] national; landesweit **I**
nature ['neɪtʃə] Natur **II U2**, 43
near [nɪə] nahe; in der Nähe von **I**
nearly ['nɪəli] fast; annähernd **II U2**, 41
with special **needs** [wɪð ˌspeʃl 'ni:dz] behindert **II U2**, 29
in **need** [ɪn 'ni:d] bedürftig; in Not **II U1**, 10
to **need** (to do) [ni:d] (tun) müssen **I**
needn't ['ni:dnt] nicht brauchen; nicht müssen **I**
to **need** (to) [ni:d] brauchen; benötigen **I**
negative ['negətɪv] negativ; verneint °**II U4**, 82
negative form ['negətɪv ˌfɔ:m] verneinte Form **I**
neighbour *(BE)* ['neɪbə] Nachbar/-in **I**
*to get on people's **nerves** [ˌget‿ɒn sʌmbɒdiz 'nɜ:vz] jemandem auf die Nerven gehen **I**
nervous ['nɜ:vəs] nervös; aufgeregt **II U1**, 12
net [net] Netz **II U4**, 68
netball ['netbɔ:l] Korbball **I**
social **network** [ˌsəʊʃl 'netwɜ:k] soziales Netzwerk **II U5**, 91
never ['nevə] nie; niemals **I**
new [nju:] neu **I**
news *(sg)* [nju:z] Nachrichten; Neuigkeiten **II U2**, 40
next [nekst] nächste/-r/-s; der/die Nächste(n) **I**
next to ['nekst tə] neben **I**
the **next** day [ðə ˌnekst 'deɪ] am nächsten Tag **II U1**, 11
next [nekst] als Nächstes **I**
nice [naɪs] nett; schön; lieb **I**
night [naɪt] Nacht **I**
all **night** [ˌɔ:l 'naɪt] die ganze Nacht **I**
night walk ['naɪt wɔ:k] Nachtwanderung **II U1**, 18
nine [naɪn] neun **I**
2nite *(= tonight)* [tə'naɪt] heute Abend **I**
no [nəʊ] kein/-e **I**
no idea [ˌnəʊ‿aɪ'dɪə] keine Ahnung **II U1**, 19
no [nəʊ] nein **I**
nobody ['nəʊbədi] niemand **II U2**, 41
noise [nɔɪz] Lärm; Geräusch **II U1**, 18
non- [nɒn] nicht- **II U1**, 10
normal ['nɔ:ml] normal **II U3**, 58
north [nɔ:θ] Norden; Nord- **II U3**, 53
nose [nəʊz] Nase **II U1**, 8
not [nɒt] nicht **I**
not any more [ˌnɒt‿eni 'mɔ:] nicht mehr **I**
not … any [nɒt … eni] kein/-e **I**
not … anything [ˌnɒt 'eniθɪŋ] nichts **I**
not … yet [nɒt 'jet] noch nicht **II U4**, 72
note [nəʊt] Notiz; Anmerkung **I**
*to make **notes** [ˌmeɪk 'nəʊts] Notizen machen **I**
*to take **notes** [ˌteɪk 'nəʊts] sich Notizen machen **I**
to **note** down [ˌnəʊt 'daʊn] notieren; aufschreiben °**II U2**, 37
nothing ['nʌθɪŋ] nichts **I**
to **notice** ['nəʊtɪs] bemerken; wahrnehmen **II U2**, 40
noticeboard ['nəʊtɪsbɔ:d] schwarzes Brett **II U1**, 10
noun [naʊn] Nomen; Hauptwort **I**
November [nə'vembə] November **I**
now [naʊ] jetzt; nun **I**
right **now** [ˌraɪt 'naʊ] jetzt gleich; sofort; gerade **II U5**, 103
number ['nʌmbə] Zahl; Nummer **I**
nut [nʌt] Nuss **I**

O

o'clock [ə'klɒk] Uhr *(Zeitangabe bei vollen Stunden)* **I**
object ['ɒbdʒɪkt] Objekt °**II U2**, 31
October [ɒk'təʊbə] Oktober **I**
of [ɒv; əv] von **I**
of course [əv 'kɔ:s] natürlich; selbstverständlich **I**
*to take **off** [ˌteɪk‿'ɒf] abnehmen; herunternehmen; ausziehen **I**
to turn **off** [ˌtɜ:n‿ɒf] abschalten; ausschalten **II U1**, 12
special **offer** [ˌspeʃl‿'ɒfə] Sonderangebot **I**
to **offer** ['ɒfə] anbieten **II U2**, 28
office ['ɒfɪs] Büro **I**
police **officer** [pə'li:s‿ɒfɪsə] Polizeibeamter **II U2**, 36
official [ə'fɪʃl] Schiedsrichter/-in **II U4**, 81
official language [əˌfɪʃl 'læŋgwɪdʒ] Amtssprache **II AC2**, 89
offline ['ɒflaɪn] offline **II U5**, 103
often ['ɒfn] oft; häufig **I**
oh [əʊ] null *(bei Telefonnummern und Uhrzeitangaben)* **I**
Oh! [əʊ] O! **I**
ointment ['ɔɪntmənt] Salbe **II U4**, 73
OK [əʊ'keɪ] o.k.; in Ordnung **I**

old [əʊld] alt **I**
How **old** are you? [haʊ͜ˈəʊld͜ə ˌjuː] Wie alt bist du?; Wie alt sind Sie? **I**
11-year-**old** [ɪˌlevnˈjɪərəʊld] 11-Jährige/-r **II U4**, 70
on [ɒn] auf; an; am; in; im **I**
*to be **on** [bi͜ˈɒn] an sein; laufen **II U5**, 102
on Mondays [ɒn ˈmʌndeɪz] montags **I**
on my own [ˌɒn maɪ͜ˈəʊn] allein; für mich **II U2**, 40
on the left [ɒn ðə ˈleft] auf der linken Seite; links **I**
on the right [ɒn ðə ˈraɪt] auf der rechten Seite; rechts **I**
on time [ɒn ˈtaɪm] pünktlich **II U2**, 37
on top [ɒn ˈtɒp] oben; obendrauf **I**
Come **on**! [ˌkʌm͜ˈɒn] Komm schon!; Komm jetzt! **I**
once [wʌns] einmal; einst **I**
one [wʌn] eins **I**
one *(sg)*/**ones** *(pl)* [wʌn/wʌnz] eine/-r/-s **II U3**, 54
online [ˌɒnˈlaɪn] online **II U1**, 21
only [ˈəʊnli] einzige/-r/-s **II U5**, 103
only [ˈəʊnli] erst; bloß; nur **I**
only child [ˈəʊnli ˌtʃaɪld] Einzelkind **I**
Oops! [uːps] Hoppla!; Huch! **I**
to **open** [ˈəʊpn] öffnen; aufmachen **I**
open [ˈəʊpn] offen; geöffnet; aufgeschlagen **I**
opinion [əˈpɪnjən] Meinung **II U5**, 92
opposite [ˈɒpəzɪt] gegenüber; auf der anderen Seite von **I**
or [ɔː] oder **I**
orange [ˈɒrɪndʒ] Orange **I**
orange [ˈɒrɪndʒ] orange **I**
order [ˈɔːdə] Reihenfolge; Ordnung **I**
word **order** [ˈwɜːd͜ˌɔːdə] Wortstellung; Satzstellung **I**
to **organise** [ˈɔːɡənaɪz] organisieren **I**
originally [əˈrɪdʒnli] ursprünglich **II AC1**, 48
other [ˈʌðə] anders; andere/-r/-s; weitere **I**
each **other** [ˌiːtʃ͜ˈʌðə] einander; sich; sich gegenseitig **I**
the **others** [ði͜ˈʌðəz] die anderen **I**
Ouch! [aʊtʃ] Aua! **II U1**, 8
our [aʊə; ɑː] unser/-e **I**
out [aʊt] außerhalb; heraus; hinaus; nach draußen **I**
to clear **out** [ˌklɪər͜ˈaʊt] ausräumen; entrümpeln **I**
out and about [ˌaʊt͜ən͜əˈbaʊt] unterwegs **II U3**, 58
a day **out** in … [ə ˌdeɪ͜ˈaʊt ɪn] ein Tag in … **II U3**, 58
outdoor [ˌaʊtˈdɔː] Freiluft-; Outdoor- **II U1**, 16
outfit [ˈaʊtfɪt] Outfit; Kleidung **II U1**, 8
outside [aʊtˈsaɪd] nach draußen; draußen; außerhalb **I**
over [ˈəʊvə] hinüber; über **I**; vorüber; vorbei **II U4**, 79
*to go **over** to [ˌɡəʊ ˈəʊvə tə] hinübergehen zu; zu jmdm. nach Hause gehen **II U5**, 95
to **overreact** [ˌəʊvəriˈækt] überreagieren **II U5**, 92
own [əʊn] eigene/-r/-s **I**
on my **own** [ˌɒn maɪ͜ˈəʊn] allein; für mich **II U2**, 40

P

p.m. [ˌpiːˈem] nachmittags *(Uhrzeit)*; abends *(Uhrzeit)* **I**
packet [ˈpækɪt] Päckchen; Paket; Packung **I**
page [peɪdʒ] Seite **I**
pain [peɪn] Schmerz **II U4**, 72
to **paint** [peɪnt] anmalen; malen **I**
painting [ˈpeɪntɪŋ] Malerei; Gemälde **II U2**, 28
pair [peə] Paar **I**
pair work [ˈpeə wɜːk] Partnerarbeit °**II U5**, 100
to **panic** [ˈpænɪk] panisch werden **II U2**, 36
piece of **paper** [ˌpiːs͜əv ˈpeɪpə] Stück Papier **I**
paper [ˈpeɪpə] Papier **I**
paradise [ˈpærədaɪs] Paradies **II U5**, 90
parcel [ˈpɑːsl] Paket; Päckchen **I**
parents *(pl)* [ˈpeərənts] Eltern **I**
park [pɑːk] Park **I**
part [pɑːt] Teil; Stadtteil **I**
*to take **part** (in) [ˌteɪk ˈpɑːt (ɪn)] teilnehmen (an) **II U5**, 90
partially sighted [ˌpɑːʃəli ˈsaɪtɪd] sehbehindert **II U2**, 32
to **participate** [pɑːˈtɪsɪpeɪt] teilnehmen °**II U2**, 29
past **participle** [ˌpɑːst pɑːˈtɪsɪpl] Partizip °**II U4**, 71
partner [ˈpɑːtnə] Partner/-in **I**
party [ˈpɑːti] Party; Feier **I**
to **pass** [pɑːs] zupassen; zuspielen **II U4**, 68
to **pass** (on) [ˌpɑːs͜ˈɒn] weitergeben **I**
past [pɑːst] Vergangenheit **II U1**, 9
past form [ˈpɑːst fɔːm] Vergangenheitsform °**II U1**, 10
past participle [ˌpɑːst pɑːˈtɪsɪpl] Partizip °**II U4**, 71
past progressive [ˌpɑːst prəˈɡresɪv] Verlaufsform der Vergangenheit °**II U2**, 29
simple **past** [ˌsɪmpl ˈpɑːst] Vergangenheitsform °**II U1**, 9
past [pɑːst] nach *(bei Uhrzeitangaben)*; vorbei (an); vorüber (an) **I**
half **past** [ˌhɑːf ˈpɑːst] halb *(bei Uhrzeitangaben)* **I**
quarter **past**/to [ˈkwɔːtə pɑːst/tə] Viertel nach/vor **I**
pasta [ˈpæstə] Pasta; Nudeln **I**
*to **pay** (for) [peɪ] bezahlen **I**
PC *(= Personal Computer)* [piːˈsiː] PC **II AC2**, 89
PE *(= Physical Education)* [ˌpiːˈiː; ˌfɪzɪkl͜ edʒʊˈkeɪʃn] Sportunterricht **II U2**, 32
to **peer-edit** [ˈpɪər͜ˌedɪt] gegenseitig kontrollieren °**II U2**, 35
pen [pen] Füller **I**
penny, **pence** *(pl)* [ˈpeni; pens] Penny *(brit. Währungseinheit)*; Pence *(brit. Währungseinheit)* **I**
pencil [ˈpensl] Bleistift; Buntstift **I**
pencil-case [ˈpensl ˌkeɪs] Federmäppchen; Mäppchen **I**
penny, **pence** *(pl)* [ˈpeni; pens] Penny *(brit. Währungseinheit)*; Pence *(brit. Währungseinheit)* **I**
people *(pl)* [ˈpiːpl] Leute; Menschen **I**
present **perfect** [ˌpreznt ˈpɜːfɪkt] das Perfekt °**II U4**, 69
perfect [ˈpɜːfɪkt] perfekt; vollkommen **I**
person, **people** *(pl)* [ˈpɜːsn; ˈpiːpl] Person; Mensch **I**
personal [ˈpɜːsnl] persönlich **I**
perspective [pəˈspektɪv] Perspektive; Blickwinkel °**II U3**, 63
to **persuade** [pəˈsweɪd] überreden **II U3**, 52
pet [pet] Haustier **I**
phone [fəʊn] Telefon; Handy **I**
to answer the **phone** [ˌɑːnsə ðə ˈfəʊn] einen Anruf entgegennehmen **I**
phone call [ˈfəʊn ˌkɔːl] Anruf; Telefonanruf **I**
photo [ˈfəʊtəʊ] Foto; Fotografie **I**
in the **photo**(s) [ˌɪn ðə ˈfəʊtəʊ(z)] auf dem Foto/den Fotos **I**
photo story [ˈfəʊtəʊ ˌstɔːri] Fotostory; Bildgeschichte **I**
*to take **photos** [ˌteɪk ˈfəʊtəʊz] fotografieren; Fotos machen **I**
phrase [freɪz] Redewendung; Ausdruck; Satz **I**
Useful **phrases** [ˌjuːsfl ˈfreɪsɪz] nützliche Ausdrücke **I**
to **pick** [pɪk] auswählen; aussuchen °**II U5**, 101
pick-up [ˈpɪkʌp] Pick-up; Wiederaufnehmen **I**
picnic [ˈpɪknɪk] Picknick **I**
picture [ˈpɪktʃə] Bild; Foto **I**
pie [paɪ] Kuchen; Pastete **I**
piece [piːs] Stück **I**
piece of paper [ˌpiːs͜əv ˈpeɪpə] Stück Papier **I**
pier [pɪə] Pier; Hafendamm **I**
pig [pɪɡ] Schwein **I**
guinea **pig** [ˈɡɪniː ˌpɪɡ] Meerschweinchen **I**
pill [pɪl] Pille; Tablette **II U4**, 73
pilot [ˈpaɪlət] Pilot/-in **II U2**, 36
pink [pɪŋk] pink; rosa **I**
pipe [paɪp] Rohr; Rohrleitung **II U2**, 34
clay **pipe** [ˈkleɪ paɪp] Tonpfeife **II U3**, 63
pitch [pɪtʃ] Spielfeld; Platz **II U4**, 68
pizza [ˈpiːtsə] Pizza **I**

place [pleɪs] Ort; Stelle; Platz I
*to take **place** [ˌteɪk 'pleɪs] stattfinden I
placemat ['pleɪsmæt] Placemat; Platzdeckchen I
plan [plæn] Plan; Entwurf I
to plan [plæn] planen I
planet ['plænɪt] Planet **II U1**, 18
planner ['plænə] Handbuch; Kalender I
to plant [plɑ:nt] pflanzen; anpflanzen **II U2**, 41
role play ['rəʊl ˌpleɪ] Rollenspiel I
to play [pleɪ] spielen I
to **play** a trick (on) [ˌpleɪ‿ə 'trɪk‿ɒn] einen Streich spielen I
player ['pleɪə] Spieler/-in; Mitspieler/-in **II U4**, 75
Please. [pli:z] Bitte. I
plural ['plʊərəl] Plural; Mehrzahl I
pocket money ['pɒkɪt ˌmʌni] Taschengeld I
poem ['pəʊɪm] Gedicht I
point [pɔɪnt] Punkt **II U4**, 68; Zeitpunkt °**II U5**, 104
point of view [ˌpɔɪnt‿əv 'vju:] Standpunkt; Ansicht; Perspektive **II U4**, 76
Point to … ['pɔɪnt tə] Zeige/Zeigt auf … I
Point. [pɔɪnt] Zeige/Zeigt darauf. I
police [pə'li:s] Polizei **II U1**, 13
police officer [pə'li:s‿ɒfɪsə] Polizeibeamter **II U2**, 36
polite [pə'laɪt] höflich I
Be **polite**. [bi: pə'laɪt] Sei/Seid höflich. I
pollution [pə'lu:ʃn] Verschmutzung **II U3**, 62
pond [pɒnd] Teich **II U2**, 33
pony ['pəʊni] Pony I
popular ['pɒpjələ] beliebt; populär I
positive ['pɒzətɪv] positiv **II U2**, 29
possessive form [pəˌsesɪv 'fɔ:m] Possessivform I
possible ['pɒsəbl] möglich I
post [pəʊst] Post *(Eintrag im Internet)* I
to post [pəʊst] online stellen; posten **II U5**, 90
poster ['pəʊstə] Poster I
class **poster** ['klɑ:s ˌpəʊstə] Klassenposter I
postman ['pəʊstmən] Briefträger **II U1**, 13
pound (£) [paʊnd] Pfund *(brit. Währungseinheit)* I
to pour [pɔ:] einschenken; eingießen; schütten I
power cut ['paʊə ˌkʌt] Stromausfall **II U5**, 103
Word **power** ['wɜ:d ˌpaʊə] die Kraft der Wörter *(Wortschatzübung)* I
practical ['præktɪkl] praktisch **II U5**, 91
to practise ['præktɪs] üben; trainieren I
practising ['præktɪsɪŋ] Üben I
to prepare [prɪ'peə] vorbereiten; zubereiten I
preposition [ˌprepə'zɪʃn] Präposition I
pre-reading [ˌpri:'ri:dɪŋ] vor dem Lesen I
prescription [prɪ'skrɪpʃn] Rezept *(für Arzneimittel)* **II U4**, 73
present ['preznt] Geschenk I; Gegenwart; Präsens °**II U1**, 14
present perfect [ˌpreznt 'pɜ:fɪkt] das Perfekt °**II U4**, 69
present progressive [ˌpreznt prə'gresɪv] Verlaufsform des Präsens/der Gegenwart I
simple present [ˌsɪmpl 'preznt] Gegenwart; Präsens I
to present [prɪ'zent] präsentieren; vorstellen I
presentation [ˌprezn'teɪʃn] Präsentation; Vortrag I
presenter [prɪ'zentə] Moderator/-in I
to press [pres] drücken; pressen **II U5**, 102
price [praɪs] Preis I
primary school ['praɪmri ˌsku:l] Grundschule I
print [prɪnt] gedruckt; Druck- **II U5**, 91
prison ['prɪzn] Gefängnis **II U3**, 56
prize [praɪz] Preis; Gewinn I
pro [prəʊ] Argument dafür **II U3**, 55
probably ['prɒbəbli] möglicherweise; wahrscheinlich **II U3**, 52
problem ['prɒbləm] Problem; Schwierigkeit I
profile ['prəʊfaɪl] Profil; Porträt I
programme ['prəʊgræm] Programm; Sendung **II U4**, 68
progress ['prəʊgres] Fortschritt °**II U2**, 33
past progressive [ˌpɑ:st prə'gresɪv] Verlaufsform der Vergangenheit °**II U2**, 29
present **progressive** [ˌpreznt prə'gresɪv] Verlaufsform des Präsens/der Gegenwart I
project ['prɒdʒekt] Projekt I
prompt card ['prɒmpt kɑ:d] Stichwortkarte; Rollenkarte °**II U2**, 32
relative pronoun [ˌrelətɪv 'prəʊnaʊn] Relativpronomen °**II U2**, 31
pronunciation [prəˌnʌnsi'eɪʃn] Aussprache I
proud (of) ['praʊd‿əv] stolz (auf) **II U1**, 9
public ['pʌblɪk] öffentlich **II U3**, 52
public transport *(no pl)* [ˌpʌblɪk 'trænspɔ:t] öffentliche Verkehrsmittel **II U3**, 52
pudding ['pʊdɪŋ] Pudding; Nachtisch I
to pull [pʊl] ziehen I
purple ['pɜ:pl] violett; lila I
to push [pʊʃ] stoßen; schieben; schubsen **II U2**, 41
*to put [pʊt] setzen; stellen; legen I
Put in … [pʊt‿'ɪn] Setze/Setzt ein … I
Put it in … [ˌpʊt‿ɪt‿'ɪn] Lege/Legt es in …; Stelle/Stellt es in … I
*to **put** through [ˌpʊt‿'θru:] verbinden I
*to **put** up [ˌpʊt‿'ʌp] aufstellen; errichten **II U2**, 33
Put … face down. [pʊt ˌfeɪs 'daʊn] Lege/Legt … umgedreht hin. I
puzzle ['pʌzl] Rätsel; Puzzle I
pyjamas [pɪ'dʒɑ:məz] Schlafanzug; Pyjama **II U1**, 12

Q

quality ['kwɒləti] Qualität I
quarter past/to ['kwɔ:tə pɑ:st/tə] Viertel nach/vor I
queen [kwi:n] Königin **II U2**, 30
question ['kwestʃən] Frage I
question tag ['kwestʃən ˌtæg] Frageanhängsel; Bestätigungsfrage °**II U5**, 94
queue [kju:] Schlange; Warteschlange I
to jump the **queue** [ˌdʒʌmp ðə 'kju:] sich vordrängeln I
quick [kwɪk] schnell I
quickly ['kwɪkli] schnell **II U2**, 40
quiet [kwaɪət] still; ruhig; leise I
quiz [kwɪz] Quiz; Rätsel I
quote [kwəʊt] Zitat °**II U2**, 28

R

rabbit ['ræbɪt] Kaninchen I
race [reɪs] Wettlauf; Rennen **II U4**, 68
camel racing ['kæml ˌreɪsɪŋ] Kamelrennen **II U4**, 68
racquet ['rækɪt] Schläger **II U4**, 68
radio ['reɪdiəʊ] Radio **II U4**, 68
raffle ['ræfl] Tombola I
to rain [reɪn] regnen **II U5**, 102
to raise money [ˌreɪz 'mʌni] Geld sammeln **II U1**, 10
rap [ræp] Rap I
to rap [ræp] rappen I
rat [ræt] Ratte I
raven ['reɪvn] Rabe **II U3**, 56
raven master ['reɪvn ˌmɑ:stə] Herr der Raben **II U3**, 56
RE *(= Religious Education)* [ˌɑ:r'i:; rɪˌlɪdʒəs‿edʒʊ'keɪʃn] Religion *(Schulfach)* **II U2**, 32
to reach [ri:tʃ] erreichen; dran kommen **II U5**, 95
reaction [ri'ækʃn] Reaktion **II U2**, 29
*to read [ri:d] lesen I
reader ['ri:də] Leser/-in I
reading ['ri:dɪŋ] Lesen I

ready ['redi] fertig; bereit **II U2**, 41
ready meal [ˌredi 'mi:l] Fertiggericht I
real [rɪəl] echt; richtig; wirklich **II U1**, 10
realistic [ˌrɪə'lɪstɪk] realistisch **II U3**, 61
really ['rɪəli] wirklich I
reason ['ri:zn] Grund **II U4**, 82
to receive [rɪ'si:v] empfangen; erhalten; bekommen **II U4**, 77
to record [rɪ'kɔ:d] aufnehmen; aufzeichnen **II U4**, 78
recording [rɪ'kɔ:dɪŋ] Aufnahme; Aufzeichnung I

recording studio [rɪ'kɔ:dɪŋ ˌstju:diəʊ] Aufnahmestudio; Tonstudio **I**
recycling [ˌri:'saɪklɪŋ] Recycling; Wiederaufbereitung **II U2**, 40
red [red] rot **I**
to **reef** the sails [ˌri:f ðə 'seɪlz] die Segel einholen **I**
region ['ri:dʒn] Region; Gegend **II AC2**, 89
registration [ˌredʒɪs'treɪʃn] Anwesenheitskontrolle **II U2**, 32
regular ['regjələ] regelmäßig; gleichmäßig **I**
relationship [rɪ'leɪʃnʃɪp] Beziehung **II U4**, 82
defining **relative** clause [dɪˌfaɪnɪŋ 'relətɪv ˌklɔ:z] notwendiger Relativsatz °**II U2**, 30
relative pronoun [ˌrelətɪv 'prəʊnaʊn] Relativpronomen °**II U2**, 31
to **relax** [rɪ'læks] sich entspannen; sich ausruhen; sich beruhigen **II U2**, 36
religious [rɪ'lɪdʒəs] religiös; gläubig **I**
to **remember** [rɪ'membə] sich erinnern (an); sich merken; denken an **I**
Remember? [rɪ'membə] Erinnerst du dich?; Erinnert ihr euch? **I**
to **repeat** [rɪ'pi:t] wiederholen °**II U5**, 94
reply [rɪ'plaɪ] Antwort; Erwiderung; Entgegnung **I**
to **reply** [rɪ'plaɪ] antworten; erwidern; entgegnen **I**
report [rɪ'pɔ:t] Bericht; Meldung **II U1**, 9
travel **report** [ˌtrævl rɪ'pɔ:t] Reisebericht **II U1**, 20
reporter [rɪ'pɔ:tə] Reporter/-in **II U4**, 75
rescue ['reskju:] Rettung **II U4**, 77
the **rest** [rest] der Rest **I**
restaurant ['restrɒnt] Restaurant; Gaststätte **I**
result [rɪ'zʌlt] Ergebnis; Resultat **II U5**, 97
*to **retell** [ˌri:'tel] nacherzählen; nochmals erzählen **I**
revision [rɪ'vɪʒn] Wiederholung °**II U1**, 15
rhyme [raɪm] Reim **I**
rhythm ['rɪðm] Rhythmus **I**
rigging ['rɪgɪŋ] Takelage **I**
right [raɪt] richtig; korrekt; rechts; rechte/-r/-s **I**
*to be **right** [bi 'raɪt] recht haben **I**
on the **right** [ɒn ðə 'raɪt] auf der rechten Seite; rechts **I**
right away [ˌraɪt‿ə'weɪ] sofort; gleich **I**
right here [ˌraɪt 'hɪə] genau hier **II U4**, 70
right now [ˌraɪt 'naʊ] jetzt gleich; sofort; gerade **II U5**, 103
*to **ring** [rɪŋ] klingeln; läuten **I**
ice **rink** ['aɪs ˌrɪŋk] Eisbahn; Schlittschuhbahn **I**
river ['rɪvə] Fluss **I**
by the **river** [baɪ ðə 'rɪvə] am Fluss **II U2**, 31
road [rəʊd] Straße **II U1**, 18
rock 'n' roll [ˌrɒk‿ən 'rəʊl] Rock 'n' Roll **II AC2**, 89
role [rəʊl] Rolle **I**
role play ['rəʊl ˌpleɪ] Rollenspiel **I**
to swap **roles** [ˌswɒp 'rəʊlz] Rollen tauschen **I**
rock 'n' **roll** [ˌrɒk‿ən 'rəʊl] Rock 'n' Roll **II AC2**, 89
to **roll** off [rəʊl] hinunterrollen; herunterrollen **II U3**, 62
Roll two dice. [ˌrəʊl ˌtu: 'daɪs] Würfle/Würfelt mit zwei Würfeln. **I**
Roman ['rəʊmən] Römer/-in; römisch **II AC1**, 48
Romanian [rʊ'meɪniən] Rumäne/Rumänin; rumänisch; Rumänisch **II AC2**, 88
room [ru:m; rʊm] Zimmer; Raum **I**
chat **room** ['tʃæt rʊm] Chatroom **II AC2**, 88
living **room** ['lɪvɪŋ rʊm] Wohnzimmer **I**
roommate ['ru:mmeɪt] Zimmergenosse/Zimmergenossin **I**
round [raʊnd] Runde **II U1**, 8
round of boxing [ˌraʊnd‿əv 'bɒksɪŋ] Boxrunde **II U1**, 8
to turn **round** [ˌtɜ:n‿(ə)'raʊnd] (sich) umdrehen; wenden **II U2**, 41
round [raʊnd] um … herum **II U5**, 103
route [ru:t] Strecke; Route **II U1**, 16
royal ['rɔɪəl] königlich **I**
rubber ['rʌbə] Radiergummi **I**
rubbish ['rʌbɪʃ] Müll; Gerümpel **I**
rude [ru:d] unhöflich; unverschämt **I**
rugby ['rʌgbi] Rugby **II U4**, 68
to **ruin** ['ru:ɪn] ruinieren; zerstören **II U4**, 81
rule [ru:l] Regel **I**
What's the **rule** for …? [ˌwɒts ðə 'ru:l fə] Was ist die Regel für …? **I**
ruler ['ru:lə] Lineal **I**
run [rʌn] Rennen; Lauf **II U4**, 70
*to **run** [rʌn] rennen; laufen **I**
*to **run** away [ˌrʌn‿ə'weɪ] wegrennen **I**
runner ['rʌnə] Läufer/-in **II U4**, 68
running ['rʌnɪŋ] Laufen; Rennen **II U4**, 70

S

sad [sæd] traurig **I**
safe [seɪf] sicher; ungefährlich **II U3**, 56
to reef the **sails** [ˌri:f ðə 'seɪlz] die Segel einholen **I**
sailor ['seɪlə] Seemann; Matrose **I**
salad ['sæləd] Salat **I**
sale [seɪl] Verkauf **II U1**, 12
the **same** way as [ˌðə seɪm 'weɪ æz] genauso wie °**II U1**, 24
the **same** [ðə 'seɪm] der-/die-/dasselbe; der/die/das gleiche **I**
sandwich ['sænwɪdʒ] Sandwich; belegtes Brot **I**
Saturday ['sætədeɪ] Samstag **I**
to **save** [seɪv] retten; bergen **I**
sax ['sæks] Saxofon **I**
saxophone ['sæksəfəʊn] Saxofon **I**
*to **say** [seɪ] sagen; aufsagen; sprechen **I**
*to **say** hello (to) [ˌseɪ hel'əʊ tə] grüßen; Grüße ausrichten (an) **I**
to **scan** [skæn] scannen; nach Details durchsuchen °**II U3**, 59
*to be **scared** (of) [bi: 'skeəd‿əv] Angst haben (vor) **I**
I'm (not) **scared** of … [ˌaɪm (nɒt) 'skeəd‿əv] Ich habe (keine) Angst vor … **I**
scary ['skeəri] unheimlich; gruselig; beängstigend **II U1**, 24
scene [si:n] Szene **I**; Schauplatz **II U4**, 77
acting a **scene** [ˌæktɪŋ‿ə 'si:n] eine Theaterszene spielen **I**
school [sku:l] Schule **I**
primary **school** ['praɪmri ˌsku:l] Grundschule **I**
schoolbag ['sku:lbæg] Schultasche **I**
Science [saɪəns] Naturwissenschaften **II U2**, 32
science fiction [ˌsaɪəns 'fɪkʃn] Science-Fiction *(Zukunftsdichtung)* **II U1**, 22
score [skɔ:] Punktestand; Spielstand **II U4**, 68
gorge **scrambling** ['gɔ:dʒ ˌskræmblɪŋ] Schluchtenklettern **II U1**, 16
to **scream** [skri:m] schreien; kreischen **II U3**, 63
sea [si:] Meer **I**
search [sɜ:tʃ] Suche; Such- **II U1**, 21
second ['seknd] zweite/-r/-s **I**
secret ['si:krət] Geheimnis **II U1**, 19
in **secret** [ɪn 'si:krət] heimlich **II U4**, 81
section ['sekʃn] Abschnitt; Paragraf °**II U1**, 22
*to **see** [si:] sehen **I**
See you! ['si: jə] Bis dann!; Bis … **I**
Wait and **see**! [ˌweɪt‿ənd 'si:] Warte ab! **I**
self-critical ['selfˌkrɪtɪkl] selbstkritisch **II U5**, 92
self-evaluation [ˌselfɪˌvælju'eɪʃn] Selbsteinschätzung **I**
selfie ['selfi] Selfie **II U4**, 81
*to **sell** [sel] verkaufen **I**
seller ['selə] Verkäufer/-in *(auf einem Flohmarkt)* **I**
*to **send** [send] schicken; senden **I**
sentence ['sentəns] Satz **I**
separate ['seprət] separat; getrennt; verschieden **II U1**, 16
September [sep'tembə] September **I**
serious ['sɪəriəs] ernsthaft; ernst **I**
*to **set** up [ˌset‿'ʌp] einrichten; aufbauen **I**
setting ['setɪŋ] Schauplatz; Rahmen °**II U3**, 58
seven ['sevn] sieben **I**
several ['sevrl] einige; mehrere; verschiedene °**II U2**, 37
to **share** [ʃeə] teilen **II U2**, 40
she [ʃi:] sie **I**
sheep, **sheep** *(pl)* [ʃi:p] Schaf **II U1**, 18
*to **shine** [ʃaɪn] scheinen; glänzen **II U2**, 33
ship [ʃɪp] Schiff **I**
shock [ʃɒk] Schock **II U4**, 79
shoe [ʃu:] Schuh **I**

shop [ʃɒp] Geschäft; Laden **I**
charity **shop** ['tʃærɪti ʃɒp] Second-Hand-Laden **I**
shopping ['ʃɒpɪŋ] Einkaufen; Einkäufe **I**
*to go **shopping** [ˌgəʊ 'ʃɒpɪŋ] einkaufen gehen **I**
shore [ʃɔː] Ufer; Küste **II U3**, 62
short [ʃɔːt] kurz **I**
short answer [ˌʃɔːt‿'ɑːnsə] Kurzantwort **I**
short form ['ʃɔːt fɔːm] Kurzform **I**
shorts *(pl)* [ʃɔːts] Shorts; kurze Hose **II U4**, 75
shot [ʃɒt] Einstellung; Kameraeinstellung °**II U5**, 98
should [ʃʊd] sollte; solltest; sollten; solltet **II U4**, 74
shouldn't ['ʃʊdnt] sollte(n) nicht **II U4**, 73
shoulder ['ʃəʊldə] Schulter **II U4**, 73
to **shout** [ʃaʊt] schreien; rufen **I**
show [ʃəʊ] Show; Schau; Aufführung **II U4**, 75
comedy **show** ['kɒmədi ˌʃəʊ] Comedy Show **II U1**, 10
talent **show** ['tælənt ˌʃəʊ] Talentwettbewerb **I**
to **show** [ʃəʊ] zeigen **I**
to **show** off [ʃəʊ‿'ɒf] angeben **II U5**, 103
shower ['ʃaʊə] Dusche **I**
shy [ʃaɪ] schüchtern **II U1**, 9
sick [sɪk] krank; unwohl **II U4**, 73
*to feel **sick** [ˌfiːl 'sɪk] Übelkeit verspüren; sich schlecht fühlen **II U4**, 73
side [saɪd] Seite **II U2**, 40
sight [saɪt] Sehenswürdigkeit; Anblick **II AC1**, 48
sightseeing ['saɪtsiːɪŋ] Sightseeing-; Besichtigungs- **II U3**, 58
sign [saɪn] Zeichen; Schild **II U1**, 18
signal word ['sɪgnəl ˌwɜːd] Signalwort **I**
silly ['sɪli] Dummkopf **II U4**, 80
silly ['sɪli] dumm; doof; albern **I**
silver ['sɪlvə] Silber **II U3**, 62
similar ['sɪmɪlə] ähnlich °**II AC1**, 49
simple past [ˌsɪmpl 'pɑːst] Vergangenheitsform °**II U1**, 9
simple present [ˌsɪmpl 'preznt] Gegenwart; Präsens **I**
*to **sing** [sɪŋ] singen **I**
I like **singing** and dancing. [ˌaɪ laɪk ˌsɪŋɪŋ‿ənd 'dɑːnsɪŋ] Ich singe und tanze gern. **I**
singer ['sɪŋə] Sänger/-in **II U1**, 15
sister ['sɪstə] Schwester **I**
half-**sister** ['hɑːfˌsɪstə] Halbschwester **I**
*to **sit** [sɪt] sitzen **I**
Sit! [sɪt] Sitz! *(Befehl für Hunde)*; Platz! *(Befehl für Hunde)* **I**
*to **sit** down [ˌsɪt 'daʊn] sich hinsetzen; sich setzen **I**
*to **sit** face to face [ˌsɪt feɪs tə ˌfeɪs] sich gegenüber sitzen **I**
site [saɪt] Webseite **II U5**, 92
situation [ˌsɪtju'eɪʃn] Situation **I**
six [sɪks] sechs **I**
Four and **six** is ten. [ˌfɔːr‿ənd ˌsɪks‿ɪz 'ten] Vier plus sechs ist zehn. **I**
size [saɪz] Größe; Kleidergröße **I**
to **skate** [skeɪt] Inlineskates fahren; Schlittschuh laufen **I**
skateboard ['skeɪtbɔːd] Skateboard **II U1**, 11
skateboarding ['skeɪtbɔːdɪŋ] Skateboardfahren **I**
skates *(pl)* [skeɪts] Inlineskates; Rollschuhe; Schlittschuhe **I**
(inline) **skating** ['ɪnlaɪn ˌskeɪtɪŋ] Inlineskatefahren **I**
skill [skɪl] Fertigkeit; Geschick **I**
to **skim** [skɪm] überfliegen °**II U3**, 59
*to **sleep** [sliːp] schlafen **I**
sleepover ['sliːpˌəʊvə] Übernachtung **I**
to **slice** [slaɪs] in Scheiben schneiden **I**
slide [slaɪd] Rutschbahn **I**
water **slide** ['wɔːtə ˌslaɪd] Wasserrutsche **I**
slogan ['sləʊgən] Slogan; Werbespruch **II U2**, 35
time **slot** ['taɪm slɒt] Zeitfenster °**II U2**, 38
slow [sləʊ] langsam **I**
small [smɔːl] klein **I**
smartcard ['smɑːtkɑːd] Chipkarte **II U3**, 52
smartphone ['smɑːtfəʊn] Smartphone **II U4**, 79
smile [smaɪl] Lächeln **I**
to **smile** [smaɪl] lächeln **I**
snack [snæk] Snack; Imbiss **I**
snack bar ['snæk ˌbɑː] Café; Imbissstube **I**
word **snake** ['wɜːd ˌsneɪk] Wortschlange **I**
to **sneak** around [ˌsniːk‿ə'raʊnd] herumschleichen **II U1**, 24
to **snore** [snɔː] schnarchen **I**
so [səʊ] so; also **I**
so far [səʊ 'fɑː] bis jetzt **II U4**, 75
social network [ˌsəʊʃl 'netwɜːk] soziales Netzwerk **II U5**, 91
sofa ['səʊfə] Sofa; Couch **I**
solution [sə'luːʃn] Lösung **II U1**, 13
to **solve** [sɒlv] lösen °**II U5**, 95
some [sʌm; səm] einige; ein paar; etwas **I**
somebody ['sʌmbədi] jemand **I**
someone ['sʌmwʌn] jemand **II U1**, 13
something ['sʌmθɪŋ] etwas **I**
sometimes ['sʌmtaɪmz] manchmal **I**
somewhere ['sʌmweə] irgendwo **II U3**, 65
song [sɒŋ] Song; Lied **I**
soon [suːn] bald **II U1**, 18
as **soon** as [əz 'suːn‿əz] sobald **II U5**, 92
Sorry! ['sɒri] Entschuldigung!; Tut mir leid! **I**
*to be **sorry** [biː 'sɒri] leid tun **I**
I'm **sorry**! [ˌaɪm 'sɒri] Tut mir leid! **I**
sound [saʊnd] Ton; Geräusch; Klang **I**
to **sound** [saʊnd] klingen **I**
south [saʊθ] Süden; Süd- **II U3**, 53
South Korean [ˌsaʊθ kə'riːən] Südkoreaner/-in; südkoreanisch; Südkoreanisch **II AC2**, 88
souvenir [ˌsuːvn'ɪə] Souvenir; Andenken **II U3**, 54
space [speɪs] Raum; Fläche; Platz; Ort **II U2**, 30
*to leave **space** [liːv 'speɪs] Platz lassen **I**
spaceship ['speɪsʃɪp] Raumschiff **II U1**, 22
*to **speak** [spiːk] sprechen **I**
speaker ['spiːkə] Redner/-in; Sprecher/-in **I**
speaking ['spiːkɪŋ] Sprechen **I**
special ['speʃl] besonders; speziell **I**
special offer [ˌspeʃl‿'ɒfə] Sonderangebot **I**
with **special** needs [wɪð ˌspeʃl 'niːdz] behindert **II U2**, 29
speech bubble ['spiːtʃ ˌbʌbl] Sprechblase **I**
*to **spell** [spel] buchstabieren **I**
spelling ['spelɪŋ] Rechtschreibung **I**
*to **spend** [spend] ausgeben *(Geld)* **I**; verbringen *(Zeit)* **II U5**, 92
spoken ['spəʊkn] gesprochen °**II U4**, 82
sponge [spʌndʒ] Rühr-; Biskuit- **I**
sport [spɔːt] Sport; Sportart **I**
... is a great **sport**. [ɪz‿ə 'greɪt ˌspɔːt] ... ist ein toller Sport. **I**
squirrel ['skwɪrəl] Eichhörnchen **I**
stadium ['steɪdiəm] Stadion **II U4**, 68
*to **stand** [stænd] stehen **I**
*to **stand** up [ˌstænd‿'ʌp] aufstehen *(von einer Sitzgelegenheit)* **I**
star [stɑː] Star; Stern **I**
to **stare** [steə] starren; anstarren **I**
to **start** [stɑːt] anfangen; beginnen; starten **I**
*to get **started** [ˌget 'stɑːtɪd] anfangen **II U2**, 33
head of **state** [ˌhed‿əv 'steɪt] Staatsoberhaupt **II AC2**, 89
statement ['steɪtmənt] Aussage; Behauptung; Erklärung **II AC2**, 88
station ['steɪʃn] Haltestelle; Bahnhof; Station **I**; Sender **II U4**, 77
bus **station** ['bʌs ˌsteɪʃn] Busbahnhof **I**
to **stay** [steɪ] bleiben **I**
to **stay** away from [ˌsteɪ‿ə'weɪ frəm] fernbleiben von; meiden **II U5**, 97
to **stay** in touch (with) [ˌsteɪ ɪn 'tʌtʃ (wɪð)] in Kontakt bleiben (mit) **II U5**, 90
to **stay** with ['steɪ wɪð] wohnen bei **II U3**, 52
steak [steɪk] Steak **I**
*to **steal** [stiːl] stehlen **II U2**, 34
step [step] Stufe; Schritt **I**
step-by-**step** [ˌstepbaɪ'step] Schritt-für-Schritt- **II U5**, 95
stepmum ['stepmʌm] Stiefmutter **I**
still [stɪl] Standbild °**II U2**, 36
still [stɪl] still **I**
still [stɪl] noch; immer noch **I**; dennoch **II U5**, 95
stomach ['stʌmək] Magen; Bauch **II U4**, 80
stomachache ['stʌməkeɪk] Bauchschmerzen; Bauchweh **II U4**, 73
stop [stɒp] Haltestelle; Halt **II U3**, 53
to **stop** [stɒp] aufhören (mit); anhalten; stoppen **I**

Stop and think [ˌstɒp‿ənd 'θɪŋk] Warte/Wartet und denk/denkt nach. **I**
Stop it! ['stɒp‿ɪt] Mach/Macht das aus!; Hör/Hört auf! **I**
storm [stɔ:m] Sturm **I**
story, **stories** *(pl)* ['stɔ:ri; 'stɔ:riz] Story; Geschichte; Erzählung **I**
photo **story** ['fəʊtəʊ ˌstɔ:ri] Fotostory; Bildgeschichte **I**
straight on [streɪt‿'ɒn] geradeaus **I**
strange [streɪndʒ] fremd; seltsam; merkwürdig **I**
street [stri:t] Straße *(in der Stadt)* **I**
in the **street** [ˌɪn ðə 'stri:t] in der Straße; auf der Straße **I**
strong [strɒŋ] stark **II U2**, 42
student ['stju:dnt] Schüler/-in; Student/-in **I**
studies *(pl)* ['stʌdiz] Studium; Lernen; Arbeit für die Schule **II U2**, 28
recording **studio** [rɪ'kɔ:dɪŋ ˌstju:diəʊ] Aufnahmestudio; Tonstudio **I**
stuff [stʌf] Zeug **I**
stupid ['stju:pɪd] dumm; blöd **II U4**, 81
subject ['sʌbdʒɪkt] Schulfach **II U2**, 28; Subjekt; Satzgegenstand °**II U2**, 31
substitute ['sʌbstɪtju:t] Ersatz; Ersatz- °**II U5**, 91
such [sʌtʃ] solch; solche/-r/-s **II U2**, 36
suddenly ['sʌdnli] plötzlich; auf einmal **I**
suggestion [sə'dʒestʃn] Vorschlag; Anregung **I**
to **sum** up [ˌsʌm‿'ʌp] zusammenfassen °**II U2**, 42
summer ['sʌmə] Sommer **II AC2**, 88
summer camp ['sʌmə kæmp] Sommerferienlager **II AC2**, 88
sun [sʌn] Sonne **II U2**, 33
Sunday ['sʌndeɪ] Sonntag **I**
superlative [su:'pɜ:lətɪv] Superlativ °**II U1**, 16
supermarket ['su:pəˌmɑ:kɪt] Supermarkt **I**
superpower ['su:pəˌpaʊə] Supermacht **II AC2**, 89
sure [ʃʊə; ʃɔ:] sicher **I**
*to make **sure** [ˌmeɪk 'ʃɔ:] sich versichern **I**
surgery ['sɜ:dʒəri] Arztpraxis; Praxis; Praxisräume **I**
surprise [sə'praɪz] Überraschung **I**
to **surprise** [sə'praɪz] überraschen **II U4**, 81
*to be **surprised** [bi sə'praɪzd] überrascht sein **II U3**, 63
surprising [sə'praɪzɪŋ] überraschend **II U1**, 24
survey ['sɜ:veɪ] Umfrage; Studie **I**
to **swap** roles [ˌswɒp 'rəʊlz] Rollen tauschen **I**
sweet [swi:t] süß **I**
sweets *(pl)* [swi:ts] Süßigkeiten; Bonbons **I**
*to **swim** [swɪm] schwimmen **I**
swimming ['swɪmɪŋ] Schwimmen **I**
*to go **swimming** [ˌgəʊ 'swɪmɪŋ] Schwimmen gehen **I**
symbol ['sɪmbl] Symbol °**II U3**, 58

T

table ['teɪbl] Tisch **I**
tablet ['tæblət] Tablet **II U5**, 95
taekwondo [ˌtækwʌn'du:] Taekwondo **II U2**, 38
question **tag** ['kwestʃən ˌtæg] Frageanhängsel; Bestätigungsfrage °**II U5**, 94
tail [teɪl] Schwanz; Schweif **I**
*to **take** [teɪk] nehmen; mitnehmen; wegnehmen; bringen; mitbringen **I**; dauern; (Zeit) brauchen **II U5**, 95
*to **take** a look at [ˌteɪk‿ə 'lʊk‿æt] einen Blick werfen auf **II U2**, 37
*to **take** a message [ˌteɪk‿ə 'mesɪdʒ] eine Nachricht entgegennehmen; jmdm. etw. ausrichten **I**
*to **take** a test [ˌteɪk‿ə 'test] einen Test machen °**II U5**, 97
*to **take** a vote [ˌteɪk‿ə 'vəʊt] abstimmen **I**
*to **take** notes [ˌteɪk 'nəʊts] sich Notizen machen **I**
*to **take** off [ˌteɪk‿'ɒf] abnehmen; herunternehmen; ausziehen **I**
*to **take** part (in) [ˌteɪk 'pɑ:t (ɪn)] teilnehmen (an) **II U5**, 90
*to **take** photos [ˌteɪk 'fəʊtəʊz] fotografieren; Fotos machen **I**
*to **take** place [ˌteɪk 'pleɪs] stattfinden **I**
Take turns. [ˌteɪk 'tɜ:nz] Wechselt euch ab. **I**
Take a deep breath. [ˌteɪk‿ə ˌdi:p 'breθ] Atme(t) tief ein. **II U2**, 36
talent ['tælənt] Talent **I**
talent show ['tælənt ˌʃəʊ] Talentwettbewerb **I**
to **talk** [tɔ:k] sprechen; reden **I**
to **talk** about ['tɔ:k‿əˌbaʊt] sprechen über; erzählen von **I**
to **talk** to ['tɔ:k tə] reden mit **I**
talking ['tɔ:kɪŋ] Sprechen **I**
tall [tɔ:l] groß; hoch **II U1**, 17
to **tap** [tæp] antippen **II U5**, 102
task [tɑ:sk] Aufgabe; Auftrag **I**
taxi ['tæksi] Taxi **II U1**, 13
tea [ti:] Tee **I**
*to **teach** [ti:tʃ] unterrichten; lehren; beibringen **II U4**, 76
*to **teach** somebody a lesson [ˌti:tʃ‿ə 'lesn] jmdm. eine Lehre/Lektion erteilen **II U4**, 76
teacher ['ti:tʃə] Lehrer/-in **I**
team [ti:m] Team; Gruppe **II U1**, 8
Technology [tek'nɒlədʒi] Technik; Computerunterricht **II U2**, 32
technology [tek'nɒlədʒi] Technologie **II AC2**, 89
teen [ti:n] Jugend- **II U5**, 92
teenager ['ti:nˌeɪdʒə] Teenager; Jugendliche/-r **I**
telephone ['telɪfəʊn] Telefon **I**
*to **tell** [tel] erzählen; sagen; mitteilen **I**
Tell me about … ['tel mi:‿əˌbaʊt] Erzähle mir von … **I**
ten [ten] zehn **I**
ten times [ten 'taɪmz] zehnmal **I**
Four and six is **ten**. [ˌfɔ:r‿ənd ˌsɪks‿ɪz 'ten] Vier plus sechs ist zehn. **I**
tennis ['tenɪs] Tennis **I**
tense [tens] Zeit; Zeitform *(grammatisch)* °**II U4**, 71
test [test] Test; Klassenarbeit; Prüfung **I**
*to take a **test** [ˌteɪk‿ə 'test] einen Test machen °**II U5**, 97
text [tekst] Text **I**
text (message) ['tekst ˌmesɪdʒ] SMS; Kurznachricht **I**
to **text** [tekst] eine SMS schicken **II U5**, 90
than [ðæn] als *(bei Vergleichen)* **II U1**, 16
more … **than** ['mɔ: ðən] mehr … als **I**
to **thank** [θæŋk] danken **II U2**, 36
Thank you. ['θæŋk ju] Danke. **I**
thankful ['θæŋkfl] dankbar **I**
Thanks. [θæŋks] Danke. **I**
that [ðæt; ðət] dass **I**
that [ðæt] das; jenes **I**
after **that** [ˌɑ:ftə 'ðæt] danach **I**
like **that** [laɪk 'ðæt] so **I**
That was close! [ˌðæt wəz 'kləʊs] Das war knapp! **I**
that's how [ðæts 'haʊ] so **II U1**, 10
That's what friends are for. [ˌðæts wɒt 'frendz‿ɑ: ˌfɔ:] Dafür sind Freunde da. **I**
that's why [ðæts 'waɪ] deshalb **II U2**, 30
That's … [ðæts] Das macht … **I**
that [ðæt] der; dem; den; die; das *(Relativpronomen)* **II U1**, 9
the [ðə; ði] der; die *(auch Pl.)*; das **I**
the others [ði‿'ʌðəz] die anderen **I**
the same [ðə 'seɪm] der-/die-/dasselbe; der/die/das gleiche **I**
the … **the** [ðə … ðə] je … desto **II U4**, 68
theatre ['θɪətə] Theater **I**
their [ðeə] ihr/-e *(Pl.)* **I**
them [ðem] sie *(Pl.)*; ihnen **I**
theme [θi:m] Thema; Motto **I**
then [ðen] dann; danach **I**
there [ðeə] da; dort; dahin; dorthin **I**
there is/are [ðər‿'ɪz/'ɑ:] da ist/sind; es gibt **I**
these [ði:z] diese (hier) **I**
they [ðeɪ] sie *(Pl.)* **I**
It's …/**They**'re … [ɪts/ðeə] Es kostet …/Sie kosten … **I**
thing [θɪŋ] Ding; Sache **I**
*to **think** [θɪŋk] denken; nachdenken; glauben **I**
Stop and **think** [ˌstɒp‿ənd 'θɪŋk] Warte/Wartet und denk/denkt nach. **I**
*to **think** of ['θɪŋk‿əv] halten von; denken über **I**
*to **think** of ['θɪŋk‿əv] (sich) ausdenken; sich etwas einfallen lassen **II U1**, 12

Think of … ['θɪŋk‿əv] Denke/Denkt an … I
third [θɜ:d] dritte/-r/-s I
thirteen [ˌθɜ:'ti:n] dreizehn I
this [ðɪs] dies; diese/-r/-s I
this afternoon [ðɪs ˌɑ:ftənu:n] heute Nachmittag II U3, 52
This is … ['ðɪs‿ɪz] Das (hier) ist … I
those [ðəʊz] diese dort; jene I
thought [θɔ:t] Gedanke °II U4, 82
thousands of ['θaʊzndz‿əv] tausende (von) I
three [θri:] drei I
through [θru:] durch I
*to throw (at) [θrəʊ] werfen (nach) I
*to **throw** away [ˌθrəʊ‿ə'weɪ] wegwerfen I
throw the dice twice [ˌθrəʊ ðə daɪs 'twaɪs] würfle zweimal °II U2, 34
thumb [θʌm] Daumen II U2, 34
thunder *(no pl)* ['θʌndə] Donner II U5, 102
Thursday ['θɜ:zdeɪ] Donnerstag I
to tick [tɪk] abhaken °II U3, 60
ticket ['tɪkɪt] Los; Ticket; Eintrittskarte I
high tide ['haɪ ˌtaɪd] Flut II U3, 62
low **tide** ['ləʊ ˌtaɪd] Ebbe II U3, 62
to tidy *(a room)* ['taɪdi] aufräumen; in Ordnung bringen I
till [tɪl] bis I
time [taɪm] Zeit I; Mal II U1, 10
all the **time** [ˌɔ:l ðə 'taɪm] die ganze Zeit II U3, 62
at the same **time** [ət ðə ˌseɪm 'taɪm] zur selben Zeit; gleichzeitig I
free **time** [ˌfri: 'taɪm] Freizeit I
on **time** [ɒn 'taɪm] pünktlich II U2, 37
ten **times** [ten 'taɪmz] zehnmal I
time line ['taɪm ˌlaɪn] Zeitstrahl I
time slot ['taɪm slɒt] Zeitfenster °II U2, 38
I can't wait till next **time**. [aɪ kɑ:nt ˌweɪt tɪl nekst 'taɪm] Ich kann es bis zum nächsten Mal kaum erwarten. II U1, 10
Time to get up! [ˌtaɪm tə ˌget‿'ʌp] Es ist Zeit aufzustehen! I
What **time**? [ˌwɒt 'taɪm] Um wie viel Uhr? I
What's the **time**? [ˌwɒts ðə 'taɪm] Wie spät ist es?; Wie viel Uhr ist es? I
timetable ['taɪmˌteɪbl] Stundenplan; Fahrplan I
tinned [tɪnd] Dosen-; aus der Dose I
tip [tɪp] Tipp; Ratschlag I
to tiptoe ['tɪptəʊ] auf Zehenspitzen gehen II U1, 19
tired ['taɪəd] müde I
title ['taɪtl] Titel; Überschrift °II U5, 104
to [tʊ; tə] zu; nach; auf; in; vor *(bei Uhrzeitangaben)* I
from … **to** [frəm … tə] von … bis I
quarter past/**to** ['kwɔ:tə pɑ:st/tə] Viertel nach/vor I
toast [təʊst] Toast I
today [tə'deɪ] heute I
together [tə'geðə] zusammen; miteinander; gemeinsam I
toilet ['tɔɪlət] Toilette I
tomato, tomatoes *(pl)* [tə'mɑ:təʊ; tə'mɑ:təʊz] Tomate I
tomorrow [tə'mɒrəʊ] morgen I
too [tu:] auch; zu I
Too bad! [ˌtu: 'bæd] Zu dumm!; Schade! I
You **too**? [ju: 'tu:] Du auch? I
top [tɒp] Spitze; oberer Teil; oberes Ende I
on **top** [ɒn 'tɒp] oben; obendrauf I
to top up [tɒp‿'ʌp] aufladen II U3, 52
topic ['tɒpɪk] Thema II U2, 37
torch [tɔ:tʃ] Fackel; Taschenlampe II U1, 18
to stay in touch (with) [ˌsteɪ ɪn 'tʌtʃ (wɪð)] in Kontakt bleiben (mit) II U5, 90
tour [tʊə] Tour; Fahrt; Rundgang II U3, 56
audio **tour** ['ɔ:diəʊ ˌtʊə] Audioführung II U3, 56
tourist ['tʊərɪst] Tourist/-in I
tourist information centre [ˌtʊərɪst ɪnfə'meɪʃn ˌsentə] Touristeninformation I
towards [tə'wɔ:dz] in Richtung; auf … zu; darauf zu II U3, 62
town [taʊn] Stadt I
toy [tɔɪ] Spielzeug I
to trace [treɪs] verfolgen; nachspüren I
to trade [treɪd] austauschen °II U4, 79
tradition [trə'dɪʃn] Tradition I
train [treɪn] Zug I
to train [treɪn] trainieren II U4, 72
training ['treɪnɪŋ] Training II U4, 80
to translate [trænz'leɪt] übersetzen I
Don't **translate** … [ˌdəʊnt trænz'leɪt] Übersetze/Übersetzt nicht … I
translation [trænz'leɪʃn] Übersetzung I
public transport *(no pl)* [ˌpʌblɪk 'trænspɔ:t] öffentliche Verkehrsmittel II U3, 52
travel ['trævl] (das) Reisen; Reise II U1, 20
travel report [ˌtrævl rɪ'pɔ:t] Reisebericht II U1, 20
to travel ['trævl] fahren; reisen II U3, 52
treasure ['treʒə] Schatz II U3, 56
tree [tri:] Baum I
family **tree** ['fæməli ˌtri:] Stammbaum I
trial [traɪəl] Qualifikation II U4, 70
trick [trɪk] Trick; Streich I
to play a **trick** (on) [ˌpleɪ‿ə 'trɪk‿ɒn] einen Streich spielen I
trifle ['traɪfl] Trifle *(englischer Nachtisch)* I
trip [trɪp] Trip; Reise; Ausflug; Fahrt II U1, 9
trouble ['trʌbl] Ärger; Probleme; Schwierigkeiten II U1, 19
*to make **trouble** [ˌmeɪk 'trʌbl] Ärger machen; in Schwierigkeiten bringen I
trowel ['traʊəl] kleiner Spaten II U3, 62
true [tru:] wahr °II U2, 34
to try [traɪ] versuchen; probieren I
to **try** on [ˌtraɪ‿'ɒn] anprobieren II U2, 31
Try … [traɪ] Versuch es mal mit …; Probier mal … I
T-shirt ['ti:ʃɜ:t] T-Shirt I
the Tube [ðə 'tju:b] die Londoner U-Bahn II AC1, 48
Tuesday ['tju:zdeɪ] Dienstag I
tunnel ['tʌnl] Tunnel I
It's your turn. [ˌɪts 'jɔ: tɜ:n] Du bist dran. I
Take **turns**. [ˌteɪk 'tɜ:nz] Wechselt euch ab. I
Your **turn**. ['jɔ: tɜ:n] Du bist dran. I
to turn [tɜ:n] einbiegen; abbiegen I
to **turn** (a)round [tɜ:n‿(ə)'raʊnd] (sich) umdrehen; wenden II U2, 41
to **turn** back [tɜ:n 'bæk] umkehren; zurückgehen II U2, 41
to **turn** off [ˌtɜ:n‿'ɒf] abschalten; ausschalten II U1, 12
tutor ['tju:tə] Klassenlehrer/-in I
tutor group ['tju:tə ˌgru:p] Klasse *(in einer englischen Schule)* I
TV [ˌti:'vi:] Fernsehen; Fernseher I
to watch **TV** [ˌwɒtʃ ti:'vi:] fernsehen I
twelve [twelv] zwölf I
to twist your ankle [ˌtwɪst jɔ:r‿'æŋkl] sich den Knöchel verrenken II U4, 72
two [tu:] zwei I
the **two** of them [ðə 'tu:‿əv ðəm] beide II U5, 92
typical ['tɪpɪkl] typisch I

U

u *(= you)* [ju:; jə] du; Sie; ihr I
UFO [ˌju:ef'əʊ] UFO II U4, 78
uncle ['ʌŋkl] Onkel I
under ['ʌndə] unter I
underground ['ʌndəgraʊnd] U-Bahn II AC1, 48
*to understand [ˌʌndə'stænd] verstehen I
understanding [ˌʌndə'stændɪŋ] Verständnis II U5, 93
unfair [ʌn'feə] unfair II U4, 72
unfriendly [ʌn'frendli] unfreundlich II U1, 24
uniform ['ju:nɪfɔ:m] Uniform I
unit ['ju:nɪt] Lektion; Kapitel; Einheit I
*to be unlucky [bi:‿ʌn'lʌki] Pech haben I
until [ʌn'tɪl] bis; erst wenn II U4, 70
to unwrap [ʌn'ræp] auswickeln; auspacken I
up [ʌp] hinauf; nach oben II U5, 94
to end **up** [ˌend‿'ʌp] enden; landen II U1, 8
*to get **up** [ˌget‿'ʌp] aufstehen *(aus dem Bett)* I
to look **up** [ˌlʊk‿'ʌp] nachschlagen; nachschauen I
upset [ʌp'set] aufgebracht; bestürzt II U2, 30
upstairs [ʌp'steəz] nach oben; im Obergeschoss; oben II U5, 102
us [ʌs] uns I
to use [ju:z] benutzen; verwenden; gebrauchen I
useful ['ju:sfl] nützlich; hilfreich I

Useful phrases [ˌju:sfl ˈfreɪsɪz] nützliche Ausdrücke I
usually [ˈju:ʒli] normalerweise; gewöhnlich; meistens I

V

verb [vɜ:b] Verb I
very [ˈveri] sehr I
very much [ˌveri ˈmʌtʃ] sehr I
vet [vet] Tierarzt/Tierärztin I
video [ˈvɪdiəʊ] Video II U5, 91
video chat [ˈvɪdiəʊ ˌtʃæt] Videochat II U3, 50
view [vju:] Aussicht; Sicht; Ausblick; Blick II U2, 30
point of **view** [ˌpɔɪnt_əv ˈvju:] Standpunkt; Ansicht; Perspektive II U4, 76
viewer [ˈvju:ə] Zuschauer/-in °II U3, 58
viewing [ˈvju:ɪŋ] Hör-/Sehverstehen I
village [ˈvɪlɪdʒ] Dorf I
visit [ˈvɪzɪt] Besuch I
to **visit** [ˈvɪzɪt] besichtigen; besuchen I
visitor [ˈvɪzɪtə] Besucher/-in I
vocabulary [vəˈkæbjəlri] Vokabular; Wortschatz I
voice [vɔɪs] Stimme I
volleyball [ˈvɒlibɔ:l] Volleyball I
*to take a **vote** [ˌteɪk_ə ˈvəʊt] abstimmen I
to **vote** [vəʊt] abstimmen; wählen I

W

to **wait** (for) [weɪt] warten (auf) I
I can't **wait** till next time. [aɪ kɑ:nt ˌweɪt tɪl nekst ˈtaɪm] Ich kann es bis zum nächsten Mal kaum erwarten. II U1, 10
Wait and see! [ˌweɪt_ənd ˈsi:] Warte ab! I
*to go for a **walk** [ˌɡəʊ fər_ə ˈwɔ:k] spazieren gehen II U1, 18
gallery **walk** [ˈɡæləri ˌwɔ:k] Museumsrundgang; Vernissage I
night **walk** [ˈnaɪt wɔ:k] Nachtwanderung II U1, 18
to **walk** [wɔ:k] gehen; laufen I
to **walk** the dog [ˌwɔ:k ðə ˈdɒɡ] den Hund ausführen; mit dem Hund spazieren gehen I
walking [ˈwɔ:kɪŋ] Wandern II U1, 16
wall [wɔ:l] Wand; Mauer I
to **want** (to) [ˈwɒnt tə] wollen; mögen I
wardrobe [ˈwɔ:drəʊb] Kleiderschrank I
to **warm** up [ˌwɔ:m_ˈʌp] aufwärmen; sich aufwärmen I
warm-up [ˈwɔ:m_ʌp] Aufwärmübung I
to **wash** [wɒʃ] waschen; sich waschen I
to **wash** up [ˌwɒʃ_ˈʌp] angespült werden II U3, 62
washing machine [ˈwɒʃɪŋ məˌʃi:n] Waschmaschine II U5, 95
to **waste** [weɪst] verschwenden II U5, 95

to **watch** [wɒtʃ] beobachten; (sich) ansehen; zuschauen I
to **watch** TV [ˌwɒtʃ ti:ˈvi:] fernsehen I
water [ˈwɔ:tə] Wasser I
water slide [ˈwɔ:tə ˌslaɪd] Wasserrutsche I
wave [weɪv] Welle I
wax [wæks] Wachs II U3, 51
wax figure [ˈwæks ˌfɪɡə] Wachsfigur II U3, 51
way [weɪ] Weg; Art und Weise I
*to be in the **way** [bi:_ɪn ðə ˈweɪ] im Weg sein/stehen I
*to get in the **way** [ˌɡet_ɪn ðə ˈweɪ] stören; im Weg stehen II U4, 80
in other **ways** [ɪn_ˈʌðə weɪz] auf andere Weise II U5, 97
the same **way** as [ˌðə seɪm ˈweɪ æz] genauso wie °II U1, 24
we [wi:; wi] wir I
We're from … [ˈwɪə frəm] Wir sind aus … I
*to **wear** [weə] anhaben; tragen *(Kleidung)* I
weather [ˈweðə] Wetter I
website [ˈwebsaɪt] Website; Internetauftritt I
wedding [ˈwedɪŋ] Hochzeit I
Wednesday [ˈwenzdeɪ] Mittwoch I
week [wi:k] Woche I
weekday [ˈwi:kdeɪ] Wochentag II U5, 100
weekend [ˌwi:kˈend] Wochenende I
at the **weekend** [ət ðə ˌwi:kˈend] am Wochenende I
weird [wɪəd] merkwürdig; seltsam; sonderbar II U5, 99
Welcome! [ˈwelkəm] Willkommen! II U1, 18
to **welcome** [ˈwelkəm] willkommen heißen II U2, 35
You're **welcome**. [ˌjɔ: ˈwelkəm] Bitte schön.; Nichts zu danken.; Gern geschehen. I
well [wel] tja; nun I
Welsh [welʃ] walisisch; Walisisch; Waliser/-in II U1, 16
west [west] Westen; West- I
wet [wet] nass II U3, 62
what [wɒt] was; welche/-r/-s; was für ein I
What about … ? [ˈwɒt_əˌbaʊt] Wie wär's mit …?; Was ist mit …? I
What are …? [ˈwɒt_ɑ:] Welche … sind es? I
What colour is …? [ˌwɒt ˈkʌlər_ɪz] Welche Farbe hat …? I
what else [ˌwɒt_ˈels] was sonst; was noch I
What is missing? [ˌwɒt_ɪz ˈmɪsɪŋ] Was fehlt? I
What is … about? [ˌwɒt_ɪz …_əˈbaʊt] Worum geht es in/im …? I
what it's like [ˌwɒt_ɪts ˈlaɪk] wie das ist II U4, 74
What on earth …? [ˌwɒt:_ɒn_ˈɜ:θ] Was um alles in der Welt …? II U5, 95
What time? [ˌwɒt ˈtaɪm] Um wie viel Uhr? I
what to … [ˈwɒt tə] was man … I

What's that? [wɒts ˈðæt] Was ist das? I
What's the rule for …? [ˌwɒts ðə ˈru:l fə] Was ist die Regel für …? I
What's your favourite …? [ˈwɒts jə ˌfeɪvrɪt] Was ist dein/-e Lieblings…? I
What's your name? [ˌwɒts jə ˈneɪm] Wie heißt du?; Wie heißen Sie? I
What's the time? [ˌwɒts ðə ˈtaɪm] Wie spät ist es?; Wie viel Uhr ist es? I
… **what** to do. [ˈwɒt tə du:] … was ich tun soll. II U5, 92
what the man looked like [ˌwɒt ðə mæn ˈlʊkt laɪk] wie der Mann aussah II U1, 13
wheel [wi:l] Rad; Steuerrad; Steuer I
wheelchair [ˈwi:ltʃeə] Rollstuhl II U3, 53
when [wen] wenn; wann; als I
whenever [wenˈevə] wann immer; jedes Mal, wenn; so oft II U5, 92
where [weə] wo; wohin I
Where … from? [ˌweə … ˈfrɒm] Woher …? I
… **where** to go. [ˌweə tə ˈɡəʊ] … wohin ich gehen kann. II U3, 54
which [wɪtʃ] welche/-r/-s I
which [wɪtʃ] der; die; das; dem; den *(Relativpronomen)* II U2, 30
a **while** [ə ˈwaɪl] eine Weile II U3, 54
while [waɪl] während I
to **whip** [wɪp] schlagen I
to **whisper** [ˈwɪspə] flüstern I
white [waɪt] weiß I
who [hu:] wer; wem; wen I
Who … for? [ˌhu: ˈfɔ:] Für wen …? I
Who is it? [ˌhu:_ˈɪz_ɪt] Wer ist es? I
Who's in? [hu:z_ˈɪn] Wer macht mit?; Wer ist dabei? II U4, 70
who [hu:] der *(Relativpronomen)*; dem *(Relativpronomen)*; den *(Relativpronomen)*; die *(Relativpronomen)* II U2, 30
whole [həʊl] ganz I
whoosh [wʊʃ] wusch I
whose [hu:z] dessen *(Relativpronomen)*; deren *(Relativpronomen)* II U2, 30
why [waɪ] warum I
that's **why** [ðæts ˈwaɪ] deshalb II U2, 30
wife, **wives** *(pl)* [waɪf, waɪvz] Ehefrau II U2, 31
wildlife [ˈwaɪldlaɪf] Tierwelt *(in freier Wildbahn)* II U2, 33
*to **win** [wɪn] gewinnen; siegen I
window [ˈwɪndəʊ] Fenster I
wine [waɪn] Wein I
winner [ˈwɪnə] Gewinner/-in; Sieger/-in I
wish [wɪʃ] Wunsch I
*to make a **wish** [ˌmeɪk_ə ˈwɪʃ] sich etwas wünschen I
with [wɪð] mit; bei I
without [wɪˈðaʊt] ohne I
witness [ˈwɪtnəs] Zeuge/Zeugin II U4, 77
wobbly [ˈwɒbli] wackelig II U3, 62
woman, **women** *(pl)* [ˈwʊmən; ˈwɪmɪn] Frau I

wonderful ['wʌndəfl] wunderbar **II U2**, 40
Woof! [wʊf] Wau! **I**
word [wɜ:d] Wort **I**
compound **word** ['kɒmpaʊnd wɜ:d] Kompositum *(zusammengesetztes Wort)* °**II U3**, 55
key **word** ['ki: wɜ:d] Stichwort; Schlüsselbegriff **I**
linking **word** ['lɪŋkɪŋ ˌwɜ:d] Bindewort **I**
signal **word** ['sɪgnəl ˌwɜ:d] Signalwort **I**
word cloud ['wɜ:d ˌklaʊd] Wörterwolke °**II U4**, 68
word order ['wɜ:d‿ˌɔ:də] Wortstellung; Satzstellung **I**
Word power ['wɜ:d ˌpaʊə] die Kraft der Wörter *(Wortschatzübung)* **I**
word snake ['wɜ:d ˌsneɪk] Wortschlange **I**
word-building ['wɜ:dˌbɪldɪŋ] Wortbildung °**II U3**, 51
work [wɜ:k] Arbeit **I**
pair **work** ['peə wɜ:k] Partnerarbeit °**II U5**, 100
to **work** [wɜ:k] arbeiten **I**; funktionieren **II U5**, 95
to **work** out [ˌwɜ:k‿'aʊt] herausfinden; ausarbeiten °**II U3**, 61
workshop ['wɜ:kʃɒp] Workshop **I**
world [wɜ:ld] Erde; Welt **I**
worm [wɜ:m] Wurm **I**
*to be **worried** [bi 'wʌrid] beunruhigt sein; besorgt sein **II U4**, 80
to **worry** ['wʌri] sich Sorgen machen **II U5**, 93
Don't **worry**! [ˌdəʊnt 'wʌri] Keine Sorge! **I**
the **worst** [ðə 'wɜ:st] der/die/das schlimmste; der/die/das schlechteste **II U1**, 16
*to be **worth** [bi: 'wɜ:θ] wert sein **I**
would love [wʊd 'lʌv] würde/-st/-n/-t sehr gern; hätte/-st-/-n/-t sehr gern **I**
would like [wʊd 'laɪk] würde/-st/-n/-t gern; hätte/-st/-n/-t gern **I**
Would you like ...? [ˌwʊd jʊ 'laɪk] Möchtest du ...?; Möchten Sie ...?; Möchtet ihr ...? °**II U4**, 70
Wow! [waʊ] Wow! **I**
to **wrap** [ræp] einwickeln; einpacken **I**
wrapping ['ræpɪŋ] Verpackung; Hülle **I**
wrist [rɪst] Handgelenk **II U3**, 62
*to **write** [raɪt] schreiben **I**
*to **write** down [ˌraɪt 'daʊn] aufschreiben **I**
writing ['raɪtɪŋ] Schreiben **I**
wrong [rɒŋ] falsch **I**
*to be **wrong** [bi: 'rɒŋ] unrecht haben; sich irren **I**
*to go **wrong** [ˌgəʊ 'rɒŋ] schiefgehen **I**

X

XOXO [ˌhʌgz‿ən 'kɪsɪz] Umarmungen und Küsse *(am Ende von E-Mails und SMS)* **I**

Y

yeah *(infml)* [jeə] ja **I**
year [jɪə] Jahr; Schuljahr **I**
11-**year**-old [ɪˌlevn'jɪərəʊld] 11-Jährige/-r **II U4**, 70
18-**year**-old [ˌeɪti:n 'jɪər‿əʊld] 18-jährig **II U3**, 52
yearbook ['jɪəbʊk] Jahrbuch **II U1**, 8
yellow ['jeləʊ] gelb **I**
yes [jes] ja **I**
yesterday ['jestədeɪ] gestern **II U1**, 11
yet [jet] schon; noch **II U4**, 72
not ... **yet** [nɒt 'jet] noch nicht **II U4**, 72
yoghurt ['jɒgət] Joghurt **I**
you [ju:; jə] du; ihr; Sie **I**
You know how to ... [ju: 'nəʊ ˌhaʊ tə] Du weißt, wie man ...; Ihr wisst, wie man ... **I**
You too? [ju: 'tu:] Du auch? **I**
You're into ... ['jɔ:r‿ˌɪntə] Du magst ...; Du stehst auf ... **I**
You're welcome. [jɔ: 'welkəm] Bitte schön.; Nichts zu danken.; Gern geschehen. **I**
You're ... [jɔ:r] Sie sind ...; Du bist ... **I**
young [jʌŋ] jung **I**
your [jɔ:; jə] dein/-e; euer/eu-e; Ihr/-e **I**
What's **your** name? [ˌwɒts jə 'neɪm] Wie heißt du?; Wie heißen Sie? **I**
Your turn. ['jɔ: tɜ:n] Du bist dran. **I**
yours [jɔ:z] dein/-er/-e/-es; eure/-r/-s; Ihr/-e **II U2**, 41
Yours ... [jɔ:z] Viele Grüße ... *(am Ende von Briefen und Mails)* **II U5**, 99
yourself [jɔ:'self] du/dir/dich/Sie/sich (selbst); selber **I**
yourselves [jɔ:'selvz] selber; ihr/euch/Sie/sich (selbst) °**II U4**, 79

Z

zero ['zɪərəʊ] null **I**
zoo [zu:] Zoo; Tierpark **II U3**, 53

Boys' names

Amir [ˌɑ:'mi:r] **II U3**, 50
Ben [ben] **I**
Bob [bɒb] **I**
Damian ['deɪmiən] **I**
Dave [deɪv] **I**
David ['deɪvɪd] **I**
Desmond ['dezmənd] **I**
Ed [ed] **II U5**, 94
Filip ['fɪlɪp] **I**
Frank [fræŋk] **II U5**, 102
Fumio ['fju:mɪəʊ] **II U2**, 41
Henry ['henri] **I**
Jack [dʒæk] **I**
Jahangir [dʒə'hʌŋgɪə] **I**
James [dʒeɪmz] **II U2**, 30
Jamie ['dʒeɪmi] **I**
Jay [dʒeɪ] **I**
Jinsoo ['dʒɪnzu:] **II U3**, 58
John [dʒɒn] **II U1**, 13
Jon [dʒɒn] **II U5**, 90
Luke [lu:k] **I**
Marley ['mɑ:li] **II U3**, 58
Mick [mɪk] **II U5**, 100
Mike [maɪk] **II U3**, 62
Nathan ['neɪθn] **II U5**, 98
Nick [nɪk] **II U3**, 58
Peter ['pi:tə] **II U1**, 13
Rokuro [rə'ku:rəʊ] **II U2**, 40
Satoshi [sə'tɒʃi] **II U2**, 40
Shahid [ʃɑ:'hi:d] **I**
Steve [sti:v] **I**
Tony ['təʊni] **I**
Tyler ['taɪlə] **I**
Will [wɪl] **II U1**, 18

Girls' names

Alice ['ælɪs] **II U2**, 33
Alicia [ə'lɪsiə; ə'lɪʃə] **I**
Amber ['æmbə] **I**
Anna ['ænə] **I**
Anne [æn] **I**
Ayla ['eɪlə] **II U4**, 74
Beata [bi'ɑ:tə] **I**
Bunko ['bʌŋkəʊ] **II U2**, 41
Carol ['kærəl] **I**
Ceri ['keri] **II U1**, 18
Claire ['kleə] **I**
Emily ['emɪli] **I**
Frances ['frɑ:nsɪs] **I**
Gwen [gwen] **II U2**, 32
Holly ['hɒli] **I**
Irina [ɪ'ri:nə] **I**
Julie ['dʒu:li] **I**
Kate [keɪt] **II U2**, 33
Laura ['lɔ:rə] **I**
Lauren ['lɔ:rən] **II U5**, 92
Lou [lu:] **I**
Lucy ['lu:si] **I**
Maisie ['meɪzi] **II U5**, 98
Mary ['meəri] **II U2**, 30
Mila ['mi:lə] **I**
Mina ['mi:nə] **II U3**, 58
Olivia [ɒl'ɪviə] **I**
Pia ['pi:ə] **I**
Polly ['pɒli] **II U2**, 36
Rose [rəʊz] **I**
Ruby ['ru:bi] **II U5**, 92
Sally ['sæli] **I**
Seeta ['si:tə] **I**
Tomoko [tə'mɒkəʊ] **II U2**, 40

Surnames

Ashton ['æʃtən] **II U4**, 75
Azad [ə'zɑ:d] **I**
Bayram ['beɪrəm] **II U4**, 74

Elliot ['eliət] **I**
Fraser ['freɪzə] **I**
Green [gri:n] **I**
Parker ['pɑ:kə] **II U4**, 81
Preston ['prestən] **I**
Richardson ['rɪtʃədsn] **I**
Swindon ['swɪndən] **I**
Thompson ['tɒmsən] **II U4**, 76
Walker ['wɔ:kə] **I**
Wright [raɪt] **II U2**, 30
Zajac ['zeɪdʒæk] **I**

Place names

Begbie Road [ˌbegbi 'rəʊd] **II U5**, 102
Bradford ['brædfəd] **II U3**, 50
Brick Lane [brɪk 'leɪn] **II U3**, 51
Brook Lane [ˌbrʊk 'leɪn] **I**
Camden Market ['kæmdən ˌmɑ:kɪt] **II U3**, 58
College Way [ˌkɒlɪdʒ 'weɪ] **I**
Cologne [kə'ləʊn] Köln **I**
Covent Garden [ˌkɒvnt 'gɑ:dn] **II U3**, 51
Cracow ['krækɒv; 'krɑ:kaʊ] Krakau **I**
Enfield [en'fi:ld] **I**
Greenwich Park [ˌgrenɪdʒ 'pɑ:k] **I**
Greenwich Pier [ˌgrenɪdʒ 'pɪə] **I**
Hollywood ['hɒliwʊd] **II AC2**, 89
Hyde Park [ˌhaɪd 'pɑ:k] **II AC1**, 48
Kidbrooke Gardens [ˌkɪdbrʊk 'gɑ:dnz] **I**
King William Walk [ˌkɪŋ 'wɪljəm ˌwɔ:k] **I**
Leicester Square [ˌlestə 'skweə] **II U3**, 65
London ['lʌndən] **I**
Nelson Road [ˌnelsn 'rəʊd] **I**
Oxford Street ['ɒksfəd ˌstri:t] **II AC1**, 48
South Street ['saʊθ ˌstri:t] **I**
Southend [saʊθ'end] **II U1**, 25
Tower Hill [ˌtaʊə 'hɪl] **II U3**, 53
Ty'n y Berth [ti:n‿ə 'bɜ:θ] **II U1**, 16
Victoria Park [ˌvɪktɔ:riə 'pɑ:k] **I**
Village Way ['vɪlɪdʒ ˌweɪ] **I**
Wimbledon ['wɪmbldən] **I**

Geographical names

America [ə'merɪkə] **II AC2**, 89
Australia [ɒs'treɪliə] Australien **II AC2**, 89
Austria ['ɔ:strɪə] Österreich **II U4**, 71
Britain ['brɪtn] Großbritannien **I**
British Empire [ˌbrɪtɪʃ‿'empaɪə] britisches Königreich **II AC2**, 89
Canada ['kænədə] Kanada **I**
China ['tʃaɪnə] China **I**
England ['ɪŋglənd] England **I**
European Union (EU) [ˌjʊərəpiən 'ju:njən (i:ju:)] Europäische Union **II AC1**, 48
France [frɑ:ns] Frankreich **II U3**, 56
Germany ['dʒɜ:məni] Deutschland **I**
India ['ɪndiə] Indien **II AC2**, 88
Isle of Dogs [ˌaɪl‿əv 'dɒgz] **I**
Italy ['ɪtəli] Italien **II U5**, 96
Kent [kent] *Grafschaft im Südosten Englands* **II U4**, 76
Normandy ['nɔ:məndi] die Normandie **II U3**, 56
Pakistan [ˌpɑ:kɪ'stɑ:n] **I**
Poland ['pəʊlənd] Polen **I**
Snowdonia National Park [snəʊˌdəʊniə ˌnæʃnl 'pɑ:k] **II U1**, 16
South Africa [ˌsaʊθ‿'æfrɪkə] Südafrika **II AC2**, 89
Spain [speɪn] Spanien **II U5**, 99
Thames [temz] **I**
United Kingdom (UK) [ju:'keɪ] Vereinigtes Königreich von Großbritannien und Nordirland **I**
USA (United States of America) [ˌju:es'eɪ (ju:ˌnaɪtɪd ˌsteɪts‿əv‿ə'merɪkə)] USA (Vereinigte Staaten von Amerika) **II AC2**, 89
Wales [weɪlz] **II U1**, 16

Other names

Arches Leisure Centre [ˌɑ:tʃɪz 'leʒə ˌsentə] **I**
Ben Briggs [ˌben 'brɪgz] **I**
Big Ben [ˌbɪg 'ben] **II AC1**, 48
British Museum [ˌbrɪtɪʃ mju:'zi:əm] **II U3**, 50
Buckingham Palace [ˌbʌkɪŋəm 'pælɪs] **II AC1**, 48
Changing of the Guards [ˌtʃeɪndʒɪŋ əv ðə 'gɑ:dz] *Wachwechsel vor dem Buckingham Palace* **II AC1**, 49
Comic Relief [ˌkɒmɪk rɪ'li:f] *wohltätige Organisation* **II U1**, 10
2Cool Performing Academy [ˌtu:ku:l pəˌfɔ:mɪŋ ə'kædəmi] **I**
Croeso i Gymru [ˌkrɔɪsəʊ‿i: 'gʌmri] **II U1**, 18
Crossharbour ['krɒsˌhɑ:bə] **II U3**, 53
Cutty Sark [ˌkʌti 'sɑ:k] **I**
Diwali [dɪ'wɑ:li] **I**
Docklands Light Railway *(DLR)* [ˌdɒklændz ˌlaɪt 'reɪlweɪ] *Regionalbahn im Osten Londons* **I**
Eid [i:d] **I**
Elephant & Castle ['elɪfənt ənd kɑ:sl] **II U3**, 53
Fan Museum [ˌfæn mju:'zi:əm] **I**
For he's a jolly good fellow [fə ˌhi:z‿ə ˌdʒɒli gʊd 'feləʊ] *Volkslied* **I**
Greenwich Foot Tunnel [ˌgrenɪdʒ 'fʊt ˌtʌnl] **I**
Guy Fawkes Night ['gaɪ fɔ:ks ˌnaɪt] **I**
Halloween [ˌhæləʊ'i:n] *Tag vor Allerheiligen* **I**
Hanukkah ['hɑ:nəkə] **I**
Honey ['hʌni] **I**
the Houses of Parliament [ðə ˌhaʊzɪz‿əv 'pɑ:ləmənt] *britisches Parlamentsgebäude* **II U3**, 50
London Eye [ˌlʌndən‿'aɪ] **II AC1**, 48
London Wall [ˌlʌndən 'wɔ:l] **II U3**, 50
London Zoo [ˌlʌndən 'zu:] **II U3**, 53
Madame Tussauds [ˌmædəm tʊ'sɔ:dz] **II U3**, 51
Manchester City [ˌmæntʃɪstə 'sɪti] *englischer Fußballclub* **II U5**, 94
Meridian Line [məˌrɪdiən 'laɪn] Nullmeridian **I**
Mickey Mouse [ˌmɪki 'maʊs] **I**
Millennium Footbridge [mɪˌleniəm 'fʊtbrɪdʒ] **II U3**, 62
Mother's Day ['mʌðəz ˌdeɪ] **I**
Mousebook ['maʊsbʊk] **II U5**, 90
Mr Fluff [ˌmɪstə 'flʌf] **I**
Mudchute Farm [ˌmʌdʃu:t 'fɑ:m] **I**
Natural History Museum [ˌnætʃrl 'hɪstri mju:ˌzi:əm] **II U2**, 40
Notting Hill Carnival [ˌnɒtɪŋ hɪl 'kɑ:nɪvl] **I**
Oyster card ['ɔɪstə ˌkɑ:d] **II U3**, 52
Pancake Day ['pænkeɪk ˌdeɪ] **I**
Pets Corner [ˌpets 'kɔ:nə] **I**
Red Nose Day [ˌred nəʊz 'deɪ] **II U1**, 8
Rocky ['rɒki] **II U3**, 56
Royal Observatory [ˌrɔɪəl‿əb'zɜ:vətri] **I**
Rugby Football Club (RFC) [ˌrʌgbi ˌfʊtbɔ:l 'klʌb (ɑ:r‿ef 'si:)] **II U4**, 75
Sherlock ['ʃɜ:lɒk] **I**
Shrove Tuesday [ˌʃrəʊv 'tju:zdeɪ] Fastnachtsdienstag **I**
Sid [sɪd] **I**
star4ever [ˌstɑ:fə'revə] **I**
Tandoori [tæn'dʊəri] **I**
Thomas Tallis School *(= TTS)* [ˌtɒməs 'tælɪs ˌsku:l] **I**
the Tower of London [ðə ˌtaʊər‿əv 'lʌndən] **II AC1**, 49
Transport Museum [ˌtrænspɔ:t mju:'zi:əm] **II U3**, 53
TTS planner [ˌti:ti:ˌes 'plænə] Handbuch für TTS-Schülerinnen und -Schüler **I**
Valentine's Day ['væləntaɪnz ˌdeɪ] **I**
Victoria [vɪk'tɔ:riə] **II U3**, 53
Whitehall ['waɪthɔ:l] *Straße in London* **II U3**, 51
World War II [ˌwɜ:ld ˌwɔ: 'tu:] Zweiter Weltkrieg **II AC2**, 89

Famous names

Christopher Wren [ˌkrɪstəfə 'ren] **II U2**, 30
Daniel Craig [ˌdænjəl 'kreɪg] **II U1**, 15
Elizabeth I [ɪˌlɪzəbəθ ðə 'fɜ:st] **II U2**, 31
James Bond [ˌdʒeɪmz 'bɒnd] **II U1**, 15
Lenny Harry [ˌleni 'hæri] *britischer Comedian* **II U1**, 10
Louis Armstrong [ˌlu:i 'ɑ:mstrɒŋ] **II U2**, 35
Prince Albert [ˌprɪns 'ælbət] **II AC1**, 49
Queen Victoria [ˌkwi:n vɪk'tɔ:riə] **II AC1**, 49
William the Conqueror [ˌwɪljəm ðə 'kɒŋkrə] **II U3**, 56;

A

abbiegen to turn I
abblocken to block II U5, 93
Abend evening I
  heute **Abend** 2nite *(= tonight)* I
Abendessen dinner I
abends in the evenings I
abends *(Uhrzeit)* p.m. I
Abenteuer adventure II U1, 16
aber but I
abfahren *to leave II U2, 30
abgeschlossen locked II U1, 19
abnehmen *to take off I
abschalten to turn off I; to turn off II U1, 12
  Schalt/Schaltet es ab! Turn it off! I
abschneiden *to cut (off) II U2, 30
abschreiben to copy I
absolut absolutely II U2, 42
Abstand gap I
abstimmen *to take a vote; to vote I
abstürzen to crash II U5, 103
acht eight I
Acker field II U1, 18
Action action I
Adresse address I
AG club I
aggressiv aggressive II U1, 24
äh er I
keine **Ahnung** no idea II U1, 19
Akku battery II U1, 19
Aktion action I
Aktivität activity I
albern silly I
alle all of them; everyone I; everybody II U3, 54
alle/-s all I
allein alone I; on my own II U2, 40
alles everything I
Alphabet alphabet I
als as II U2, 30
als *(bei Vergleichen)* than II U1, 16
als when I
also so I
alt old I
  Wie **alt** bist du? How old are you? I
  Wie **alt** sind Sie? How old are you? I
am on I
  am besten best I
  am Fluss by the river II U2, 31
  am Wochenende at the weekend I
aus **Amerika** American II U1, 9
Amerikaner/-in American II U1, 9
amerikanisch American II U1, 9
Amtssprache official language II AC2, 89
sich **amüsieren** *to have fun I
an on; at I
  an Bord aboard I
  an sein *to be on II U5, 102
anbieten to offer II U2, 28
Anblick sight II AC1, 48
Andenken souvenir II U3, 54
die **anderen** the others I
andere/-r/-s other I
  ein/-e **andere**/-r/-s another I
Einerseits …, (aber) **andererseits** … On the one hand …, (but) on the other hand … II U4, 82
(sich) **ändern** to change II U5, 90
anders different; other I
Anfang beginning II U1, 22
anfangen to start I; *to get started II U2, 33; *to begin II U5, 99
anfeuern to cheer II U4, 72
angeben to show off II U5, 103
Und ein **Angeber**! With a very big head! II U5, 95
von **Angesicht** zu **Angesicht** face-to-face II U5, 93
angespült werden to wash up II U3, 62
Angst fear II U4, 82
  Angst haben (vor) *to be scared (of) I
  Ich habe (keine) **Angst** vor … I'm (not) scared of … I
anhaben *to wear I
anhalten to stop I
Anhänger/-in fan II U4, 83
anhören to listen (to) I
anmalen to paint I
Anmerkung note I
annähernd nearly II U2, 41
anonym anonymous II U1, 13
anpflanzen to plant II U2, 41
anprobieren to try on II U2, 31
Anregung suggestion I
Anruf phone call I
  einen **Anruf** entgegennehmen to answer the phone I
Anrufbeantworter answering machine I
anrufen to call I
Anrufer/-in caller I
anschauen to look at I; *to have a look (at) II U4, 73
sich **anschließen** to join II U2, 33
ansehen to look at I
(sich) **ansehen** to watch I
Ansicht point of view II U4, 75
anstarren to stare I
antippen to tap II U5, 102
Antwort answer; reply I
antworten to answer; to reply I
Anweisung instruction I
Anwesenheitskontrolle registration II U2, 32
Apfel apple I
App app II U5, 97
Apparat machine I
April April I
Arbeit job; work I
Arbeit für die Schule studies *(pl)* II U2, 28
arbeiten to work I
Architekt/-in architect II U2, 30
Areal area II U4, 70
Ärger trouble II U1, 19
  Ärger machen *to make trouble I
Argument dafür pro II U3, 55
  Argument dagegen con II U3, 55
Arm arm II U2, 41
Art kind I
  Art und Weise way I
Artikel article II U2, 33
Arzt/**Ärztin** doctor II U4, 72
Arztpraxis surgery I
Assistent/-in assistant II U4, 78
Atlas atlas II AC2, 88
atmen to breathe II U4, 80
Atmosphäre flair II U3, 51
Attraktion attraction II U3, 59
Aua! Ouch! II U1, 8
auch too I; also II U1, 10
  Du **auch**? You too? I
Audio- audio I
Audioführung audio tour II U3, 56
auf on; at; to I
  auf dem Foto/den Fotos in the photo(s) I
  auf der anderen Seite von across; opposite I
  auf der Straße in the street I
  auf einmal suddenly I
  auf Wiedersehen goodbye I
  auf … zu towards II U3, 62
aufbauen *to set up I
aufbewahren *to keep I
Aufführung show II U4, 75
Aufgabe task; exercise; job I
aufgebracht upset II U2, 30
aufgeregt excited I; nervous II U1, 12
aufgeschlagen open I
aufhängen *to hang up II U2, 33
aufhören to finish I
  Hör/Hört auf! Stop it! I
aufhören (mit) to stop I
aufladen to top up II U3, 52
aufmachen to open I
Aufmerksamkeit attention II U5, 93
Aufnahme recording I
Aufnahmestudio recording studio I
aufnehmen to record II U4, 78
aufpassen to look out II U4, 70
  aufpassen auf to look after I
  Pass/Passt auf! Be careful! I
aufräumen to tidy *(a room)* I
aufrechterhalten *to keep going II U1, 12
aufregend exciting I
aufsagen *to say I
aufschreiben *to write down I
aufstehen *(aus dem Bett)* *to get up I
  Es ist Zeit **aufzustehen**! Time to get up! I
aufstehen *(von einer Sitzgelegenheit)* *to stand up I
aufstellen *to put up II U2, 33
Auftrag task I
aufwärmen to warm up I
  sich **aufwärmen** to warm up I
Aufwärmübung warm-up I
aufzeichnen to record II U4, 78

Aufzeichnung recording I
Auge eye II U1, 9
Er traute seinen Augen nicht. He couldn't believe his eyes. II U2, 40
Augenblick moment II U2, 40
Augenzeuge/Augenzeugin eyewitness II U4, 77
August August I
aus from I
ausblasen *to blow out I
Ausblick view II U2, 30
Auschecken Check-out I
(sich) ausdenken *to think of II U1, 12
Ausdruck phrase I; expression II AC2, 89
nützliche Ausdrücke Useful phrases I
ausflippen *to go crazy II U5, 95
Ausflug trip II U1, 9
den Hund ausführen to walk the dog I
ausgeben (Geld) *to spend I
sich ausgeschlossen fühlen *to feel left out II U5, 104
(sich) ausleihen to borrow II U5, 103
Mach/Macht das aus! Stop it! I
auspacken to unwrap I
auspusten *to blow out I
ausräumen to clear out I
jmdm. etw. ausrichten *to take a message I
sich ausruhen to relax II U2, 36
Ausrüstung equipment II U4, 69
Aussage statement II AC2, 88
ausschalten to turn off I; to turn off II U1, 12
Schalt/Schaltet es aus! Turn it off! I
aussehen to look I
wie der Mann aussah what the man looked like II U1, 13
außerhalb outside; out I
Außerirdische/-r alien I
Äußerung expression II AC2, 89
Aussicht view II U2, 30
Aussprache pronunciation I
Ausstattung equipment II U4, 69
aussteigen *to get out of II U5, 102
aussteigen (aus einem Bus/Zug) *to get off (a bus/train) II U3, 53
Ausstellung display II U3, 59
Ausstellung in der Klasse class display I
Australien Australia II AC2, 89
Auswahl choice II U3, 58
auswählen *to choose II U2, 30
Wähle/Wählt … aus. Choose … I
auswendig lernen *to learn … by heart I
auswickeln to unwrap I
Auszeichnung award II U4, 74
ausziehen *to take off I
Auto car I
Automat machine I

B

Baby baby I
Bad bath I
Badewanne bath I
Badezimmer bathroom I
Badminton badminton I
Bahnhof station I
bald soon II U1, 18
Ball ball I
Banane banana I
Bär bear II U3, 56
Basketball basketball I
Batterie battery II U1, 19
Bauch stomach II U4, 80
Bauchschmerzen stomachache II U4, 73
Bauchweh stomachache II U4, 73
bauen *to build II U2, 30
Bauernhof farm I
Baum tree I
Beachtung attention II U5, 93
beängstigend scary II U1, 24
beantworten to answer I
bedeckt cloudy II U1, 19
bedeuten *to mean II U3, 54
Bedeutung meaning II U1, 21
bedürftig in need II U1, 10
sich beeilen to hurry I
beeindruckt impressed II U2, 36
beeinflussen to influence II AC2, 89
beenden to finish I; to end II U4, 79
sich befassen mit *to deal (with) II U3, 54
befestigen to fix II U5, 95
befolgen to follow II U3, 54
befragen to interview I
Befragung interview I
Befürchtung fear II U4, 82
begeistert excited I
Beginn beginning II U1, 22
beginnen to start I; *to begin II U5, 99
behalten *to keep I
Behauptung statement II AC2, 88
behindert with special needs II U2, 29
bei with; at I
beibringen *to teach II U4, 76
beide both II U4, 81
beide the two of them II U5, 92
Bein leg II U4, 71
beinahe almost II U4, 75
Beispiel example I
zum Beispiel for example II AC2, 89
beißen *to bite II U3, 56
beitreten to join II U2, 33
bekommen *to get I; to receive II U4, 77
belebt busy I
beliebt popular I
bellen to bark I
bemerken to notice II U2, 40
benötigen to need (to) I
benutzen to use I
beobachten to watch I
bequem comfortable II U3, 65
bereit ready II U2, 41
bereits already I
Berg mountain II U1, 16
bergen to save I
Bericht report II U1, 9
Bericht (in einer Zeitschrift, Zeitung) article II U2, 33
sich beruhigen to relax II U2, 36; to calm down II U2, 41
berühmt famous I
beschäftigt busy I
beschreiben to describe I
besichtigen to visit I
Besichtigungs- sightseeing II U3, 58
besiegen *to beat II U3, 54
besitzen *to have got I
besonders special I
besorgen *to get I
besorgt sein *to be worried II U4, 80
besser better I
(der/die/das) Beste (the) best II U1, 10
besteigen to climb I
beste/-r/-s best I
am besten best I
bestürzt upset II U2, 30
Besuch visit I
besuchen to visit I
Besucher/-in visitor I
betreten to enter II U2, 40
Betreuer/-in instructor II U1, 18
Bett bed I
ins Bett gehen *to go to bed I
beunruhigt sein *to be worried II U4, 80
bevor before I
(sich) bewegen to move I
Bewegung move I
bewölkt cloudy II U1, 19
bezahlen *to pay (for) I
Beziehung relationship II U4, 82
Biene bee II U2, 33
Bild picture I
bilden *to make I
Bildgeschichte photo story I
billig cheap I
Bindewort linking word I
Bis … CU (= See you); See you! I
Bis dann! CU (= See you); See you! I
bis jetzt so far II U4, 75
von … bis from … to I
bis till I; until II U4, 70
Biskuit- sponge I
ein bisschen a bit II U1, 18
Bitte. Please. I
Bitte schön. Here you are.; You're welcome. I
bitten to ask I
bitten um to ask for I
blau blue I
bleiben to stay I
Bleistift pencil I
Blick look I; view II U2, 30
einen Blick werfen auf *to take a look at II U2, 37
Blitz lightning (no pl) II U5, 102
blockieren to block II U5, 93
blöd stupid II U4, 81
bloß only I

Blume flower II U2, 41
BMX BMX II U4, 68
weiße Bohnen in Tomatensoße baked beans (pl) I
Bonbons sweets (pl) I
Boot boat I
an Bord aboard I
böse angry; bad I
Botschaft message I
Bowlingbahn bowling alley I
Box box I
Boxen boxing II U1, 8
Boxrunde round of boxing II U1, 8
brauchen to need (to) I
nicht brauchen needn't I
(Zeit) brauchen *to take II U5, 95
braun brown I
brechen *to break I
schwarzes Brett noticeboard II U1, 10
Brief letter II U5, 91
Briefträger postman II U1, 13
Brille glasses (pl) II U4, 80
bringen *to bring; *to get; *to take I
in Schwierigkeiten bringen *to make trouble I
jmdn. dazu bringen, etw. zu tun *to make somebody do something II U5, 92
Brite/Britin British I
britisch British I
Broschüre brochure I
Brot bread I
belegtes Brot sandwich I
Brücke bridge II U3, 62
Bruder brother I
Buch book I
Büchse can I
Buchstabe letter I
buchstabieren *to spell I
bunt colourful I
Buntstift pencil I
Burg castle II U3, 56
Büro office I
Bus bus I
Busbahnhof bus station I

C

Café café; snack bar I
Cafeteria cafeteria I
Camping camping II U5, 99
Cent (Währung) cent I
Center centre I
Chance chance II U5, 100
Charakter character I
Chatroom chat room II AC2, 88
chatten (sich online unterhalten) to chat I
China China I
Chipkarte smartcard II U3, 52
circa about I
Clown clown II U4, 80
Cola coke I
Comedian comedian II U1, 10
Comedy Show comedy show II U1, 10
Comic comic II U4, 82
Comicheft comic II U4, 82
Computer computer I
Computerunterricht Technology II U2, 32
cool cool I
Couch sofa I
Cousin/Cousine cousin I
Creme cream I
Cricket cricket II U4, 69
Curry (Gewürz oder Gericht) curry I

D

da because I
da there I
da ist/sind there is/are I
dabei sein *to be in II U4, 70
Dachboden loft I; attic II U4, 76
dahin there I
danach then; after that I
dankbar thankful I
Danke. Thank you.; Thanks. I
danken to thank II U2, 36
Nichts zu danken. You're welcome. I
dann then I
darauf zu towards II U3, 62
das the I
das that I
Das (hier) ist … This is … I
Das macht … That's … I
Das war knapp! That was close! I
das (Relativpronomen) which II U2, 30
dass that I
Datum date I
dauern *to take II U5, 95
Daumen thumb II U2, 34
die Daumen drücken *to keep your fingers crossed I
davonkommen mit *to get away with II U4, 76
Deck deck I
dein/-e your I
dein/-er/-e/-es yours II U2, 41
Dekoration decorations (pl) I
dekorieren to decorate I
dem (Relativpronomen) who; which II U2, 30
den (Relativpronomen) who; which II U2, 30
denken *to think I
Denke/Denkt an … Think of … I
denken an to remember I
denken über *to think of I
dennoch still II U5, 95
der the I
der; dem; den; die; das (Relativpronomen) that II U1, 9
der (Relativpronomen) who; which II U2, 30
deren (Relativpronomen) whose II U2, 30
der-/die-/dasselbe the same I
Desaster disaster II U5, 102
deshalb that's why II U2, 30
Design design II U2, 30
dessen (Relativpronomen) whose II U2, 30
deutlich clear I
Deutsch German I
deutsch German I
Deutsche/-r German I
aus Deutschland German I
Deutschland Germany I
Dezember December I
Diagramm diagram I
Dialog dialogue I
die (auch Pl.) the I
die (Relativpronomen) who; which II U2, 30
Dienstag Tuesday
dies this I
diese (hier) these I
diese dort those I
diese/-r/-s this I
Ding thing I
Dinosaurier dinosaur II U2, 40
Diskussion discussion II U5, 90
diskutieren to discuss I
Distanz distance II U3, 60
doch after all I
Donner thunder (no pl) II U5, 102
Donnerstag Thursday I
doof silly I
Dorf village I
dort there I
dorthin there I
Dose can I
aus der Dose tinned I
Dosen- tinned I
Drama drama II U2, 28
dramatisch dramatic II U3, 63
dran kommen to reach II U5, 95
Du bist dran. Your turn.; It's your turn. I
draußen outside I
nach draußen out I
dreckig dirty II U2, 40
drei three I
eine Dreiergruppe a group of three I
dreizehn thirteen I
drin inside I
dritte/-r/-s third I
Druck- print II U5, 91
drücken to press II U5, 102
die Daumen drücken *to keep your fingers crossed I
du you; u (= you) I
du/dir/dich/Sie/sich (selbst) yourself I
Du auch? You too? I
Du bist dran. Your turn.; It's your turn. I
Du bist … You're … I
Du weißt, wie man … You know how to … I
dumm silly I; stupid II U4, 81
Zu dumm! Too bad! I
Dummkopf silly II U4, 80
dunkel dark II U1, 18
Dunkelheit the dark II U1, 18
durch through I

durchdrehen *to go crazy **II U5**, 95
dürfen can **I**; *to be allowed to (do sth); *to be able to (do sth); may **II U5**, 95
nicht **dürfen** mustn't **I**
Dusche shower **I**
DVD DVD **I**

E

Ebbe low tide **II U3**, 62
echt real **II U1**, 10
Ecke corner **II U2**, 34
Ehefrau wife, wives *(pl)* **II U2**, 31
Ehemann husband **II U2**, 30
Ei egg **I**
Eichhörnchen squirrel **I**
eifersüchtig sein (auf) *to be jealous (of) **I**
eigene/-r/-s own **I**
eilen to hurry **I**
Eimer bucket **II U3**, 62
ein/-e a; an **I**
ein paar a couple of **I**
ein wenig a little **I**
ein/-e andere/-r/-s another **I**
noch **ein**/-e another **I**
einander each other **I**
Atme(t) tief ein. Take a deep breath. **II U2**, 36
einbiegen to turn **I**
Einchecken Check-in **I**
eine/-r/-s one *(sg)*/ones *(pl)* **II U3**, 54
Einerseits …, (aber) andererseits … On the one hand …, (but) on the other hand … **II U4**, 82
einfach easy **I**
einfach just **I**
Einfall idea **I**
sich etwas **einfallen** lassen *to think of **II U1**, 12
Einführung introduction **II U2**, 29
eingießen to pour **I**
Einheit unit **I**
die Segel **einholen** to reef the sails **I**
einige some; a few **I**
Einkäufe shopping **I**
Einkaufen shopping **I**
einkaufen gehen *to go shopping **I**
einladen to invite **I**
Einladung invitation **I**
Einleitung introduction **II U2**, 29
einmal once **I**
einpacken to wrap **I**
einrichten *to set up **I**
eins one **I**
einsam lonely **I**
einschenken to pour **I**
einschlafen *to fall asleep **I**
Setze/Setzt **ein** … Put in … **I**
einst once **I**
einsteigen *to get into **I**
eintreten to enter **II U2**, 40
Eintrittskarte ticket **I**

einwickeln to wrap **I**
Einzelkind only child **I**
einzeln individual **II U4**, 69
einzige/-r/-s only **II U5**, 103
Eis ice; ice cream **I**
Eisbahn ice rink **I**
Eiscreme ice cream **I**
elektronisch electronic **II U1**, 21
elf eleven **I**
Eltern parents *(pl)* **I**
E-Mail e-mail **I**
per **E-Mail** schicken to mail **II U5**, 97
empfangen to receive **II U4**, 77
Ende ending; end **I**
enden to finish **I**; to end up **II U1**, 8; to end **II U4**, 79
endlich at last **I**; finally **II U2**, 31
eng close **I**
aus **England** English **I**
England England **I**
Engländer/-in English **I**
Ich bin **Engländer**/-in. I'm English. **I**
Englisch English **I**
englisch English **I**
englischsprachig English-speaking **I**
entdecken to discover **II U2**, 28
auf **Entdeckungsreise** gehen to explore **I**
Entfernung distance **II U3**, 60
eine Nachricht **entgegennehmen** *to take a message **I**
einen Anruf **entgegennehmen** to answer the phone **I**
entgegnen to reply **I**
Entgegnung reply **I**
entlang along **I**
entlanggehen *to go down **I**
entrümpeln to clear out **I**
(sich) **entscheiden** to decide **I**
Entschuldigen Sie! Excuse me … **I**
Entschuldigung! Sorry!; Excuse me … **I**
entsetzt horrified **I**
sich **entspannen** to relax **II U2**, 36
entsprechen to match **I**
enttäuscht disappointed **I**
entwerfen to design **II U2**, 31
Entwurf plan; draft **I**; design **II U2**, 30
er he **I**
Erdboden earth **II U2**, 40
Erde world **I**; earth **II U2**, 40
die **Erde** earth **II U2**, 40
Ereignis event **I**
Erfahrung experience **II U4**, 69
erfinden to create **I**
erforschen to explore **I**
ergänzen to add **I**
Ergebnis result **II U5**, 97
ergreifen to grab **II U3**, 62
erhalten to receive **II U4**, 77
Erinnerst du dich? Remember? **I**
sich **erinnern** (an) to remember **I**
Erinnert ihr euch? Remember? **I**
Erinnerung memory **II U1**, 19

Erkältung cold **II U4**, 73
erklären to explain **I**
Erklärung statement **II AC2**, 88
erkunden to explore **I**
ernst serious **I**
ernsthaft serious **I**
erraten to guess **I**
erreichen *to get to **I**; to reach **II U5**, 95
errichten *to put up **II U2**, 33
erschaffen to create **I**
erst only **I**
erst wenn until **II U4**, 70
erstaunlich amazing **II U1**, 18
erste/-r/-s first **I**
als **Erstes** first **I**
ertappt caught on camera **II U1**, 8
Erwachsene/-r adult **II U3**, 58
erwähnen to mention **II AC2**, 88
erwidern to reply **I**
Erwiderung reply **I**
erzählen *to tell **I**
erzählen von to talk about **I**
nochmals **erzählen** *to retell **I**
Erzähle mir von … Tell me about … **I**
Erzählung story, stories *(pl)* **I**
es it **I**
Es ist super zum/für … It's great for … **I**
Essen food **I**; meal **II U1**, 18
(ein Bonbon) essen *to have *(a sweet)* **I**
essen *to eat **I**
etwa about **I**
etwas some; something; a little **I**
euer/eure your **I**
eure/-r/-s yours **II U2**, 41
Euro *(Währung)* euro **I**
Europäische Union European Union (EU) **II AC1**, 48
ewig forever **II U5**, 93
Examen exam **II U2**, 28
extra extra **I**

F

Fackel torch **II U1**, 18
fähig sein zu *to be able to (do sth) **II U5**, 95
fahren *to go **I**; to travel **II U3**, 52
Fahrer/-in driver **II U1**, 13
Fahrplan timetable **I**
Fahrrad bike **I**
Fahrradmotocross bicycle motocross **II U4**, 83
Fahrt trip **II U1**, 9; tour **II U3**, 56
fair fair **I**
Fakt fact **II U2**, 37
fallen *to fall **I**
fallen (lassen) to drop **II U3**, 62
falls if **I**
falsch wrong **I**
fälschen to fake **II U4**, 76
Familie family **I**
Fan fan **II U4**, 83
fangen *to catch **II U4**, 68

Fantasie fantasy I
fantastisch fantastic II U2, 29
Fanzeitschrift fanzine II U2, 38
Farbe colour I
Welche **Farbe** hat …? What colour is …? I
farbenfroh colourful I
Farm farm I
Farmer/-in farmer II U1, 13
fast nearly II U2, 41; almost II U4, 75
Fastnachtsdienstag Shrove Tuesday I
Februar February I
Federmäppchen pencil-case I
Feedback feedback II U2, 29
Was fehlt? What is missing? I
fehlend missing II U1, 13
Fehler mistake I
Feier party I
feiern to celebrate I
Feiertag holiday I
Feld field II U1, 18
Fenster window I
Ferien holidays *(pl)* I
fernbleiben von to stay away from II U5, 97
Fernsehen TV I
fernsehen to watch TV I
Fernseher TV I
fertig ready II U2, 41
Fertiggericht ready meal I
Fertigkeit skill I
fertigstellen to finish I
Fest festival I
festhalten *to hold I
Festival festival I
festnehmen to arrest II U1, 13
Feuerwerk fireworks *(pl)* I
Fieber fever II U4, 73
Figur character I; figure II U3, 51
Film film I
Filmemacher/-in filmmaker II U1, 24
finden *to find I
Finger finger I
Fisch fish, fish *(pl)* I
fit werden *to get fit I
Fläche space II U2, 30; area II U4, 70
Flair flair II U3, 51
Flasche bottle I
Flohmarkt flea market I
Flughafen airport II AC1, 48
Fluss river I
am **Fluss** by the river II U2, 31
flüstern to whisper I
Flut high tide II U3, 62
Flyer flyer I
folgen to follow II U3, 54
Form form I
in **Form** kommen *to get fit I
verneinte **Form** negative form I
hier: sich fortbewegen *to get around II U3, 53
fortfahren *to go on I
Forum forum II U5, 90
Foto photo; picture I
auf dem **Foto**/den **Fotos** in the photo(s) I
Fotos machen *to take photos I
Fotoapparat camera II U1, 8
Fotografie photo I
fotografieren *to take photos I
Fotostory photo story I
Frage question I
fragen to ask I
Frage/Fragt nach … Ask about … I
fragen nach to ask for I
Französisch French II U2, 32
französisch French II U2, 32
Frau woman, women *(pl)* I
Frau *(Anrede)* Mrs I
frei free I
Freiluft- outdoor II U1, 16
Freitag Friday I
Freizeit free time; leisure I
Freizeitzentrum leisure centre I
fremd strange I
Fremdsprache foreign language II U2, 38
fressen *to eat I
Freude fun I
Freudenfeuer bonfire I
sich freuen auf to look forward to II U2, 33
sich **freuen** an to enjoy II U1, 12
Freund/-in friend I
Dafür sind **Freunde** da. That's what friends are for. I
Freundin *(in einer Paarbeziehung)* girlfriend II U3, 54
freundlich friendly II U1, 14
Freundschaft friendship II U5, 94
Freundschaft schließen *to make friends II U2, 43
frisch fresh I
uns frisieren *to do our hair I
froh happy I
fröhlich happy; fun I
Frucht fruit I
früh early I
Frühstück breakfast I
frühstücken *to have breakfast I
Frühstückszerealie cereal *(no pl)* I
Fuchs fox II U2, 34
fühlen *to feel I
sich **fühlen** *to feel I
sich ausgeschlossen **fühlen** *to feel left out II U5, 104
sich schlecht **fühlen** *to feel sick II U4, 73
Führer/-in guide II U3, 56
Füller pen I
fünf five I
fünfzehn fifteen I
funktionieren to work II U5, 95
für mich on my own II U2, 40
Für wen …? Who … for? I
Furcht fear II U4, 82
furchtbar awful I
Fuß foot, feet *(pl)* I
zu **Fuß** on foot II U3, 60
Fußball football I
Fußboden floor I
Fußgelenk ankle II U4, 72
Fußknöchel ankle II U4, 72

G

ganz all I
den **ganzen** Tag all day II U1, 14
ganz whole I
Garage garage I
garstig nasty II U5, 91
Garten garden I
Gaststätte restaurant I
Gebäude building I
geben *to give I
es **gibt** there is/are I
Gebiet area II U4, 70
gebrauchen to use I
gebrochen broken I
Geburtstag birthday I
Alles Gute zum **Geburtstag**! Happy Birthday! I
Herzlichen Glückwunsch zum **Geburtstag**! Happy Birthday! I
Gedächtnis memory II U1, 19
Gedicht poem I
gedruckt print II U5, 91
gefährlich dangerous I
Mir gefällt … I like … I
Gefängnis prison II U3, 56
Gefühl feeling II U1, 9
gegen against II U1, 19
Gegend region II AC2, 89
sich gegenseitig each other I
gegenüber opposite I
Geheimnis secret II U1, 19
gehen *to go; to walk I
ins Bett **gehen** *to go to bed I
nach unten **gehen** *to go down I
zu jmdm. nach Hause **gehen** *to go over to II U5, 95
Wie **geht** es dir? How are you? I
Wie **geht** es euch? How are you? I
Wie **geht** es Ihnen? How are you? I
gehören (zu) to belong (to) II U2, 29
gehören zu *to go with I
zueinander **gehören** *to go together I
Geist ghost II U2, 30
gelangweilt bored I
gelb yellow I
Geld money I
Geld sammeln to raise money II U1, 10
Geld verdienen *to make money I
Gelee jelly I
Gelegenheit chance II U5, 100
Gemälde painting II U2, 28
gemein nasty II U5, 91
Gemeindezentrum community centre I
gemeinsam together I
genau exactly II AC2, 88
genau hier right here II U4, 70

Genie genius **II U5**, 95
genießen to enjoy **II U1**, 12
genug enough **I**
genügend enough **I**
geöffnet open **I**
gerade just; at the moment **I**; right now **II U5**, 103
geradeaus straight on **I**
Gerät machine **I**
Geräusch sound **I**; noise **II U1**, 18
gerecht fair **I**
Gern geschehen. You're welcome. **I**
  gern haben to like **I**
  gern mögen to love **I**
  hätte/-st/-n/-t **gern** would like **I**
  hätte/-st-/-n/-t sehr **gern** would love **I**
  würde/-st/-n/-t **gern** would like **I**
  würde/-st/-n/-t sehr **gern** would love **I**
Gerümpel rubbish **I**
Geschäft shop **I**
geschehen to happen **I**
Geschenk present **I**
Geschichte story, stories *(pl)* **I**; history **II U2**, 30
geschichtlich historical **I**
Geschick skill **I**
Gesicht face **I**
Gespräch dialogue; conversation **I**
Gestalt figure **II U3**, 51
gestalten to design **II U2**, 31
Gestaltung design **II U2**, 30
gestern yesterday **II U1**, 11
gesund healthy **I**
Gesundheit health **II U4**, 69
Getränk drink **I**
getrennt separate **II U1**, 16
gewaltig huge **II AC1**, 48
Gewinn prize **I**
gewinnen *to win **I**
Gewinner/-in winner **I**
gewöhnlich usually **I**
Gitter grid **I**
glänzen *to shine **II U2**, 33
Glas glass **I**
glauben *to think; to believe **I**
gläubig religious **I**
der/die/das **gleiche** the same **I**
gleich right away **I**
  jetzt **gleich** right now **II U5**, 103
gleichmäßig regular **I**
gleichzeitig at the same time **I**
Glocke bell **II AC1**, 48
Glück haben *to be lucky **II U3**, 62
  … hat/haben **Glück**. … is/are lucky. **I**
glücklich happy **I**
Glücksbringer lucky charm **I**
Götterspeise jelly **I**
graben *to dig **II U2**, 33
grau grey **I**
greifen to grab **II U3**, 62
Griff knob **II U5**, 95
groß big **I**; tall; high **II U1**, 17; large **II AC1**, 48
großartig great **I**; fantastic **II U2**, 29
Großbritannien Britain **I**
Großbuchstabe capital letter **I**
Größe size **I**
Großeltern grandparents *(pl)* **I**
Großstadt city **I**
grün green **I**
Grund reason **II U4**, 82
Grund- basic **II U3**, 59
grundlegend basic **II U3**, 59
Grundschule primary school **I**
Gruppe group **I**; team **II U1**, 8
gruselig scary **II U1**, 24
Gruß greeting **I**
  Grüße ausrichten (an) *to say hello (to) **I**
  Herzliche **Grüße** *(am Briefende)* Love … **I**
  Liebe **Grüße** *(am Briefende)* Love … **I**
  Viele **Grüße** … *(am Ende von Briefen und Mails)* Yours … **II U5**, 99
grüßen *to say hello (to) **I**
gut good; fine **I**
  gut sein in *to be good at **I**
  Guten Morgen. Good morning. **I**
  Mir geht's **gut**. I'm fine. **I**
Guthaben credit **II U3**, 52

H

unsere **Haare** machen *to do our hair **I**
haben *to have got; *to have **I**
  hätte/-st/-n/-t gern would like **I**
  hätte/-st-/-n/-t sehr gern would love **I**
Hafendamm pier **I**
Hähnchen chicken **I**
halb *(bei Uhrzeitangaben)* half past **I**
halb half **I**
Halbjahresferien half-term break **I**
Halbschwester half-sister **I**
die **Hälfte** half, halves *(pl)* (of) **I**
Halle hall **II U2**, 29
Hallo. Hello.; Hi.; Hey! **I**
Tag vor Allerheiligen Halloween **I**
Halt stop **II U3**, 53
halten *to hold; *to keep **I**
  halten von *to think of **I**
Haltestelle station **I**; stop **II U3**, 53
Hamburger burger **I**
Hammer hammer **II U2**, 34
Hand hand **I**
  Klatsch/Klatscht in die **Hände**. Clap your hands. **I**
Handbuch planner **I**
  Handbuch für TTS-Schülerinnen und -Schüler TTS planner **I**
sich **handeln** um *to be about **I**
Handgelenk wrist **II U3**, 62
Händler merchant **II AC2**, 89
Handlung action **I**
Handlungsort location **II U3**, 58
Handschuh glove **I**
Handy phone **I**; mobile **II U5**, 91
hart hard **II U1**, 12
hassen to hate **II U2**, 42
häufig often **I**
  häufig gefragt frequently asked **I**
Haupt- main **I**
Hauptstadt capital **II AC1**, 48
Hauptwort noun **I**
Haus house **I**
  nach Hause home **I**
  zu Hause at home **I**
  zu jmdm. nach **Hause** gehen *to go over to **II U5**, 95
Hausaufgabe(n) homework **I**
Haustier pet **I**
Haustür front door **II U5**, 102
He! Hey! **I**
Heim home **I**
heimlich in secret **II U4**, 81
Ich **heiße** … My name is … **I**
  Wie **heißen** Sie? What's your name? **I**
  Wie **heißt** du? What's your name? **I**
helfen to help **I**
heraus out **I**
herausfinden *to find; *to find out **I**
Herausforderung challenge **II U1**, 16
Herd cooker **I**
herein in **I**
Herr *(Anrede)* Mr **I**
  Herr der Raben raven master **II U3**, 56
um … **herum** around **I**
herumschleichen to sneak around **II U1**, 24
herunter down **II U3**, 62
herunterfallen *to fall off **II U2**, 34
herunterkommen *to come down **I**
herunterladen *(aus dem Internet)* to download **II U5**, 97
herunternehmen *to take off **I**
herunterrollen to roll off **II U3**, 62
Herz heart **II U3**, 62
Herzliche Grüße *(am Briefende)* Love … **I**
heute today **I**
  heute Abend 2nite *(= tonight)* **I**
  heute Nachmittag this afternoon **II U3**, 52
Hi. Hi.; Hey! **I**
hier here **I**
  genau **hier** right here **II U4**, 70
  Hier ist … Here's … **I**
Highlight highlight **II U1**, 9
Hilfe help **I**
  ohne fremde **Hilfe** alone **I**
hilflos helpless **I**
hilfreich useful; helpful **I**
hilfsbereit helpful **I**
hinauf up **II U5**, 94
hinaus out **I**
hinausfließen to flow out **II U3**, 62
hinein inside **I**
hineingehen to enter **II U2**, 40
hineingelangen *to get into **I**
hinfallen *to fall over; *to fall **I**
hinkommen *to get there **I**
Lege/Legt … umgedreht **hin**. Put … face down. **I**

sich **hinsetzen** *to sit down **I**
hinter behind **I**
Hintergrund background **I**
hinterhergehen to follow **II U3**, 54
hinüber over; across **I**
hinübergehen zu *to go over to **II U5**, 95
hinunter down **II U3**, 62
hinunterfallen *to fall off **II U2**, 34
hinuntergehen *to go down **I**
hinunterrollen to roll off **II U3**, 62
Hinweis clue **II U1**, 13
hinzufügen to add **I**
historisch historical **I**
Hobby hobby, hobbies *(pl)* **I**
hoch tall; high **II U1**, 17
hochleben lassen *to give the bumps **I**
Hochzeit wedding **I**
Hockey hockey **II U4**, 69
hoffen to hope **I**
Hoffnung hope **II U4**, 82
hoffnungsvoll hopeful **I**
höflich polite **I**
Sei/Seid **höflich**. Be polite. **I**
Höhepunkt highlight **II U1**, 9
holen *to get **I**
Homepage homepage **I**
Hoppla! Oops! **I**
Hör- audio **I**
horchen auf to listen for **I**
Hören listening **I**
hören *to hear **I**
Ich habe **gehört**, dass … I hear … **I**
Hör-/Sehverstehen viewing **I**
kurze **Hose** shorts *(pl)* **II U4**, 75
Hospital hospital **II U2**, 30
Hotel hotel **II U2**, 33
hübsch beautiful **II U2**, 30
Huch! Oops! **I**
Huhn chicken **I**
Hülle wrapping **I**
Hund dog **I**
den **Hund** ausführen to walk the dog **I**
mit dem **Hund** spazieren gehen to walk the dog **I**
Ich bin **hundemüde**. I'm dog-tired. **I**
hungrig hungry **I**
Husten cough **II U4**, 73
Hut hat **I**
hüten to look after **I**

I

ich I; me **I**
Ich bin aus … I'm from … **I**
Ich bin Engländer/-in. I'm English. **I**
Ich bin … I'm … **I**
Ich heiße … My name is … **I**
Ich mache … nicht gern. I don't like … **I**
Ich mag … nicht. I don't like … **I**
Ich möchte … I'd like to … *(= I would like to)* **I**
Ich weiß (es) nicht! I don't know! **I**
Ich würde gern … I'd like to … *(= I would like to)* **I**
Idee idea **I**
Identität identity **II AC1**, 49
Idiot/-in idiot **II U2**, 41
ihm him **I**
ihn him **I**
ihnen them **I**
ihr you; u *(= you)* **I**
Ihr/-e your **I**; yours **II U2**, 41
ihr/-e her; its **I**
ihr/-e *(Pl.)* their **I**
Ihr wisst, wie man … You know how to … **I**
im in; on **I**
im Innern inside **I**
im Moment at the moment **I**
im Weg sein/stehen *to be in the way **I**
Imbiss snack **I**
Imbissstube snack bar **I**
immer always **I**
für **immer** forever **II U5**, 93
immer noch still **I**
immerhin after all **I**
in in; on; at; to; into; inside **I**
in der Nähe von near **I**
in der Straße in the street **I**
in Not in need **II U1**, 10
in … hinein into **I**
in Ordnung OK; fine **I**
indem as **I**
Inder/-in Indian **I**
indisch Indian **I**
individuell individual **II U4**, 69
Infinitiv infinitive **I**
Information information *(no pl)* **I**
Informationen information *(no pl)* **I**
Inlineskates fahren to skate **I**
Inlineskatefahren inline skating **I**
Inlineskates skates *(pl)* **I**
innen inside **I**
Instruktion instruction **I**
interessant interesting **I**
Interesse interest **II U5**, 90
sich **interessieren** (für) to care (about) **II U5**, 93
sich **interessieren** für *to be interested in **II U2**, 31
interessiert sein an *to be interested in **II U2**, 31
Interkulturelles Across cultures **I**
international international **I**; multi-ethnic **II AC1**, 48
Internet internet **I**
Internetauftritt website **I**
Interview interview **I**
interviewen to interview **I**
irgendein/-e/-er any **I**
irgendwelche any **I**
irgendwo anywhere **II U3**, 54; somewhere **II U3**, 65
sich **irren** *to be wrong **I**
Italien Italy **II U5**, 96

J

ja yes; yeah *(infml)* **I**
jagen to chase **I**
Jahr year **I**
Jahrbuch yearbook **II U1**, 8
Jahrhundert century **II U3**, 62
18-**jährig** 18-year-old **II U3**, 52
11-**Jährige**/-r 11-year-old **II U4**, 70
Januar January **I**
je … desto the … the **II U4**, 68
jedenfalls anyway **II U3**, 62
jede/-r/-s every; each **I**
jeder everybody **II U3**, 54
jeder everyone **I**
jede Menge lots (of) **I**
jedes Mal, wenn whenever **II U5**, 92
jemals ever **II U2**, 33
jemand somebody **I**; someone **II U1**, 13
jemand anderes anyone else **II U2**, 40
jene those **I**
jenes that **I**
jetzt now **I**
jetzt gleich right now **II U5**, 103
Job job **I**
Joghurt yoghurt **I**
Jonglieren juggling **II U2**, 38
jubeln to cheer **II U4**, 72
Jugend- teen **II U5**, 92
Jugendliche/-r teenager **I**
Juli July **I**
jung young **I**
Junge boy **I**
Juni June **I**

K

Kaffee coffee **I**
Kalender planner **I**
kalt cold **II U1**, 18
kalt stellen *to leave it to cool **I**
Kamelrennen camel racing **II U4**, 68
Kamera camera **II U1**, 8
mit der **Kamera** festgehalten caught on camera **II U1**, 8
Kampf fight **II U2**, 41
kämpfen *to fight **II U5**, 102
Kanada Canada **I**
Kaninchen rabbit **I**
Kapitän/-in captain **I**
Kapitel unit **I**
kaputt broken **I**
Karneval carnival **II AC1**, 48
Karotte carrot **I**
Karte card **I**
Kartoffelchip crisp *(BE)* **I**
Käse cheese **I**
Kasten box **I**
Katastrophe disaster **II U5**, 102

Katze cat I
kaufen *to buy; *to get I
Käufer/-in buyer I
Kaufmann merchant II AC2, 89
keine Ahnung no idea II U1, 19
Keine Sorge! Don't worry! I
kein/-e no; not … any I
Keks biscuit I
keltisch Celtic II U1, 16
kennen *to know I
Kerl guy II U1, 9
Kerze candle I
Kerzenlicht candlelight (no pl) II U5, 103
Kfz-Mechaniker/-in mechanic II U1, 13
Kind child, children (pl) I
Kino cinema I
Kirche church I
Kiste box I
Klang sound I
klar clear I
Klasse group; class I
Klasse (in einer englischen Schule) tutor group I
Ausstellung in der Klasse class display I
Klassenarbeit test I
Klassenkamerad/-in classmate I
Klassenlehrer/-in tutor I
Klassenposter class poster I
Klassenzimmer classroom I
klatschen to clap I
Klatsch/Klatscht in die Hände. Clap your hands. I
Kleider clothes (pl) I
Kleidergröße size I
Kleiderschrank wardrobe I
Kleidung clothes (pl) I; outfit II U1, 8
klein small; little I
Klettern climbing II U1, 16
klettern to climb I
Klick click II U5, 103
Klicken click II U5, 103
klingeln *to ring I
klingen to sound I
Klub club I
klug clever II U2, 41
knapp close I
Das war knapp! That was close! I
sich den Knöchel verrenken to twist your ankle II U4, 72
Koch-AG Cooking Club I
Kochen cooking I
kochen to cook II U5, 103
Kokosnuss coconut II U3, 63
Kollektion collection II U1, 10
Köln Cologne I
Kolonie colony II AC2, 89
komfortabel comfortable II U3, 65
Komiker/-in comedian II U1, 10
kommen *to come I
kommen nach *to get to I
kommen zu *to get to I
Komm jetzt! Come on! I
Komm schon! Come on! I
Kommentar comment II U1, 12
kommentieren to comment (on) II U5, 97
kommunizieren to communicate II AC2, 89
Kompromiss compromise II U5, 93
König king I
Königin queen II U2, 30
königlich royal I
königlicher Leibgardist Beefeater II U3, 56
können can I; *to be able to (do sth) II U5, 95
könnte/-n could II U2, 40
kann nicht can't I; cannot II U5, 95
können nicht can't I; cannot II U5, 95
(vielleicht) können may II U5, 95
Kannst du … nennen? Can you name …? I
Kontakt contact II U2, 37
in Kontakt bleiben (mit) to stay in touch (with) II U5, 90
kontrollieren to check I
Konversation conversation I
Konzept draft I
Kopf head I
Kopfhörer headphones (pl) II U5, 102
Kopfschmerzen headache (no pl) II U4, 73
Kopfweh headache (no pl) II U4, 73
kopieren to copy I
Korbball netball I
Koreaner/-in Korean II U4, 76
Koreanisch Korean II U4, 76
koreanisch Korean II U4, 76
menschlicher Körper human body II U3, 62
korrekt correct; right I
Korrigiere/Korrigiert … Correct … I
kosten *to cost I
Es kostet …/Sie kosten … It's …/ They're … I
Wie viel kostet/kosten …? How much is/ are …? I
kostenlos free I
Kostüm costume I; fancy dress II U4, 80
die Kraft der Wörter (Wortschatzübung) Word power I
Krakau Cracow I
Krampf cramp II U4, 74
krank sick II U4, 73
Krankenhaus hospital II U2, 30
kreativ creative I
Kreis circle I
kreischen to scream II U3, 63
kreuzen to cross II AC2, 89
Kronjuwelen crown jewels II U3, 56
Küche kitchen I
Kuchen cake; pie I
Küchenschrank cupboard I
Kühlschrank fridge I
Kultur culture I
Kummerkastentante agony aunt II U5, 92
sich kümmern (um) to care (about) II U5, 93
sich kümmern um to look after I
Kunst art II U2, 29
Kunstunterricht Art I
Kurs course II U1, 16
kurz short I
Kurzantwort short answer I
Kurzform short form I
Kurznachricht text (message) I
Küste shore II U3, 62

L

Lächeln smile I
lächeln to smile I
lachen to laugh I
Laden shop I
Lage location II U3, 58
Lagerfeuer bonfire I
Lamm lamb I
Lämmchen lamb I
Lampe light II U5, 102
Land country, countries (pl); land I
landen to end up II U1, 8; to land II U4, 78
landesweit national I
Landkarte map I
Landwirt/-in farmer II U1, 13
lang long I
… lang for … II U1, 12
langsam slow I
langweilig boring I
Laptop laptop II U5, 97
Lärm noise II U1, 18
lassen *to let I; *to leave II U2, 30
Lass/Lasst uns … Let's … I
Lassi lassi I
Lauf run II U4, 70
Laufen running II U4, 70
laufen *to run; to walk I; *to be on II U5, 102
Läufer/-in runner II U4, 68
Laune mood II U1, 24
laut loud I
läuten *to ring I
Leben life, lives (pl) II U2, 39
leben to live I
lebendig lively II U2, 29
Lebensmittel food I
legen *to put I
Lege/Legt es in … Put it in … I
jmdm. eine Lehre/Lektion erteilen *to teach somebody a lesson II U4, 76
lehren *to teach II U4, 76
Lehrer/-in teacher I; instructor II U1, 18
königlicher Leibgardist Beefeater II U3, 56
leicht easy I
leid tun *to be sorry I
Tut mir leid! Sorry!; I'm sorry! I
leise quiet I
Leiter ladder II U2, 34
Lektion unit I
jmdm. eine Lehre/Lektion erteilen *to teach somebody a lesson II U4, 76
Lernen studies (pl) II U2, 28

lernen *to learn I
viel zu **lernen** a lot to learn I
auswendig **lernen** *to learn … by heart I
Lesen reading I
vor dem **Lesen** pre-reading I
lesen *to read I
Leser/-in reader I
letzte/-r/-s last I
letztlich finally II U2, 31
Leute people *(pl)* I
(Pl.) Leute guy II U1, 9
Licht light II U5, 102
lieb nice I
Lieber … Dear … I
Liebe … *(Anrede in Briefen)* Dear … I
Liebe Grüße *(am Briefende)* Love … I
lieben to love I
Ich **liebe** dich. I love you. I
Ich **liebe** … I love … I
lieber better I
Lieblings- favourite I
Mein/e **Lieblings …** My favourite … I
Was ist dein/-e **Lieblings**…? What's your favourite …? I
Lied song I
liegen *to lie II U2, 40
lila purple I
Limonade lemonade I
Lineal ruler I
Linie line I
Link link II U3, 59
linke/-r/-s left I
links on the left; left I
auf der **linken** Seite on the left I
Liste list I
Loch hole II U2, 33
LOL LOL (= laughing out loud) II U1, 8
Londoner/-in Londoner I
Los ticket I
losgehen *to leave II U4, 72
loslassen *to let go (of) II U4, 80
Lösung solution II U1, 13
Löwe lion II U3, 56
Lücke gap I
lügen to lie II U1, 9
lustig funny; fun I

M

Maat mate I
machen *to do; *to make I
Fotos **machen** *to take photos I
sich Notizen **machen** *to take notes I
Machst du so …? Is this how you (do) …? I
Mädchen girl I
ein **Mädchen** aus Deutschland a girl from Germany I
Magen stomach II U4, 80
Mahlzeit meal II U1, 18
Mai May I
mailen to mail II U5, 97
Mal time II U1, 10
malen to paint I
Malerei painting II U2, 28
Mama mum I
manchmal sometimes I
Manga *(japanischer Comic)* manga II U2, 38
Mango mango I
Mann man, men *(pl)* I
wie der **Mann** aussah what the man looked like II U1, 13
Mannschaftsführer/-in captain I
Mäppchen pencil-case I
Mappe folder I
Marathon marathon II U4, 68
Markt market I
März March I
Maschine machine I
Match match II U4, 68
Material material II U3, 61
Mathe Maths II U2, 32
Mathematik Maths II U2, 32
Matrose sailor I
Mauer wall I
Maus/Mäuse mouse *(sg)*, mice *(pl)* I
Mechaniker/-in mechanic II U1, 13
Medien media II U5, 91
Meer sea I
Meerschweinchen guinea pig I
mehr more I
mehr … als more … than I
Mehrzahl plural I
meiden to stay away from II U5, 97
Meile *(brit. Längenmaß)* mile II U4, 72
mein/-e my I
Mein/e Lieblings… My favourite … I
mein/-er/-e/-es mine II U2, 41
meinen *to mean II U3, 54
Meinung opinion II U5, 92
die meisten (the) most I
der/die/das **meiste** (the) most I
meistens usually I
Meldung report II U1, 9
eine Menge a lot of I
jede **Menge** lots (of) I
Mensch person, people *(pl)* I
Menschen people *(pl)* I
Menschenmenge crowd II U3, 58
menschlicher Körper human body II U3, 62
sich merken to remember I
merkwürdig strange I; weird II U5, 99
Meter metre II U3, 62
mich me I
Milch milk I
Million million II AC1, 48
Ich habe das schon eine **Million** Mal gemacht. I've done this a million times before. II U5, 95
Mini- mini II U4, 70
Minute minute I
mir me I
Mir geht's gut. I'm fine. I
mit with I
mit *(dem Fahrrad)* by *(bike)* I
mitbringen *to bring; *to take I
miteinander together I
Mitglied member II U2, 33
mithalten (mit) *to keep up (with) II U4, 80
mitmachen *to be in II U4, 70
mitnehmen *to take I
Mitschüler/-in classmate I
Mitspieler/-in player II U4, 75
Mittagessen lunch I
Mittagspause lunch break I
Mitte middle I
mitteilen *to tell I
Mittwoch Wednesday I
Mobiltelefon mobile II U5, 91
Mode fashion II U2, 28
Model model I
Modell model I
Moderator/-in presenter I
modern modern II U3, 64
mögen to like; *to be into; to want (to) I
gern **mögen** to love I
nicht **mögen** to hate II U2, 42
Du **magst** … You're into … I
Ich **mag** dich. I love you. I
Ich **mag** … I like … I
Ich **mag** … nicht. I don't like … I
Ich **mag** … total gern. I love … I
Ich **möchte** … I'd like to … *(= I would like to)* I
möglich possible I
möglicherweise probably II U3, 52
Möglichkeit chance II U5, 100
Möhre carrot I
Moment moment II U2, 40
im **Moment** at the moment I
Monat month II U1, 10
Monster monster I
Montag Monday I
montags on Mondays I
Morgen morning I
Guten **Morgen**. Good morning. I
morgen tomorrow I
morgens in the mornings I
motivieren to motivate I
Motto theme I
müde tired I
Müll rubbish I
Mund mouth I
Training für den Mund mouth jogging I
Münze coin I
Museum museum I
Museumsrundgang gallery walk I
Musik music I
Musiker/-in musician II U3, 53
müssen must I; *to have to II U2, 40
(tun) müssen to need (to do) I
nicht **müssen** needn't I
mutig brave I
Mutter mother I
Muttersprache first language II AC2, 89

N

nach unten down II U3, 62
nach to I
nach drinnen inside I
nach Hause home I
nach unten downstairs II U5, 102
nach *(bei Uhrzeitangaben)* past I
nach *(zeitlich)* after I
nach draußen outside; out I
nach oben up II U5, 94; upstairs II U5, 102
Nachbar/-in neighbour *(BE)* I
nachdenken *to think I
Warte/Wartet und denk/denkt nach. Stop and think I
nacherzählen *to retell I
nachjagen to chase I
Nachmittag afternoon I
heute Nachmittag this afternoon II U3, 52
nachmittags *(Uhrzeit)* p.m. I
Nachricht message I
eine Nachricht entgegennehmen *to take a message I
eine Nachricht hinterlassen *to leave a message I
Nachrichten news *(sg)* II U2, 40
nachschauen to look up I
nachschlagen to look up I
nachspüren to trace I
nächste/-r/-s next I
der/die Nächste(n) next I
als Nächstes next I
am nächsten Tag the next day II U1, 11
Nacht night I
die ganze Nacht all night I
Nachtisch pudding I
Nachtwanderung night walk II U1, 18
in der Nähe von near I
nahe near I; close II U3, 56
Name name I
Namenstag name day I
Nase nose II U1, 8
nass wet II U3, 62
national national I
Natur nature II U2, 43
natürlich of course I
Naturwissenschaften Science II U2, 32
neben next to I
(ein Bonbon) nehmen *to have *(a sweet)* I
nehmen *to take I
neidisch sein (auf) *to be jealous (of) I
nein no I
benennen to name I
Kannst du … nennen? Can you name …? I
nennen to name; to call I
jemandem auf die Nerven gehen *to get on people's nerves I
nervös nervous II U1, 12
nett nice I; friendly II U1 14
Netz net II U4, 68
soziales Netzwerk social network II U5, 91
neu new I
Neuigkeiten news *(sg)* II U2, 40
neun nine I
nicht not I
nicht mehr not any more I
nicht mögen to hate II U2, 42
noch nicht not … yet II U4, 72
nicht- non- II U1, 10
nichts nothing; not … anything I
Nichts zu danken. You're welcome. I
nie never I
niedlich cute I
niedrig low II U1, 17
niemals never I
niemand nobody II U2, 41
noch still I; yet II U4, 72
noch ein/-e another I
noch einmal again I
noch mal again I
noch nicht not … yet II U4, 72
Nomen noun I
Nord- north II U3, 53
Norden north II U3, 53
normal normal II U3, 58
normalerweise usually I
in Not in need II U1, 10
Notiz note I
Notizen machen *to make notes I
sich Notizen machen *to take notes I
November November I
Nudeln pasta I
null zero I
null *(bei Telefonnummern und Uhrzeitangaben)* oh I
Nullmeridian Meridian Line I
Nummer number I
nun now I
nun well I
nur only; just I
Nuss nut I
nützlich useful I
nützliche Ausdrücke Useful phrases I

O

O! Oh! I
o.k. OK I
ob if I
oben on top I; upstairs II U5, 102
nach oben up II U5, 94
obendrauf on top I
oberer Teil top I
oberes Ende top I
im Obergeschoss upstairs II U5, 102
Obst fruit I
oder or I
offen open I
öffentlich public II U3, 52
offline offline II U5, 103
öffnen to open I
oft often I
so oft whenever II U5, 92
ohne without I
ohne fremde Hilfe alone I
Öko- Eco II U2, 33
Oktober October I
Oma grandma; granny I
Onkel uncle I
online stellen to post II U5, 90
online online II U1, 21
Opa grandad I
Orange orange I
orange orange I
Ordner folder I
Ordnung order I
in Ordnung fine I
in Ordnung bringen to tidy *(a room)* I
organisieren to organise I
Ort place I; space II U2, 30
Ost- east I
Osten east I
Ostern Easter I
Österreich Austria II U4, 71
Outdoor- outdoor II U1, 16
Outfit outfit II U1, 8

P

Paar pair I
ein paar some; a few; a couple of I
Päckchen packet; parcel I
Packung packet I
Paket packet; parcel I
panisch werden to panic II U2, 36
Papa dad I
Papier paper I
Stück Papier piece of paper I
Paradies paradise II U5, 90
Park park I
Partner/-in partner I
Party party I
zueinander passen *to go together I
passen zu *to go with; to match I
passieren to happen I
Pasta pasta I
Pastete pie I
Pause break II U2, 40
PC PC *(= Personal Computer)* II AC2, 89
Pech haben *to be unlucky I
peinlich embarrassing II U1, 8
Pence *(brit. Währungseinheit)* penny, pence *(pl)* I
Peng! Bang! II U5, 102
Penny *(brit. Währungseinheit)* penny, pence *(pl)* I
perfekt perfect I
Person person, people *(pl)* I
pro Person each I
persönlich personal I; face-to-face II U5, 93
Perspektive point of view II U4, 76
Pferd horse I
pflanzen to plant II U2, 41
Pfund *(brit. Währungseinheit)* pound (£) I
Picknick picnic I

Pick-up pick-up I
Pier pier I
Pille pill II U4, 73
Pilot/-in pilot II U2, 36
pink pink I
Pizza pizza I
Placemat placemat I
Platzdeckchen placemat I
Plan plan I
planen to plan I
Planet planet II U1, 18
Platz place I; space II U2, 30; pitch II U4, 68
Platz! *(Befehl für Hunde)* Sit! I
plaudern to chat I
plötzlich suddenly I
Plural plural I
Polen Poland I
Polizei police II U1, 13
Polizeibeamter police officer II U2, 36
Pommes frites chips *(pl) (BE)* I
Pony pony I
populär popular I
Porträt profile I
positiv positive II U2, 29
Possessivform possessive form I
Post *(Eintrag im Internet)* post I
Poster poster I
praktisch practical II U5, 91
Präposition preposition I
Präsentation presentation I
präsentieren to present I
Praxis surgery I
Praxisräume surgery I
Preis price; prize I; award II U4, 74
preiswert cheap I
pressen to press II U5, 102
pro Person each I
  pro Stück each I
probieren to try I
  Probier mal … Try … I
Problem problem I
Probleme trouble II U1, 19
Profil profile I
Programm programme II U4, 68
Projekt project I
Prospekt brochure I
prüfen to check I
Prüfung test I; exam II U2, 28
Publikum audience II U2, 37
Pudding pudding I
Punkt point II U4, 68
Punktestand score II U4, 68
pünktlich on time II U2, 37
Puzzle puzzle I
Pyjama pyjamas II U1, 12

Q

Qualifikation trial II U4, 70
Qualität quality I
quer durch across I
Quiz quiz I

R

Rabe raven II U3, 56
  Herr der **Raben** raven master II U3, 56
Rad wheel I
Radfahren cycling I
Radiergummi rubber I
Radio radio II U4, 68
Rap rap I
rappen to rap I
Raster grid I
Rat advice II U2, 36
raten to guess I
Ratschlag tip I; advice II U2, 36
Rätsel puzzle; quiz I
Ratte rat I
Raum room I; space II U2, 30
Raumschiff spaceship II U1, 22
Reaktion reaction II U2, 29
realistisch realistic II U3, 61
recht haben *to be right I
rechte/-r/-s right I
rechts on the right; right I
  auf der **rechten** Seite on the right I
Rechtschreibung spelling I
Recycling recycling II U2, 40
reden to talk I
  reden mit to talk to I
Redewendung phrase I
Redner/-in speaker I
Regel rule I
  Was ist die **Regel** für …? What's the rule for …? I
regelmäßig regular I
Region region II AC2, 89
regnen to rain II U5, 102
Reihenfolge order I
Reim rhyme I
rein in I
reinigen to clean I
Reise trip II U1, 9; travel II U1, 20
Reisebericht travel report II U1, 20
Reisebus coach II U1, 13
Reiseführer guide II U3, 56
(das) Reisen travel II U1, 20
reisen to travel II U3, 52
Religion *(Schulfach)* RE *(= Religious Education)* II U2, 32
religiös religious I
Rennen race II U4, 68; running; run II U4, 70
rennen *to run I
reparieren to fix II U5, 95
Reporter/-in reporter II U4, 75
der Rest the rest I
Restaurant restaurant I
Resultat result II U5, 97
retten to save I
Rettung rescue II U4, 77
Rettungsboot lifeboat I
Rettungsring lifebuoy I
Rezept *(für Arzneimittel)* prescription II U4, 73
Rhythmus rhythm I
richtig correct; right I; real II U1, 10
Richtung direction I
  in **Richtung** towards II U3, 62
riesengroß huge II AC1, 48
riesig huge; large II AC1, 48
Ring circle I
Rock 'n' Roll rock 'n' roll II AC2, 89
Rohr pipe II U2, 34
Rohrleitung pipe II U2, 34
Rolle role I
  Rollen tauschen to swap roles I
Rollenspiel role play I
Rollschuhe skates *(pl)* I
Rollstuhl wheelchair II U3, 53
Rolltreppe escalator I
Römer/-in Roman II AC1, 48
römisch Roman II AC1, 48
rosa pink I
rot red I
Route route II U1, 16
Rücken an Rücken back to back I
Rückenschmerzen backache II U4, 73
Rückenweh backache II U4, 73
Rückmeldung feedback II U2, 29
rufen to shout; to call I; to cry II U5, 102
Rugby rugby II U4, 68
ruhig quiet I
Rühr- sponge I
ruinieren to ruin II U4, 81
Rumäne/Rumänin Romanian II AC2, 88
Rumänisch Romanian II AC2, 88
rumänisch Romanian II AC2, 88
Runde round II U1, 8
Rundgang tour II U3, 56
Rutschbahn slide I

S

Saal hall II U2, 29
Sache thing I
Saft juice I
sagen *to say; *to tell I
Sahne cream I
Salat salad I
Salbe ointment II U4, 73
sammeln to collect I
  Geld **sammeln** to raise money II U1, 10
Sammlung collection II U1, 10
Samstag Saturday I
Sandwich sandwich I
Sänger/-in singer II U1, 15
Satz phrase; sentence I
Satzstellung word order I
säubern to clean I
Säugling baby I
Saxofon saxophone; sax I
Schach chess II U2, 28
Schachtel box I
Schade! Too bad! I
Schaf sheep, sheep *(pl)* II U1, 18

schaffen to create I
Wir haben es **geschafft**! We did it! II U4, 81
Schälchen bowl I
Schale bowl I
Schatz treasure II U3, 56
Schau show II U4, 75
schauen to look I
Schau/Schaut mal! Look! I
Schauplatz scene II U4, 77
Schauspieler actor II U2, 36
in Scheiben schneiden to slice I
scheinen *to shine II U2, 33
schenken *to give I
scherzen to joke II U5, 102
schicken *to send I
schieben to push II U2, 41
Schiedsrichter/-in official II U4, 81
schiefgehen *to go wrong I
schießen to kick II U4, 68
Schiff ship I
Schiffsjunge cabin boy I
Schiffsoffizier mate I
Schild sign II U1, 18
Schinkenspeck bacon I
Schlafanzug pyjamas II U1, 12
schlafen *to sleep I; *to be asleep II U1, 19
Schlafzimmer bedroom I
schlagen *to hit; to whip I; *to beat II U3, 54
Schläger racquet II U4, 68
Schlamm mud II U3, 62
schlammig muddy II U3, 62
Schlange queue I
schlau clever II U2, 41
der/die/das schlechteste the worst II U1, 16
sich **schlecht** fühlen *to feel sick II U4, 73
schlecht bad I
schließen to close I
Schließfach locker I
schließlich at last; after all I; in the end II U1, 10; finally II U2, 31
der/die/das schlimmste the worst II U1, 16
schlimm *(ugs.)* bad I
Schlittschuh laufen to skate I
Schlittschuhbahn ice rink I
Schlittschuhe skates *(pl)* I
Schloss castle II U3, 56
Schluchtenklettern gorge scrambling II U1, 16
Schluss end I
zum **Schluss** in the end II U1, 10; finally II U2, 31
Schluss *(einer Geschichte)* ending I
Schlüssel key II U3, 63
Schlüsselbegriff key word I
Schmerz pain II U4, 72
Schmuck jewellery; decorations *(pl)* I
schmücken to decorate I
schmutzig dirty II U2, 40
Schnäppchen bargain I
schnappen to grab II U3, 62
schnarchen to snore I
schneiden *to cut (off) II U2, 30
in Scheiben **schneiden** to slice I
schnell fast; quick I
schnell quickly II U2, 40
Schock shock II U4, 79
Schokolade chocolate I
schön nice; fine I; beautiful II U2, 30
schon already I; yet II U4, 72
schon einmal before II U4, 71
Schrank cupboard I
schrecklich awful I
Schreiben writing I
schreiben *to write I
schreien to shout I; to scream II U3, 63; to cry II U5, 102
Schritt step I
Schritt halten (mit) *to keep up (with) II U4, 80
Schritt-für-**Schritt**- step-by-step II U5, 95
schubsen to push II U2, 41
schüchtern shy II U1, 9
Schuh shoe I
Schule school I
Schüler/-in student I
Schulfach subject II U2, 28
Schuljahr year I
Schulklasse class I
Schulstunde lesson I
Schultasche schoolbag I
Schulter shoulder II U4, 73
Schüssel bowl I
schütten to pour I
Schwanz tail I
schwarz black I
schwarz werden *to go black II U5, 102
schwarzes Brett noticeboard II U1, 10
Schweif tail I
Schwein pig I
schwer hard II U1, 12
Schwester sister I
schwierig hard II U1, 12; difficult II U4, 77
Schwierigkeit problem I
in **Schwierigkeiten** bringen *to make trouble I
Schwierigkeiten trouble II U1, 19
Schwimmen swimming I
Schwimmen gehen *to go swimming I
schwimmen *to swim I
Science-Fiction *(Zukunftsdichtung)* science fiction II U1, 22
sechs six I
Vier plus **sechs** ist zehn. Four and six is ten. I
Second-Hand-Laden charity shop I
See lake I
See zum Rudern boating lake I
Seemann sailor I
die Segel einholen to reef the sails I
sehbehindert partially sighted II U2, 32
sehen *to see; to look I
Sehenswürdigkeit sight II AC1, 48; attraction II U3, 59
sehr very; very much I
Hör-/Sehverstehen viewing I
sein *to be I
Sei/Seid höflich. Be polite. I
sein/-e his; its I
Seite page I; side II U2, 40
auf der anderen **Seite** von across; opposite I
selber yourself I; himself II U1, 8; myself II U5, 93
selbst even I
du/dir/dich/Sie/sich (selbst) yourself I
er/sich (selbst) himself II U1, 8
ich/mir/mich (selbst) myself II U5, 93
selbstbewusst confident II U1, 16
Selbsteinschätzung self-evaluation I
selbstkritisch self-critical II U5, 92
selbstsicher confident II U1, 16
selbstverständlich of course I
Selfie selfie II U4, 81
seltsam strange I; weird II U5, 99
senden *to send I
Sender station II U4, 77
Sendung programme II U4, 68
separat separate II U1, 16
September September I
Sessel chair I
setzen *to put I
sich **setzen** *to sit down I
Shorts shorts *(pl)* II U4, 75
Show show II U4, 75
Comedy **Show** comedy show II U1, 10
sich each other I
sicher sure I; safe II U3, 56
Sicht view II U2, 30
Sie you; u *(= you)* I
Sie sind … You're … I
sie her; she I
sie *(Pl.)* them I
sie *(Pl.)* they I
sieben seven I
siegen *to win I
Sieger/-in winner I
Sightseeing- sightseeing II U3, 58
Signalwort signal word I
Silber silver II U3, 62
singen *to sing I
Ich **singe** und tanze gern. I like singing and dancing. I
Sinn meaning II U1, 21
Situation situation I
Sitz! *(Befehl für Hunde)* Sit! I
sich gegenüber **sitzen** *to sit face to face I
sitzen *to sit I
Skateboard skateboard II U1, 11
Skateboardfahren skateboarding I
Slogan slogan II U2, 35
Smartphone smartphone II U4, 79
SMS text (message) I
eine **SMS** schicken to text II U5, 90
Snack snack I

so like this; so; like that I; that's how II U1, 10
so oft whenever II U5, 92
so … wie as … as I
sobald as soon as II U5, 92
Sofa sofa I
sofort right away I; right now II U5, 103
sogar even I
solch such II U2, 36
solche/-r/-s such II U2, 36
sollte(n) nicht shouldn't II U4, 73
sollte should II U4, 74
sollten should II U4, 74
solltest should II U4, 74
solltet should II U4, 74
Sommer summer II AC2, 88
Sommerferienlager summer camp II AC2, 88
Sonderangebot special offer I
sonderbar weird II U5, 99
Song song I
Sonne sun II U2, 33
Sonntag Sunday I
Sonst noch etwas? Anything else? I
Keine Sorge! Don't worry! I
sich Sorgen machen to worry II U5, 93
sorgfältig careful II U3, 56
Sorte kind I
Souvenir souvenir II U3, 54
sowieso anyway II U3, 62
soziales Netzwerk social network II U5, 91
Sozialwissenschaften Humanities *(pl)* II U2, 32
Spalt gap I
Spanien Spain II U5, 99
spannend exciting I
Spaß fun I
Spaß haben *to have fun I
Es macht Spaß. It's fun. I
spät late I
zu spät late I
zu spät kommen *to be late I
Wie spät ist es? What's the time? I
zu spät dran sein *to be late I
kleiner Spaten trowel II U3, 62
später later I
mit dem Hund spazieren gehen to walk the dog I
spazieren gehen *to go for a walk II U1, 18
Speck bacon I
speziell special I
Spiel game I; match II U4, 68
spielen to play I
eine Theaterszene spielen acting a scene I
einen Streich spielen to play a trick (on) I
spielen *(Theater)* to act I
Spieler/-in player II U4, 75
Spielfeld field II U1, 18; court; pitch II U4, 68
Spielkarte card I
Spielstand score II U4, 68
Spielzeug toy I
Spind locker I
Spitze top I
Sport sport I
… ist ein toller Sport. … is a great sport. I
Sportart sport I
Sportunterricht PE *(= Physical Education)* II U2, 32
Sprache language I
Sprachmittlung mediation I
Sprechblase speech bubble I
Sprechen speaking; talking I
sprechen *to say; to talk; *to speak I
sprechen über to talk about I
Sprecher/-in speaker I
Sprechgesang chant II U4, 72
springen to jump I
Spur clue II U1, 13
Staatsoberhaupt head of state II AC2, 89
Stadion stadium II U4, 68
Stadt city; town I
Stadtplan map I
Stadtteil part I
Stammbaum family tree I
ständig always I
Standort location II U3, 58
Standpunkt point of view II U4, 76
Star star I
hier: stark hard II U3, 56
stark strong II U2, 42
starren to stare I
starten to start I
Station station I
stattfinden *to take place I
Steak steak I
stehen *to stand I
stehen auf *to be into I
Du stehst auf … You're into … I
stehlen *to steal II U2, 34
steigen to climb I
Stelle place I
stellen *to put I
online stellen to post II U5, 90
Stelle/Stellt es in … Put it in … I
Stern star I
Steuer wheel I
Steuerrad wheel I
Stichwort key word I
Stiefmutter stepmum I
still quiet; still I
Stimme voice I
Stimmung mood II U1, 24
stolz (auf) proud (of) II U1, 9
stoppen to stop I
stören *to get in the way II U4, 80
Story story, stories *(pl)* I
stoßen to push II U2, 41
Strand beach II U5, 99
Straße road II U1, 18
auf der Straße in the street I
in der Straße in the street I
Straße *(in der Stadt)* street I
Strecke route II U1, 16
Streich trick I
einen Streich spielen to play a trick (on) I
Streit fight II U2, 41
(sich) streiten *to fight II U5, 102
Stromausfall power cut II U5, 103
Stück piece I
pro Stück each I
Stück Papier piece of paper I
Student/-in student I
Studie survey I
Studium studies *(pl)* II U2, 28
Stufe step I
Stuhl chair I
Stunde hour II U3, 53
Stundenplan timetable I
Sturm storm I
Such- search II U1, 21
Suche search II U1, 21
suchen nach to look for I
Süd- south II U3, 53
Südafrika South Africa II AC2, 89
Süden south II U3, 53
Südkoreaner/-in South Korean II AC2, 88
Südkoreanisch South Korean II AC2, 88
südkoreanisch South Korean II AC2, 88
summen to hum II U2, 33
super great; cool I
Es ist super zum/für … It's great for … I
Supermacht superpower II AC2, 89
Supermarkt supermarket I
süß cute; sweet I
Süßigkeiten sweets *(pl)* I
Szene scene I

T

Tabelle grid I
Tablet tablet II U5, 95
Tablette pill II U4, 73
Taekwondo taekwondo II U2, 38
Tag day I
am nächsten Tag the next day II U1, 11
den ganzen Tag all day II U1, 14
ein Tag in … a day out in … II U3, 58
eines Tages one day II U2, 36
Takelage rigging I
Talent talent I
Talentwettbewerb talent show I
Talisman lucky charm I
Tante aunt I
tanzen to dance I
Ich singe und tanze gern. I like singing and dancing. I
Tänzer/-in dancer II U2, 36
tapfer brave I
Tasche bag I
Taschengeld pocket money I
Taschenlampe torch II U1, 18
Tatsache fact II U2, 37
Rollen tauschen to swap roles I
tausende (von) thousands of I
Taxi taxi II U1, 13

Team team II U1, 8
Technik Technology II U2, 32
Technologie technology II AC2, 89
Tee tea I
Teenager teenager I
Teich pond II U2, 33
Teil part I
teilen to share II U2, 40
teilnehmen (an) *to take part (in) II U5, 90
Telefon phone; telephone I
Telefonanruf phone call I
Tennis tennis I
Teppich carpet II U3, 65
Test test I
teuer expensive I
Text text I
Theater theatre I; drama II U2, 28
eine Theaterszene spielen acting a scene I
Thema theme I; topic II U2, 37
Ticket ticket I
Tier animal I
Tierarzt/Tierärztin vet I
Tierpark zoo II U3, 53
Tierwelt *(in freier Wildbahn)* wildlife II U2, 33
Tipp tip I
Tisch table I
Titel heading I
tja well I
Toast toast I
Toilette toilet I
toll great I; amazing II U1, 18
... ist ein **toller** Sport. ... is a great sport. I
Tomate tomato, tomatoes *(pl)* I
Tombola raffle I
Ton sound I
Tonmodell model I
Tonpfeife clay pipe II U3, 63
Tonstudio recording studio I
Tor goal I
Torte cake I
Tortenguss jelly I
tot dead II U3, 62
Tour tour II U3, 56
Tourist/-in tourist I
Touristeninformation tourist information centre I
Tradition tradition I
tragen *(Kleidung)* *to wear I
Trainer/-in coach I
trainieren to practise I; to train II U4, 72
Training training II U4, 80
Training für den Mund mouth jogging I
Er **traute** seinen Augen nicht. He couldn't believe his eyes. II U2, 40
Traum dream II U1, 15
Traum- fantasy I
traurig sad I
treffen *to meet; *to hit I
sich **treffen** *to meet I
treten to kick II U4, 68
Trick trick I
Trifle *(englischer Nachtisch)* trifle I
trinken *to drink I
Trip trip II U1, 9
trotzdem anyway II U3, 62
Tschüss! Bye! II U4, 72
T-Shirt T-shirt I
tun *to do; *to make I
tun als ob to act like II U5, 92
Tunnel tunnel I
Tür door I
Turnier competition II U2, 29
Turteltauben lovebirds *(pl)* II U1, 9
Tüte bag I
Typ guy II U1, 9
typisch typical I

U

U-Bahn underground II AC1, 48
die Londoner **U-Bahn** the Tube II AC1, 48
Übelkeit verspüren *to feel sick II U4, 73
Üben practising I
üben to practise I
über about; over; across I
überall everywhere I
überall (in) all over I
überall (egal, wo) anywhere II U3, 54
überhaupt at all I
Übernachtung sleepover I
überprüfen to check I
überqueren to cross II AC2, 89
überraschen to surprise II U4, 81
überraschend surprising II U1, 24
überrascht sein *to be surprised II U3, 63
Überraschung surprise I
überreagieren to overreact II U5, 92
überreden to persuade II U3, 52
Überschrift heading I
übersetzen to translate I
Übersetze/Übersetzt nicht ... Don't translate ... I
Übersetzung translation I
übrig left I
Übung exercise I
Übungsheft exercise book I
Ufer bank; shore II U3, 62
UFO UFO II U4, 78
Uhr clock I
Um wie viel **Uhr**? What time? I
Wie viel **Uhr** ist es? What's the time? I
Uhr *(Zeitangabe bei vollen Stunden)* o'clock I
um *(bei Uhrzeitangaben)* at I
um halb acht at 7:30 I
um ... herum around I; round II U5, 103
Um wie viel Uhr? What time? I
umarmen to hug I
(sich) umdrehen to turn round II U2, 41
Umfrage survey I
Lege/Legt ... umgedreht hin. Put ... face down. I
umgehen mit *to deal (with) II U3, 54
umher around I
umkehren to turn back II U2, 41
umkippen *to fall over I
sich umschauen to explore I
umsteigen (in) to change (onto) II U3, 53
und and I
unfair unfair II U4, 72
Unfall accident II U4, 69
unfreundlich unfriendly II U1, 24
ungefähr about I
ungefährlich safe II U3, 56
Ungeheuer monster I
unglaublich amazing II U1, 18
Unglück disaster II U5, 102
unheimlich scary II U1, 24
unhöflich rude I
Uniform uniform I
unrecht haben *to be wrong I
unregelmäßig irregular I
uns us I
unser/-e our I
unten downstairs II U5, 102
nach **unten** down II U3, 62
nach **unten** gehen *to go down I
unten below I
unter under I
im Untergeschoss downstairs II U5, 102
unterhalb below I
Unterhaltung conversation I
unternehmen wegen *to do about II U5, 100
Unterricht lesson I; class II U2, 40
unterrichten *to teach II U4, 76
Unterrichtsstunde lesson I
Unterschied difference I
unterschiedlich different I
unterwegs out and about II U3, 58
unverschämt rude I
unwohl sick II U4, 73
Urlaub holiday I
Seid ihr im **Urlaub**? Are you on holiday? I
Sind Sie im **Urlaub**? Are you on holiday? I
ursprünglich originally II AC1, 48

V

Vanillepudding custard I
Vanillesoße custard I
Vater father I
Veranstaltung event I
verärgert angry I
Verb verb I
verbessern to improve I
sich **verbessern** to improve I
verbinden *to put through I; to join II U2, 33; to link II U5, 104
Verbindung link II U3, 59
verbringen *(Zeit)* *to spend II U5, 92
verdienen to earn I; to deserve II U4, 76
Geld **verdienen** *to make money I
Verein club I
verfolgen to trace I
Vergangenheit past II U1, 9

vergeben *to forgive **II U4**, 81
vergessen *to forget **I**
vergleichen (mit) to compare (with/to) **I**
verhaften to arrest **II U1**, 13
Verkauf sale **II U1**, 12
verkaufen *to sell **I**
Verkäufer/-in assistant **II U4**, 78
Verkäufer/-in *(auf einem Flohmarkt)* seller **I**
öffentliche Verkehrsmittel public transport *(no pl)* **II U3**, 52
Verkleidung fancy dress **II U4**, 80
verlassen *to leave **II U2**, 30
verlegen embarrassed **II U1**, 9
verletzen *to hurt **II U4**, 72
verletzt hurt **II U1**, 24
Verletzung injury **II U4**, 76
verlieren *to lose **II U4**, 68
vermuten to guess **I**
verneinte Form negative form **I**
Vernissage gallery walk **I**
Verpackung wrapping **I**
verpassen to miss **II U5**, 99
sich den Knöchel verrenken to twist your ankle **II U4**, 72
verrückt crazy **I**; mad **II U5**, 97
verrückt werden *to go crazy **II U5**, 95
Versammlung assembly **II U2**, 29
versäumen to miss **II U5**, 99
verschieden different **I**; separate **II U1**, 16
Verschmutzung pollution **II U3**, 62
verschwenden to waste **II U5**, 95
verschwunden missing **II U1**, 13
verschwunden sein *to be gone **II U4**, 81
sich versichern *to make sure **I**
sich verständigen to communicate **II AC2**, 89
Verständnis understanding **II U5**, 93
verstehen *to understand **I**
versuchen to try **I**
Versuch es mal mit ... Try ... **I**
verursachen to cause **II U4**, 82
Vervollständige/Vervollständigt ... Complete ... **I**
verwenden to use **I**
verzeihen *to forgive **II U4**, 81
verzieren to decorate **I**
Video video **II U5**, 91
Videochat video chat **II U3**, 50
viel much **I**
viel/-e lots (of); a lot of **I**
viel a lot **I**
viel zu lernen a lot to learn **I**
viele many **I**
vielleicht maybe **I**
Vielvölker- multi-ethnic **II AC1**, 48
vier four **I**
Vier plus sechs ist zehn. Four and six is ten. **I**
Viertel nach/vor quarter past/to **I**
violett purple **I**
Vogel bird **II U2**, 33
Vogelbeobachtung birdwatching **II U2**, 28
Vokabular vocabulary **I**
voll (von) full (of) **I**
Volleyball volleyball **I**
völlig absolutely **II U2**, 42
vollkommen perfect **I**
von from; about; of **I**
von ... bis from ... to **I**
vor in front of **I**
vor dem Lesen pre-reading **I**
vor *(bei Uhrzeitangaben)* to **I**
vor *(zeitlich)* before **I**; ago **II U1**, 10
vorbei over **II U4**, 79
vorbei (an) past **I**
vorbereiten to prepare **I**
sich vordrängeln to jump the queue **I**
vorher before **II U4**, 71
Vormittag morning **I**
vormittags in the mornings **I**
vormittags *(Uhrzeit)* a.m. **I**
Vorschlag suggestion **I**
Vorsicht! Be careful! **I**
vorsichtig careful **II U3**, 56
vorstellen to present **I**
sich (etwas) **vorstellen** to imagine **I**
Stelle/Stellt ... **vor**. Introduce ... **I**
Vorstellung introduction **II U2**, 29
vortäuschen to fake **II U4**, 76
Vortrag presentation **I**
vorüber over **II U4**, 79
vorüber (an) past **I**

W

Wache guard **II AC1**, 49
Wachs wax **II U3**, 51
Wachsfigur wax figure **II U3**, 51
Wächter/-in guard **II AC1**, 49
wackelig wobbly **II U3**, 62
Wackelpudding jelly **I**
Wahl choice **II U3**, 58
wählen to vote **I**; *to choose **II U2**, 30
während *(+ Nomen)* during *+ noun* **II U1**, 9
während while; as **I**
wahrnehmen to notice **II U2**, 40
wahrscheinlich probably **II U3**, 52
Wald forest **II U1**, 16
Waliser/-in Welsh **II U1**, 16
Walisisch Welsh **II U1**, 16
walisisch Welsh **II U1**, 16
Wand wall **I**
Wandern walking **II U1**, 16
wann when **I**
wann immer whenever **II U5**, 92
warten (auf) to wait (for) **I**
Warte/Wartet und denk/denkt nach. Stop and think **I**
Warte ab! Wait and see! **I**
Warteschlange queue **I**
warum why **I**
was what **I**
was für ein what **I**
Was fehlt? What is missing? **I**
Was ist das? What's that? **I**
Was ist dein/-e Lieblings...? What's your favourite ...? **I**
Was ist die Regel für ...? What's the rule for ...? **I**
Was ist mit ...? What about ...? **I**
was man ... what to ... **I**
was noch what else **I**
was sonst what else **I**
Was um alles in der Welt ...? What on earth ...? **II U5**, 95
... **was** ich tun soll. ... what to do. **II U5**, 92
waschen to wash **I**
sich **waschen** to wash **I**
Waschmaschine washing machine **II U5**, 95
Wasser water **I**
Wasserrutsche water slide **I**
Wau! Woof! **I**
Webseite site **II U5**, 92
Website website **I**
wechseln to change **II U5**, 90
Wechselt euch ab. Take turns. **I**
Wecker alarm clock **II U2**, 43
Weg way **I**
im **Weg** sein/stehen *to be in the way **I**
im **Weg** stehen *to get in the way **II U4**, 80
weg away **I**
weg sein *to be gone **II U4**, 81
Es ist **weg**. It's gone. **II U3**, 62
wegen because of **II U4**, 81; for **II U5**, 91
wegnehmen *to take **I**
wegrennen *to run away **I**
wegwerfen *to throw away **I**
weh tun *to hurt **II U4**, 72
Weide field **II U1**, 18
Weihnachten Christmas **I**
weil because **I**
eine Weile a while **II U3**, 54
Wein wine **I**
auf andere Weise in other ways **II U5**, 97
weiß white **I**
weit far **II U3**, 55
weitere more; other **I**
weiterführen *to go on **I**
weitergeben to pass (on) **I**
weitergehen *to go on **I**
weitermachen *to go on **I**
welche/-r/-s what; which **I**
Welche Farbe hat ...? What colour is ...? **I**
Welche ... sind es? What are ...? **I**
Welle wave **I**
Welt world **I**
Was um alles in der **Welt** ...? What on earth ...? **II U5**, 95
wem who **I**
wen who **I**
Für **wen** ...? Who ... for? **I**
wenden to turn round **II U2**, 41
Wendung expression **II AC2**, 89
ein wenig a little **I**; a bit **II U1**, 18
wenige a few **I**; few **II U1**, 18

wenn when; if I
wer who I
Wer ist dabei? Who's in? II U4, 70
Wer ist es? Who is it? I
Wer macht mit? Who's in? II U4, 70
Werbespruch slogan II U2, 35
werden *to become II U3, 56
werfen (nach) *to throw (at) I
wert sein *to be worth I
West- west I
Westen west I
westeuropäische Zeit Greenwich Mean Time (= GMT) I
Wettbewerb contest I; competition II U2, 29
ich wette I bet II U3, 54
Wetter weather I
Wettkampf contest I
Wettlauf race II U4, 68
wichtig important I
wichtig nehmen to care (about) II U5, 93
wie like I
wie as II AC2, 88
wie how I
Wie viele …? How many …? I
Wie alt bist du? How old are you? I
Wie alt sind Sie? How old are you? I
wie das ist what it's like II U4, 74
wie der Mann aussah what the man looked like II U1, 13
Wie geht es dir? How are you? I
Wie geht es euch? How are you? I
Wie geht es Ihnen? How are you? I
Wie heißen Sie? What's your name? I
Wie heißt du? What's your name? I
Wie man … How to … I
Wie spät ist es? What's the time? I
Wie viel (kostet/kosten) …? How much is/are …? I
Wie viel Uhr ist es? What's the time? I
Wie wär's mit …? What about …? I
wieder again I
Wiederaufbereitung recycling II U2, 40
Wiederaufnehmen pick-up I
auf Wiedersehen goodbye I
Wiese field II U1, 18
Willkommen! Welcome! II U1, 18
willkommen heißen to welcome II U2, 35
wir we I
Wir sind aus … We're from … I
wirklich real II U1, 10
wirklich really I
wissen *to know I
Du weißt, wie man … You know how to … I
Ich weiß (es) nicht! I don't know! I
Ihr wisst, wie man … You know how to … I
Witz joke I
witzig funny; fun I
wo where I
Woche week I
Wochenende weekend I
am Wochenende at the weekend I
Wochentag weekday II U5, 100
Woher …? Where … from? I
wohin where I
… wohin ich gehen kann. … where to go. II U3, 54
Wohlfahrt charity I
wohltätige Zwecke charity I
Wohltätigkeitsverein charity I
wohnen to live I
wohnen bei to stay with II U3, 52
Wohnung flat I
Wohnzimmer living room I
wollen to want (to) I
Workshop workshop I
Wort word I
die Kraft der Wörter *(Wortschatzübung)* Word power I
Wörterbuch dictionary I
Wörternetz *(eine Art Schaubild)* mind map I
Wortschatz vocabulary I
Wortschlange word snake I
Wortstellung word order I
Worum geht es in/im …? What is … about? I
Wow! Wow! I
wunderbar beautiful II U2, 30; wonderful II U2, 40
Wunsch wish I
sich etwas wünschen *to make a wish I
Ich würde gern … I'd like to … *(= I would like to)* I
würde/-st/-n/-t gern would like I
würde/-st/-n/-t sehr gern would love I
Würfle/Würfelt mit zwei Würfeln. Roll two dice. I
Wurm worm I
wusch whoosh I
wütend angry I

Z

z.B. *(= zum Beispiel)* e.g. *(= for example)* I
Zahl number I
zählen (auf) to count (on) I
auf Zehenspitzen gehen to tiptoe II U1, 19
zehn ten I
Vier plus sechs ist zehn. Four and six is ten. I
zehnmal ten times I
Zeichen sign II U1, 18
zeichnen *to draw I
Zeichnung drawing I
zeigen to show I
Zeige/Zeigt auf … Point to … I
Zeige/Zeigt darauf. Point. I
Zeile line I
Zeit time I
(Zeit) brauchen *to take II U5, 95
zur selben Zeit at the same time I
die ganze Zeit all the time II U3, 62
Es ist Zeit aufzustehen! Time to get up! I
Zeitschrift magazine I
Zeitstrahl time line I
Zelten camping II U5, 99
zentral central II U3, 62
Zentral- central II U3, 62
hier: Zentrum heart II U3, 62
Zentrum centre I
zerbrechen *to break I
zerstören to ruin II U4, 81
Zeug stuff I
Zeuge/Zeugin witness II U4, 77
ziehen to pull I
Ziel goal I
Ziellinie finish line II U4, 81
Zimmer room I
Zimmergenosse/Zimmergenossin room-mate I
Zitrone lemon II U1, 24
Zoo zoo II U3, 53
zornig angry I
zu too I
Zu dumm! Too bad! I
zu to I
zu Hause at home I
zubereiten to prepare I
zuerst first I; at first II U3, 63
Zug train I
Zuhause home I
zuhören to listen (to) I
Hör/Hört noch einmal zu. Listen again. I
Zuhörer/-in listener II U4, 77
zujubeln to cheer II U4, 72
zum Beispiel for example II AC2, 89
zumachen to close I
zunächst at first II U3, 63
zuordnen to match I
zupassen to pass II U4, 68
zurück back I
zurückgehen to turn back II U2, 41
hier: zurückschrecken to jump back II U3, 57
zurückspringen to jump back II U3, 57
zusammen together I
in Zusammenhang stehen *to be connected II U2, 37
zusammenhängen *to be connected II U2, 37
zusätzlich extra I; additional II U2, 28
zuschauen to watch I
zuspielen to pass II U4, 68
zuvor before II U4, 71
zwei two I
zweite/-r/-s second I
zwischen between I
zwölf twelve I;

In the classroom

Asking for help and information

Can you help me, please?	Kannst du / Können Sie mir bitte helfen?
How do you do this exercise?	Wie macht man diese Übung?
How do you spell … , please?	Wie schreibt man … , bitte?
Is this right? I'm not sure.	Ist das richtig? Ich bin mir nicht sicher.
Is it OK to …?	Ist es in Ordnung, wenn ich / wir …?
Is it true or false?	Ist das richtig oder falsch?
Sorry, I don't know. Ask …	Tut mir leid, das weiß ich nicht. Frag …
Sorry. Can you say that again, please?	Wie bitte? Können Sie das bitte wiederholen?
What does that mean?	Was bedeutet das?
What's for homework?	Was haben wir als Hausaufgabe auf?
What's that in English / German?	Was heißt das auf Englisch / Deutsch?

Vocabulary for instructions and activities

Act (out) one of the scenes. / Act (out) the dialogues.	Spiele eine der Szenen. / Spiele die Dialoge.
Add more words / ideas.	Füge weitere Wörter / Ideen hinzu.
Ask your partner questions.	Stelle deinem Partner / deiner Partnerin Fragen.
Answer your partner's questions.	Beantworte die Fragen deines Partners / deiner Partnerin.
Check your partner's text.	Überprüfe den Text deines Partners / deiner Partnerin.
Collect ideas.	Sammle Ideen.
Compare English and German.	Vergleiche das Englische und Deutsche.
Complete the answers.	Vervollständige die Antworten.
Copy the grid / the mind map.	Schreibe die Tabelle / das Wörternetz ab.
Correct the wrong sentences.	Korrigiere die falschen Sätze.

Describe your room.	Beschreibe dein Zimmer.
Decide who writes which part.	Entscheidet, wer welchen Teil schreibt.
Discuss different ideas.	Diskutiert verschiedene Ideen.
Draw a picture.	Zeichne ein Bild.
Exchange your flyers / questions.	Tauscht eure Flyer / Fragen untereinander aus.
Explain your answer. / Explain why.	Erkläre deine Antwort. / Erkläre warum.
Fill in your grid / the form.	Fülle deine Tabelle / das Formular aus.
Find the rule / the right word order.	Finde die Regel / die richtige Wortstellung.
Finish your brochure.	Stelle deine Broschüre fertig.
Form expert groups.	Bildet Expertengruppen.
Get organised.	Organisiert euch.
Go back to your home group.	Gehe zurück zu deiner ersten Gruppe.
Guess the new words.	Errate die neuen Wörter.
Imagine you're one of the people in the story.	Stelle dir vor, du bist eine der Personen in der Geschichte.
Improve your text / part of the report.	Verbessere deinen Text / Teil des Berichts.
Learn your text by heart.	Lerne deinen Text auswendig.
Listen to the sentences / the dialogue.	Höre dir die Sätze / den Dialog an.
Look at the picture / the examples.	Schau dir das Bild / die Beispiele an.
Look up the words.	Schlage die Wörter nach.
Make a poster / a grid / a mind map.	Fertige ein Poster / eine Tabelle / ein Wörternetz an.
Match the sentence parts.	Ordne die Satzteile einander zu.
Name more sports.	Nenne mehr Sportarten.
Note down what is missing.	Notiere, was fehlt.
Peer-edit each other's work.	Kontrolliert eure Arbeiten gegenseitig.
Plan the scenes.	Plane die Szenen.
Record your final report / dialogue.	Nehmt euren fertigen Bericht / Dialog auf.
Scan the text for details.	Suche den Text nach Details ab.
Share the information with your partner.	Teile die Informationen mit deinem Partner / deiner Partnerin.
Skim the text for the gist.	Überfliege den Text und finde die wichtigsten Aussagen.
Sum up what happens in the story.	Fasse zusammen, was in der Geschichte passiert.
Practise your scenes / the dialogues.	Übe deine Szenen / die Dialoge.
Present the information from your text.	Präsentiere die Informationen aus deinem Text.
Put in the correct forms.	Setze die richtigen Formen ein.
Read your text aloud.	Lies deinen Text laut vor.
Repeat the sentences / the dialogues.	Wiederhole die Sätze / die Dialoge.
Say the words / the sounds.	Sage die Wörter / die Laute.
Show your brochure.	Zeige deine Broschüre.
Swap roles.	Tauscht die Rollen.
Take a card.	Nimm eine Karte.

In the classroom

Take notes.	Mache dir Notizen.
Take turns.	Wechselt euch ab.
Talk with your partner.	Sprich mit deinem Partner / deiner Partnerin
Tell your partner about your hobby.	Erzähle deinem Partner / deiner Partnerin von deinem Hobby.
Think of ideas for …	Überlege dir Ideen für …
Trade your part with somebody else.	Tausche deinen Teil mit jemandem.
Translate the words / sentences.	Übersetze die Wörter / Sätze.
Use the ideas / the vocabulary.	Verwende die Ideen / die Vokabeln.
Work with a partner or in a group.	Arbeite mit einem Partner / einer Partnerin oder in einer Gruppe.
Write dialogues / a short text / a reply.	Schreibe Dialoge / einen kurzen Text / eine Antwort.
Write about your friends.	Schreibe über deine Freunde.
Write down school words.	Schreibe Wörter zum Thema „Schule" auf.

Useful words

activity – Aktivität
answer – Antwort
class display – Ausstellung in der Klasse
collocation – Wortverbindung
description – Beschreibung
dialogue – Dialog
dice – Würfel
draft – Entwurf; Konzept
drawing – Zeichnung
example – Beispiel
fact – Tatsache; Fakt
folder – Ordner; Mappe
game – Spiel
grid – Gitter; Tabelle; Raster
heading – Überschrift
information – Information(en)
key word – Schlüsselwort
list – Liste
mind map – Wörternetz
order – Reihenfolge
perspective – Perspektive
phrase – Redewendung; Ausdruck
picture story – Bildergeschichte
point of view – Standpunkt; Ansicht
presentation – Präsentation; Vortrag
prompt card – Rollenkarte
puzzle – Rätsel; Puzzle
pros and cons – Vor- und Nachteile
question – Frage
quiz – Quiz; Rätsel
quote – Zitat
report – Bericht
revision – Wiederholung
rhyme – Reim
role play – Rollenspiel
rule – Regel
scene – Szene
signal word – Signalwort
slogan – Slogan; Werbespruch
speech bubble – Sprechblase
story – Geschichte; Erzählung
task – Aufgabe
theme – Thema
title – Titel; Überschrift
unit – Lektion; Kapitel
useful phrases – nützliche Ausdrücke
vocabulary – Vokabular; Wortschatz
word cloud – Wörterwolke

Irregular verbs

■ ■ ■ Grundform, *simple past* und *past participle* sind identisch
■ ● ● Grundform unterscheidet sich vom *simple past* und *past participle*
■ ● ■ Grundform und *past participle* sind identisch, nur das *simple past* hat eine andere Form
■ ● ▲ Grundform, *simple past* und *past participle* haben alle eine andere Form

■ Grundform	■ simple past	■ past participle	Deutsch
cost [kɒst]	cost [kɒst]	cost [kɒst]	kosten
cut [kʌt]	cut [kʌt]	cut [kʌt]	schneiden
hit [hɪt]	hit [hɪt]	hit [hɪt]	schlagen, treffen
hurt [hɜːt]	hurt [hɜːt]	hurt [hɜːt]	verletzen, sich weh tun
let [let]	let [let]	let [let]	lassen
put [pʊt]	put [pʊt]	put [pʊt]	legen, setzen, stellen
set up ['set ˌʌp]	set up ['set ˌʌp]	set up ['set ˌʌp]	erbauen, errichten

■ Grundform	● simple past	● past participle	Deutsch
bring [brɪŋ]	brought [brɔːt]	brought [brɔːt]	(mit)bringen
build [bɪld]	built [bɪlt]	built [bɪlt]	bauen
buy [baɪ]	bought [bɔːt]	bought [bɔːt]	kaufen
feel [fiːl]	felt [felt]	felt [felt]	fühlen
find [faɪnd]	found [faʊnd]	found [faʊnd]	finden
get [get]	got [gɒt]	got [gɒt]	bekommen, erhalten
have [hæv]	had [hæd]	had [hæd]	haben
hear [hɪə]	heard [hɜːd]	heard [hɜːd]	hören
hold [həʊld]	held [held]	held [held]	halten
keep [kiːp]	kept [kept]	kept [kept]	(auf)bewahren, behalten
learn [lɜːn]	learned [lɜːnd] / learnt [lɜːnt]	learned [lɜːnd] / learnt [lɜːnt]	lernen
leave [liːv]	left [left]	left [left]	(ver)lassen
make [meɪk]	made [meɪd]	made [meɪd]	machen, tun
meet [miːt]	met [met]	met [met]	treffen
pay [peɪ]	paid [peɪd]	paid [peɪd]	(be)zahlen
read [riːd]	read [red]	read [red]	lesen
retell [ˌriː'tel]	retold [ˌriː'təʊld]	retold [ˌriː'təʊld]	nacherzählen
say [seɪ]	said [sed]	said [sed]	sagen
sell [sel]	sold [səʊld]	sold [səʊld]	verkaufen
send [send]	sent [sent]	sent [sent]	senden, verschicken
sit [sɪt]	sat [sæt]	sat [sæt]	sitzen
sleep [sliːp]	slept [slept]	slept [slept]	schlafen
spell [spel]	spelt [spelt]	spelt [spelt]	buchstabieren

spend [spend]	spent [spent]	spent [spent]	ausgeben, verbringen
stand (up) [stænd]	stood (up) [stʊd]	stood (up) [stʊd]	(auf)stehen
tell [tel]	told [təʊld]	told [təʊld]	erzählen
think [θɪŋk]	thought [θɔ:t]	thought [θɔ:t]	(nach)denken, glauben
understand [ˌʌndə'stænd]	understood [ˌʌndə'stʊd]	understood [ˌʌndə'stʊd]	verstehen
win [wɪn]	won [wʌn]	won [wʌn]	gewinnen, siegen

■ Grundform	● simple past	■ past participle	Deutsch
become [bɪ'kʌm]	became [bɪ'keɪm]	become [bɪ'kʌm]	werden
come [kʌm]	came [keɪm]	come [kʌm]	kommen
run [rʌn]	ran [ræn]	run [rʌn]	laufen, rennen

■ Grundform	● simple past	▲ past participle	Deutsch
be [bi:]	was / were [wɒz / wɜ:]	been [bi:n]	sein
blow (out) [bləʊ]	blew [blu:]	blown [bləʊn]	(aus)blasen, (aus)pusten
break [breɪk]	broke [brəʊk]	broken ['brəʊkn]	(zer)brechen, kaputt machen
choose [tʃu:z]	chose [tʃəʊz]	chosen [tʃəʊzn]	(aus)wählen
do [du:]	did [dɪd]	done [dʌn]	machen, tun
draw [drɔ:]	drew [dru:]	drawn [drɔ:n]	zeichnen
drink [drɪŋk]	drank [dræŋk]	drunk [drʌŋk]	trinken
eat [i:t]	ate [et]	eaten [i:tn]	essen
fall [fɔ:l]	fell [fel]	fallen ['fɔ:lən]	fallen
fly [flaɪ]	flew [flu:]	flown [fləʊn]	fliegen
forget [fə'get]	forgot [fə'gɒt]	forgotten [fə'gɒtn]	vergessen
give [gɪv]	gave [geɪv]	given['gɪvn]	geben
go [gəʊ]	went [went]	gone [gɒn]	gehen, fahren
know [nəʊ]	knew [nju:]	known [nəʊn]	kennen, wissen
see [si:]	saw [sɔ:]	seen [si:n]	sehen
show [ʃəʊ]	showed [ʃəʊd]	shown [ʃəʊn]	zeigen
sing [sɪŋ]	sang [sæŋ]	sung [sʌŋ]	singen
speak [spi:k]	spoke [spəʊk]	spoken ['spəʊkn]	sprechen
swim [swɪm]	swam [swæm]	swum [swʌm]	schwimmen
take [teɪk]	took [tʊk]	taken ['teɪkn]	nehmen
throw [θrəʊ]	threw [θru:]	thrown [θrəʊn]	werfen
wear [weə]	wore [wɔ:]	worn [wɔ:n]	anhaben, tragen
write [raɪt]	wrote [rəʊt]	written ['rɪtn]	schreiben

Check-out solutions

Unit 1 Page 25

Exercise 1

They talked about the 'dreams' page. / They put the sports pages together. / They looked at Jay's ideas for the music pages. / They collected ideas for the puzzles page. / They took a photo of the yearbook team. / They made a list of jobs for next week.

Exercise 2

1. went
2. was
3. wasn't
4. invited
5. did you go
6. did
7. were
8. was
9. was
10. didn't stay

Exercise 3

1. When did you get up this morning?
2. Where did you go?
3. What did you see?
4. Why did your classmates laugh at you?

Exercise 4

1. Luke's dog Sherlock is **the craziest** animal in England. There's nothing **funnier** than when he chases his tail. It's always **faster** than he is!
2. The **cutest** pets for Holly are her two guinea pigs. Mr Fluff likes to explore. He thinks a trip in a bag is **more interesting** than a game on the floor! Honey isn't as **brave** as Mr Fluff.
3. Cats are **the most popular** pets in the class. Dave's cat Sid brings presents for the family. Some presents are **better** than others. The **worst** thing for Dave is a mouse in his bed!

Unit 2 Page 43

Exercise 1

a) 1. which / that
2. which / that
3. who / that
4. whose
5. who / that

b) Contact clause possible in sentence 1 and 3

Exercise 2

1. Dave was washing his face when Sid came into the bathroom.
2. He sent Jay a text while his mother was making breakfast.
3. He was getting his bike when his father left the house.
4. He arrived at school while Luke was still sleeping.

Exercise 3

a) 1. Geography
2. Music
3. Technology
4. History
5. Art

b) Phrases: I really like … / I like … best because … / … is interesting/great/so much fun because … / I like to learn about … / …

Unit 3 Page 65

Exercise 1

1. The Frasers are going to have a picnic. / The Frasers are going to go on a picnic.
2. Luke and Sherlock are going to play ball in the park. / Luke and Sherlock are going to play in the park.
3. Mr and Mrs Azad are going to visit / see / go to the Tower of London.
4. Holly is going to go (inline) skating. / Holly is going to have fun on her skates.
5. Amir is going to take (lots of) photos / pictures.
6. Shahid is going to meet someone / his girlfriend / a friend (somewhere).

Exercise 2

1. anybody
2. someone
3. everybody
4. something
5. somewhere
6. everything
7. anywhere
8. nothing

Exercise 3

1. fast
2. comfortably
3. excitedly
4. slowly
5. clearly
6. well
7. loudly
8. sadly

Unit 4 Page 83

Exercise 1

1 c)
2 e)
3 b)
4 a)
5 f)
6 d)

Exercise 2

1. Luke: Have you found any interesting information on the internet yet?
   Dave: Yes, I have. I found some (information) yesterday after school.
2. Luke: Has Jay drawn any mangas for his report (yet)?
   Dave: Yes, he has. He drew some cool new characters at lunch.
3. Dave: Have you seen the two new manga comics yet?
   Luke: Yes, I have. I've already finished one of them.
4. Luke: Have you seen Olivia today?
   Dave: No, I haven't. But she sent me a text an hour ago. / But I sent her a text an hour ago.
5. Dave: Has Holly written about guinea pigs?
   Luke: I hope not! She wrote about guinea pigs last year.

Exercise 3

The full name of BMX is 'bicycle motocross'. It is a sport that **has become** *very* popular with young people. It **started** with children in the USA in about 1970. At first, the children **used** normal bikes on mud roads; there **were** no special BMX bikes. But then a few bicycle companies **discovered** the sport, and the world **had** its first BMX bikes. It's a fast, dangerous sport, and there **have been** many serious accidents. That's why many parents are *not* big fans. In one survey with parents last year, BMX **wasn't** at the top of the list of 'favourite sports'. One mother said: "**I've seen** dirty football and rugby uniforms, but my children's BMX clothes after a race? They're the worst!"

Unit 5 Page 105

Exercise 1

1 e) When my dad wants to relax, he watches football on TV.
2 d) When I want to know the words of a song I've heard, I look it up on the internet.
3 b) When my mum works away from home, she sends me text messages.
4 a) When I want to tell all my friends how great my holiday is, I post it on my social network profile.
5 c) When my sister wants to know about the coolest new clothes, she reads girls' magazines.

Exercise 2

1. Lösungsvorschlag:
   A: I really hurt my foot. I hope it isn't broken. / I think it could be broken.
   B: Does it really hurt?
   A: Yes, it does.
   B: Well, you should go to the doctor's. / Why don't you go to the doctor's?
   A: Yes, maybe you're right.

2. Lösungsvorschlag:
   A: I can't believe I missed my favourite show last night!
   B: Well, you could watch it on the internet. / Why don't you watch it on the internet?
   A: The interent doesn't always have everything.
   B: Have you tried looking yet?
   A: Well, no.

3. Lösungsvorschlag:
   A: Oh no, something is wrong with my bike!
   B: What's the problem?
   A: I don't know.
   B: Have you tried looking on the internet yet? / Have you asked Mum and Dad / Ben / … for help?

4. Lösungsvorschlag:
   A: I can't believe she posted those photos – they're really embarrassing.
   B: Have you talked to her yet?
   A: Yes, I have. She doesn't think they're embarrassing. And she thinks she looks really good in them.
   B: Well, why don't you tell her to cut you off the photos?
   A: OK, that's a good idea.

5. Lösungsvorschlag:
   A: I'm not allowed to use my phone for a week because my parents are really angry with me.
   B: Well, maybe you should tell them that you're sorry.
   A: I've already told them, but they still took my phone.
   B: Just use my phone when you need it.

Exercise 3

When I was young, we **weren't able to** make phone calls from everywhere because there were no mobile phones. Now you **can** use your smartphones nearly everywhere. But you **aren't allowed to** use them at school, are you? There **must** be rules for using them, right? 30 years ago you **had to** look for information in books. Today you **can** look things up on the internet. When we were young, we **were able to** watch TV only sometimes, but today you **can** watch videos online all day.

Grammar solutions

Unit 1

G1 Two years ago we raised lots of money.

Dear Olivia,
Thank you for your e-mail and the photos. I like them a lot.
You **wanted** to know about our charity event. Well, last month we **organised** an event in the park and we **planned** lots of activities. First there **were** games for students, parents and teachers. After that we **sold** cakes. In the afternoon the students in Year 7 **did** some really cool tricks. And then it **was** the turn of the students in Year 8. They **created** a comedy show. The girls **wanted** to look funny so they **painted** their faces and **wore** some funny costumes too. In the evening the school band **sang** in the park – lots of people **came** to listen. Michael **was** the real star of their show.
He **did** some cool moves!
We **raised** 400 euros in just one day!
Write soon.
Pia

G2 How did they know?

Lösungsvorschlag:
How old was he? – He was about twenty years old.
When did you see him? – I saw him at 10 o'clock.
Where did you see him? – I saw him in front of the sports shop in Trafalgar Road.
Did you see what he took from the shop? – Well, he had two bags full of T-shirts and shoes.
Was he alone? – Yes, he was.

G3 The police didn't know what the man looked like.

Man arrested
Greenwich. On 4th September a young man **broke into** a sports shop in Trafalgar Road. Yesterday the police **arrested** him. They **didn't know** what he **looked** like at first. But then they **got** an anonymous phone call. The caller **didn't give** them much information, but she **gave** them an address in Greenwich. When the police **got to** the house, two women **were** there but the man **wasn't**. So they **waited** till he **came** home and then they **arrested** him – he **didn't try** to run away. The police **found** the sports shoes and the T-shirts in the loft, but they **didn't find** the bike.

G4 An adventure course helps students to be more confident.

a) big – bigger – the biggest
bad – worse – the worst
happy – happier – the happiest
important – more important – the most important

b) 1. Luke is tall. Holly is taller. But Olivia is the tallest of the three.
2. The red car is expensive. The blue car is more expensive. But the black car is the most expensive of the three.
3. Hook Lane is a busy road. King's Street is busier. But London Road is the busiest of the three.
4. Luke has got a good idea. Holly's idea is better. But Dave has got the best idea of the three.

G5 Outdoor activities are as important as lessons in the classroom.

Lösungsvorschlag:
The Rhine is longer than the Spree/Oder.
The Spree is shorter than the Oder/Rhine.
Düsseldorf is as big as Stuttgart.
Cologne is bigger than Düsseldorf/Stuttgart.
The Feldberg is the highest mountain. It is higher than the Brocken/the Großer Arber.
The Großer Arber is about as high as the Feldberg.
The Saarland is the smallest state/region. It is smaller than Hesse/Saxony.
Hesse is bigger than Saxony.

Unit 2

G6 The queen who loved parties

a) 1. Dave: Have you got any music **which/that** people listened to at Anne's parties? You can use it in your presentation.
Luke: Yes, I have. But I'm not sure. I don't like the songs **which/that** they played in the 17th century.
Dave: Well, don't worry about that. Luke, what's that under the table?
Luke: Oh, thanks, Dave. This is the photo of the Queen's House **which/that** I'm looking for.

2. Jay: Who was Christopher Wren?
Olivia: He was the famous architect **whose** designs you can see in London.
Jay: Really?
Olivia: Yes, he was the man **who/that** designed the Royal Naval College, the Royal Observatory, St Paul's Cathedral and many other buildings.
Jay: Cool! Those are all buildings **which/that** I know.

b) 1. Have you got any music people listened to at Anne's parties?
I don't like the songs they played in the 17th century.
This the photo of the Queen's House I'm looking for.
2. Those are all buildings I know.

G7 What were they doing when Sally fell into the pond?

Lösungsvorschlag:
B: What were Holly and Olivia doing?
A: While Holly was practicing / learning new signs, Olivia was playing netball.

Unit 3

G8 It's going to be fun.

Jay is going to go to Covent Garden. He's going to listen to the buskers there.
Amir is going to send / write a postcard home.
Olivia and Holly aren't going to see / visit Brick Lane with its street art / graffiti.
Shahid is going to go to a café with his girlfriend.
Mrs Azad isn't going to go shopping / to the supermarket.
Mr Azad is going to wash his car.

G9 It's something important.

Amir: Listen, **everybody**. I want to buy a little present for my aunt to say 'thank you'. Is there a good shop **anywhere**?
Olivia: What are you thinking of?
Amir: Well, it must be **something** special, but it mustn't be **anything** expensive.
Jay: **Everything** is expensive in London!
Holly: That's not true! I know a good shop where **nothing** costs more than £10.
Amir: OK. Let's go there and see if we can find **something** for her.

G10 Now we're going slowly past the Tower of London.

1. Buy an Oyster card and travel by public transport **cheaply** and **comfortably**.
2. Stand on Westminster Bridge and take **fantastic** photos of Big Ben.
3. On a **nice** day, take a picnic with you and have lunch in one of London's **great** parks.
4. Go to the British Museum and learn about money, animals and ships. It's **free**!
5. Visit Madame Tussauds. The museum shows famous people very **realistically**.
6. If you're in London for a day or two only, take a sightseeing bus. Most guides know London and its history **well**.

G11 You can see London faster and more easily with a guide.

Lösungsvorschlag:
A bear runs faster than a pig or a cat. A horse runs fastest.
A pig eats less than a bear. A cat eats least.
A bear sleeps longer than a horse. A cat sleeps longest.
A bear weighs more than a lion. A horse weighs most.

Unit 4

G12 Have you ever run in a marathon?

Lösungsvorschlag:

a) 1. Have you prepared for Sports Day yet?
2. Have you bought new sports shoes yet?
3. Have you already started eating healthy food?
4. Have you ever hurt your foot while you were playing sports?
5. Have you found a name for your team yet?

b) 2. Have you bought new sports shoes yet?
- No, I haven't. I don't need any new shoes. My old ones/shoes are OK.
- Yes, I have. I've just bought some new shoes. Look, they are in this bag.
- Yes, I have. I bought them last week.

3. Have you already started eating healthy food?
- Yes, I have. I've already eaten two apples today.

4. Have you ever hurt your foot while you were playing sports?
- Yes, I have. I've hurt my leg twice/two times. When I was little, I broke my leg at the ice rink. And last year I twisted my ankle while I was playing basketball.
- No, I haven't.

5. Have you found a name for your team yet?
- Yes, I have. But I'm not going to tell you.
- No, I haven't found a nice name yet.

Unit 5

G13 I'm writing to you because I need your advice.

Joe: I like your magazine **because** it's always got the interesting news on my favourite stars in it.
Ginny: I buy *TeenLife* **as soon as/when** I get my pocket money from my parents. I love it!
Michael: The concert photos are fantastic. When I look at them, it's **like** I'm there.
Lisa: **Whenever/When** I read Ruby's advice, I think she really understands our problems.
Sheila: **After** I tried the make-up which came with the magazine last week, I'm not going to buy *TeenLife* again! It looked awful on my face.

G14 You watched the match last night, didn't you?

1. Olivia: Miss Brown played an interesting song in class today, **didn't she**?
Holly: Its title was *Life before media technology*, **wasn't it**?
Jay: Yes, and it's a really cool song, **isn't it**?
Holly: Well, yeah. I liked it.

2. Luke: We're going to work on our media project this afternoon, **aren't we**?
Dave: Of course. Let's meet in front of the school after lessons and go to my house.
Luke: Good idea. With Jamie and Irina it's always very noisy at our house, **isn't it**?
Dave: That's true! If we concentrate, perhaps we can finish the project today.
Luke: I'm not sure. We haven't worked on this kind of project before, **have we**? So we don't really know how long it's going to take us, **do we**?
Dave: That's right. But you've already collected some ideas, **haven't you**?
Luke: Well, erm …

G15 I wasn't allowed to go over to Jay's house yesterday.

Hi,
Guess what. When I came home from school, there was water everywhere on the kitchen floor. Something was wrong with the washing machine and Dad **had to** fix it before Mum came home. Dad had no idea what he was doing … But I **was allowed to** use his tablet and check for advice in a forum. I **was able to** find a great website quickly. It was very helpful. All we **had to** do was turn the knob off. So we **were able to** solve the problem in 20 minutes and Mum **was able to** use the washing machine when she came home.
See you at school on Monday.
Luke

G16 You could look at a forum for help.

Lösungsvorschlag:
1. You should say sorry (to her). / You could ask if she needs help. / You should be more careful when you play netball.
2. You should tell Dave. / You could buy him a new book. / You could ask how much the book was and give him the money.
3. You shouldn't pull him out from under the bed. / You could put some food in front of the bed. / You could leave a gap between the bed and the wall. Then it's easier to pick him up.
4. You should say sorry (to her). / You could buy her new flowers for her garden. / Next time if you are not sure, you should ask her first.

Bildquellennachweis:
U.1 February Films (Andrew Kemp), London; **U.2** plainpicture GmbH & Co. KG (Design Pics), Hamburg; **2.1** February Films (Andrew Kemp), London; **2.2** February Films (Andrew Kemp), London; **2.3** February Films (Andrew Kemp), London; **02.4ff** shutterstock.com (suicidecrew), New York, NY; **3.1** February Films (Andrew Kemp), London; **3.2** February Films (Andrew Kemp), London; **3.3** February Films (Andrew Kemp), London; **4.1** February Films (Andrew Kemp), London; **4.2** iStockphoto (andrearoad), Calgary, Alberta; **4.3** February Films (Andrew Kemp), London; **5.1** February Films (Andrew Kemp), London; **5.2** Thinkstock (Salah Malkawi), München; **5.3** February Films (Andrew Kemp), London; **6.1** Fotolia.com (visoook), New York; **6.2** February Films, London; **6.3** February Films (Andrew Kemp), London; **7.1** February Films (Andrew Kemp), London; **7.2** February Films, London; **7.3** February Films, London; **8.1** February Films (Andrew Kemp), London; **8.2** February Films (Andrew Kemp), London; **9.1** February Films (Andrew Kemp), London; **9.2** February Films (Andrew Kemp), London; **10.1** Getty Images (Stuart Wilson), München; **12.1** shutterstock.com (Studio 37), New York, NY; **16.1** Fotolia.com (Jakub Cejpek), New York; **16.2** Thinkstock (Ammit), München; **16.3** Dream Maker Software (RF), Colorado; **19.1** February Films (Andrew Kemp), London; **20.1** Hath, Jessica Alice, Freiburg; **21.1** shutterstock.com (granata1111), New York, NY; **21.2** February Films (Andrew Kemp), London; **22.1** Fotolia.com (evron.info), New York; **22.2** ddp images GmbH (Newscom/UPI), Hamburg; **22.3** Fotolia.com (toolklickit), New York; **24.1** February Films, London; **28.1** February Films (Andrew Kemp), London; **28.2** February Films (Andrew Kemp), London; **28.3** February Films (Andrew Kemp), London; **28.4** February Films (Elke Bock), London; **29.1** February Films (Andrew Kemp), London; **30.1** laif (Pawel Libera/Loop Images), Köln; **31.1** February Films (Andrew Kemp), London; **32.1** February Films (Andrew Kemp), London; **34.1** Imago, Berlin; **35.1** Fotolia.com (calaratjada), New York; **35.2** shutterstock.com (dw1), New York, NY; **35.3** Thinkstock (Peter Elvidge), München; **35.4** Fotolia.com (Stephen Coburn), New York; **35.5** Thinkstock (Josh Rinehults), München; **35.6** shutterstock.com (Martijn Wisse), New York, NY; **36.1** February Films, London; **43.1** Thinkstock (Simon Greig), München; **43.2** Fotolia.com (matttilda), New York; **43.4** akg-images, Berlin; **43.5** shutterstock.com (S-BELOV), New York, NY; **47.1** Getty Images (Blend Images), München; **48.1** Getty Images, München; **48.2** shutterstock.com (Bikeworldtravel), New York, NY; **48.3** shutterstock.com (Carsten Medom Madsen), New York, NY; **48.4** shutterstock.com (Francesco Carucci), New York, NY; **48.5** dreamstime.com (Emanuel Corso), Brentwood, TN; **48.6** Fotolia.com (geckospake), New York; **49.1** February Films, London; **50.1** February Films (Andrew Kemp), London; **51.1** iStockphoto (andrearoad), Calgary, Alberta; **51.2** laif (Polaris Images), Köln; **51.3** Corbis (Mike Kemp/In Pictures), Berlin; **51.4** February Films (Andrew Kemp), London; **54.1** February Films (Andrew Kemp), London; **54.2** February Films (Andrew Kemp), London; **54.3** February Films (Andrew Kemp), London; **54.4** February Films (Andrew Kemp), London; **54.5** February Films (Andrew Kemp), London; **54.6** February Films (Andrew Kemp), London; **56.1** Argus (Peter Frischmuth), Hamburg; **56.2** Corbis (Alison Wright), Berlin; **57.1** shutterstock.com (Arvydas Kniuksta), New York, NY; **57.2** shutterstock.com (Jacek Chabraszewski), New York, NY; **57.3** Fotolia.com (kateignatenko), New York; **57.4** BigStockPhoto.com (toxawww), Davis, CA; **57.5** Thinkstock (boggy22), München; **57.6** Thinkstock (Søren Sielemann), München; **58.1** February Films, London; **58.2** February Films, London; **60.1** Google Inc. (Kartendaten © 2014 Google), Mountain View, CA 94043; **62.1** Thinkstock (John Pavel), München; **65.1** shutterstock.com (Four Oaks), New York, NY; **65.2** February Films (Andrew Kemp), London; **65.4** February Films (Andrew Kemp), London; **65.5** dreamstime.com (Woo Bing Siew), Brentwood, TN; **65.6** February Films (Andrew Kemp), London; **68.1** Thinkstock (Salah Malkawi), München; **68.2** shutterstock.com (Bikeworldtravel), New York, NY; **68.3** Klett-Archiv (Thomas Weccard), Stuttgart; **68.4** shutterstock.com (Eoghan McNally), New York, NY; **69.1** Picture-Alliance (Uli Gasper), Frankfurt; **71.1** Hath, Jessica Alice, Freiburg; **72.1** February Films (Andrew Kemp), London; **72.2** February Films (Andrew Kemp), London; **74.1** shutterstock.com (Glayan), New York, NY; **75.1** Thinkstock (AlbertoChagas), München; **76.1** February Films, London; **77.1** dreamstime.com (A1shutterbug), Brentwood, TN; **82.1** shutterstock.com (Michaelpuche), New York, NY; **82.2** February Films (Andrew Kemp), London; **83.1** Fotolia.com (José 16), New York; **86.1** Mauritius Images (Alamy), Mittenwald; **87.1** Alamy Images (David Robertson), Abingdon, Oxon; **88.1** February Films, London; **88.2** February Films, London; **89.1** Thinkstock (Ramon Purcell), München; **89.2** Ullstein Bild GmbH (ullstein - iT), Berlin; **90.1** February Films (Andrew Kemp), London; **91.1** Fotolia.com (visoook), New York; **91.2** Getty Images (Photodisc), München; **91.3** Thinkstock (Purestock), München; **91.4** February Films (Andrew Kemp), London; **92.1** iStockphoto (RF/Matt Ramos), Calgary, Alberta; **94.1** Picture-Alliance (PhotoAlto), Frankfurt; **98.1** February Films, London; **98.2** February Films, London; **98.3** February Films, London; **100.1** Getty Images (Photodisc), München; **104.1** www.CartoonStock.com (Cook, Gary), Bath; **105.1** Thinkstock (Elena Elisseeva), München; **108.1** dreamstime.com (Oleg Shipov), Brentwood, TN; **109.1** dreamstime.com (Ingrid Hogenbijl), Brentwood, TN; **109.2** Klett-Archiv (Simianer & Blühdorn), Stuttgart; **109.3** shutterstock.com (Michaelpuche), New York, NY; **109.4** shutterstock.com (criben), New York, NY; **112.1** Getty Images (LatitudeStock - Allan Hartley), München; **115.1** Getty Images (Sonya Hurtado), München; **115.2** Getty Images (Digital Vision), München; **119.1** Getty Images (E+), München; **119.2** Fotolia.com (Sophie James), New York; **120.1** Getty Images (Vetta), München; **121.1** Getty Images (Brand X Pictures), München; **122.1** February Films (Andrew Kemp), London; **122.2** February Films (Andrew Kemp), London; **125.1** Getty Images (E+), München; **126.1** February Films (Andrew Kemp), London; **133.1** shutterstock.com (Ferencz Teglas), New York, NY; **138.1** February Films, London; **138.2** February Films, London; **142.1** February Films (Andrew Kemp), London; **145.1** Thinkstock (RTimages), München; **146.1** February Films (Elke Bock), London; **150.1** iStockphoto (laartist), Calgary, Alberta; **150.2** Thinkstock (Stephen Finn), München; **152.1** February Films (Elke Bock), London; **152.2** February Films (Elke Bock), London; **152.3** February Films (Andrew Kemp), London; **152.4** February Films (Elke Bock), London; **154.1** Corbis (David Batterbury, Eye Ubiquitous), Berlin; **154.2** shutterstock.com (Orion-v), New York, NY; **154.3** shutterstock.com, New York, NY; **154.4** iStockphoto (Kohlerphoto), Calgary, Alberta; **154.5** shutterstock.com, New York, NY; **154.6** iStockphoto (slobo mitic), Calgary, Alberta; **154.7** February Films (Andrew Kemp), London; **156.1** Alamy Images (Holmes Garden Photos), Abingdon, Oxon; **165.1** February Films (Andrew Kemp), London; **170.1** iStockphoto (craftvision), Calgary, Alberta; **175.1** iStockphoto (Joshua Hodge Photography), Calgary, Alberta; **180.1** shutterstock.com (CREATISTA), New York, NY; **184.1** dreamstime.com (Alenmax), Brentwood, TN; **186.1** shutterstock.com (Willyam Bradberry), New York, NY; **195.1** shutterstock.com (Monkey Business Images), New York, NY; **236.1** February Films (Elke Bock), London; **249.1** Pulse Creative Limited - Transport for London, Heaton Mersey, Stockport

Text- und Liedquellen:
S. 26 From *Middle School: How I Got Lost in London* by James Patterson. Published by Random House Children's Publishers. Reprinted by permission of the Random House Group Ltd.; **S. 44** Excerpt from *Horrid Henry Rules the World* by Francesca Simon, Orion Children's Books, an Imprint of The Orion Publishing Group Ltd, London, July 1, 2008 © Francesca Simon, 2008 (adapted); **S. 66** Excerpt from *The Copper Treasure* by Melvin Burgess, A & C Black Publishers Ltd, London, 1999/2002 © Francesca Simon, 2008 (adapted); **S. 73** Excerpt from the brochure *Erkennen – Bewerten – Handeln: Zur Gesundheit von Kindern und Jugendlichen in Deutschland*, Robert Koch-Institut, Bundeszentrale für gesundheitliche Aufklärung, p. 33, Berlin und Köln, 2008 © Robert Koch-Institut; **S. 84** „The Summer Table" from WONDER by R. J. Palacio, copyright © 2012 by R.J. Palacio. Reprinted by permission of R.J. Palacio and Alfred A. Knopf, an imprint of Random House Childrens's Books, a division of Random House LLC. All rights reserved; **S. 94** „Friends" Text: Armato, Antonina/Dione, Aura marie/James, Tim/Jost, David © Akashic Field Music/Antonina Songs/Good Songs Publishing A/S/ Universal/MCA Music Publishing GmbH, Berlin/Universal Music Publishing GmbH, Berlin/Rolf Budde Musikverlag GmbH, Berlin/Jost Music Publisching David Jost, Berlin; **S. 106** Excerpt from *Ratburger* by David Walliams, HarperCollins Children's Books, a division of HarperCollins Publishers Ltd, London, 2012 © David Walliams 2012 (adapted); **S. 131** Excerpt from *Ratburger* by David Walliams, HarperCollins Children's Books, a division of HarperCollins Publishers Ltd, London, 2012 © David Walliams 2012 (adapted)

Sollte es in einem Einzelfall nicht gelungen sein, den korrekten Rechteinhaber ausfindig zu machen, so werden berechtigte Ansprüche selbstverständlich im Rahmen der üblichen Regelungen abgegolten.

LONDON
0km
1km
CAMDEN
Camden Market
Regent's Park
Outer Circle
Albany Street
Hampstead Road
Park Road
Maida Vale
SHERLOCK HOLMES
Sherlock Holmes Museum
Madame Tussauds
Marylebone Road
Westway A40
Gloucester Place
Baker Street
Edgware Road
Wigmore Street
Oxford Circus
Regent Str
Oxford Street
Marble Arch
Notting Hill Carnival
NOTTING HILL
Bayswater Road
Bond Street
Picc
Ci
Hyde Park
Piccadilly
The Serpentine
Green Park
Rotten Row
Kensington Road
Buckingham Palace
National History Museum
Brompton Road
Sloane Street
Vic
Heathrow Airport
Cromwell Road
Victoria Station
Brompton Road
Fulham Road
King's Road
Wimbledon
Chelsea Embankment
Grosvenor

Highbury
King's Cross Station
Pancras
tation
City Road
Gray's Inn Road
Place
Old Street
Great Eastern St.
Farringdon Road
Clerkenwell Road
City of London
Brick Lane
British Museum
ry St.
High Holborn
St. Paul's Cathedral
London Wall
Avenue
Covent Garden
Covent Garden
ross Road
Fleet Street
Tower of London
Millennium Bridge
Embankment
Strand
Blackfriars Bridge
Southwark Bridge
Tate Modern
Victoria
Waterloo Bridge
London Eye
Globe Theatre
Southwark Street
The Shard
Tower Bridge
Trafalgar Square
London Dungeon
SOUTHWARK
Blackfriars Road
Borough High Street
Docklands
Thames Barrier
Horse Guards
Waterloo Station
Waterloo Road
ses of
iament
Westminster Bridge
nster
ey
River Thames
TER
Lambeth Bridge
Millbank
Albert Embankment
Vauxhall Bridge
Mudchute Farm
Trinity Hospital
Thames
Swimming Pool (Arches Leisure Centre)
London
Greenwich
Cutty Sark
Playground
Greenwich Market
Boating Lake
Vanbrugh Castle
Planetarium
Royal Observatory
Greenwich Station
Fan Museum
Deer Park
Tennis Court
Rose Garden
GREENWICH
Thomas Tallis School

Bakerloo	Metropolitan	Interchange stations
Central	Northern	Step-free access from street to train
Circle	Piccadilly	Step-free access from street to platform
District	Victoria	National Rail
District open weekends, public holidays and some Olympia events	Waterloo & City	Riverboat services
Hammersmith & City	DLR	Tramlink
Jubilee	London Overground	Airport
	Emirates Air Line	Emirates Air Line

† **Covent Garden**
Exit only from late February until early November 2015. Also, on Saturdays and Sundays, westbound trains will not stop. Please use Leicester Square instead

Stanmore
Step-free access via a steep ramp

Tottenham Court Road
Central line trains will not stop at this station from early January until early December 2015

West Ham
Until late February 2015 step-free access will only be to the DLR and c2c

MAYOR OF LONDON

tfl.gov.uk

*Service and network charges may apply. See tfl.gov.uk/terms for details.

24 hour travel information
0343 222 1234*

Sign up for email updates
tfl.gov.uk/emailupdates

@TfLTravelAlerts

UNDERGROUND

TRANSPORT FOR LONDON
EVERY JOURNEY MATTERS

© Transport for London

Reg. user No. 14/E/2757/P

Improvement works may affect your journey, please check before you travel

Version A TfL 12.2014

Correct at time of going to print

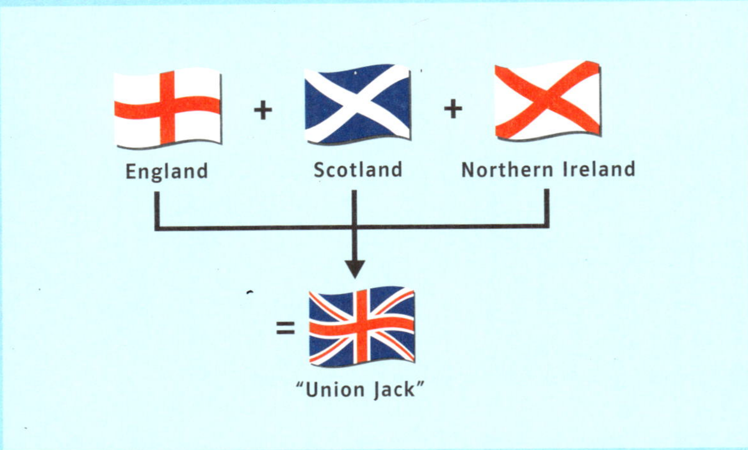
England
+
Scotland
+
Northern Ireland
=
"Union Jack"

Atlantic Ocean
Galway
REPUBLIC OF IRELAND
Cor